23672   H3   £4

CAMBRIDGE STUDIES IN INTE[

C0000179232

SOUTH AFRICA'S ~~~~~
POLICY

Editorial Board

STEVE SMITH (*Managing editor*)
LAWRENCE FREEDMAN FRED HALLIDAY KAL HOLSTI
ROY JONES ROBERT S. LITWAK PETER NAILOR
WILLIAM OLSON ADAM ROBERTS JOHN SIMPSON
JACK SPENCE ROGER TOOZE JOHN A. VASQUEZ
JOHN VINCENT

Cambridge Studies in International Relations is a joint initiative of Cambridge University Press and the British International Studies Association (BISA). The series will include a wide range of material, from undergraduate textbooks and surveys to research-based monographs and collaborative volumes. The aim of the series is to publish the best new scholarship in International Studies from Europe, North America and the rest of the world.

CAMBRIDGE STUDIES IN INTERNATIONAL RELATIONS

SOUTH AFRICA'S FOREIGN POLICY

The search for status and security 1945–1988

JAMES BARBER

Master of Hatfield College and Pro-Vice-Chancellor, University of Durham

and

JOHN BARRATT

Director General, South African Institute of International Affairs and Honorary Professor of International Relations, University of Witwatersrand

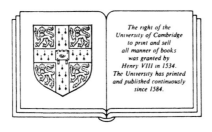

The right of the
University of Cambridge
to print and sell
all manner of books
was granted by
Henry VIII in 1534.
The University has printed
and published continuously
since 1584.

CAMBRIDGE UNIVERSITY PRESS

Published in association with

THE SOUTH AFRICAN INSTITUTE OF INTERNATIONAL AFFAIRS

Cambridge

New York   Port Chester

Melbourne   Sydney

CAMBRIDGE UNIVERSITY PRESS
Cambridge, New York, Melbourne, Madrid, Cape Town,
Singapore, São Paulo, Delhi, Tokyo, Mexico City

Cambridge University Press
The Edinburgh Building, Cambridge CB2 8RU, UK

Published in the United States of America by Cambridge University Press, New York

www.cambridge.org
Information on this title: www.cambridge.org/9780521388764

© Cambridge University Press 1990

This publication is in copyright. Subject to statutory exception
and to the provisions of relevant collective licensing agreements,
no reproduction of any part may take place without the written
permission of Cambridge University Press.

First published 1990
Re-issued 2011

A catalogue record for this publication is available from the British Library

Library of Congress Cataloguing in Publication data
South Africa's foreign policy: the search for status
and security, 1945–1988/James Barber and John Barratt.
    p.   cm. – (Cambridge studies in international relations: 12)
Includes index.
ISBN 0-521-37313-1. – ISBN 0-521-38876-7 (pbk.)
1. South Africa – Foreign relations – 1948–1961.
2. South Africa – Foreign relations – 1961–1978.
3. South Africa – Foreign relations – 1978–
I. Barratt, John.   II. Title.   III. Series.
DT779.9.B37 1990
327.68 – dc20   89-35773 CIP

ISBN 978-0-521-37313-5 Hardback
ISBN 978-0-521-38876-4 Paperback

Cambridge University Press has no responsibility for the persistence or
accuracy of URLs for external or third-party internet websites referred to in
this publication, and does not guarantee that any content on such websites is,
or will remain, accurate or appropriate.

For June and Valerie

CONTENTS

ACKNOWLEDGMENTS

This book was proposed and encouraged by the South African Institute of International Affairs in its role of promoting independent and non-partisan research on South African foreign policy. The authors are indebted to the Institute, but the Institute is in no way responsible for viewpoints expressed, or for anything else contained in this work which is entirely the responsibility of the authors.

Special thanks are due to the following individuals: Bryan Bench and Chris Schoeman for their work in compiling the statistical tables and charts in the Appendix, Ruth Liber, Cynthia Connolly and Dorothy Anson for typing the manuscript; and Jackie Kalley, Jan Smuts House Librarian, for willing help from her wide bibliographical knowledge.

We are also indebted to many individuals – scholars, civil servants, politicians, businessmen and journalists – with whom we discussed aspects of the subject and from many of whom we gained valuable insights and information.

As always, we are most grateful to our wives, June and Valerie, for their support and endurance, without which the writing of this book would not have been possible.

SOUTHERN AFRICA

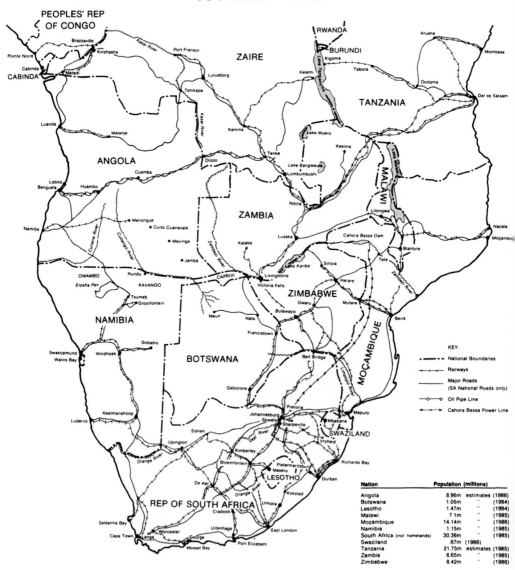

PEOPLES' REP
OF CONGO

Brazzaville
Pointe Noire
Cabinda
CABINDA
Matadi
Kinshasha
Kasai River
Port Franqui
Luluaborg
Tshikapa
Kasai River

ZAIRE

RWANDA
BURUNDI
Kigoma
Kelemi
Lake Tanganyika

Arusha
Mombasa

TANZANIA
Tabora
Dodoma
Dar es Salaam

Luanda
Malanje

ANGOLA

Lobito
Benguela
Huambo
Cuemba
Dilolo

Kamina
Tenke
Lake Muero
Lake Bangweula
Lumbumbushi
Kasima
Ndola

MALAWI

Namibe
Menongue
Curto Cuanavale
Mavinga
Jamba

ZAMBIA

Kataba
Lusaka
Cahora Bassa Dam

Lake Tanganyika
Lilongwe

Nacala
Moçambi

Cunene River
Cubango River
Zambezi River

OWAMBO
Etosha Pan
Rundu
KAVANGO
CAPRIVI
Tsumeb
Grootfontein

Livingstone
Victoria Falls
Lake Kariba
Sinoia
Blantyre
Tete

Cahora Bassa Dam

ZIMBABWE
Gweru
Harare
Mutare

NAMIBIA
Maun
Nata
Bulawayo

Francistown

Zambezi River
Beira

Swakopmund
Walvis Bay
Windhoek
Gobabis

BOTSWANA

Gaborone

Beit Bridge

MOÇAMBIQUE

KEY:

National Boundaries
Railways
Major Roads
(SA National Roads only)
Oil Pipe Line
Cahora Bassa Power Line

Luderitz
Keetmanshoop

Sishen
Upington
Orange River

Johannesburg
Soweto
Sharpeville
Pretoria
Mbabane
Maputo

SWAZILAND
Vryheid

Kimberley
Bloemfontein
Maseru
Pietermaritzburg
Richards Bay

De Aar
Orange River
Kokstad
LESOTHO
Umtata
Durban

REP OF SOUTH AFRICA
Cradock

Saldanha Bay
Cape Town
Langa
Worcester
George
Mossel Bay
Uitenhage
Port Elizabeth
East London

Limpopo River
Vaal River

Nation	Population (millions)		
Angola	8.96m	estimates	(1986)
Botswana	1.05m	"	(1984)
Lesotho	1.47m	"	(1984)
Malawi	7.1m	"	(1985)
Mozambique	14.14m	"	(1986)
Namibia	1.15m	"	(1985)
South Africa (incl homelands)	30.36m	"	(1985)
Swaziland	.67m	(1986)	
Tanzania	21.75m	estimates	(1985)
Zambia	6.65m	"	(1985)
Zimbabwe	8.42m	"	(1986)

Source The Statesman's Year-Book, 1987-88

1 INTRODUCTION

This book is an account of South Africa's foreign policy between 1945 and 1988. It sets out to describe and examine critically the main developments during that period. The study of foreign policy focuses attention on the government, and in particular the executive – its aims, its resources, how it employed those resources, the pressures on it at home and abroad, who made the decisions on what basis. Other groups, institutions and organisations are examined only in so far as they influenced or played a part in the government's foreign policy activities. The limits this imposes are striking in South Africa's case because the black majority has no say in government. However, the status and rights of blacks, and the activities of black movements, are central issues of foreign as well as domestic policy, not least because the international community identifies them as matters of concern. Therefore developments in black politics are outlined. Also examined are the domestic, regional and international settings, which impose limits and provide opportunities in which Pretoria seeks to achieve its aims.

THE GOVERNMENT'S AIMS

The overriding aim of South African governments in this period was the preservation of a white controlled state, although the means employed to maintain white power and identity changed as the challenges increased. That aim shaped and dominated domestic and foreign policy as Pretoria fought to ensure the security, status and legitimacy of the state within the international community. To identify the aim does not imply that all whites supported it, although the great majority did. Nor does it imply an absence of competition for power among whites, but the rival parties competed within a political system which (in almost all cases) they sought to control not to change from its racial structure. Nor does it imply that the whites formed a uniform

1

socio-economic group, for they were divided by class, language, culture, urban and rural interests which were reflected in political allegiances, but whenever the state was threatened most whites subordinated other loyalties to defend the established order. Nor, finally, does it imply that race will continue indefinitely as the major division in South Africa, but it was in the period of this study.

The commitment to the white state was already firmly in place in 1945, and was reinforced by the election in 1948 of a National Party (NP) Government which introduced apartheid – the legally entrenched separation of people by racial classification. Successive Prime Ministers confirmed this. After World War II Jan Smuts stated: 'We have developed a white community here, and I can visualise no future government will ever dare to touch the basis on which South Africa has been developed.'[1] In 1955 Johannes Strijdom stated: 'Our task in South Africa is to maintain the identity of the white man: in that task we will die fighting.'[2] Ten years later his successor, Hendrik Verwoerd, was telling the world: 'Our motto is to maintain white supremacy for all time to come over our own people and our own country, by force if necessary.'[3] John Vorster who followed, assured the white electorate that the world should know that in defending itself white South Africa 'will fight to the end with all that we have got'.[4]

At first the maintenance of white control was explained in terms of racial superiority based on past achievements and a continuing ability of whites to rule over all for the benefit of all. In 1960, responding to Harold Macmillan's 'Wind of Change' speech, Verwoerd declared that whites had brought civilisation, economic development, order and education to Africa, and the continent's future rested on them.[5] However, under persistent criticism Pretoria shifted its emphasis (or at least its presentation) away from racial superiority to group rights, stressing in particular the right of whites to a separate identity and control of their own destiny. In 1970 Vorster argued that the whites had every right to be in South Africa because their roots were in the land which they had gained legitimately: 'I believe they have the right to maintain themselves as white people . . . That right which I claim for myself I also grant to every non-white person living here, to be itself.'[6] The priority given to the group, and especially the white group, overrode other considerations including individual rights. In 1946 Smuts denied that racial discrimination infringed elementary human rights, arguing that discrimination was necessary to protect 'the more backward sections of our multiplex society', and adding that failure to do so 'was tantamount to saying that the most

2

progressive races should be retarded by the less progressive if the latter were a majority'.[7] Almost forty years later, during the 1983 constitutional referendum, J. C. Heunis, Minister of Constitutional Development, spoke of 'unity in diversity' within a 'multinational heritage', and he said that although in one sense South Africa was made up of millions of individuals, in fact 'well nigh all of them prize their membership of distinct entities . . . and these nations and groups compete for political power'.[8]

During the 1970s the government, in its determination to emphasise South Africa's multinationalism, carved 'independent' African homelands or Bantustans from the existing state, while others were granted 'self-governing' status. This policy was presented as equivalent to the imperial powers granting independence to their colonies. Although this policy implied a reduction in the state's territory, the great bulk remained under white control, for even if all the homelands were to gain independence whites would still have control of 87 per cent of the total area, including the major urban centres and ports. Pretoria's intention was both to achieve a smaller, more secure 'white' state by externalising the blacks, and to counter international criticism by granting Africans political rights in their own areas. It was radical social engineering, in which large numbers of Africans were forcibly removed to the homelands. Yet increasingly blacks were drawn into white areas because the main economic activity remained there, but they were denied rights because their assumed home was in the Bantustans. The homeland concept was rejected by black nationalists and failed to gain international recognition. By the 1980s even Pretoria's enthusiasm had waned, but the policy continued from inertia and from lack of agreed alternatives. Pretoria, without abandoning the apartheid framework, introduced a new constitution, based on 'power sharing', with separate legislative chambers for whites, coloureds and Asians (the latter two groups not having homelands). There was no chamber of Africans, but some were offered residential rights in white South Africa, consultative councils, and the possibility of negotiating some political rights. Control of the government remained firmly in white hands under an executive white President.

FOREIGN POLICY MAKING

Deon Geldenhuys has described foreign policy making in South Africa as an 'oligarchic–bureaucratic' process, in which decision making is concentrated in the hands of a small group of senior ministers and officials, and in which not only blacks, but the white

3

electorate, pressure groups, and even members of the ruling party have had little say.[9] The oligarchy included the Prime Minister (State President from 1984), the Foreign and Defence Ministers and their senior officials, the military, and the Intelligence Agencies. From time to time others played a part. In the 1970s the Department of Information made a flamboyant if short lived contribution, while more consistent if less spectacular roles were played by departments responsible for trade, finance, minerals, and regional transport. Relationships and roles within the governing groups varied with changing circumstances and personalities. For example, the colonial withdrawal from southern Africa created a security problem as Pretoria found itself surrounded by black and potentially hostile states, and therefore the military came more into prominence as policy makers. An example of different personalities was provided by the three Foreign Ministers. Two of them (Eric Louw and 'Pik' Botha) were outgoing and assertive men who forced themselves into strong positions in the government, whereas the third (Hilgard Muller) was unassuming and had little influence outside his own department.

Although decision making was concentrated in few hands the external challenges brought foreign policy into political prominence. The white public may not have had a direct part but they were aware of the broad issues, reacted strongly to external pressures, and set a mood within which the government operated. The electorate and its own party supporters consciously judged its performance on foreign policy issues, which were often interlocked with domestic concerns. The policy makers themselves influenced, and were influenced by, the public debate and shared its assumptions. That led to clashes externally because prevailing international values ran counter to those of white South Africa. The government thus had great difficulty in reconciling demands arising from its domestic and foreign settings. While the pressure from its followers at home was to preserve white control, the pressure abroad (backed by black demands at home) was to abandon it. The problems were intensified by clashing perceptions. Most whites saw themselves as members of a Western, Christian, anti-communist society committed to a mixed/capitalist economy; whereas abroad the overriding perception was of a racist, authoritarian, exploitative society. In consequence white South Africans often felt betrayed by the West, which they believed should be their natural ally, whereas the West treated them with ambivalence: balancing continuing economic links with persistent criticism of racial policies.

The growing criticism underlined the constant interaction between foreign and domestic issues. The question in foreign policy analysis is not whether domestic affairs are to be examined, but rather how much attention should be paid to them, what sectors are to be investigated, and in what depth. In South Africa's case the relationship was strong and obvious, and much of her foreign policy was a product of, or response to, internal events. It was obvious, for example, in the dispute over the relationship between economic and political developments. As attempts to isolate South Africa foundered on the strength of economic links, a bitter dispute raged between the main trading partners and militant critics who advocated the imposition of economic sanctions. A related dispute concerned the connection between apartheid and capitalism. Does apartheid serve capitalism? Can capitalist expansion undermine apartheid? Do Western economic links strengthen or undermine apartheid? The questions were easy to put; the answers difficult to find.

FOREIGN POLICY SETTINGS

South Africa's foreign policy was pursued in three overlapping but distinctive settings: the regional context of southern Africa; relations with the West; and the broader world context including international organisations. There was activity outside these settings, such as Pretoria's efforts to build links with black states to the north, with other 'pariah' states (which became more important as isolation increased), and with South American states and Australia in an attempt to form a southern oceans alliance. However, these were either intermittent contacts or marginal to the main settings.

Southern Africa provided the most immediate and, from the late 1960s, the most active setting. Within the region Pretoria's aim was to surround itself with friendly, or at least compliant, neighbours willing to accept the prevailing political order in South Africa. Until the 1960s the rest of the region was under the control of colonial powers, with imperial economic/political systems operated by the metropolitan powers (Britain and Portugal). Even after Britain's decision to withdraw in the mid 1960s the colonial story was not over, as the Rhodesian dispute dragged on, and the Portuguese struggled to retain control in Mozambique and Angola. Although Pretoria opposed Britain's withdrawal, it had no choice but to come to terms with the new situation. A white security bloc was formed with South Africa as its most powerful member, and, somewhat to Pretoria's surprise, it discovered that in Britain's absence its economic and military strength created opportunities to demonstrate its regional power and to build links with the new black states. Yet while Pretoria demonstrated its

5

strength it failed to break the hostility of most black states. The best that was achieved was a 'live and let live' situation, and even that became more difficult from the mid 1970s when Portuguese rule collapsed in Angola and Mozambique. The white bloc disintegrated, the white regime in Rhodesia was defeated, and South Africa was left surrounded by black states. To a greater or lesser extent they were all dependent on her for vital services, and Pretoria tried to tie them to her through co-operation, but the black states resented their dependence (even if they could not break it) and they remained bitter opponents of apartheid. They were not always prepared meekly to subordinate their political interests to economic advantage.[10]

From the late 1970s Pretoria overtly used her military power to try to gain regional dominance. At the same time, the global powers were drawn into the region, as communist states and the US tried to influence the course of events, particularly in Angola where South African forces clashed with Cubans backed by the Soviet Union. Their entry and the hostility of neighbouring black states continued to limit Pretoria's regional power despite its relatively great strength. For all Pretoria's efforts the region did not provide a platform to launch its influence further into Africa. Instead the military imperatives of state security became dominant. By 1988, although functional and economic links continued, the emphasis on co-operation with others was more than matched by the assertion of regional military power.

The government saw South Africa as a natural part of the Western world – sharing its values, its economic system and its security concerns. Furthermore it saw itself as a bridge between Africa and the West ('the white world'). 'We look upon ourselves', said Verwoerd, 'as indispensable to the white world . . . We are the link. We are white, but we are in Africa. We link them both, and that lays on us a special duty.'[11] In the 1950s the government sought co-operation with the colonial powers, and tried to gain membership of a Western military alliance, but there was only limited co-operation and no alliance. Pretoria's perception of South Africa as a Western bastion standing firm against communist expansion gained little external support. Despite these disappointments South Africa was integrated into the Western international economic system, with increasing two way flows of trade, capital, and technology. The most powerful Western states – the US, Britain, West Germany, France, together with Japan (Japanese businessmen in South Africa became 'honorary whites') – tried to separate economic from political relations. They failed, because the militant opponents of apartheid challenged and attacked all links with South Africa, whatever their nature. From a combination of prudence and conviction the Western states kept their diplomatic distance from Pretoria, adopting an aloof stance, ignoring calls for defence agreements and special status in Africa, and eventually they imposed limited sanctions.

Pretoria's disappointment at its failure to gain Western support was matched by the bitterness of its militant opponents at the West's failure to act against apartheid. To the black states and anti-apartheid groups the Western states were appeasers at best, and partners of apartheid at worst. International organisations, including the United Nations (UN), provided stages from which to display the bitterness and launch the attacks. From the 1960s South Africa became increasingly isolated as she was forced out of many international organisations, starting with the Commonwealth. Despite the hostility, Pretoria clung to UN membership because this confirmed its international legitimacy and sovereign status while to withdraw might create the opportunity for the recognition of a black government in exile. However, the criticism persisted, and South Africa had no diplomatic friends. The Western states continued to support her UN membership (on the principle of universal membership) but they too were persistent, if less militant, critics. Wherever Pretoria turned, its activities were blighted by its internal racial policies. It clung to hopes that the international climate would change, or that attention would move elsewhere, or that its policies would succeed in transforming the situation. The hopes were not realised. South Africa remained a pariah state.

THE PATTERN OF POLITICAL DEVELOPMENT

This study is chronological. The framework is provided by a pattern of challenge and response which shaped South Africa's political development after 1945. The state faced periods of severe challenge and even crisis, when domestic and international threats together prompted great fears and uncertainty among whites, and high expectation among blacks. At times the state appeared to be on the point of collapse, with its resources apparently inadequate or inappropriate to meet the challenges. Yet recovery followed as the government, business community and the white society responded with strong security and economic measures, together with social and political readjustments, while at the same time the opponents were unable to sustain their challenge. Recovery led to periods of white confidence when the government was convinced that it could meet any continuing danger, only for a new set of challenges to appear.

7

Between 1945 and 1988 four cycles can be identified, each starting with a period of challenge. The earliest came in the years immediately following the Second World War when South Africa felt the first impact of international hostility and militant black nationalism at home. The United Party Government neither anticipated the problems nor handled them with conviction, and although the challenges were mild compared with those that followed, at the time they had a great impact because they were outside previous experience. Smuts's indignation and despair over his treatment at the UN in 1946 was no less than that of his successors, for he and his colleagues were convinced that they were unjustly treated, and they rightly feared that new international forces were threatening the established South African order. The government's uncertainty over the two central issues of racial policy and foreign affairs contributed to its defeat at the 1948 election. It was replaced by the National Party (NP) which preached three unequivocal messages: that the society must be structured on rigid racial lines; that the whites must have exclusive control; and that foreign interference must be resisted. The NP was suspected abroad because of its opposition to the Allies during the war, and its racial commitments compounded the immediate problems. The apartheid policies of the new government were viewed with profound hostility by black nationalists and attracted strong international criticism. To its enemies the government was intransigent and racist; to its supporters it was clear and determined. Despite the hostility, it overcame the early problems and uncompromisingly pushed ahead with apartheid. As it did so it consolidated support among the white electorate, and by the late 1950s the NP Government was in firm control. White South Africa enjoyed a period of confidence.

That confidence was undermined in the early 1960s. Harold Macmillan, the British Prime Minister, warned that the colonial powers were withdrawing from Africa and white South Africans could not expect support if they tried to stand against black nationalism. Shortly afterwards, after police fired on black demonstrators at Sharpeville, a sustained struggle developed between black nationalists and the government. The government banned the nationalists who then committed themselves to revolution by launching an underground struggle inside the country and training guerrilla fighters abroad. Pretoria's increasing international problems led to withdrawal from the Commonwealth and constant attacks from the new black states at the UN. Under this combined pressure there were many (inside and outside South Africa) who believed that revolution was imminent. It did not come. The government's response to the crisis was fivefold: to

unify whites in defence of the state; to intensify security arrangements; to exploit its economic strength; to push ahead with apartheid;
and to join a white regional security bloc. Inside South Africa Pretoria
emphasised the concept of a multinational state in which blacks could
gain rights and even independence in their own homelands. Although
the government failed to convince its international opponents (who
were reinforced by the exiled black parties) such was its success at
home in suppressing black nationalism and promoting economic
growth that from the mid 1960s the whites enjoyed a decade of
confidence. At home the government's grip was firm; the economy
continued to grow; the ring of white territories held firm; and the
threat of international sanctions receded as they proved ineffective
against Rhodesia. Pretoria became so confident that it launched
initiatives into black Africa.

That period of confidence was shattered by a new wave of domestic
and international challenges. It started with the 1974 coup in Portugal
where the new government announced it would withdraw from
Angola and Mozambique, thereby breaking the white security ring,
making Rhodesia indefensible, and leading to black Marxist government on South Africa's borders. Pretoria's response to its changing
regional setting was mixed, with weary resignation to a Marxist state
in Mozambique, attempts to foster a 'moderate' government in Rhodesia, but armed intervention in Angola. Soon Pretoria faced major
internal problems inspired in part by the regional upheaval. In 1976
black youths rose in defiance of apartheid: first in Soweto and then
across the country. The government's harsh response, with the
shooting of youths and the killing of Steve Biko, the Black Consciousness leader, intensified opposition and the sense of crisis. Again,
predictions of the imminent overthrow of the state were rife. Even the
Prime Minister, John Vorster, spoke of prospects too ghastly to
contemplate. On the international front the presence of Cuban troops
in Angola signalled the entry of global conflict into the region, raising
further problems. Military action in Angola failed and led to a
humiliating retreat after the entry of Cuban troops and the withdrawal
of US support, while after Soweto and Steve Biko's death, the West
demonstrated its opposition by supporting a UN mandatory arms ban
against South Africa. At the same time the ANC staged a revival:
mobilising international opposition, launching a sabotage campaign
inside South Africa, and recruiting young blacks fleeing the country.

Surrounded by challenges the government vacillated at first but
when it recovered its nerve it responded with characteristic vigour:
repressing opposition, strengthening the security forces, pushing

ahead with apartheid by granting 'independence' to Bantustans, and reducing its international dependence (for example, by expanding the arms industry). Pretoria also recognised that repression had its limits and started a process of reform in two sensitive areas: the constitution and labour relations. The process led eventually to a new constitution – with an executive President and a tricameral parliament of coloured, Indian and white chambers. The constitution was opposed by most Africans, who saw their exclusion as confirmation of their lack of rights. It was also opposed by an unusual alliance of whites: 'liberals' who criticised the absence of Africans, and 'right wingers' who criticised Coloured and Indian participation: and both groups opposed the increased executive powers. However, a referendum of whites gave the government a clear majority for the constitution. At the same time a security agreement with Mozambique, welcomed in the West, aroused hopes of greater regional stability. These developments restored Pretoria's confidence which was based on regaining order in the black townships; on regional developments, in which the carrot of economic co-operation, the stick of military action, and the weaknesses of black neighbours gave Pretoria a strong hand; and on improved relations with the West, where in the US, Britain and West Germany conservative governments adopted policies of 'constructive engagement'. In one important respect, however, there were grounds for concern because the economy failed to recover from a combination of adverse external circumstances and internal mismanagement. While between 1960 and 1974 the real economic growth rate had averaged 5.5 per cent per annum, in the following ten years it was only 1.9 per cent, and while until 1974 the main sources of foreign capital had been investment, after that there was increasing reliance on foreign loans, leaving the economy exposed for the future. Despite that, with domestic security strengthened, controlled reform under way, regional power displayed for all and more sympathy in the West, white South Africa enjoyed another period of confidence. As P. W. Botha toured European states in 1984 there were hopes in Pretoria that pariah status was ending.

However, shortly after Botha's return from Europe the most serious and sustained black risings yet spread across the country. While in previous crises black disturbances had been patchy and confined to major centres, this time they spread quickly across the whole country and into small rural towns. Previously the police had been able to regain order but this time the army had to be summoned, and it took nearly two years and stringent emergency regulations to suppress the opposition. The fuel for the risings was, as ever, opposition to

10

apartheid – sparked off this time by the new constitution, as well as deteriorating economic conditions. Groups (in particular the United Democratic Front) were formed to campaign against the constitution, and to confront the government. The result was that the government's reforms which had been designed to solve socio-political problems had set off a new wave of black opposition on one side, and a powerful 'right-wing' reaction on the other. The black risings and the government's response led to renewed international condemnation. In the West television coverage of the protests and violence had a profound impact, implanting South Africa into domestic politics, especially in the US where the public outcry led to limited economic sanctions and the withdrawal of many companies. The region was also unstable, as Pretoria increasingly turned to force rather than diplomacy in its relations with neighbours.

Yet the government did regain its security grip. An uneasy order was imposed on the black townships, and regional threats were countered by the assertion of military power. The government's success was only partial. Its policy towards Africans was in disarray: even moderate leaders refused to work with it, the local government system had broken down, and the 'independent' homelands were chronically unstable. Economic difficulties increased further. Although full international sanctions were not imposed, the economy was facing greater problems than at any time since 1945. The constitution had not provided the government with a secure base and even its hold on the white electorate (especially Afrikaners) was less certain. At the time this book was completed Pretoria had reimposed order, the economy was showing a few signs of recovery and an international agreement had been reached on Namibia, but there were too many doubts and fears to say that white South Africa was enjoying another period of confidence.

Two final points can be made about the pattern of challenge and response. First, although the government has so far always succeeded in regaining order, each period of challenge has been sharper and more profound than its predecessor, and therefore more difficult to counter. Second, the periods of crisis have produced clear changes in government policy. In efforts to solve the crises new policies have been introduced or existing ones modified. The post-Second World War challenge produced a change of government and the introduction of apartheid; the shootings at Sharpeville and their aftermath saw a surge in apartheid activity (especially in the Bantustans) and a substantial increase in military strength; Soweto and the regional challenge of the 1970s set off the labour and constitutional changes and an

11

increased military role in policy making. So far it is difficult to detect if further shifts in government policy will follow the black risings of the mid 1980s, for they came while the government was still trying to implement the post-Soweto changes. What can be said, however, is that the shifts of policy and attempts at social engineering have so far failed because they have not resolved the central problem of giving black South Africans full rights in their own country. Until that is achieved the search for international status and security cannot succeed. Success will come only if the government abandons its principal aim of ensuring the preservation of a white controlled state.

PART I

THE POST-WAR CHALLENGE
AND
THE FOUNDATION OF
APARTHEID: 1945–1960

2 SMUTS AND THE AFTERMATH OF WAR

Like all the victorious allies, South Africa entered the post-war years anticipating the fruits of victory.[1] In the Union itself the war had caused little physical hardship – the battlefields were far away and the economy had expanded as demand for minerals increased and as local manufacturers flourished in the absence of foreign competition.[2] However the war had imposed a heavy political price on the white government. Immediately following Britain's declaration of war in 1939 General J. B. M. Hertzog, the South African Prime Minister, introduced a neutrality motion into the House of Assembly, but there he was opposed by eight cabinet colleagues including his Deputy, General Jan Smuts. Smuts moved an amendment to enter the war, and in a dramatic parliamentary confrontation he carried the day by eighty votes to sixty-seven. Smuts immediately formed a new government and led the Union into war. He had no doubt that the decision was right but he also had no doubt about the sacrifices involved. Among his white opponents memories of a bitter past came flooding back – a past in which Boer had fought Briton, and in which there had been deep divisions among the Afrikaners (Boers) themselves.[3] It was to heal these wounds and to seek a cure for economic ills that Smuts and Hertzog, both Afrikaners, had formed the United Party in 1934. Their message then had been one of reconciliation among all whites, but that was now lost in the decision to go to war.

While Smuts and Hertzog had been united in seeking white reconciliation at home they had differences on foreign policy. At that time South Africa's external affairs were dominated by the relationship with Britain – the major African colonial power, the leader of the Commonwealth, and the 'imperial factor' in the Union's own history. Smuts was a great Commonwealth man. He was convinced that his country's best interests were served by working within a strong British Commonwealth and Empire. Hertzog did not share these enthusiasms. He was not, like the Nationalists, a bitter opponent of the British connection, but he accepted rather than enthused about it. For him South Africa had separate interests, although often these could be forwarded by working with Britain. To Hertzog, and even more to the Nationalists, the decision to go to war was another example – as in 1914–18 – of being drawn into a conflict which was not of direct concern to the Union. That view was rejected by most English speaking whites and a substantial number of Afrikaners, but there was enough of the old division of Boer against Briton to reopen old wounds.

The main opposition to the war came from the National Party, led by Dr D. F. Malan. The Nationalists saw themselves as the bearers of the true Afrikaner traditions, culture, and history – a history in which they had struggled against the twin threats of black Africa and imperial Britain. As the Nationalists' criticism of the war continued, so the future shape of post-war white politics emerged. Although the United Party retained Afrikaner leadership and many Afrikaner followers, its main strength was among the English speakers. In contrast the National Party was almost exclusively Afrikaner. Behind the conflict which arose over the symbols of the state – the Union Jack against the Republican Tricolour; 'God Save the King' against 'Die Stem' – there was a deep division of loyalty and identity among the whites.

The chief Nationalist ogre was Smuts – in their eyes he was a traitor to his Afrikaner inheritance who had sent 'Africa's sons to die for Britain'[4] and had become the creature of 'Hoggenheimer', a capitalist caricature dominated by economic motivation.[5] In contrast Smuts was idolised in his own party where his authority was accepted almost without question. That had adverse long term implications for the party, because beneath the protective shadow of Smuts's last years there was little room for vigorous new ideas or leaders.[6] The Nationalists complained that the Prime Minister spent too much time and energy on international affairs and was prepared to sacrifice his country's interests for those of his global ambitions. Malan suggested that if a monument were erected to Smuts it should stand next to that for the first Dutch Governor, Jan van Riebeck, but while van Riebeck's 'had its back to the sea and faces South Africa' Smuts's 'should have its back to South Africa and face overseas'.[7]

SMUTS AND THE INTERNATIONAL COMMUNITY

While at home Smuts was a controversial figure, abroad he had enormous prestige. Like previous Prime Ministers he acted as his own Foreign Minister, but he brought a personal and distinctive breadth of vision by linking the Union's interests to those of the whole international community.[8] His ideas and policies had a grand, panoramic sweep which his successors never emulated, or perhaps never had the opportunity to emulate. Even during the war years he was busy sketching his ideas for the future international system – such as the creation of a new major organisation, and the rebuilding of Europe. In Smuts's lifetime international relations had been dominated by two world wars whose origins were in Europe. For him, therefore, the overriding task for the future was the prevention of a third world war, and to that end he supported three interlocking developments – the creation of the United Nations, the restoration of Europe, and the reinforcement of the British Commonwealth.

As President of the Commission on the General Assembly Smuts played a leading part in the formation of the United Nations. He drafted the preamble to the Charter with its ringing declaration of 'faith in fundamental human rights, in the dignity and worth of the human person, in the equal rights of men and women'[9] – words which ironically were soon to be used against his country in the Assembly he had helped to create. However, his main concern was international order and securing the peace, and it was in that light that he supported the special status for the Great Powers, although he had doubts about both of the future superpowers. He saw the US as a giant full of promise but unsophisticated and unsure of its international role. The USSR was an enigma, but he hoped that if its world status were recognised it too would work for peace.[10] In the search for peace Europe was the focus of Smuts's attention. 'The restoration of Europe', he said, 'is the supreme problem of the coming peace, and beyond all doubt, the most urgent problem before the world.'[11] His concern probably also reflected the central place Europe held for white South Africans who saw themselves as representatives of its culture and values in a difficult and often alien continent.

Smuts hoped that Britain would take the lead in building a third world power. There were two strands to his thinking – the Commonwealth and Western Europe. He saw 'scattered sprawling across the seas the British group' standing as a third Great Power between the US and the USSR – 'an area of stability between the two power poles'.[12] In a world of uncertainty, he saw the Commonwealth as a rock on which to build order. In 1945 Britain still had a vast Empire, alongside a small tightly-knit Commonwealth in which full membership was confined to five states, all of which were ruled by whites – Australia, Canada, New Zealand, South Africa and Britain itself. Membership gave each an enhanced international status, and for

17

Smuts a stage of global dimensions. Tested in the fires of two world wars the Commonwealth had achieved an almost spiritual quality for Smuts. It was, he said, bound by 'unbreakable spiritual bonds which are stronger than steel'.[13] With the traditional Commonwealth acceptance of no interference in each others' internal affairs, with Britain still the ruler of a great Empire, it was easy for Smuts to believe that the future Commonwealth would be a projection of the past – intimate, like minded, and predominantly white. He failed to anticipate the concern with racial discrimination that was soon to plague the Union's membership of all international organisations, including the Commonwealth. On occasion he linked his hopes for the Commonwealth with the restoration of Europe. He urged Britain to take the lead in Europe, and speculated about the possibility of linking the Commonwealth with some of the Western European states. He said: 'If Western Union, with British membership is thus consummated, a third or middle power group will arise, at least equal to either of the other two, the security set-up of the world will rest on a triangle of power, and will not continue to be precariously poised between two great powers facing each other across a broken Europe.'[14]

South Africa's defence arrangements were closely associated with the Commonwealth, but there was no formal alliance, and when questioned by the Nationalists, Smuts always emphasised the Union's independence. Yet for him there was the reassuring assumption that the relationship with Britain was so close, the interests of the two countries so interlocked, that there was no need for formal agreements. Independence and commitment were compatible because South Africa's interests lay in a strong Commonwealth, including military co-operation. When it became clear that Britain could no longer shoulder all her old military commitments Smuts called on other members to contribute more to Commonwealth defence.[15]

Another potential advantage of the Commonwealth was the extension of the Union's influence across Africa. Smuts had always harboured expansionist ambitions to move north into Central and East Africa, and he believed that the Commonwealth would provide the instrument for achieving this. During the war he had asked Britain to transfer to the Union the three neighbouring High Commission Territories of Bechuanaland, Basutoland and Swaziland, but the British postponed a decision until after the war. Unwilling to jeopardise the relationship, Smuts had not mentioned that disappointment, and in 1943 he called for a Commonwealth reorganisation in which the dominions would become 'sharers and partners in the Empire', to 'take both interest and pride in the Colonies within their sphere, and in that way to create, in our great world-wide Commonwealth, a new "esprit de corps", a common patriotism, and a larger-human outlook'.[16] Smuts was thinking in particular of South Africa's 'sphere of influence' in Africa. When, in March 1945, he was urged in parliament to help create a massive federal state embracing South Africa, the Rhodesias, Kenya and Tanganyika, and incorporating the High Commission Territories, Smuts, without going into detail, confirmed that he had always striven to knit together 'the parts of Southern Africa that belong to each other, parts that must necessarily work together for a stable future on the continent of Africa'.[17]

SMUTS CABINED AND CONFINED

As the post-war years unfolded it became clear that Smuts had made false assumptions about the international setting in which his country would operate. The war aims proclaimed by the Allies – to counter Nazi racism and German and Japanese oppression – were translated into post-war values against all racism and in favour of majority rule. To its surprise and consternation the South African Government became a target for attack because of its internal racial policies. When Smuts climbed onto the international stage he continued to see himself as the experienced world statesman, but many of his audience now saw him first and foremost as the leader of a racist government imposing its control in a divided society. As the pressure mounted so Smuts was forced away from his grand design to defend his country and the structure of its society. He had failed to anticipate the tough reality that South Africa's international relations would increasingly be shaped by her internal racial policies.

It seems ironic that a South African leader should underrate the importance of race relations. It was not that Smuts was unconscious of the problem – that was impossible for any South African – and he was wise enough to appreciate that increased attention would be detrimental to the Union, but he had no firm answers. He appreciated that injustices and discrimination grew from racial divisions, but said 'I don't see clearly what can be done about it.'[18] On another occasion he wrote: 'I am suspected of being a hypocrite because I can be quoted on both sides. The Preamble of the [United Nations] Charter is my own work and I also mean to protect the European position in a world which is tending the other way.'[19] Yet when choice had to be made he favoured 'the European position'. For instance, when he set himself up as peacemaker in a dispute between the Indian and white communities in Natal he recognised that both sides 'suffer from a form of hysteria', but added, 'In the last resort I take the side of the European and what he stands for in this continent.'[20] He expressed a commonly held white South African fear of India unloading its surplus population into Africa. In more general terms he claimed that 'South Africa is a little epic of European civilization on a dark continent . . . I frankly am a Westerner, although I love and respect the whole human family, irrespective of colour or race.'[21] Faced by such a dilemma he tried to push the problem aside, as something to be settled by future generations, but in doing so he opted for the 'status quo' in which whites were dominant.

The ambiguity that Smuts recognised in himself left his government open to criticism from all sides. The National Party attacked it for failing to defend the white position. They pointed to the liberalism of the Deputy Prime Minister, Jan Hofmeyr, and to the government's acceptance of the Fagan Report (1948) which stated that territorial segregation of the races was an unrealisable dream, that blacks must be recognised as a permanent part of the urban population, and that the system of migratory labour was obsolete. In response the Nationalists turned to their own report (the Sauer Report) which said that the races could and should be separated and live apart. In the enclosed world of white politics some of the opposition accusations against the government stuck. Therefore, although Smuts's instincts and political judgement kept him from grasping the nettle of racial reform, although under pressure he always supported the white position, although he openly stated that Hofmeyr's views were too idealistic, and although he had no intention of giving blacks political rights, an air of uncertainty surrounded the government's racial policies. Malan said of Smuts: 'On the colour problem he never sounded a clear note.'[22]

BLACK STIRRINGS

In contrast to the white National Party, the black nationalists accused the government of practising racial discrimination and denying blacks their rights. A larger, more militant African nationalism emerged in the 1940s, the product of changing circumstances at home and abroad. The economic boom drew blacks into the towns, doubling the black urban population between 1939 and 1952. There was a revival in black trades unions and in the major black political party, the African National Congress (ANC). A. B. Xuma, the ANC leader, was an efficient organiser rather than a magnetic public figure but black public support for the party steadily increased, and Xuma consolidated its position by working with the Indian Congress and the

Communist Party. Inside the ANC an important Youth League was formed which was determined to push the party into a more active and radical stance. It emphasised indigenous leadership, and black self-determination. It was wary of outside interference, including that of the Communist Party which, by 1945, had black representatives on the ANC executive.[23]

Alongside the changing domestic scene the international situation gave the black nationalists new hope. The Second World War, with its blood-letting in Europe, the defeat of the colonial powers in Asia, the Atlantic Charter and unanimous allied condemnation of Nazi racism, stimulated their ambitions. In December 1945 the ANC issued a Declaration of Rights which demanded equality for blacks, with full citizenship rights, the abolition of discrimination, and an equal share of material resources. However, when calling for the unity of the masses, the leaders recognised that a long struggle lay ahead 'entailing great sacrifices of time, means and even life itself'.[24] In its struggle the ANC found a platform at the UN, where its message was heard by the international community and the whites at home. In 1946 Smuts was embarrassed by the appearance at the UN of Dr Xuma, the first of a long line of black nationalist and anti-apartheid leaders who followed that road. However, the United Party Government had no sympathy with these black aspirations nor any intention of giving ground to them. A major strike by black gold miners in 1946 was broken by dismissing workers and by brutal police methods which led to deaths and injuries. Instead of a direct say in government Africans were given an advisory body – the Native Representative Council – but in 1946 during the strike even that moderate body unanimously refused further co-operation and disbanded itself after attacking government policy.

EARLY ATTACKS AT THE UNITED NATIONS

At the UN the early attacks against South Africa were centred on two main issues – the status of South West Africa (Namibia) and the treatment of Indians in the Union – but behind these was a broader hostility to Pretoria's racial policies. As the attacks developed the UN become unrecognisable to Smuts as the organisation he had helped to form or as the one he believed was needed. Instead of concentrating on global order and security it became, in Smuts's words, 'a cockpit of emotion, passion and ignorance'[25] against the Union's racial policies. In March 1947 Smuts confessed that the UN 'has been a great disappointment to me – not only personally, but from the larger viewpoint'.[26] His reactions characterised those of South African governments over the next forty years. The details and intensity of their responses changed but not the spirit. Smuts, like those who followed, protested that the attacks were against policies that fell within the Union's domestic jurisdiction, and were therefore outside the UN's competence. He pointed to Article 2(7) of the Charter which excluded internal affairs from the UN's competence. 'There', said Smuts, 'is my veto.'[27] His indignation was greater because he believed that the main attacks came from governments which were incompetent, prejudiced, ill-informed, and ignored their own sins. In replying to the Indian delegate in 1946 Smuts asked whether there was greater discrimination anywhere than that based on caste, community and religion in India.

The case of South West Africa was usually presented at the UN in constitutional cum legal terms, but again the real issue was racial discrimination. The territory had come under Pretoria's administration after the First World War as a League of Nations Mandate.[28] Because of its small population, its geographical position, and its lack of development, it was designated as 'C' class mandate, whereby it was to be administered under the Union's laws as an integral part of the country. However South Africa, like other mandatory powers, undertook to 'promote to the utmost the material and moral well-being and social progress of the inhabitants'.[29] She was obliged to make annual reports and accept the principle 'that the well-being and development of the peoples formed a sacred trust of civilisation'.[30] There had been some criticism of South Africa's administration before World War Two but generally the League's yoke was light, and Pretoria had administered the vast, harsh territory largely free from interference.[31]

With the disappearance of the League, Smuts went to the UN to seek the incorporation of South West Africa into the Union. In that, said his Nationalist critics, he made his first mistake. They said the government should have absorbed the territory by right because the UN had no legitimate claims in the matter, whereas by raising the issue Smuts had undermined the South African position. Smuts went to the UN because he was confident of success, believing that the case for incorporation was irrefutable, and because of his early commitment to the organisation. His position was that while there was no legal obligation on the Union to reach agreement with the UN there was a moral obligation to try, but if that failed the 'status quo' would remain.[32]

At the UN the South African delegates argued that of all the old

mandate territories South West Africa was the most suited for incorporation because economically and geographically it was a natural part of
the Union, and was essential for her defence. It was only the
dilatoriness of the Cape Government that had prevented its absorp-
tion before the German occupation and that been remedied by the
successful invasion in World War One. If on no other grounds, the
Union could claim the territory by right of conquest, but it was also
what the people of South West Africa themselves wanted. The
government claimed that in the white Legislative Council and at black
tribal meetings there had been clear majorities who wanted 'to remain
under the Union flag and form part of the Union'.[33]

In November 1946 South Africa's request to incorporate the territory
was rejected. The General Assembly then adopted – by thirty-seven
votes to zero, with nine abstentions – a resolution recommending that
South West Africa be put under a trusteeship agreement. Three
reasons were given: first, that the Union's discriminatory policies were
detrimental to the interests of the African inhabitants; second, that
incorporation would be contrary to the UN trusteeship system which
had superseded the mandate agreement; and third, the Africans may
not have understood the advantages of the trusteeship system when
presented by Pretoria. For Smuts it was a grave blow. 'South Africa',
he wrote, 'is dazed and amazed at the rebuff at New York.'[34]

The early clashes over South West Africa coincided with the Indian
Government's first attacks on Pretoria for the treatment of South
Africa's Indian population. The majority of the quarter million Indians
were concentrated in Natal, which with its predominantly English
speaking white population was a United Party stronghold. Shortly
before the 1943 election, and under pressure from his own party,
Smuts had introduced the 'Pegging Act', which restricted Indian
settlement and land ownership. That brought bitter opposition from
both the local Indians and the Indian Government. In the following
years the government sought a compromise between the Indian
claims for greater rights and the white claim for more restrictions. In
March 1946 Smuts personally introduced new legislation – the Asiatic
Land Tenure and Indian Representation Act, which on the one hand
limited Indian land ownership and occupation to certain areas in
Natal, and on the other offered them a form of political representation.
However, while the Indian representatives (two members) on the
Natal Provincial Council could be drawn from their own people, their
representatives in the House of Assembly and the Senate (three and
two respectively) would be whites. The compromise satisfied nobody.
On their side the Natal Indians rejected 'The Ghetto Act', and

23

launched a passive resistance campaign, which was supported by the Indian Government, while among whites the Nationalists and 'right-wing' government supporters were unhappy about the 'liberal' franchise proposals. Although Smuts forced the legislation through parliament his party was split and supported him with little enthusiasm.

At the UN the Indian Government sponsored a resolution criticising the Union for denying human rights to its Indian population and impairing friendly relations between two member states. When Pretoria failed to change its position India recalled its High Commissioner and imposed a symbolic economic boycott. As with South West Africa, Pretoria was on the defensive – harried and attacked on an issue which it regarded as exclusively within her jurisdiction – and again there was miscalculation. 'We feel our case to be so judicially secure that it only had to be stated to be realised', wrote the High Commissioner in London.[35] Caught on the horns of a dilemma Smuts agreed to discuss the resolution 'without admitting the right of the United Nations to intervene in this matter'. The Nationalists immediately pointed out that discussion was a form of interference. At the UN Smuts said that the Indians were outside the UN's competence because they were South African nationals. He denied that racial discrimination in South Africa had infringed elementary human rights: on the contrary the distinctions drawn between the races avoided friction by creating safeguards for 'the more backward sections of our multiplex society'.[36] As there was no definition of 'human rights' in the Charter there could be no obligation to meet them. 'Political rights and freedoms . . . were not fundamental'. Such an argument, Smuts contended, 'was tantamount to saying that the most progressive races should be retarded by the less progressive if the latter were in a majority. Equality in fundamental rights and freedoms could be assured in a multiracial state only by a measure of discrimination in respect of non-fundamental rights.'[37] He suggested that an advisory opinion be sought from the International Court of Justice on whether this was an internal issue covered by Article 2(7) of the Charter.

As in the South West African dispute Pretoria had been forced to retreat to a legalistic defence of its position, but again it failed to quell the criticism. In January 1947 the General Assembly resolved that friendly relations had been impaired between two member states (India and South Africa), that the treatment of Indians in the Union came within the Charter provisions, and that India and South Africa should abide by a 1927 agreement which Pretoria denied was a binding international treaty.[38] When the General Assembly next met in September 1947 India immediately complained that South Africa had failed to implement the resolution and that Smuts had abused the UN by denouncing the principle of human equality.

The conflict with India implied more than a clash of interests between two states. It confirmed that irrespective of South Africa's wishes the Union's racial policies would be treated as a matter of concern by international bodies, and that opposition would come from inside the Commonwealth.[39] South Africa was not yet diplomatically isolated but she was fast becoming an embarrassing friend. Smuts's government had been the first to face the dilemma that while political survival at home rested on a commitment to white domination, internationally the same commitment brought hostility and isolation.

THE COMMONWEALTH AND BRITAIN

Although the post-war Commonwealth was not developing as Smuts had anticipated, it remained an important forum for South Africa's external affairs. Central to it was the bilateral relationship with Britain, in whom Smuts retained considerable, if not uncritical faith. By 1947, disillusioned by the UN, he said, 'I look upon Britain as a safer guarantee of peace in the world than the United Nations itself.'[40] He saw the introduction of Marshall Aid in 1947 as a great opportunity for Britain to take the lead in Europe where 'proudly she should once more resume her glorious role in world affairs'.[41] The strength of the continuing link with Britain was symbolised by the visit of the royal family to the Union in 1947 – its first post-war overseas tour. Nothing could have given Smuts greater pleasure. He believed that the visit strengthened the ties between the two countries and eased the task of reconciliation between Afrikaners and English speaking whites at home. Yet while for Smuts and most of his supporters the royal tour was an unqualified success, the Nationalists were critical (Dr Verwoerd, then editor of *Die Transvaaler* refused even to mention it in his paper) and there were even doubts among some United Party supporters who believed that Smuts had overplayed his hand by fawning too much on the royal party. He had humbled himself too much and in doing so had humbled his country.

The royal tour may have masked the reality that while the bilateral relationship with Britain was still strong the two sides were steadily moving apart. An early indication of change (which came like a hammer blow for Smuts) was the defeat of Churchill by the Labour Party in the 1945 election. In the event relations with the new government were not as difficult as Smuts feared. Great respect was given to him personally, and the Labour Government was grateful for the Union's economic help to Britain and to the whole sterling area as it struggled to counter the dominance of the dollar. Yet there was less intimacy. Heaton Nicholls, the High Commissioner in London, wrote: 'During the Churchill regime, Smuts's advice was always given grave consideration and more often than not accepted. With the Labour Party, of course, his advice was not always so welcome . . . Nevertheless his advice always carried weight.'[42]

White South African doubts about the Labour Party were reinforced when Attlee's government accepted that the aim of imperial policy was to direct the colonies towards self-government. By 1947, with India, Pakistan and Ceylon independent, with further decolonisation in prospect, and with Britain economically weak and uncertain of her international role, a new Commonwealth was emerging. The Commonwealth of like mindedness was giving way to that of diversity. Publicly Smuts accepted it, said he admired British realism, and came to see some creative elements in the changes, but it was not what he had foreseen or liked. Privately he thought the decision to quit India 'an awful mistake',[43] and when Ceylon was granted independence he wrote: 'Ceylon a Dominion this year? Am I mad or is the world mad?'[44] Smuts had hoped to see a stronger Commonwealth built on the old foundations – hence the proposal to link it with Western European recovery – not a vehicle for British decolonisation.

The clash between South Africa and the Asian Commonwealth members left Britain in an invidious position. The Indians did not raise the dispute directly at Commonwealth Conferences because, in Nehru's view, that might have inferred that the Commonwealth could be 'considered as some kind of superior body which sometimes acts as a tribunal, or judge, or in a sense supervises the activities of its member nations'. In December 1946 India's UN delegate appealed to Britain to vote against South Africa to show that on racial discrimination the Charter was not just 'a scrap of paper'.[45] Britain avoided any commitment, but the Indian appeal marked the start of a conflict in which the demands of the newly independent states for racial equality clashed with the ties of loyalty to an old dominion. When at home the Nationalists pressed Smuts about the dangers of Commonwealth interference he replied that the government had always stood firmly against it, and when pressure had been exerted at Commonwealth Conference the response had been clear: 'Namely, that we in South Africa did not recognise equal rights . . . that we did not recognise such a thing [equality] and had never recognised it and would never recognise it.' He accepted that the matter would probably be raised again, but he asserted, 'The position of South Africa remains unchanged. We are a sovereign state and our future and status will not be decided by another body . . . We have developed a white community here and I can visualise no future government which will ever dare to touch the basis on which South Africa has been developed.'[46]

A DELICATE AND EVEN DANGEROUS SITUATION

While in the post-war years South Africa was accepted without question into the Western economic system, political/ diplomatic relations became ambivalent. The Western states did not lead the attacks against the Union but they were already reluctant to accept guilt by association in defending her racial politics. By 1947 Smuts was deep in gloom. He spoke of a 'solid wall of prejudice' and 'floods of emotion fanned by mischievous propaganda' against the Union's racial policies.[47] Early in 1947 he told the House that 'the past four months have been some of the most difficult of my life', and when he was asked what would be the situation if the UN applied sanctions against South Africa, he did not dismiss it as an absurd idea. 'Sanctions', he said, 'constitute a war measure . . . and South Africa must treat this matter very seriously . . . We are in a delicate and even dangerous situation.'[48] He said he had learned 'during the past few months that South Africa is in a much more dangerous and much more difficult position than ever before. We have built up a community in the southern part of the continent which is not without its dangers . . . We have built up . . . a monument among the nations, something that we cannot sacrifice.'[49]

As Smuts agonised, the Nationalists used the international situation as a rod to beat his back. Not only, they said, had he spent too much time on international affairs, he had spent it unsuccessfully. Why, the Nationalists asked, had he responded so lamely to the Indian attacks? Why had he taken the South West Africa case to the UN? Why had he accepted the UN Charter when it contained the principle of equality for all? Jan Strijdom, a future Nationalist Prime Minister, concluded that Smuts 'will be recorded in the history of South Africa as the man who has accomplished the downfall of white civilization'.[50] Malan said that Smuts gave 'the impression that he is first a United Nations man and then he is a South African. I am in the first instance a South African man.'[51] Smuts's replies to these attacks were those of a sad, perplexed and disillusioned man. Because it had been assumed that his great knowledge and prestige would give South Africa an advantage in international affairs the failure seemed all the greater. 'The

Opposition', wrote Smuts, 'naturally rejoice and put this all to my account, and to the liberalism (!) with which I have led the world astray.'[52]

In retrospect two images of Smuts remain. One, which his admirers remember, comes from the days when he was a dominant, international figure with the vitality which is captured in his statue in Parliament Square, London – the lithe, stretched body, the confident forward thrust of the head. The other remains in the memory of his detractors, when in the final years the certainty had gone, when he had become the heavy, brooding figure of the statue in the Cape Town Gardens. Smuts's experience reveals that while in the immediate post-war years the international pressures on South Africa were much less severe than they became later, they were no less keenly felt. The criticism was so unexpected and, in white eyes, so unwarranted that it was deeply resented. The resentment persisted, but as time passed the whites came to expect less, and with fewer hopes learned to cope with the increasing hostility.

The early challenges faced by the United Party Government were not intense enough to be described as 'a crisis' but the government's response lacked confidence and conviction, and that had its influence on the 1948 election when the United Party lost power. There are a number of explanations for the government's defeat – the unbalanced constituencies which meant that although the Nationalists gained fewer votes they had more seats; a poor electioneering performance by the government; discontent among urban whites at the government's housing record; discontent among the farming community (especially in the Transvaal) at its agricultural pricing policy; and the success of the Nationalists in drawing the Afrikaners together. However, over and above these was the government's uncertainty in responding to the interlocking problems of race relations at home and international pressures abroad.

3 THE NATIONALISTS ESTABLISH THEIR RULE AND LOOK TO AFRICA

The results of the 1948 election came as a surprise even to the National Party. Internationally the new government was treated with suspicion because it had opposed involvement in the war, and because its rigid racial policies offended against the growing commitment to racial equality. There was a short term adverse international economic reaction with reserves dropping by £37m. and the withdrawal of some industrial investments.[1] At home the government's apartheid policies met with strong resistance from the black nationalists, while within the white political system the United Party challenged it on constitutional and economic issues. However, as the 1950s progressed the government became secure. Refusing to be diverted by opposition from home or abroad it imposed apartheid and its position was reinforced with the return of international economic confidence. With further election victories in 1953 and 1958 the National Party transformed itself from a party with no experience of government and a narrow electoral base to South Africa's natural party of government.[2] By the late 1950s white South Africa was enjoying a period of confidence and a sense of security.

THE NATIONALISTS IMPOSE THEIR AUTHORITY

The new government sought to distance itself from its predecessor in foreign as well as domestic policies. Having criticised Smuts for paying too much attention to international affairs it proclaimed that South Africa must always come first. The first two Nationalist Prime Ministers, were different in character – Malan (1948–54) quiet, charming and intellectual; Strijdom (1954–8) the 'Lion of the North', aggressive and forthright – but both were mainly interested in domestic affairs and had little international experience. However, they were drawn into foreign policy making because domestic and foreign affairs were intertwined, and because as chief

29

executives they had to represent their country. Malan made a number of trips abroad and retained the practice of acting as his own Foreign Minister. Strijdom broke this in 1955 by appointing Eric Louw as Minister of External Affairs.[3] Strijdom, for all his reputation as a militant politician, was not a strong Prime Minister, and for a time Louw, who had previous diplomatic experience, became the most prominent figure in foreign policy making. Louw was known for his energy, skill in debating, and loyalty to his staff, but he was a fiery, combative man and while that style may have impressed the faithful at home it made few friends abroad. However, irrespective of style, Louw would have encountered difficulties. Like Smuts, the Nationalists found themselves operating in a harsh international environment with very limited options. The result was a continuity in South Africa's foreign policy based on the constraints in which it operated.

At home and abroad the National Party presented a monolithic, authoritarian face to its opponents. Although like all parties it had internal differences, it succeeded in confining these to itself and subordinating them in its determination to retain power. Unity was enhanced by the work of exclusive Afrikaner societies, of which the most powerful was the secret Broederbond to which most cabinet ministers belonged.[4] For the committed Nationalists the 1948 election was more than a change of government: it was a people inheriting their God given right. Malan declared that 'In the past we felt like strangers in our own country but today South Africa belongs to us once more.'[5] The Nationalists saw other groups as less than 'true' South Africans – the blacks because South Africa was a white state; the white English speakers because their loyalties were torn between Britain and the Union.

The NP leaders sought to ensure that their views and policies impregnated the government. No English speaker was appointed to the cabinet until 1961, battle-hardened English speaking army officers were replaced by inexperienced but loyal Afrikaners. Some individuals were removed, including Colonel C. B. Powell, the Director of Military Intelligence, who may have reported on the Nationalists during the war. Yet there were limits. When Malan announced that he intended to appoint Dr Otto du Plessis, who had a pro-Nazi reputation, as Minister to the Hague and Brussels, the Dutch and Belgian Governments refused to accept him. At home, although Afrikaners were appointed to senior civil service positions, there were not enough to fill all the places, and 'Smuts's men' retained important posts, including D. D. Forsyth, the Secretary for Foreign Affairs. Forsyth, like many of the senior Foreign Affairs officials, remained an

Anglophile. A British minute of 1951 said that Forsyth 'has grown in stature since the Nationalists came to power and undoubtedly has an influence on Doctor Malan . . . Forsyth is a very good friend of ours. His main aim is to maintain the British connection and avoid the establishment of a Republic in South Africa. In present circumstances he needs, however, to tread warily.'[6] It was not until 1956 that Forsyth was replaced by an Afrikaner Nationalist, G. P. Jooste.

Ironically the United Party (UP) continued to be led by Afrikaners: J. G. Strauss until 1955 and Sir de Villiers Graaf until the 1970s. The early years of opposition were especially galling for the UP, as it could still gain a majority of votes but not a majority of parliamentary seats. The UP was no less committed to white rule than the Nationalists, but it represented different white sections and its racial policies were more pragmatic. Reinforced by pressure groups, such as the Torch Commandos, it fought bitter battles against the government on such issues as the Afrikanerisation of the forces, constitutional changes, and the symbols of state (flag and anthem). The struggle over the government's decision to remove the Cape Coloureds from the common voters' roll became a focus of conflict, but it also revealed the limits within which the white political system operated. Although the government's proposals met with fierce opposition from the UP and its allies, what became clear was that most white opponents were less concerned with the rights of the Coloureds than the government's dictatorial approach and its contempt for the constitution. For them it was a struggle to defend the constitution – in which the Coloureds happened to have a vote – rather than a fight to preserve Coloured rights.

Another area of controversy in white politics was immigration. Permanent immigration was confined to whites (as opposed to the temporary black immigrants who came to work in the mines and white farms). The UP government had encouraged large scale immigration, partly to satisfy the need for skilled workers, but also to strengthen the white population and the British element in particular. 'Let them come', said Smuts 'the good and the bad, let them come in their thousands, their tens of thousands, their hundreds of thousands, we shall absorb them all.'[7] They had come, in their tens of thousands at least, but for the new Nationalist government they created a dilemma. It too wanted to strengthen the white community and the economy, but it also wanted to ensure Afrikaner dominance. For men like Strijdom that dominance was threatened by immigrants especially those from Britain. He accused the UP of seeking to 'plough under' the Afrikaners through immigration.[8] To counter such a possibility the new government substantially cut the number of immigrants, and diluted the political effect further through a new citizenship act, by which British subjects had to be resident five years before they could apply for a vote, whereas previously they had gained it automatically after two.

APARTHEID AND THE BLACK RESPONSE

The main focus of attention at home and abroad was on apartheid. The government was determined to separate people by race under white control, and so in rapid succession it introduced its apartheid legislation – the Prohibition of Mixed Marriages Act (1949); the Population Registration Act (1950); the Group Areas Act (1950); the Bantu Authorities Act (1951); the Bantu Education Act (1955). The United Party opposed apartheid on constitutional grounds and because they said it was impractical, but some whites fought it because of its racial discrimination. These included the Liberal Party formed in 1953 and the Black Sash Movement of liberal women.

The chief opponents of apartheid were the black nationalists. As the new government was establishing its position so the ANC was strengthening and extending its activities. In 1949 Xuma, who believed that the party was not ready for militant mass action, was replaced by Dr James Moroka. Moroka, like Chief Albert Luthuli who succeeded to the leadership in 1952, was prepared to support a Programme of Action proposed by the Youth League under the forceful leadership of men like Anton Lembede, Nelson Mandela, Walter Sisulu and Oliver Tambo. The Programme called for national freedom, which implied the end of segregation and apartheid and 'freedom from White domination and the attainment of political independence'. To achieve that the Programme proposed employing 'immediate and active boycott, strike, civil disobedience and non-co-operation', if the government did not respond sympathetically. Inevitably the government did not respond in that way and boycotts and strikes were organised.[9] These included a 'stay away' from work on May Day 1950, which resulted in clashes with the police leading to eighteen deaths. Early in 1952 the ANC demanded that the government repeal six 'unjust laws', otherwise a Defiance Campaign would be waged in which blacks would openly defy apartheid laws. Launched in a 'mood of religious fervour' the Defiance Campaign reached its zenith in September 1952 when 2,500 resisters were arrested.[10] In the following months it faltered and then came to a halt in the face of a determined, harsh response from the police, and as central control was lost it led to outbursts of local violence.

The Defiance Campaign helped to turn the nationalist cause into a mass black movement, and helped it to gain considerable international sympathy. However, success created its own problems. As the ANC grew in size organisational demands at central and local levels were not always met, and the existing internal ideological divisions – 'Africanist', 'socialist', and 'liberal' – were intensified. The main thrust was still to exert strong pressure for a place in the system rather than overthrow it by revolution, but the movement was an amalgam of interests, and not all were satisfied with the main thrust or the methods being used. The presence of communists created persistent tension. The Youth League complained that the communists were patronising and introduced views which 'obscure the fundamental fact that we are oppressed not as a class but, as a people, a Nation'. However, even non-communists, like Luthuli challenged this view. He argued that the party was prepared to recruit all who subscribed to its constitution and aims. He stated that the Congress's 'primary concern is liberation, and we are not going to be side tracked by ideological clashes and witch hunts'.[11]

The internal differences were not fully reconciled at the Congress of the People in 1955 – a gathering drawn from all races and most of the main extra-parliamentary opposition, including the ANC, the Indian Congress, and the Congress of Democrats (a small white organisation led by communists). The meeting issued the Freedom Charter, which demanded equal political rights and freedoms irrespective of race, a socialist reordering of the economy, an end to colonialism, and peaceful relations with neighbouring states. The ANC hesitated before accepting the Charter because militant members regarded it as far too mild and reformist, and even Luthuli admitted that it 'is uneven – sometimes it goes into unnecessary detail and at other times it is a little vague'.[12] Because of that vagueness the Charter is open to different interpretations and fails to specify the means to be used to achieve the objectives. However, once it was accepted by the ANC it became a rallying point for the Congress movements. In contrast the 'Africanists' refused to accept it because they said it had been too influenced by whites, was multiracial in its aims, and did not endorse Pan Africanism. It was, in their eyes, 'a "sell out" of the African's birthright, and of his prerogative in his land'.[13]

In meeting the black nationalist challenge the government had broad support across the white community. The UP opposed the government within the white political system, but when the system was challenged it rallied to the government's side. During the ANC's Defiance Campaign Strauss called on 'the people of South Africa' (i.e.

the whites) to forget their differences. The government-led response was a combination of fierce legislation and police action, including bannings and mass arrests. By the end of 1955 many leaders from the ANC, the Congress of Democrats and the Indian Congress were under banning orders. In December 1956 the Treason Trial started of 156 political opponents drawn from all races, and it was not until March 1961 that the last of the accused were acquitted. From the government's point of view the trial had the advantage of blunting the edge of nationalist activities while the energies of the leaders were diverted away from political activity, but there was a price to be paid as the trial gave the accused international prominence, unity in their opposition to apartheid, and eventually a triumph on their acquittal.

The government frequently identified black nationalism with communism. The perception of an all-pervasive communism was common among white South Africans, irrespective of party. While it was a deeply held fear it also offered reassurance, for if hostility to the white society – whether it came from black nationalists or international organisations – could be explained as part of an evil international movement the burden of guilt was lifted from the whites. Perceived in this way opposition to white rule did not stem from an unjust social order but from communism. In 1950 the government introduced the Suppression of Communism Act, which defined communism so widely that all who advocated change through 'the promotion of disturbances or disorders' were covered by it, and the act was used against black nationalists. Certainly there were links between the communists and black nationalists, and some black nationalists were communists, but most were not. At the time of its banning the South Africa Communist Party had a membership of about 3,000 of whom about 1,200 were black. After the banning Moses Kotane, the Communist Party's Secretary General, advised members to infiltrate the ANC, the Indian Congress and the Congress of Democrats. In this they had some success and there were accusations that despite their small numbers the communists dominated the ANC. However, while they exercised influence they certainly did not dominate and the communists met regular resistance from the 'Africanists' and the 'liberals'.

Internationally the black nationalists and white critics, like the novelist Alan Paton and the Anglican churchmen Michael Scott and Trevor Huddleston, gained attention. They found sympathetic audiences at the UN and in liberal Western circles. 'Apartheid' became an international smear word symbolising racial oppression. The struggles within the Union – the Defiance Campaign, the bannings, the Treason

Trial – were given prominence in the Western media, and while the hostility was less intense than it became later, the government was resentful and bitter because it could not accept that the international opposition was based on principle. It explained it away as expediency – the West currying favour with the new states and the new states diverting attention away from their own defects. Nobody was more resentful than Eric Louw who accused foreign journalists of distorting the truth and unjustly treating South Africa as an international butt. He tried to counter the criticism by developing the government's information services, which were brought under the wing of the Department of External Affairs in 1955, but little progress could be made in reforming the image of South Africa abroad because that image was based on the racial policies at home.

The UP accused the government of isolating the country through its racial policies. In 1957 Strijdom thrust back at the opposition saying: 'The ideological policy to which the outside world objects is that we will not allow political equality between white and non-white.' He asked the UP if it was opposed to legislation which 'has the effect of retaining in the hands of the white man power to govern the country'. If it were not 'I ask what then is the difference between that party and us. If we are unfair to the non-whites in this respect are they not then just as unfair?'[14] The United Party had no answer.

FRUSTRATED HOPES IN AFRICA

Shortly after the 1948 election Malan, speaking about South Africa's place in Africa, accepted that she could not dissociate herself from the destinies of the continent. He said:

> We are a part of Africa . . . and our actions here in South Africa are largely influenced by what takes place in the rest of Africa. Not only do we wish to be on friendly terms with the territories of Africa for that reason, but we also have a growing trade with these territories. It is inevitable that by trade, by the attempt to control disease, South Africa is integrated with these [territories] . . . South Africa also has the right by virtue of its population as a white man's country, and its experience during the course of years in connection with the native problem and the coloured problem to aspire to leadership in this matter and to act as adviser to the peoples of the Northern territories.[15]

Malan never changed these views – the acceptance of an African identity, the eagerness to forge material links, the assumption of a natural white leadership – but soon there were signs that the context in

35

which they were pursued would change dramatically over the coming years. In 1948 Malan assumed that colonial rule in Africa would remain indefinitely, and he was dismayed when, by the mid 1950s, it was becoming clear that independent black states would emerge, although the pace and scope of the development was still uncertain. In 1956 the British withdrew from the Sudan and in 1957 Ghana was granted independence. With a natural temptation to let desire dictate to judgement, white South Africans first refused to believe that decolonisation could happen at all, then assumed that it would be a very slow and selective process stretching over generations. They had the difficult task of absorbing unpalatable ideas which carried dangers for them. Strijdom appealed for time to adjust.

The government tried a number of African initiatives. In 1949 Charles Te Water was appointed roving ambassador, with a brief to travel widely on the continent and to the colonial capitals, 'to put matters in the right light'.[16] However, little came of the efforts because of the different perceptions between Pretoria and the colonial powers. That was equally apparent when Malan introduced his 'African Charter'. It was not an 'off the cuff' idea (he first spoke about it in 1945 while in opposition and he was still referring to it in 1953) nor was it a formal document; rather a set of values and aims. Although it was Malan's personal view it reflected the hopes of many whites, so that *Die Burger* could applaud him for his foresight and imagine him 'standing on Kilimanjaro' surveying all Africa.[17]

The Charter set out five main aims for Africa – to protect it from Asian domination; to preserve it for Africans; to ensure that its development was on Western Christian lines; to keep out communism; and to make it 'non-militarised'. The first of these aims – the protection of Africa against Asian domination – was a recurring theme. However ill-founded, there were strongly held white fears that Asians, and Indians in particular, would seek to flood the continent. Malan claimed that India 'already had a firm footing in parts of Africa and with its population of over 400 million people is seeking a place where it can unload its superfluous population and the most obvious place to unload them is Africa'.[18]

In advancing the catch phrase for the Charter's second aim – 'Africa for the Africans' – Malan naturally included the White Africans. He said: 'Africa should be safeguarded for the European in so far as he is settled here permanently because he has borne civilization on his shoulders . . . For the rest Africa should be there for the benefit of the natives.' However, he was convinced that the 'benefit of the natives' involved continued European leadership either directly by white residents or through the colonial powers. Malan hoped that the colonial powers would co-operate with Pretoria to 'see if we can retain Africa as a reserve, if I may call it that, for the future development of the Western European Christian civilization'. This led him to the ironic conclusion that British imperialism, which the Nationalists had resisted so fiercely, 'is indispensable as a civilizing influence. England's leadership and guardianship cannot, in the interests of the natives themselves, be spared.' The alternative was to sink into barbarism and accept dictatorship. The fourth aim was to keep Africa free from communism, 'the curse of the underdeveloped and backward peoples', as Malan described it. The anti-communist legislation at home and the search for defence alliances abroad were part of the same endeavour. The final aim was to prevent Africa becoming militarised. Here was another apparent paradox, for this was proposed when South Africa was trying to form an African military alliance. What Malan meant in fact was that 'the natives' should not be armed. 'Do not allow', he said, 'the natives of Africa to become militarised. One does not hand a rifle to a child.' The 'white' governments, including the colonial governments, would continue to have military forces, but black men in these forces should not be given arms.[19]

Nothing came of Malan's Charter but its ideas and values indicate the scale of the problem for white South Africans in coming to terms with the changes taking place in the continent and their fears about the impact of these changes on blacks inside the Union. This concern led to important statements on 'native policy' from both Malan and Dr Hendrik Verwoerd, then Minister of Native Affairs. In 1951 Malan denied a United Party claim that the government's Bantustan policy would lead to independent black states. While he accepted that Africans would gradually acquire more responsibility, he added: 'In their own areas they will always have to stand under the guardianship and the domination of the white man in South Africa. Call it "baaskap", call it what you like. We have always used the expression that we are their guardians and we remain their guardians.'[20] Two years later he said that he was against the creation of independent black states 'within the South African boundaries', and he was referring to the British High Commission Territories as well as the Bantustans.[21] Verwoerd took a similar line. In 1951 he said: 'The answer is obvious. It stands to reason that White South Africa must remain their guardian. How could small scattered states arise? The areas will be economically dependent on the Union. It stands to reason that when we talk of the Natives' right to self-government in these areas we cannot mean that we intend to cut large slices of South Africa and turn them into independent states.'[22]

Malan never came to terms with the prospect of sovereign black states. When he heard that Britain intended granting independence to Ghana he called it 'a thoughtless action' and 'a disastrous step'.[23] In the mid 1950s, however, the government's attitude started to change. This roughly coincided with Malan's retirement and the appearance of Strijdom and Louw, but the change is better explained by new circumstances than new personalities. The South Africans had no choice but to accept that major changes were taking place in the continent. When he took office, Strijdom – always a militant advocate of white rights – was arguing for close co-operation with the colonial powers and the continuation of white supremacy in Africa. He described 'African policy' as co-operation between the white communities to ensure their survival.[24] Soon, however, he started to shift his position – making the best of a bad job – and spoke of 'extending the hand of friendship' to the new states.[25] In 1956 he told the House of Assembly: 'We do not regard each other as enemies, but as Nations and Governments acknowledging and respecting each other's rights to exist.' He hoped that the Union could give guidance and direction.[26]

The other circumstantial change was within the government. For the first time there was a minister, and a forceful one, responsible for foreign affairs who was backed by an expanding department staffed by able men. While in the past concern with foreign affairs had fluctuated with the personal interest of the Premiers, there was now a more consistent pattern in which the department, with its awareness of the international situation, played a more prominent role in government policy making. This awareness and a new flexibility was revealed in an important speech Louw made at Pretoria University in 1957. He told the students that the Union must 'accept its future role in Africa as a vocation and must in all respects play its full part as an African power'. Based upon its technical and economic power South Africa could become 'a permanent link between the Western nations on the one hand and the population of Africa south of the Sahara on the other'. The African states would come to realise that apartheid was no threat to them and all Africa could combine together against external interference.[27] Louw's speech revealed the two main ways in which Pretoria hoped to achieve its ends. The first was to accept with reasonable grace the changing scene despite the deep doubts. When Ghana achieved its independence Louw said that good relations with the new state were fundamental to the government's policy, and although Strijdom did not personally attend the celebrations

Nkrumah wrote to thank him for sending a delegation of such high quality. Louw and Nkrumah even reached an informal agreement for the exchange of diplomats.[28] The second step was to extend trade, economic and technical links. These would be mutually advantageous, and because of South Africa's economic strength they would give her influence over others. Louw was able to draw encouragement from Nkrumah's statement that while he deplored apartheid Ghana was prepared to trade with South Africa, accept her technical aid and was hesitant about interference in her internal affairs unless world opinion led the way.[29] In 1957 Louw announced that a Roving Trade Commission for Africa and some permanent representatives were to be appointed, and the government would give a subsidy to a shipping line to develop links with the West coast. Earlier, in the technical field, the Union had become a founder member (1950) of the Commission for Technical Co-operation in Africa South of the Sahara (CTCA) and the Bureau for Soil Conservation. In 1958 the Union became a founder member of another co-operative organisation – the Foundation for Mutual Assistance in Africa South of the Sahara (FAMA) which was made up of colonial authorities and independent states.

In 1959 the Department of External Affairs underlined the increasing importance attached to the continent by establishing a separate African Division – its first geographical division. Yet these attempts to come to terms with the changing continent have to be set alongside the persistent opposition to decolonisation and scepticism about the ability of blacks to govern themselves. In the government there was constant vacillation – acceptance of the new states one moment, criticism the next, and always opposition to further decolonisation. Louw captured Pretoria's internal tensions when in 1959 he said: 'We in South Africa see no danger in states attaining their independence. Of course not, we cannot stop it.' He went on to say: 'Some of these leaders are not yet one generation removed from the primitive conditions of their forefathers. There are many of them whose fathers and mothers were completely primitive, barbaric people.'[30]

The uncertainty led to hesitation in seizing or responding to initiatives. At the time of Ghana's independence Louw, who had reached an informal agreement with Nkrumah, broached with his cabinet colleagues the possibility of exchanging diplomats with black states and setting aside a special residential area at home for black diplomats. He gained no support, and was soon reminded of white sensitivity on such matters when there was a storm of protest from the United Party and unease among Nationalists because a Ghanaian attending an international conference was given the same treatment as whites. Louw met similar cabinet opposition in 1959 when he proposed to visit black states and exchange representatives.[31] The government's eagerness to keep the colonial powers in Africa was another brake on co-operation. When Ghana invited South Africa to a conference of independent states in Addis Ababa Strijdom refused, explaining to Nkrumah that he favoured a conference of 'all governments with direct responsibility in Africa including the colonial powers'.[32] In the late 1950s Pretoria tried to reassure itself that so far only a handful of territories had achieved independence, that these were far from the Union's borders, that they had not included any with white settler populations. It clung to the hope that for the foreseeable future most of Africa would remain under colonial control. Meanwhile South Africa could offer economic and technical co-operation, which, as Louw told the Pretoria students, would demonstrate the value of a society that had preserved its white identity and its Western culture.

THE SOUTHERN AFRICAN SUBCONTINENT

Within Africa Pretoria's main concern was naturally with its immediate neighbours. Reassuringly for her they were all at that time under colonial control – the Portuguese were in Mozambique and Angola; the British in three High Commission Territories (Basutoland, Bechuanaland, Swaziland), and in Central Africa. In 1953 the British formed Southern and Northern Rhodesia and Nyasaland into the Central African Federation, with local whites in control of internal affairs. In the 1950s the South Africans, and indeed the colonial authorities, did not foresee early independence for any of these territories, with the possible exception of the Federation.

If the Union were to have a leadership role in Africa the obvious starting point was the subcontinent. However, the colonial situation placed constraints on Pretoria. In economic terms, although the neighbouring territories relied on South Africa for many services they were also tied into the economic and financial systems of the colonial powers. There were overlapping colonial and regional economic structures. In political terms, the situation was ambivalent. The subcontinent remained under white control, as the South Africans wished, but they did not have a strong voice in its development. The history of the Central African Federation illustrates this. The Federation was established with a variety of aims, not all of which were easy to reconcile. For example, while the British wanted to build a large economically viable unit and establish racial 'partnership', the white

Rhodesians saw it as a way to retain their pre-eminent position and gain independence under a white government. However, both the British and the Federation leaders were determined to restrict South Africa's influence, especially after the National Party victory. Patrick Gordon Walker, the Colonial Secretary in the British Labour Government, explained that although the creation of the Federation did not imply hostility to the Afrikaner government it was designed to limit its influence. Southern Rhodesia he saw as 'the key stone' where whites must be drawn away from the Union to counter Afrikaner influence, to enhance Britain's position, and to demonstrate that racial partnership and not apartheid was the way forward. It was on those grounds that he recommended the establishment of the Federation, which would be reinforced by vigorous British immigration, capital investment, and railway development.[33] The Labour Party lost office before it could implement these plans (and indeed in opposition it voted against the Federation because of black fears inside the territories) but the new Conservative Government went ahead with similar motives to those of Gordon Walker.

More immediately frustrating for Pretoria was the position of the three British High Commission Territories of Basutoland, Bechuanaland, and Swaziland. Their geographical position gave these territories an importance for South Africa which was out of all proportion to their size or wealth. Despite warnings from A. L. K. Geyer, the High Commissioner in London, that it was a hopeless cause, the government reopened the claim that the territories should be transferred to South Africa under the 1910 Act of Union. For the Nationalists it was more than a formal constitutional matter; rather it was an issue that involved South Africa's dignity and independence, but Malan also argued, with justification, that the British had made few efforts to develop the territories. The South African case was that it was both economically advantageous, and constitutionally correct to effect the transfer. When a South African commission (the Tomlinson Commission) reported in 1956 on the future development of black areas in the Union it included the three British territories.

To forward the case for the transfer Malan used private negotiations, public appeals and threats of retaliation. In February 1951 he made his feelings clear at a dinner given for Patrick Gordon Walker, who was visiting the Union. Malan said:

> Whether the delay is due to the fact that we are not trusted with the protection or promotion of Native interests you will best be able to judge . . . But apart from the question of grievous mistrust there is another aspect of this outstanding question . . . It affects our equal

41

status and place among the other members of the Commonwealth
. . . Constitutionally [the Union] stands on a footing of equality with
the other members . . . But in one vital respect she differs from them
all, and that is . . . actually within her borders, she is compelled to
harbour territories, entirely dependent on her economically and
largely also for their defence, but belonging to and governed by
another country. Such a condition . . . will not for a single moment be
tolerated [by other members]. And so long as this is tolerated by
South Africa, there can be no real equality nor even full independence for her . . . And no one can blame her if under such circumstances she feels herself relegated to a position of inferiority and in
fact to the position of a semi-independent and third class country.[34]

If the territories were not transferred what did the future hold? One
possibility was that the British would stay on indefinitely, a prospect
no Nationalist government could accept with equanimity. Yet the
alternative that they might become independent black states seemed
ludicrous. In 1953 Malan said the British could do as they pleased in
the Gold Coast and Nigeria. 'But can they make any of these Protectorates a free and independent country? Can we in South Africa, who
are a free and independent State, permit Negro States, Bantu States, to
arise within our borders – States which are free and independent and
which can lay down their own policies in every respect? We cannot
possibly do so.'[35] Malan's concern was a combination of the old fear of
'liberal' native policies on the borders unsettling the Union's blacks,
and a new security concern that the territories would become centres
of subversion for black nationalists – veritable Trojan horses in their
midst. Accusations were made that Basutoland had already become 'a
breeding ground for communists'.[36]

The British trod a delicate path. They did not want to antagonise the
South Africans, but decisions in southern Africa could not be divorced
from the broad thrust of colonial policy, or domestic political concern
about South Africa's racial policies. However, in the 1950s the British
were as confused as Pretoria over the future of the territories. On the
one hand, successive British Governments emphasised that there
could be no transfer to the Union without consulting the inhabitants
and gaining the approval of the Westminster Parliament, which in fact
meant that there would be no transfer. However, on the other hand,
British colonial policy had not reached the stage of envisaging the
independence of such small territories. Sir John Redcliff-Maud, who
went to Pretoria as British High Commissioner in 1959, later wrote that
the idea that each of these territories 'might achieve sovereign independence had never occurred to anyone – and if it had I think it would
have been dismissed as moonshine'.[37]

The British therefore moved warily, as was illustrated by the drama surrounding Seretse Khama, the designated Chief of the Bamangwato of Bechuanaland. In 1948, while at Oxford, Seretse married an English girl, Ruth Williams. As he did this without following tribal custom there were divisions about it among his own people, but the big question for the British was the effect the marriage might have on relations with the Union. If there were doubts on this score they were soon dispelled by a strongly worded telegram from Malan, and a report from Sir Evelyn Baring, the British High Commissioner. Malan said that the consequences of allowing the Khamas to return 'would be deplorable', and if it did happen South Africa would consider action, including economic measures.[38] It was not only the Nationalists who disapproved. There were strong warnings from Smuts and from Sir Geoffrey Huggins, the Prime Minister of Southern Rhodesia. Smuts said that the Nationalist Government might demand incorporation of Bechuanaland or threaten to blockade the territory, and the United Party 'would be unable to oppose such a move because of the emotions roused, for white South Africans were hardly sane on the subject of miscegenation'.[39] Although the British never admitted it, the main reason for their decision to ban Seretse from Bechuanaland was the reaction of the South African and Rhodesian Governments. In response to a proposal from Gordon Walker that Seretse must renounce his claims and leave the territory, the Prime Minister, Attlee, minuted: 'It is as if we had been obliged to agree to Edward VIII's abdication so as not to annoy the Irish Free State and the USA.'[40] Nevertheless, the British cabinet gave its reluctant support to Gordon Walker's proposal. (In 1956, after surrendering claims to the chieftainship for himself and his family, Seretse Khama was allowed to return to Bechuanaland with no protest from South Africa.)

As the 1950s progressed, Pretoria continued to make ritual noises about the transfer of the Territories, but without hope of success. The uncertainty about their future persisted. In an article published in March 1959, Dr W. W. M. Eiselen, the Secretary for Native Affairs, referred to a statement by the retiring British High Commissioner, Sir Percival Liesching, that while the Protectorates were advancing towards greater self-government that did not imply that they would even achieve full independence. Similarly, wrote Eiselen, the Union was prepared to give the Bantustans greater autonomy, but would stop short of full independence. There would be no surrender of European trusteeship.[41]

In the late 1950s Pretoria was still struggling to come to terms with change and impending change across the continent. It profoundly distrusted the replacement of European colonialism with independent black states, and it was frustrated at its failure to influence the colonial powers in general, particularly to secure the incorporation of the High Commission Territories and to convince the British that the racial 'partnership' in Central Africa could never work. Yet Pretoria retained hopes. So far the colonial withdrawal had been limited and was far from the Union's borders. The government was prepared to throw its weight against further change and to use what powers it had to extend its influence, especially in southern Africa.

4 THE NATIONALISTS SEARCH FOR AN INTERNATIONAL ROLE

The South African Government identified communism as its main threat both at home and abroad. Because communists challenged white rule across Africa there was a temptation in Pretoria to believe that all who challenged white rule were therefore communists. When Louw visited London in 1952 he asserted that disturbances throughout Africa were of one piece. He made specific reference to the Mau Mau rising in Kenya and recent troubles in Northern Rhodesia. These, he said, were communist inspired, and backed by the United Nations, Western liberals, British socialists and misguided clerics who were either duped by communists or under their influence. He said that the threat increased with every retreat of white control.[1] Earlier Malan had said that 'communism makes a special appeal to the country's non-European population', and if the communists had their way, 'the death knell will have been sounded for white civilization'.[2]

The banning of the Communist Party in 1950 was not followed by an immediate break in diplomatic links with the USSR. The possibility was discussed by the cabinet, but for the time being, and influenced by British advice, it was decided to retain the Consul General's Office which had been established during the war.[3] However, the Nationalists' suspicion had made the Soviet diplomats virtual recluses before 1956 when Louw announced that diplomatic ties were to be severed. Explaining the decision he accused the Soviets of encouraging subversion and flouting the Union's laws. His specific complaints ranged from contacting revolutionary groups to holding racially mixed drinks parties.[4]

As Pretoria assumed a natural hostility towards the Eastern bloc so it assumed a natural identity of interests with the West. 'We are', declared Malan, 'a country which shares Western civilization, and Western interests and dangers.'[5] In many ways the claim to a Western identity was well founded. South Africa was integrated into the Western economic system, she had defence arrangements with

Britain, her forces contributed to the Western military efforts in Korea and the Berlin airlift, and culturally the whites were linked to Europe. Nevertheless the situation was not clear cut. For some Western states South Africa was of peripheral interest – geographically remote, of no direct military concern, consumed by a unique racial problem – a little understood country, and one that was becoming an increasingly embarrassing international acquaintance. Even for those with strong links there was despair and bewilderment at South African and especially Afrikaner attitudes. Following his 1951 visit to South Africa Patrick Gordon Walker compared the Afrikaner Nationalists to Irish nationalists. 'They have', he said, 'a logic of their own that is grounded on emotion and hatred that is practically impossible for us to understand.'[6] On their side the South Africans rejected the aspects of Western society which they associated with their strongest Western critics – socialism, liberalism, and the permissive society. A frustrated Malan declared: 'One finds in the world today and especially in England that there is a sickly sentiment in regard to the black man . . . They venerate the black skin.'[7]

There were two main South African complaints about the behaviour of the Western states. First, that there was persistent and unwarranted criticism of apartheid. Normally this was initiated by groups and individuals outside the Western governments but the South Africans expected the governments to counter it. Second, they complained at the failure of Western governments to stand alongside South Africa in international organisations. The South Africans resented the situation whereby there were close business and financial contacts but cool diplomatic attitudes. Yet the West was also under pressure. In 1951 the Indian delegate at the UN repeated the challenge that 'If the discriminatory policies of South Africa were permitted to flourish free from censure by the Western democracies, the Asian and African peoples could give little credence to the avowed desire of the West to unite for peace and to achieve collective security based on respect for human rights and fundamental freedoms.'[8] The Western states were never to escape this dilemma. They tried to alleviate it by keeping South Africa at a diplomatic distance, while accusing the Afro-Asians of advancing emotional and impractical suggestions. The Western approach was cautious and legalistic, stressing the importance of procedures as well as substance, balancing the desirability of change with the need for international order, and searching for compromise. Yet, in an increasingly polarised situation that search looked ambivalent and uncertain, breeding distrust from both sides.

RELATIONS WITH BRITAIN AND THE USA

Among the Western states, the relationship with Britain remained the most important. For the Nationalists it was a complex, love–hate affair in which attitudes from the past were freely mixed with those of the present. The traditional Nationalist hostility was tempered by the fact that Britain was the devil they knew, and one who in the 1950s was clearly Africa's major external power. Furthermore Britain was the Union's most reliable diplomatic ally – consistently supporting her at the UN against interference in internal affairs based on Article 2(7).[9] Yet the Nationalists never completely threw off their suspicions. 'South Africa', said Malan, 'has during her history come to know . . . two Englands. The one is England at her worst. The other is England at her best. South Africans this side of the house and the Afrikaner-speaking section of our people know them both.'[10] Diplomatic relations between the two governments remained close, reinforced for a time by the personal contacts of the older English speaking officials, but at a political level they were cooler and more formal than in Smuts's day. The family atmosphere disappeared, and 'instead of the friendly standing from which the High Commissioner could call on and talk to any minister in London without notice in the Press, such friendly visits now began to assume the appearance of visits between representatives of foreign states'.[11]

However, Britain and the Union continued to be drawn together by interests if not by sentiment. Britain was the continent's major colonial power; South Africa its strongest independent state; several British colonies bordered the Union; both were anti-communist and had common defence concerns not only in the southern oceans but stretching north as far as the Middle East; and both were bound together by economic links. These common interests were recognised in a British policy document which Patrick Gordon Walker laid before the Labour cabinet in September 1950. Recognising South Africa's importance to Britain the document advised fostering friendship with Pretoria because of the common interests, but at the same time checking the spread of its influence in British territories to the north. A dilemma for the British Government, as outlined by Gordon Walker, was to retain the loyalty of the whites in British possessions in East and Central Africa while encouraging black political advancement. He feared that in these circumstances the whites might wish to throw in their lot with the Union. Southern Rhodesia in particular he saw as 'the keystone to the policy of containing South Africa', and, as noted, advised that an effort should be made to orientate it away from the

Union by increased British support and by creating a Central African Federation. Of the High Commission Territories the document said that efforts should be made not to offend Pretoria by such actions as returning Seretse Khama, while on the broader international front Britain should seek to strengthen relations, especially in economic and security matters. Although the Union's racial policies could not be supported it would be a mistake to isolate her, as greater influence could be exerted by contact and therefore Britain should give Pretoria what help she could at the UN.[12] Labour lost office soon after endorsing this policy, but the new Conservative Government adopted a similar approach.

Although the governments on both sides were aware of the common interests, there was increasing British public criticism of apartheid. That caused deep resentment in Pretoria. In January 1957, when Louw heard that British civil rights organisations were sending observers to the Treason Trial, he wrote to *The Times* saying: 'If this impudent interference in our internal affairs is sought to be justified (as has been suggested) by the fact that South Africa is a member of the Commonwealth, then the sooner we get out of the Commonwealth the better!' He asserted that the criticisms were not based on a concern for liberties, but were a 'manifestation of the campaign of hate that has been conducted against South Africa for the past eight years by a section of the British Press, by the Communists and Socialists, and also by individuals like Canon Collins, Father Huddleston and the Revd Michael Scott'.[13] The reference to 'socialists' was probably directed at the Labour Party, which, following its election defeat in 1951, took such a critical stance towards apartheid that Pretoria openly questioned whether it could ever work again with a Labour government.

In the search for Western links the government recognised the importance of the US, but there was continued uncertainty about her attitudes. Washington had few ties with either the Union or Africa in general, and did not perceive any immediate communist danger to either. Instead, and much to the fury of Pretoria, it sometimes associated the Union with its critical approach to European colonialism. At home the American Government (unlike its South African counterpart) was endeavouring to build a multiracial society which bred a predisposition against apartheid. However, as a foreign policy issue South Africa had a low priority. It was an irritant which embarrassed the US at the General Assembly, but Washington saw no point either in confronting Pretoria or becoming associated with it. In 1948 the Truman administration accepted a position paper which was based on the assumptions that the region was stable and outside the arena of East/West confrontation. The paper, which was critical of the Union's racial policies, was opposed to any attempt by Pretoria to extend its influence in Africa, and argued that the Union had a moral but not a legal obligation to place South West Africa under UN supervision. However, as no US vital interests were involved, it was suggested that the 'status quo' of friendly if limited relations with Pretoria was maintained, while keeping open the possibility that the region might later gain in importance. This policy of benign neglect was pursued for a decade, but in the late 1950s there was a small shift of emphasis by the Eisenhower administration, as independent black states began to emerge in Africa and at home the Civil Rights Movement gained momentum. In 1958 a Bureau of African Affairs was created in the State Department, and in October of that year the US cast its first vote against apartheid at the UN instead of abstaining as in the past.[14]

The South African hopes and frustrations in the relationship were again captured by the volatile Louw. In 1957, an American rebuff at the UN was met by a characteristic outburst in which he said that the West could not continue to push South Africa 'around today as it has been doing in the last eleven years and tomorrow expect us to support them on some issue'.[15] Yet two years later he was in a much more conciliatory mood when he argued that an adverse US vote cast at the UN did not represent a change of policy. Somewhat unconvincingly he tried to explain it away as the result of heavy pressures brought on the US, and the chance that its delegation at the time was led by a prominent labour leader known for his dislike of South Africa. Louw added that the Americans had moderated the wording of the resolution.[16]

ECONOMIC LINKS

While there were signs of the West distancing itself diplomatically from the Union, economic ties were being reinforced. Between 1949 and 1959 the South African economy had an average annual growth rate of 5.4 per cent based on a broad expansion in the traditional agricultural and mining sectors and continued progress in manufacturing.

The government was directly concerned with the economy. It controlled large areas of it, and shared common interests with private business in such matters as retaining cheap labour, attracting overseas capital and advanced technology. However, there were differences between the government and the companies, and the United Party claimed that the economy grew despite government policies, which, said the opposition, frightened away investors, restricted the inflow of skilled white labour, and disrupted the supply of black labour through rigid apartheid regulations. Despite such criticisms the government encouraged home industries because 'not only was "Made in South Africa" identified in the Nationalist Party creed as sound nationalism, but the balance of payments crisis attendant on its accession to power gave it a new imperative'.[17]

In manufacturing industry a substantial proportion of the goods were absorbed in the domestic market, but the West supplied capital, skilled manpower, and technology, and new markets were opened up in neighbouring African states. Agriculture held steady, with its main external market in Britain, while there was a substantial expansion in the mineral industries, which came about in two ways. First, the range of minerals was greatly extended, as the country's vast and varied resources were exploited by an expanding world economy. Some minerals came into prominence for the first time, including uranium for which agreements were signed with the US and the UK atomic energy authorities. The second great mineral development was a growth in gold production. Although its importance declined as a proportion of all mineral output (gold accounted for 82 per cent of total mineral exports in 1945, but by 1965 had fallen to 60 per cent) it remained the single most important product not only of the mining industry but also of the whole economy, and gave the Union a distinctive place in the Western financial scene. The expansion came through the use of new technologies and the opening up of major fields in the Orange Free State. These developments required massive financial investments – 'overall the largest and most spectacular financial undertaking ever conducted in South Africa'[18] – of which more than half came from overseas. As the major gold producer the Union also had a direct interest in the management of the international monetary system. She gained benefits from this, but her interests as a producer sometimes led to confrontation with the international agencies and with the US, who were attempting to peg the official price of gold at $35 per ounce.[19]

The international impact of the economy was therefore most clearly seen in two sets of relations – with southern African neighbours, and with the West. Yet in both cases the single major strand was the relationship with Britain: the major colonial power in southern and central Africa, and the Union's main trading and financial partner in the West. The links with neighbouring territories were built on South

Africa's advanced communications, her financial and trading structures (including a customs and monetary union with the British High Commission Territories), trade in manufactured goods, and, perhaps most striking of all, the movement of vast numbers of black workers to the mines and farms of the Union. The economic relations with the West were both extensive and complex. The post-war expansion of the global economy increased the contacts and saw a growth in the activities of multinational companies. In bilateral terms the British link became less dominant but remained the most important. In 1960 Britain held 52 per cent of all foreign investment, followed by the US with 19 per cent and other European states with 16 per cent. In trade the distribution was more even, although Britain again had a clear lead – 30 per cent of the Union's imports and 28 per cent of exports, against the US with 17 per cent of the imports and 9 per cent exports, and West Germany with 10 per cent imports and 5 per cent exports.[20]

The impact of Western economic relations varied both in their size and their relative importance. While, for example, the value of US trade was important to South Africa it was relatively insignificant in the total American economy, although there were areas of special concern, including the provision of minerals. For Britain, with a smaller economy and suffering economic hardships, the links had a much greater importance. In general, however, where economic ties existed they improved the climate for South African foreign policy making. There was reluctance among those Western states with a substantial stake to adopt too critical an attitude, and their own business and financial interests were constantly reminding them of the Union's importance. There is no direct evidence of Pretoria using economic pressure in its dealings with Western states, but in their diplomatic and political relations both sides were conscious of the mutual benefits they derived from economic links. Overall the economic interests of South Africa and her major Western trading partners were reasonably well balanced, and it served both sides to foster and reinforce them.[21]

UNDER ATTACK AT THE UNITED NATIONS

From the beginning the Nationalist Government was wary of international organisations in general and the UN in particular. In the UN General Assembly the stream of votes and speeches against South Africa continued unabated. In 1952 the pretence was dropped that the attacks were concerned only with the specific issues of South West Africa and the position of the Indians. Fourteen Arab and Asian states

51

placed 'Apartheid' on the General Assembly's agenda, declaring that it 'is creating a dangerous and explosive situation which contributes both a threat to international peace and a flagrant violation of basic principles of human rights and fundamental freedoms'.[22]

Like Smuts the Nationalist Government tried to take refuge behind Article 2(7) of the Charter, putting forward legal objections while refusing to discuss the merits of the issue. However the critics challenged this, not only with the old claims that South West Africa was an international territory and that the treatment of Indians threatened good relations between two member states, but also with what had been implicit in the earlier attacks; that racial discrimination could not be confined behind state boundaries. It involved all men and was a threat to world peace. Pretoria's response was no less vigorous. At a National Party Conference in October 1953 (a setting in which he need feel no inhibitions) Malan called the UN 'a failure, a cancer eating at the peace and tranquillity of the world'.[23] Four years later, in the less heady atmosphere of the House of Assembly, Louw said that the UN was 'in decline' and 'at the crossroads' and predicted that it might soon destroy itself.[24]

The Nationalists considered leaving the UN. After only a few months in office Louw told the General Assembly that if there were no changes the question 'will have to be faced whether consideration of our own national interests is compatible with continued membership'.[25] In 1955 the Union withdrew from a UN agency – the United Nations Educational, Scientific and Cultural Organisation (UNESCO) – which Louw described as a 'futile' organisation, staffed by woolly headed academics, and used as a sounding board for anti-South African agitation.[26] In the next year the government came near to leaving the UN itself. It was over a recurring dispute about the inclusion of items in the General Assembly agenda which were unacceptable to the Union. Louw told Parliament that South Africa would retain only token representation and play no part, other than voting when Article 2(7) was at issue or in exceptional circumstances. Yet the final break never came, and soon the South Africans were back in the fray. Louw claimed that the policy of 'token representation' had achieved its purpose, that attitudes were more reasonable, and that in future the Union would be a more active member. He announced that he would personally attend the next session, and the Union's permanent UN representative would be enhanced to the rank of Minister.[27]

The claim of a change in attitude at the UN was at best a selective interpretation of the situation. The South Africans could point to the appointment of a moderate Good Offices Commission for South West Africa, and to Louw's election as a Vice President of the General Assembly (although that was more in the spirit of 'Buggin's turn' among Commonwealth states than a new enthusiasm for Pretoria in the Assembly). Also the Western states were concerned at suggestions of withdrawal because they believed in the value of contact, and because they feared that if one state were forced out others might follow. However, if Pretoria took these signs as a general shift in attitudes it was mistaken. The UN agenda continued to be set largely by the opponents of apartheid, and hostile resolutions continued to rain down on South Africa. The decision to remain in the UN was based less on a shift of international attitudes than on the outcome of an internal debate in Pretoria in which arguments for withdrawal – that there was nothing but criticism and humiliation at the UN, that once the Union as a target was removed international attention would move elsewhere and withdrawal would show the contempt in which the organisation was held by the white electorate at home – proved less persuasive than those for staying – the opportunity to respond directly to criticism, the network of contacts both formal and informal, the value of the specialised institutions (such as the IMF), the fear of recognition of a black government in exile, and because membership gave the Union the accolade of a sovereign state. For all the criticism of her racial policies, sovereign status distinguished the Union from colonial territories. A challenge to her could be seen as an attack on the principle of sovereignty which was so treasured by the new states. The South African decision to remain in the UN rested on a hard-headed calculation of interests.

At the UN no other government supported apartheid. The critics were divided into two broad streams – the 'militants', comprising the communist and Afro-Asian states, who wanted direct action; and the 'moderates', mainly the Western states, who adopted a legalistic approach and sought compromises. It was the militants who normally seized the initiative, and, following the condemnation of apartheid in 1952, there were persistent General Assembly resolutions against South Africa. One example will serve for all. In January 1957 the General Assembly resolved by fifty-six votes to five, with twelve abstentions, to deplore South Africa's failure to observe her obligations under the Charter, and her extension of discriminatory measures. The Assembly called on the Union to reconsider her apartheid policies and to co-operate constructively.[28] In such resolutions the South African Government was 'condemned', its policies 'deplored', it was 'urged' to mend its ways, but there was no direct UN action because the Western states on whom effective action depended were not prepared to go further. Although Pretoria was often critical of them the Western states formed a diplomatic shield around her.

That shield was less willingly used in the case of South West Africa. While Pretoria could cite Article 2(7) to defend its internal racial policies, uncertainty persisted about the old mandate. The militants called for the removal of the Union's administration because she refused to accept UN rulings and because her racial policies contravened the Charter. The South Africans would never agree to that but in 1950 they sought a compromise following an advisory decision from the International Court of Justice which unanimously found that the mandate was a treaty still in force and that the status of the territory could not be altered without UN approval. By majority vote the court advised that the General Assembly had supervisory functions, but limited to those under the mandate. Finally, by a vote of eight to six, the court found that the Union was not obliged to place the territory under the Trusteeship system. The South African Government, relieved about the Trusteeship finding but unenthusiastic about the rest, re-emphasised that it was under no obligation to comply with the findings. It refused to recognise the UN right of supervision, but as an alternative proposed a new agreement with Britain, the US and France (the three remaining Principal Allied Powers from the First World War) which would be confirmed by the UN and supervised by the International Court of Justice. Although implicitly this was an acceptance by Pretoria that it could not act unilaterally, the terms of the proposal were unacceptable to a UN *ad hoc* Committee and no agreement was reached.

A further attempt at compromise was made by the UN in 1957 with the appointment of a Good Offices Committee to find 'a basis for an agreement which would continue to accord to the territory of South West Africa an international significance'.[29] The Committee, in its membership (Britain, the US and Brazil) and its terms of reference (with no mention of UN supervision) was the creature of 'the moderates'. For a time it seemed that progress might be made on a novel proposal from the Committee that the territory be divided between the north, where the bulk of the black population lived, and the south, where there was a greater racial mixture. The north would have a strong international presence in its administration, whereas the south would remain under South Africa. However, the proposal failed to gain sufficient support in the General Assembly, while for its part Pretoria rejected renewed plans for international supervision of the whole territory.

54

Neither the South Africans nor the militants were prepared to give enough ground to satisfy the other. Pretoria did not formally incorporate the territory but otherwise worked on the assumption that it was part of the Union. As early as 1948 Malan said the government was preparing legislation 'from which it will be clearer than ever before that we regard South West Africa as an integral part of the Union . . . there will be practically no difference between what is usually described as formal incorporation and the position that will be created'.[30] Louw said that the government was resolved to keep the territory in the hands of 'representatives of European culture' lest it fall into the hands of a 'black proletariat with strong communist backing'.[31] In 1949 the South West Africa Amendment Act gave the whites (but not the blacks) of the territory their first direct representation in the central legislative bodies of the Union, with six members in the House of Assembly and two in the Senate. That had the advantage for the government of strengthening its parliamentary position as it could rely on gaining these seats, but Malan explained the move in terms of rights for the white inhabitants. 'We will never', he said, 'throw the whites of South West Africa "to the wolves".'[32] A further important step was taken towards incorporating the territory when 'native affairs' were transferred from the Administrator in the territory to the Union Minister of Native Affairs, and all Native Reserves in South West Africa were placed under the South African Native Trust.

THE SEARCH FOR ALLIANCES

Pretoria sought security alliances on the basis of its self-perceived image as the leading Western state in Africa. Early uncertainty that the Nationalist Government might withdraw into itself, reflecting the party's traditional suspicion of foreign alliances and the use of armed forces outside the Union, disappeared as international communism was identified as a major threat. In response Pretoria adopted a two-pronged strategy – to gain a place for itself in a major Western alliance, and to commit the West to the defence of Africa. In addition it sought to regain from Britain sovereignty of the Simonstown naval base. In pursuit of these aims small but symbolic units were sent to fight in Korea and to help in the Berlin airlift. Within Africa Malan declared that the government's aim 'is to take responsibility, in so far as agreement can be reached with other countries [the colonial powers] for territories to the north of South Africa. We want to help in the protection of our neighbours.'[33]

Yet the government continued to see the Union as a 'small power' and assumed that the main military burden of defending Africa and the surrounding oceans would fall on the leading Western states. One of its major aims was therefore to gain membership of a Western alliance. While the security of the state was an important motive in this it was not the only one. Rich political rewards would follow membership of an alliance: it would signal a general acceptance of the Union by the West, it would please party members because it would mean less reliance on Britain as the chief ally, and among whites generally it would enhance the government's reputation. Paul Sauer told Ernest Bevin, the British Foreign Secretary, that while only half the whites had supported participation in World War Two, 'if there was trouble with Russia 90 per cent of the South African people [whites] would be wholeheartedly in it'.[34] Pretoria's hopes were that NATO would extend its operational area to the southern hemisphere and/or that NATO would associate itself with an African defence alliance. Malan argued that a future war could not be contained in the area north of the tropic of Cancer, and added that as many NATO members had territories in Africa they had direct defence interests in the continent.[35] On one occasion he referred to the Union as 'an auxiliary of the NATO alliance'.[36]

Although Pretoria was eager to demonstrate its independence from Britain, Britain remained the major power in southern Africa and her co-operation was needed both in bilateral defence arrangements and in the search for alliances. From the late 1940s there were regular defence consultations and negotiations, senior military personnel exchanged visits, and Britain continued as the main arms supplier (including destroyers, tanks and aircraft). In their negotiations the two sides sought to agree 'a package' of proposals which would further their mutual interests. However, there were differences in what they both wanted in the package. The South African priorities – NATO membership, an African alliance, and sovereignty over Simonstown – have been noted. On their part the British were keen to involve South Africa in the defence of the Middle East; they were not opposed to an African defence arrangement but it was not a high priority, and they vacillated about Simonstown. Pretoria was prepared to show interest in Middle Eastern defence because it wanted British support for its other aims. Therefore, while it backed Britain's proposed Middle East Defence Organisation (MEDO), and allocated forces for use there, these steps did not represent an enthusiasm for a new commitment but were taken to please Britain. In the event MEDO was stillborn because other states would not give it their backing, and although, under British urging, Pretoria continued to declare its support for Middle East defence, and Malan repeated the British view that the region was 'the gateway to Africa', Pretoria did not become directly involved.

In the search for African defence arrangements South Africa and Britain co-sponsored a defence conference in Nairobi 1951 where they were joined by representatives from the other major colonial powers – France, Portugal, Belgium and Italy – and observers from the US and Southern Rhodesia. The British persuaded Pretoria that the conference should be concerned with 'practical and technical matters' rather than with a general alliance. Opening the conference Lord Ogmore, the chief British representative, explained that the aim was to ensure that in the event of conflict the flow of men, machines and equipment (in particular from southern Africa to the north and the east) would not be hindered by territorial boundaries. Sauer, the chief South African representative, spoke of considering 'what facilities they can give on a mutual basis to help one another in the unfortunate event of a war to check communist aggression'. He added that South Africa would not seek facilities from others that it would not grant in return. 'Let us', he said, 'take the big view throughout.'[37] Within this 'big view' Pretoria saw the Nairobi Conference as the seed from which an alliance could grow. The colonial powers were much more cautious. The British and Portuguese underlined that the conference could make recommendations but not decisions, and when the French suggested that the scope should be extended to cover West Africa Ogmore said that further preparation would be required, and perhaps invitations sent to additional countries. He suggested a separate conference, and although that was organised it was not done with the urgency desired by Pretoria. The second conference – attended by France, Belgium, Portugal, Britain and South Africa – assembled at Dakar in 1954. Its results, except that it was concerned with West rather than East Africa, were similar to those of Nairobi. After the two conferences F. C. Erasmus, the Minister of Defence, claimed that South Africa had undertaken substantial commitments in the event of communist aggression in Africa and had become closely associated with other governments in continental defence.[38]

If Pretoria was 'committed', the other governments were not. The NATO powers neither extended the area of the alliance nor offered South Africa a formal relationship, and no African alliance emerged. There had been no lack of effort on Pretoria's part but by 1959 Erasmus was publicly accepting defeat. He spoke of 'the tragedy' of the West having no defence plans for South Africa – 'the Gibraltar of southern

Africa' – with its strategic importance, mineral wealth and control of the sea routes.[39] The only military agreement which the government achieved was a revision of the Simonstown Agreement with Britain (see below).

There were several reasons for Pretoria's failure. One was her refusal to arm black men or have mixed race forces, which undermined direct operational co-operation with the colonial powers who relied on black troops.[40] More important, however, were differences in perception. No other government shared Pretoria's view that the Union faced a direct communist threat, and there were differences about Africa's future. While most of the continent was under colonial control there were early signs among the colonial powers of uncertainty about the long term costs and commitment of staying on. In a continent with an uncertain future the colonial powers questioned the desirability of an alliance, and especially one with an increasingly unpopular state. Finally the Union's armed forces had little to offer. On the assumption that the Union was a small power and the main burden would fall on others, the government restricted defence expenditure. In 1955 it was only 8 per cent of the revenue budget (R39.4m. from a total of R501.6m.) and by 1960 it has fallen to 6 per cent (R39.2m. from R602.8m.).[41] There were also doubts about the efficiency and effectiveness of the forces. Those funds which were allocated to defence were not always spent; Erasmus, the Minister, lacked drive and administrative skill; inexperienced Afrikaner officers were promoted at the expense of battle-tried English speakers; and although some new equipment was bought much was outdated. The state of the forces was not likely to tempt potential allies. Sir Percival Liesching, Under Secretary of State at the British Commonwealth Relations Office, commenting in 1955 on a possible contribution to Middle East defence, said the condition of the South African forces was so deplorable that it was a moot point whether a commitment was worth having.[42] The low military expenditure and the poor state of the forces suggest that despite the regular references to the communist threat and the need for alliances to counter external foes, the government did not have a strong sense of imminent danger. The search for alliances doubtless had a military dimension but it was more an attempt to satisfy the government's domestic and international political ambitions by confirming its Western identity and gaining a continuing Western commitment to Africa.

The negotiations with Britain over the naval base at Simonstown are best seen in the political and military context that surrounded the search for alliances. The existing naval agreement not only gave

Britain use of the base but also sovereignty over it. Pretoria wanted to regain sovereignty and have responsibility for running it but was willing to agree to Britain's continued use. The negotiations spluttered on and off for some years because of divided views in the British Government over such matters as the importance of the Cape route and how closely an agreement on Simonstown should be tied to a Union commitment to the Middle East. The doubters among the British argued that despite all Pretoria's promises the facility might be withdrawn once sovereignty was surrendered, and that caution must be exercised in handing the National Party Government a potentially powerful political gift at the expense of the United Party. On the other side of the British debate was an eagerness to reduce commitments, a recognition that Simonstown was not of much value without South African goodwill, and in practice the proposals made by Pretoria would give Britain adequate facilities.

Eventually an agreement was reached in 1955 in an exchange of correspondence between Erasmus and Selwyn Lloyd, the British Foreign Secretary. The base was to be transferred to South African sovereignty in return for guaranteed use by Britain, an increased Union contribution to sea defence of the Cape route, the purchase of naval vessels from Britain and an implicit agreement that the South African navy would be under the command of the Royal Navy if both were together at war. The purchases from Britain were to include six anti-submarine frigates, ten coastal mine-sweepers, and four seaward defence boats. These specific points were set in the context of the earlier broader discussions. One memorandum, concerned with regional defence, reflected the aims of MEDO, and the meetings at Nairobi and Dakar. It stated that 'South Africa and the sea routes round southern Africa must be secured from aggression without', and that 'the defence of Southern Africa against external aggression lies not only in Africa, but also in the gateway to Africa, the Middle East'. Britain would therefore contribute forces for the defence of Africa while the Union's forces would aim 'to keep the potential enemy as far as possible from the borders of South Africa'.[43]

Neither side gained all it wanted from the new agreement. The British failed to achieve a clear South African commitment to the Middle East; Pretoria failed to gain a broader alliance. But there were advantages for both. For Pretoria the agreement was politically advantageous, it extended its naval strength, and it had negotiated a formal defence treaty, albeit less extensive than it had hoped. For the British they continued to have use of the base (even in a war in which South Africa was not involved), the Union was to make a greater contribution to the sea defences, and the reduced responsibility was in line with Britain's general withdrawal from a global role.

THE COMMONWEALTH

As Britain remained the Union's main international partner, so the Commonwealth remained its most important international grouping outside the UN. Yet the Nationalists remained ambivalent towards it. While for the UP the Commonwealth bound the country to Britain and the Crown, the Nationalists' emotional pull was towards a Republic and away from the old imperial master. The UP had declared that the government could not have it both ways – Commonwealth membership and a Republic – but in 1949 the decision to allow India to retain her membership after declaring a Republic suggested otherwise. Malan was delighted with the admission of a Republic, and at the time even said some kind words about India. However, he did not force the Republican issue at home because he appreciated that any attempt to do so would split the white community and might fail to gain majority support.

In calculating its position the government recognised that Commonwealth membership had advantages. At a time when the Union was becoming diplomatically isolated, it provided a network of formal and informal links, it led to military co-operation with Britain and access to her information and intelligence services, and it reinforced ties with 'friends', such as Australia. On his arrival for the 1956 conference, Strijdom said: 'There is a need in these days of danger and uncertainty in the international field of maintaining ties of friendship and for the promotion of co-operation between all states who hold the same views or similar views as we do.'[44] At the other end of the scale the Commonwealth also provided the opportunity for informal contacts with some of the sternest critics – such leaders as Jawaharlal Nehru and Kwame Nkrumah – and that may have temporarily blunted the edge of their criticism. As late as May 1959, Louw was claiming that South Africa had established good relations with the new Commonwealth countries in Africa: Nigeria and Ghana.[45]

Despite these advantages the government was often frustrated by and resentful of Commonwealth behaviour. A particular, if unusual, example of this was Pretoria's cool attitude towards Britain during the Suez crisis of 1956. The UP clamoured to support Britain, but the government would not be drawn. It spoke of achieving a peaceful solution while retaining the friendship of all, and, much to the fury of the UP, abstained on a UN vote condemning the Anglo–French invasion. In one sense the crisis served South Africa's interests by underlining the importance of the Cape route following the closure of the Suez canal. Also Pretoria was at this time suspicious of Israel as it tried to build its influence in black Africa. However, it was not these factors that explained the government's aloof stance. At the beginning of the crisis Strijdom had said: 'It is best to keep our heads out of the beehive',[46] and the beehive image captures well the furious activity, the subterfuge and self-inflicted wounds that surrounded the affair – including the breakdown of Commonwealth consultation, which infuriated Louw, undermined UP criticism and embarrassed the British High Commissioner, Sir Percival Liesching. Pretoria's attitude during the Suez crisis reflected more a judgement on Britain's ham-fisted policy, than any desire to remain uncommitted. Once the crisis was over the government was quickly back into its stride criticising the Afro-Asian states, and Egypt in particular – with its USSR ties and its support for black nationalists. Years later Verwoerd argued that Britain's mistake at Suez had been to draw back: 'If Britain had been prepared to execute the policy which she had believed to be the correct one and had not allowed herself to be dissuaded, I am sure there would be less unrest in the world and especially in Africa today.'[47]

Verwoerd's regret at the failure to stand firm against the anti-colonial challenge was characteristic of the government's view towards the Commonwealth. Essentially Pretoria wanted a Commonwealth that was anti-communist, that was concerned with security and the preservation of Western values and avoided interference in internal affairs. It certainly did not want a convenient instrument to ease the decolonisation process. As early as 1951 Malan accused Britain of 'killing the Commonwealth' by announcing that African and West Indian colonies would be led to independence on the same footing as old members. He accused Britain of unilaterally admitting India, Pakistan and Ceylon without the consent of other members, and said her policy would lead to ferment in Africa with attempts to expel the white man. 'The Commonwealth', he said, 'can exist only as a result of a feeling of solidarity between the members . . . [which rests on] two things, namely specific common interest and sufficient homo-geneity of culture and political outlook.' He asked rhetorically whether South Africa had more in common with India than it had with Western European states.[48] He warned Britain against hasty indepen-dence for the colonies, and had it confirmed that membership required general and not just British approval.

Yet the tide would not turn. Pretoria's resentment steadily increased, as in 1956 when Louw said it was unbelievable that Mr

K. A. Gbedemah, the Ghanaian Finance Minister, could suggest that colonialism would be dead in five years and that African states would not tolerate the continued subjections of South Africa's black majority. By the late 1950s South Africa's position in the Commonwealth was very uneasy. A Commonwealth agenda was emerging influenced by the new members with its emphasis on non-alignment, anti-colonialism and opposition to racial discrimination.

The changing pattern of South Africa's relations within the Commonwealth reflected its more general position. Although it belonged to the community of states and participated fully in terms of economic and diplomatic activity, its relationships were increasingly judged in terms of its racial policies. This made other governments reluctant to associate too closely, and brought mounting criticism in international organisations. During the 1950s international pressures had grown steadily.

PART II

SHARPEVILLE AND THE CHALLENGE OF THE EARLY 1960s: 1960–1965

5 THE STATE UNDER THREAT – THE INTERNAL AND INTERNATIONAL SETTINGS

On Strijdom's death in 1958 Dr Hendrik Verwoerd became Prime Minister. Each step in the chain of succession was seen by the government's opponents as a further hardening of attitudes – from Malan, the father of modern Nationalism; to Strijdom, the advocate of 'baaskap'; to Verwoerd, the architect of apartheid. Like his predecessors, Verwoerd's main concern had been with internal developments, but like them he too became drawn into foreign policy making, and in his case he dominated the scene. He was a man of great determination, burning conviction and formidable powers of work. His personal style was earnest and sincere without flamboyance, but he drew admirers to him, convinced of his vision and foresight.

Verwoerd retained Louw as Foreign Minister until the latter's retirement in 1964. Louw lost none of his aggression. He was even censured by the UN General Assembly in 1961 for questioning the ability of the new states to assume their responsibilities, accusing them of falling under the influence of Moscow and Peking and favourably comparing the lot of blacks in South Africa with the rest of the continent.[1] Yet as Verwoerd established his authority Louw had less freedom of action, and when he retired Verwoerd chose a very different character to replace him – Dr Hilgard Muller, a quiet, courteous man, with little drive; an implementor not an initiator of policy, an ideal subordinate for Verwoerd. With Muller in charge there were fewer personality clashes at international gatherings, but there was also less thrust in the department. As Secretary for Foreign Affairs (the chief official) Verwoerd retained G. P. Jooste who had succeeded Forsyth in 1956. Jooste, a formal, meticulous man was a firm Nationalist and an admirer of Verwoerd. The two worked so closely together

65

that the Prime Minister sometimes operated directly through him, circumventing Louw and later Muller. In 1963 Verwoerd asked Jooste instead of Louw to lead the delegation to the UN, a decision that may have prompted Louw's resignation.

Verwoerd's domestic political inheritance was very different from Malan's ten years earlier. Now the party had a grip on the government, the great bulk of Afrikaners were massed behind it, the white opposition was weaker, the framework of apartheid was in place, and although black nationalism was more active it was not yet a serious threat to the state. The international scene was less secure as political developments in Africa moved against Pretoria, but again there was no sense of immediate danger. In the late 1950s the government and the white society were enjoying a period of confidence.

That confidence did not last. The early 1960s were years of crisis for white South Africa. Many of the dangers were rooted in the past but they gained a new intensity from the rising expectations and militancy of blacks inside the country and international pressures outside. For the whites there was a cumulative sense of danger as the challenges mounted upon each other. However, the government fought back and piloted the state through the crisis and the years of uncertainty that followed. As it did so the tension eased and the sense of crisis disappeared. Because of the interplay of challenge and response much of the evidence for the early 1960s is contradictory. While the government emphasised its successes, claiming that the ordeal had shown the strength and stability of the country, the opponents equally pointed to the conflicts, the social divisions and the commitment of those at home and abroad to overthrow the existing order. Whatever the government's claims, South Africa would never be the same again. The unquestioning assumption of white dominance died in the early 1960s, and with that came changes in government policy, in black nationalism and in the international context in which South Africa operated.

REPUBLICANISM AND MACMILLAN'S MESSAGE

1960 opened dramatically when Verwoerd announced that the white electorate would vote in October to decide whether South Africa should become a Republic. Like many Nationalists Verwoerd had nursed the Republican dream throughout his political life and he went ahead with the referendum despite the opposition of the UP, the doubts of some of his own supporters, and the findings of a National Party survey which indicated that the majority of the white electorate might vote against it. When asked what majority would be required Verwoerd replied that one vote would do, and added that if he failed through a referendum he would try other means – presumably calling a general election on the issue. Among the whites there were a few unheeded voices calling for black participation, but greater controversy arose over the right of the whites of South West Africa to participate. Uncharacteristically Verwoerd hesitated, but then decided in their favour, perhaps calculating that most of them were Nationalists and their votes might tip the balance. In the event their votes were not required. There was a clear majority for the Republic – 850,458 votes in favour and 775,878 against.[2] Although the voting reflected the old divisions – based on provinces, rural and urban dwellers, and Afrikaans and English speakers – it also revealed that an increasing number of whites were rallying behind the government. The referendum was a triumph for Verwoerd. Despite the opposition and the doubts, he had achieved one of the great goals of Afrikaner Nationalism.

In itself the Republican issue would have made 1960 a year of intense political activity, but in the months between the announcement of the referendum and the voting in October the Union was shaken by a chain of events. Although they took place inside the country their importance was intensified by an African setting in which colonial territories were being transformed into independent states. In 1960 itself – the 'Year of Africa' – sixteen colonies gained independence. In southern Africa, however, the white rulers were determined to hold onto power, but they could not prevent the impact of the new developments spilling into the subcontinent, promoting hope among black nationalists and fear and anxiety among whites. When white refugees passed through the Union fleeing from the violence that followed the Congo's independence, many white South Africans saw it as living proof that their anxieties were well founded and vowed never to let it happen to them.

Inside South Africa the first major event to follow the announcement of the referendum was the visit of Harold Macmillan, the British Prime Minister. He came in February as part of an African tour. The government welcomed the visit and would have resented omission from the itinerary, but the pleasure was short-lived. On his arrival Macmillan asked to meet leaders of the ANC and the Liberal Party, who, in the government's eyes, were too radical to operate in the existing political system. The requests were ignored. Then Macmillan privately told Verwoerd that Britain could not continue to support South Africa's claim that her racial policies were outside the competence of international organisations. That was blow enough, but worse followed when Macmillan made his 'Wind of Change' speech to the combined Houses of Parliament. Although the British Prime Minister did not say anything that had not been said before the speech came as a shock. The reason lies partly in Britain's leading position in Africa so that Macmillan was seen as speaking for the West. It also lies in the setting of the speech – where it was said as much as what was said. If Macmillan had spoken elsewhere it might have been explained away as another example of Britain currying favour with the blacks; but when the whites were told straight to their faces, in their own Parliament, it could not be brushed aside. Finally Macmillan unearthed and exposed the whites' own fears – fears about decolonisation, about Western attitudes and about the strength of African nationalism. He exposed the fears and stripped away the illusions, and was bitterly resented for doing so. Mr Fred Barnard, Verwoerd's private secretary, wrote that the speech 'was to come as a surprise attack, a move calculated to drive Dr Verwoerd into a corner and to embarrass him in the eyes of his own Parliament, of his country and of the world'. Barnard believed that Macmillan consciously tried to place Verwoerd at a disadvantage by breaking the convention of presenting his host with a copy of the speech before it was delivered.[3]

Macmillan's broad theme was that anti-colonial nationalism which had swept across Asia was now sweeping through Africa, and Western interests were best served by coming to terms with it. 'The great issue' of the second half of the twentieth century said Macmillan 'is whether the uncommitted peoples of Africa will swing to the East or the West. The struggle is joined and it is a struggle for the minds of men.' British policy in Africa was not, however, simply based on power politics, or opportunism, but on a conviction of right. The British were concerned to raise standards of living and 'to create a society which respects the rights of individuals – a society in which men are given the opportunity to grow to their full stature', with 'an increasing share in political power and responsibility'. Macmillan recognised that Britain's policy would create difficulties for South Africa because development in one part of the continent must influence the rest, but he was sure that they would appreciate that Britain had to do her duty as she saw it.

Macmillan tried to sugar the pill by stating that the British Government was opposed to sanctions, that existing differences would eventually disappear, and meanwhile friendly co-operation would continue. Sugared or not, the pill was there. The British were coming to terms with African nationalism and the South Africans could not expect support if they chose to stand against it. It was the tone as well as the content of the speech that angered many whites and frightened others. There was a smugness in the British Prime Minister's message of having backed a winner and a just cause. Macmillan spoke on a grand historical scale, stretching back to the Roman Empire and reaching forward to generations yet unborn. It was a speech hinting at historical inevitability, for while the growth of an 'African national consciousness' took many forms it could not be stopped – 'it is happening everywhere. The wind of change is blowing through the continent.'[4]

Verwoerd replied immediately. Without a copy of Macmillan's speech he had to speak impromptu, but for many whites, and not only his own supporters, it was one of his finest hours. After thanking Macmillan for his frankness he said that despite differences South Africa and Britain could remain friends, for both were committed to peace and Western values. However, they had differences in Africa. South Africa's policies were in full accord with the new developments, whereas he warned of changes in British policies: 'The very objective at which you are aiming may be defeated by them.' The attempt to do justice to all 'does not only mean being just to the Black man in Africa, but also to be just to the Whites'. It was the whites 'who brought civilization here, who made the development of Black nationalism possible'. Whites had made southern Africa their motherland, but 'we also see ourselves as a part of the Western world, a true White state in Africa, with the possibility of granting a full future to the Black man in our midst'. This made South Africa 'indispensible to the White world . . . We are the link. We are White, but we are in Africa. We link with both, and that lays upon us a special duty.'[5]

SHARPEVILLE AND BLACK NATIONALISM

The dust had not settled from Macmillan's visit before the tragedy of Sharpeville. Sharpeville was the bloodiest of a series of confrontations between the police and demonstrators who had been called out by the Pan-African Congress (PAC) to defy the pass laws. The response to the call was patchy but at Sharpeville the police fired into a large crowd which had surrounded the police station. 67 Africans were killed and 186 wounded. On the same day in Langa, near Cape Town, three Africans were killed and about fifty wounded. Because of the scale of the tragedy, Sharpeville would have stood out in South Africa's history whenever it had happened, but it was not the first time that the police had killed demonstrators. The others are forgotten; Sharpeville remains. It remains because it was seen as part of the broader struggle which was sweeping Africans into power across the continent, and which, said Robert Sobukwe, the PAC leader, would bring 'freedom and independence' to South Africa by 1963.[6] Within that framework of expectations those who had died at Sharpeville were martyrs for a cause in which the righteous majority would quickly and inevitably inherit the state.

After Sharpeville, black nationalism changed. Earlier the movement had passed through two broad phases. In the first – which lasted to the Second World War – black nationalists were reformers drawn from a small middle class who were prepared to work, by peaceful means, for a place in the existing structure. In the second period – roughly 1945 to 1960 – the movement became more broadly based; it employed mass civil action; it sought a radical change in the existing social and political orders, but still through non-violent means. Sharpeville marked the start of another phase.[7] In this there were two new characteristics. First, the movement became revolutionary in its aims and methods as protest turned to resistance. Alongside continuing non-violent activities, small dedicated groups organised a campaign of violence against the state. Second, the movement spread its activities abroad and with the backing of sympathetic governments and non-state organisations it became internationalised.

Before Sharpeville the black nationalist movement had split into two main streams – the long established ANC, and the Pan-African Congress (PAC) which was formed in 1959 by a breakaway group from the ANC. The PAC presented itself as an 'Africanist' party, the party of the black 'have nots' compared with the white 'haves', committed to black values, black control of the state, and in tune with the spirit of Pan-Africanism preached by such leaders as Kwame Nkrumah and Sekou Toure. The PAC manifesto proclaimed that South Africa's Africans 'recognise themselves as part of one African nation, stretching from Cape to Cairo, Madagascar to Morocco' and it pledged the party to work for a United States of Africa.[8] The PAC criticised the ANC for its multiracialism, for the influence exerted by whites including communists, for its acceptance of the 'reformist' Charter, and for its failure to take militant action. The ANC responded vigorously, confirming its commitment to multiracialism and argued that South Africa could not be bracketed with states like Ghana that were almost exclusively black. It denied that it was dominated by whites or communists or that it had failed to act firmly.

Following the break there was bitter rivalry between the two parties. In the wake of Sharpeville both organised strikes, marches and mourning for the dead. The size of these demonstrations revealed to many whites for the first time the enormous potential strength of mass black action. In Cape Town a peaceful march by many thousands of blacks became a living witness of black demands, but it also revealed the ruthlessness of the government in arresting Philip Kgosana the march leader after promising him a meeting with government leaders. Later there was a day of mourning for the dead, a national 'stay at home', and a major conference at Pietermaritzburg in March 1961 – the 'All In Conference', which in the event was not 'all in' as the PAC refused to attend. The conference called for a national convention of all races to draw up a democratic constitution. Although these activities captured the enthusiasm of many blacks and kept the nationalists in the public eye, they ran into increasing difficulties. Some arose in the organisations themselves – inadequate funds, poor communications, internal rivalries, and inexperienced leadership – but the greatest problem was the government's fierce opposition, which reflected both its determination and its concern. Early in 1961, when faced by the threat of another 'stay at home' Verwoerd admitted: 'We regard the present situation as very serious', but asserted that the government was well equipped 'to halt the reign of terror'.[9]

The government's action included banning the black parties, the arrest of their leaders, intensive police activity in the townships, and the introduction of new legislation. Conflicting claims were made about the success of these steps, and although in retrospect it seems obvious that the weight of the government's resources and manpower would always succeed against the weakly organised and funded black parties, that did not seem so clear at the time. As the nationalists' mass action began to falter, so underground revolutionary groups were organised. There were two revolutionary movements – 'Umkhonto we Sizwe' (Spear of the Nation) linked to the ANC, and 'Poqo' (meaning 'only' or 'pure' implying a purely African movement) linked to the PAC. Both were formed in 1961 but it was more than a year before they were operating. Umkhonto launched its sabotage campaign by attacking power stations and government buildings in Port Elizabeth and Johannesburg on 16 December, 1962 – a day revered by Afrikaners for their victory over the Zulu. According to Nelson Mandela, it was 'only when all else failed, when all channels of peaceful protest had been barred to us, that the decision was made to embark on violent forms of political struggle . . . We did so not because we desired such a course, but solely because the Government had left us with no other choice.'[10]

The relationship between the parent bodies and Umkhonto and

Poqo was not always clear and they must often have acted independently. Like all such organisations they suffered from rivalries and incompetence, and they were sometimes penetrated by government informers, but they also attracted able and dedicated members who were soon active in attacking government targets and recruiting young men to leave the country for guerrilla training. The government and the nationalists became locked in a fierce struggle which was fought out in secret meetings, night raids, intimidation, infiltration, torture, sabotage, imprisonment without trial, killings, emergency laws, dramatic escapes and arrests. Umkhonto concentrated its attacks on government property, while Poqo was prepared to attack people and operated in rural as well as urban areas. It was accused of the murder of two headmen in Pondoland, an attempt on the life of Chief Matanzima of the Transkei, the terrorist murder of five whites at Bashee River Camp, and promoting riots in Paarl which led to the death of five blacks and two whites. Violence was also used by a small group of radical whites, The African Freedom Movement, who organised sabotage against property. They had plans to release prisoners from Robben Island, and one of their members, John Harris, planted a bomb at Johannesburg railway station in July 1964 which killed one person and injured many others, but the group was soon broken by the police.[11]

At first the government had considerable difficulties in countering this new, violent resistance. Bombs and sabotage became common. Between September 1961 and June 1963 at least 193 cases of sabotage came before the courts, ranging from such minor acts as placing burning matches in letter boxes to blowing up power lines and throwing bombs into houses.[12] However, the black movements wanted more than sabotage. They planned revolution. The ambitious scale of their thinking was revealed in Umkhonto's plans for 'Operation Mayebuye'. The operation was to start with the landing by sea or air of small groups of trained 'freedom fighters'. Their tasks were to establish bases, recruit and train new fighters from the local communities, and gain the political support of the black population. Once the ground had been laid a massive onslaught was to be launched in four areas – Port Elizabeth, Port Shepstone, the north west Transvaal, and the north western Cape. It was anticipated that strong international support would follow – diplomatic, economic, and even military. Although the plan envisaged a protracted war there was a prospect 'that the state structure will collapse sooner than we at the moment envisage' because of Pretoria's international isolation and the commitment of the African and Socialist governments against her.

In no other guerrilla operation, it was claimed, had the international situation been such a vital factor operating against the enemy.[13]

Such ambitious plans were never realised because the nationalists greatly overestimated their own strengths and underrated that of the government. After early uncertainty the government succeeded in arresting many of the leaders. Nelson Mandela was arrested in August 1962, and in the next year the government had its greatest triumph when seventeen of the Umkhonto High Command were captured at Rivonia. That was a grievous blow to the movement, and Poqo also suffered. In June 1964 John Vorster, then Minister of Justice, claimed that Poqo had been smashed with 3,264 of its members arrested.[14] During 1963 there were press reports of the trials of more than 1,000 members of the ANC and PAC, of whom 46 received the death penalty. These government successes came in part through improved intelligence from captured nationalists and penetration by informers. With this improved information, and in contrast with the early mass arrests which were designed to intimidate the African population as much as capture known nationalists, the government acted with precision. These major set-backs marked the 'death knell of amateurism' for the nationalists. In the 'post-mortems' that followed they recognised that they had acted without adequate bases, strong organisation and discipline, and without sufficient funds. They also recognised that they had failed to contain infiltration by government informers, in part because they had not mobilised the people. Joe Mathews of the ANC spoke of the masses having no knowledge of what was happening. 'We were going to war', he said, 'without the people with us. The vanguard was isolated and this allowed the police to easily infiltrate.'[15]

Banned and under fierce attack at home, the nationalists moved their operations abroad. In this new setting they found considerable sympathy. International recognition for their struggle had already been symbolised in the award of the 1960 Nobel Peace Prize to Chief Albert Luthuli, the ANC President. In the words of the citation, 'in spite of the unmerciful South African race laws, Luthuli had always urged that violence should not be used. To a high degree it is due to him that struggles in South Africa have not taken the form of bloody conflicts.' The government was furious but gave Luthuli a ten-day passport to receive the prize in person. The ANC leader made the most of his temporary international audience – appearing on British television, giving a press conference in Oslo in which he called for economic action against Pretoria, and at a dinner in his honour reaffirming his commitment to non-racial democracy and non-violence.[16]

Luthuli's award came in recognition of the non-violent stage of the nationalists' campaign, and international support for that approach continued. However, as they organised the revolutionary stage, the nationalists sought new forms of support, for violent as well as peaceful activities. Even before Sharpeville, Oliver Tambo had been sent abroad to organise the ANC's international activities and he was soon reinforced by the arrival of political refugees. Most of these were black Africans who formed the bulk of the parties in exile, but there were exiles from the other races, some of whom were to play leading roles in the international anti-apartheid campaign. Although there were no precise figures, several thousand people fled in the early 1960s. Amnesty International reported that between the 1960 emergency and late 1963, 1,200 refugees passed through Bechuanaland alone. In March 1964 Vorster stated that 562 people who had been charged with sabotage had left the country and that estimates of those who were receiving guerrilla training varied between 900 and 5,000.[17]

The main routes for the flights (and the subsequent re-entry) were through the British High Commission Territories. Inevitably friction arose between the authorities on either side of the borders. Pretoria complained that the British were giving passage to the Republic's enemies, allowing them to establish bases, hold conferences, and organise raids. In turn the British complained about border raids and hot pursuit into their territory. Yet neither side saw it in their interests to push the dispute too far. Pretoria apologised for the border infringements claiming (albeit unconvincingly) that they were mistakes, and concentrated on greater efficiency in policing the border areas. Threats to close the borders, which could have strangled the small territories economically, were not carried out, but new regulations were introduced. From 1962 passports were required to cross into Basutoland; in the following year stringent laws were introduced against people committing offences outside the Republic's border; an extradition treaty was concluded with Southern Rhodesia; tighter controls were introduced on aircraft movements and East African Airways, which had been involved in transporting refugees, were refused a licence to fly to South Africa. The police also arrested people crossing back into the Union and gained important information from them. For their part the British, who were criticised by the nationalists for not giving them enough support and by the South Africans for giving them too much, tightened their attitude towards the nationalists. While they were not prepared to turn the refugees back they hurried them on, introduced legislation against violence abroad and became increasingly vigilant about potential guerrilla bases. In 1963, for example, the Basutoland police raided a Poqo centre in Maseru and seized a list of party members which was said to contain between 10,000 and 15,000 names. Despite British denials, Poqo suspected that Pretoria was given the list or succeeded in gaining access to it.[18] The attitude of the white government of the Central African Federation was even tougher. It began to return black South Africans who did not have valid papers. For example, in February 1963 a dozen young men en route for guerrilla training crossed through Bechuanaland, but when they reached Northern Rhodesia they were arrested and returned to the Republic where they were imprisoned for two years.[19]

Elsewhere in Africa the nationalists found great sympathy. In 1962, before his arrest, Nelson Mandela slipped out of South Africa to attend a PAFMECSA conference (Pan-African Freedom Movement of East, Central and South Africa). His reception there exceeded expectations. 'Wherever I went', he said, 'I found sympathy for our cause and promises of support.'[20] Mandela continued his overseas trip to Britain where he received considerable public attention and met opposition leaders, but, more significantly for this stage of black nationalism, he took the opportunity to study literature about war and revolution, attended a military training course in Algeria and made arrangements for South African recruits to receive military training.

Through such contacts the nationalists gained international recognition and support, but the attempts by friendly governments to bring the ANC and PAC together failed. However the internationalisation of the movements continued and the range of support expanded. In brief, the main aim of the international activities was to mobilise support for the continuing struggle by such activities as training guerrilla fighters, fund-raising, propaganda, diplomatic support, working alongside anti-apartheid groups and rallying public support. The emphasis differed according to the setting. In the West (where London was the main centre) the aim was to gain 'the support and sympathy of the governments and people for the freedom struggle',[21] to combine with anti-apartheid groups to exert pressure on governments, banks and companies, and to build a public mood against apartheid through the media and anti-apartheid campaigns. In black Africa, activities increased as more states gained independence. Cairo, already established for nationalist broadcasting, was joined by new centres at Dar es Salaam, Addis Ababa (the OAU headquarters), and military training camps in Algeria and Tanzania. The communist states gained in influence because they were prepared to give military support to the armed struggle, and this enabled communists within the ANC to become more prominent. While Nelson Mandela was at the PAFMECSA conference, Arthur Goldreich (a white communist

ANC member) was visiting Eastern Europe to make contacts which led to the provision of military support in arms and training. However, divisions among the communist states and the black nationalists led to the ANC gaining support from the USSR while the PAC was aided by China.

THE AFRICAN SETTING

In Africa decolonisation gained pace. Even colonial possessions like the High Commission Territories, which previously had been considered too small and impoverished to become sovereign states, were now being groomed for independence. In April 1960 Louw accurately predicted that white rule would soon be confined to the Portuguese territories, Southern Rhodesia and South Africa itself. He said that even Northern Rhodesia was 'practically over the wall'.[22] Pretoria persistently criticised the withdrawal. It accused the colonial powers of appeasement, of betraying the white man and his civilisation, and of exposing the continent to communist penetration by handing over power to immature regimes. Verwoerd stated that British colonial policy had passed through three stages – first 'baaskap'; second 'partnership'; and finally 'running away'.[23] He claimed that 'non-racialism' was a euphemism for promoting black interests at the expense of whites, and while the British claimed to find apartheid abhorrent, he found their treatment of white men in Kenya and Tanganyika abhorrent.

Pretoria's attempts to come to terms with the changing scene met with little success. Briefly it seemed that there might be advantage in the chaos that followed the Belgian Congo's independence, as Moise Tshombe, the leader of Katanga Province, sought South African aid in his unsuccessful attempt to secede from the rest of the country, and later in his short reign as Prime Minister of the whole Congo. There was also encouragement for South Africa in statements made by black leaders in southern Africa who stressed that on gaining their independence they would have to learn to live alongside their powerful neighbour. However, these were exceptions. The characteristic response from the emerging states was one of hostility. As Louw had stated in 1957, the main card South Africa could play was to offer economic and technical co-operation, but in the early 1960s the newly independent states were in 'the middle belt' of Africa. They had few links with the Republic and they were unwilling to create new ones. They saw South Africa not as a potential economic partner but as a racist state.

Racism intruded into diplomatic relations. The issue had been discussed by Louw (with particular reference to Ghana) at the 1960 Commonwealth Conference. Following the conference, Sir Robert Menzies wrote to Verwoerd saying that much of the heat could be taken out of Pretoria's relations with Afro-Asian states if it would exchange diplomats on equal terms. Verwoerd disagreed. He said that South Africa already received 'coloured' diplomats from Egypt and Taiwan, and was prepared to consider restoring relations with India and Pakistan if those countries so wished, but he had strong doubts about diplomats from black Africa. He wrote of the danger of their embassies becoming centres of agitation as they favoured a 'multi-racial or Bantu government here'. It was best, therefore, to postpone the matter until separate development had advanced further in South Africa, and until the black states showed less inclination to interfere in internal affairs. Verwoerd also mentioned the social problems that would arise if representatives of the black states 'moved in Government social circles'. The same social rights would then be claimed by South Africa's own educated Bantu and Bantu national leaders which would endanger 'the whole position of the white man'. 'We have', he concluded, 'to tread warily.'[24]

Black diplomatic representation was not an issue on which Pretoria was prepared to bend to Commonwealth opinion, but within its self-imposed limits it made occasional attempts to resolve the problem. There was renewed talk of a diplomatic suburb, and in 1964 Verwoerd said that he favoured the old idea of a roving ambassador who would keep contact with the black states while their representatives could fly to South Africa for day visits. He said that this would save money, but that excuse deceived nobody. Verwoerd's proposal came in response to press reports that Kenneth Kaunda, the President of the newly independent Zambia, had offered to exchange diplomats provided they received equal treatment at both ends. To that Verwoerd stated that while South Africa's representatives would act in accordance with the customs of other countries, foreign representatives must 'act in accordance with South Africa's customs'.[25] Black leaders interpreted that as accepting 'the custom' of white racial superiority.

In these circumstances, and despite the emergence of many new states, South Africa's few diplomatic links in the continent were reduced further. The Egyptian representative withdrew in 1961; South Africa's Consul General was asked to leave the Congo; and when Pretoria decided to withdraw the Consul from Nairobi shortly before Kenya's independence, the last links outside white-controlled Africa were lost. Instead of diplomatic contacts there was increasing hostility. In Ghana South Africans were refused entry unless they signed a statement condemning apartheid; Ethiopia and Liberia had instigated the Namibia case; leaders like Dr Julius Nyerere of Tanganyika were persistent critics; and many states proclaimed the imposition of economic sanctions.

THE INTERNATIONAL SETTING

The entry of the new black states heightened international awareness of apartheid. In attacking South Africa the new states brought with them a burning conviction of right, and a confidence that a society built on apartheid could not stand. They saw themselves as introducing a new morality into international affairs by which South Africa was judged and found wanting. As those that gained independence in the early 1960s were geographically remote and had few economic links with the Republic, their moral fervour was not blunted by fears of material loss. They combined with the other opponents of apartheid to place it high on the international agenda. In doing so they were supported by the communists led by the USSR.

Relations between South Africa and the USSR had never been good and they had deteriorated further in the late 1950s. In the same year as the government closed the Soviet Consulate (1956) President Kruschev at the 20th Party Congress shifted the emphasis of Soviet policy away from direct East/West confrontation towards 'the world of socialism' which offered help to the liberation of colonial peoples, and South Africa was placed within that framework. At international gatherings Moscow was in the forefront of those calling for her diplomatic and economic isolation, and more particularly it gave support to the ANC which it recognised as the sole legitimate liberation movement. However, there was a difference of emphasis between Moscow and the black states. While the Africans wanted the UN to organise action, the Soviet Union, following the Congo experience, wanted it to remain a political forum not an enforcement agency.[26]

Despite the diplomatic antagonism between Moscow and Pretoria there was also limited economic co-operation. Following the news of substantial Russian diamond discoveries in the early 1950s, Harry Oppenheimer, the Chairman of Anglo American, moved swiftly to bring the marketing of Soviet gems into the established de Beers Group operation which dominated the world market. Agreement was reached whereby the USSR gem production was bought at an annually agreed price. There was also co-operation, although less formal, on gold prices. Later Moscow claimed that the co-operation in mineral marketing was a means of strengthening the USSR so that it was able to help the liberation movements.[27]

The combination of condemnation on one hand and co-operation on the other was more exposed in the case of the Western states – partly because of the more open nature of their societies, but more because of the scale and range of their contacts with South Africa. Although Western governments became more critical of Pretoria, there was no direct confrontation and economic links were openly encouraged. Britain remained the most prominent because southern Africa still had a low priority for the US. However, following Sharpeville and the inauguration of President Kennedy, US attention increased. Apartheid was more readily condemned; South Africa was kept at diplomatic arm's length as Washington sought to build bridges to the new black states; Menon Williams, the new Assistant Secretary of State for Africa, offended the colonial powers as well as Pretoria by his open sympathy with black nationalism; and a suggestion that Verwoerd should make a private visit to Washington to explain South Africa's case in person was rebuffed. For its part Pretoria ignored President Kennedy's appeal to dismantle apartheid following which the US imposed a selective and largely symbolic arms ban.[28] The South Africans viewed these developments in American policy as the products of ignorance and opportunism.

A significant development in the West was the growth of anti-apartheid movements. They had started to emerge in the late 1950s and were given a substantial boost by Sharpeville and the arrival of South African political exiles. At a rally in Trafalgar Square, London, in February 1960, Father Trevor Huddleston, Julius Nyerere, Hugh Gaitskell (the leader of the Labour Party), and Trade Union leaders launched the Boycott Movement in response to a call from the ANC and the black states. Following Sharpeville they extended its activities to total opposition to Pretoria, and renamed it the Anti-Apartheid Movement (AAM). As the movement spread, South Africa's international environment was increasingly influenced by these non-governmental organizations which created a hostile public mood through demonstrations, media attention, and the recruitment of major public figures. They combined with the black states to ensure persistent anti-apartheid international pressure, and often undertook the groundwork of collecting information and organising campaigns while the black states gained international legitimacy for these activities by bringing them to the attention of international organisations.

However, the AAM and the black states were treated with suspicion by some Western governments and ran into direct opposition from right-wing political groups, such as the American–South African Council, and business associations, including the United Kingdom–South Africa Trade Association and the South African Foundation, which was backed by South African interests.[29]

There were persistent calls for economic sanctions. The anti-apartheid groups and the black states saw sanctions both as a moral gesture and as a means of undermining apartheid. Those who opposed them marshalled a range of arguments from the need to retain a firm ally against communism, to claims that apartheid was undermined by economic expansion. Both sides were convinced of their case. As Ronald Segal, himself an advocate of sanctions, wrote: 'Those who wanted sanctions dismissed all arguments against them as trivial or irrelevant, while those who opposed such action denounced it as illegal, impractical and economically calamitous. It was a dialogue of pulpits, with the phrases of revelation.'[30] However, for Western governments with a strong stake in South Africa, sanctions were not a clear cut issue. It involved a maze of moral questions, material interests, international and domestic considerations and pressures. What would be the impact on southern Africa as a whole? What would be the economic cost at home? How would the whites respond politically? Would force be needed to impose sanctions? Might the economy be wrecked leaving the country under an unstable and potentially hostile regime? Is apartheid so morally reprehensible that sanctions should be imposed whatever the cost? How would the electorate at home respond?

Without the moral fervour of the black states, and conscious of their economic and strategic interests and political divisions at home, the leading Western states shied away from sanctions. In reaching their decision they were influenced by shifting predictions of the future. As Macmillan had indicated, the Western states were coming to accept radical change in Africa but they were unsure what shape this would take in South Africa. In the wake of Sharpeville it was widely assumed that without rapid and radical change there would be a black revolution. 'Sitting on a volcano', and 'Standing on the edge of a precipice' were the images of the day. However, as the 1960s wore on it became clear that 'the inevitable' was not imminent. The prospect of internal revolution faded and change seemed to rest increasingly on external action. That bred doubts all round. If there were no imminent internal revolution might it not be better to wait, to hope that economic development would bring change, to play a passive role and see what emerged? The views of the US Government exemplified this shift. On taking up his post as US Ambassador to South Africa in 1960, Joseph Satherthwaite was advised by the State Department to prepare for black rule within eighteen months to five years. By the end of 1963 that appeared so 'absurdly unrealistic' that a State Department report recommended concentration on limited achievable goals in black labour and education.

Despite the increasing doubts the advocates of sanctions kept up their pressure. In 1962 the General Assembly, by sixty-seven votes to sixteen with twenty-three abstentions, asked member states to break off diplomatic relations with the Republic, to boycott her goods, stop all exports, and close access to her ships and aircraft. In April 1964 there was a major sanctions conference in London which drew delegates from more than forty countries. Usually there was little to show for these efforts – words without substance – but late in 1963 the black states prompted the Security Council to call on all members to ban the sale of arms to South Africa. This was not a mandatory resolution, and some Western states ignored it, but it was a warning to Pretoria that international hostility could lead to action.

THE WITHDRAWAL FROM THE COMMONWEALTH

Following the decision to declare a Republic, South Africa had to reapply for Commonwealth membership. Like many Nationalists Verwoerd had little enthusiasm for the Commonwealth, but to gather support at the referendum he subordinated his views and urged the voters to back 'a democratic Republic within the Commonwealth'.[31] Following the referendum victory he decided to attend the 1961 conference himself, and there is no reason to doubt that he set out to retain membership provided certain conditions were fulfilled. The conditions were: no interference in internal policies, no sacrifice of principles, and no loss of sovereignty or national honour. Macmillan, who was eager to keep South Africa in the Commonwealth, had privately contacted other members in search of compromise, but alongside the private soundings a public debate developed which exposed the conflict. On one side were those like Julius Nyerere, the future President of Tanganyika, who proclaimed that his country would not join the Commonwealth if South Africa remained in it, and on the other large advertisements advocating her membership appeared in the British press, covertly funded by South African businessmen.

At the conference Verwoerd agreed to discuss his government's racial policies, but while some Commonwealth leaders were prepared to separate that issue from continued membership others were not. Opposition from the Afro-Asian states had been anticipated but it was an attack from Mr Diefenbaker of Canada that finally undermined Macmillan's search for compromise. After long, fruitless discussions Verwoerd withdrew South Africa's application. While formally it was a 'withdrawal', in reality the Republic had been forced out of the Commonwealth. 'In substance', wrote Robert Menzies, 'he had to withdraw unless he was prepared to depart from the politics which, however criticised, are the settled policies of his own government.'[32] In one sense it was a personal blow for Verwoerd, who prided himself on his ability to persuade others, yet he had few doubts that South Africa's interests lay outside the organisation. Even if he had gained readmission in 1961 there was no future in the new Commonwealth. The question at stake was not Republican status but racial policies. If Macmillan was downcast at having failed to patch up an agreement, Nyerere was elated. 'Marvellous', he said, the Commonwealth 'is cemented on a firm moral foundation.'[33]

When Verwoerd reported to the House of Assembly he said that four possibilities had faced him. First, he could have given way to the pressures by agreeing to radical policy changes. Second, he could have stood his ground but accept a conference communiqué critical of South Africa. Third, he could have sat back to let the others fight it out. Finally, he had the choice of withdrawal. The first two options he dismissed because they infringed South Africa's sovereignty. The third he rejected because it would place friends, like Britain and Australia, in an impossible position which could have destroyed the Commonwealth. He concluded, therefore, that the only step left, which would retain both South Africa's dignity and her strong bilateral ties with individual Commonwealth members, was a voluntary withdrawal.[34]

On his return Verwoerd was treated as a hero by his followers. At the airport he told them: 'We do not come back as people who have had a defeat. It's a happy day for South Africa. What happened was no less than a miracle. So many nations have had to get their complete freedom by armed struggle . . . But here we have reached something which we never expected.'[35] On that occasion he was speaking to Afrikaners and 'freedom' was freedom from the old British imperial dominance, but once the initial euphoria was over Verwoerd broadened his appeal in search of English speaking support. His tone became one of hard-headed interest in which he played down the Commonwealth's advantages, saying it offered neither military protection nor diplomatic support, and later he went on to claim that the relationship with Britain had become more relaxed as Britain no longer felt obliged to steer South Africa into line with other Commonwealth members.[36] Finally, Verwoerd dismissed predictions of an economic crisis, because South Africa's economic relations and trading concessions with Commonwealth members, and notably Britain, would continue. Yet, even if he ignored them, there were disadvantages – increased diplomatic isolation, loss of information sources and defence links with Britain, and the break in informal ties with friends and foe alike. However, once the decision was taken the debate among whites died because most of them believed that membership could only be bought at the cost of abandoning white dominance. It was that, and not the commitment to a Republic, that killed the Commonwealth issue. The most striking change came in the UP whose members came to accept that their Commonwealth image – of crown and flag, of like-minded men, and of being 'British' – was now irrelevant. Only a few months after the withdrawal, de Villiers Graaf said that there was a price that the UP was not prepared to pay for readmission, and that included white leadership.[37] Two months later the party conference agreed that it would only reapply for membership if it was 'in South Africa's interests'. After that nothing was heard of returning to the Commonwealth.

THE ORGANISATION OF AFRICAN UNITY – A NEW THREAT

The strength of feeling among black African states against South Africa was reflected in their own international body, the Organisation of African Unity (OAU). At the first meeting in 1963 the members resolved to support freedom fighters against colonial and white minority governments with arms, military training, shelter and transit.[38] This was a threat that Pretoria could not ignore, but from the beginning the OAU's rhetoric was more impressive than its actions. Already by the time the OAU was formed Pretoria had broken the immediate black nationalist challenge, and in these circumstances if an external threat was to be mounted it required a sustained and substantial financial and military effort. The OAU was unable to offer that. In 1964 a proposal to establish an African High Command was rejected when the cost and organisational demands became clear. Instead a Liberation Committee was formed. That had limited impact, for while OAU members gave it generous verbal support, their material aid was disappointing and there were disputes about strategy and which of the nationalist movements to support.

Following an OAU decision to impose sanctions all members declared trade boycotts and refused to handle South African shipping or aircraft. The greatest impact was the withdrawal of overfly rights to South African Airways which forced its aircraft to fly around 'the bulge' of Africa, adding 900 miles to the flight to Europe. To help counter this Pretoria contributed R3,800,000 to an airfield on the Portuguese island of Ilha do Sol which offered stop-over facilities. Otherwise the African boycotts put little pressure on the Republic. Few of the new states had established contacts, and those that had often only gave lip-service to sanctions. It was clear to the black states, as to everyone else, that economic sanctions could only hurt South Africa if they were applied by the Western states, and so they directed their pressure against them.

Although the OAU's efforts proved less effective than its members hoped or Pretoria feared, the South Africans remained concerned. They had hoped that once the early fires of independence were spent the black states would turn their attention elsewhere. They did not. Although OAU members often tried to disguise their limited powers in wild rhetoric, they succeeded in keeping apartheid high on the international agenda by constant criticism and diplomatic pressure, so that Pretoria was forced to recognise that while the organisation's efforts were often ineffective its members were persistent and determined critics.

THE UNITED NATIONS – PERSISTENT HOSTILITY

At the UN pressure against South Africa intensified. The established issues – apartheid, the Indians and Namibia – were discussed in an atmosphere which, according to Louw, was 'charged with unbridled emotion'. 'Never', he declared, 'except in a state of war had there been such concentrated opposition against a state.'[39] There was bitter reaction to Sharpeville. For the first time South Africa appeared on the agenda of the Security Council (rather than the General Assembly) and the critics included Western states. Supported by the US, and with only Britain and France abstaining, the Security Council resolved that South Africa's racial policies had 'led to international friction and if continued might endanger international peace and security'. The US action marked a clear change of attitude, and Britain quickly followed by voting for a General Assembly resolution requesting all states 'to consider taking such separate and collective action as is open to them, in conformity with the Charter of the United Nations, to bring about the abandonment of [apartheid] politics'.[40]

The culmination of UN opposition in this period was the Security Council's call for an arms embargo. The resolutions passed were not mandatory but the US voted for them, and there was limited support from Britain and France who said they would only sell arms for 'external' use. In the General Assembly a stream of resolutions continued to be directed against South Africa. In 1962 two thirds of the Assembly supported a resolution recommending economic sanctions and establishing a Special Committee on Apartheid which became a focus for UN opposition. However it would be tedious to detail all the resolutions, for it was the pattern of the past only more so. With the 'militants' reinforced and the Western states more openly critical, Pretoria's chief hope was that the resolutions, although sharply worded and widely supported, would not be translated into action by the Security Council where the Western powers had vetoes. Alongside the censure there were occasional attempts at dialogue. The most significant, which followed the UN Sharpeville resolution, was a visit to South Africa by the Secretary General, Dag Hammarskjold, early in 1961. Although there were clear differences of view, Verwoerd was impressed by Hammarskjold and realised that changes would have to be made to meet international pressures. Both men agreed that the talks had been useful and should be resumed.[41] However, tragically, Hammarskjold was killed in an air accident and his successor, U Thant, was not invited to continue the talks.

The gulf of attitudes between Pretoria and other UN members was underlined in 1964 when U Thant appointed a group to investigate ways of resolving the South African deadlock. Mrs Gundar Myrdal of Sweden was appointed leader, with members from Britain, Yugoslavia, Ghana and Morocco. At the UN this seemed a balanced, mainly moderate group with reasonable terms of reference. (Indeed the Yugoslav resigned because he thought it was too moderate.) The South Africans saw it differently. They rejected the right of any group to interfere in their internal affairs, and refused entry visas. In Pretoria's eyes the suspicions were fully justified when the committee reported that majority rule must come, and stated: 'What is now at issue is not the final outcome, but the question whether on the way the people of South Africa are to go through a long ordeal of blood and hate.' To avoid that it proposed the abolition of all racial discrimination and called for a National Convention to plan a representative government. If Pretoria failed to respond an expert committee should investigate the imposition of economic sanctions. The South Africans were furious. They had no intention of calling a National Convention (which was an ANC demand), even less of establishing a representative government or giving way to a sanctions threat. Verwoerd said that the UN report 'consists to a large extent of a number of inaccuracies, distortions and erroneous conclusions based on false premises'.[42]

The government did not let its case at the UN go by default. As it could no longer anticipate support from the West, it added to the old concentration on sovereignty a new emphasis on the costs and difficulties of taking action against the Republic. It pointed to the conflict and confusion that had followed UN involvement in the Congo with a third of the members refusing to pay their dues and others, including South Africa, withholding their contributions to the operation itself, and underlined the reluctance in both the East and West to give more autonomy to the UN or to support further African 'adventures'.

Although the black states slowly absorbed the lesson that international action was difficult to organise and uncertain in its outcome, they continued to seek ways to challenge South Africa. One was to turn the legalistic approach favoured by Pretoria into a two-edged sword. Although neither side believed that legal arguments were decisive, they used them but with contradictory intentions – one to promote action, the other to counter it. The Namibian issue, which continued to be the main legal dispute, entered a new and potentially dangerous phase for South Africa in November 1960 when Ethiopia and Liberia (as ex-members of the League of Nations) asked the International Court of Justice for a binding judgement that Namibia was still a mandatory territory; that South Africa had obligations under the old Covenant; that apartheid was contrary to those obligations; and that Pretoria had failed to promote the well-being of the inhabitants. The danger for South Africa was that a binding judgement could be referred to the Security Council for enforcement, and both Britain and the US informed Pretoria that they would feel bound by the decision. Pretoria, recognising the importance of the case, sent a powerful legal team, but in 1962 its application that the Court had no jurisdiction in the case was rejected by eight votes to seven. This decision, alongside previous 'advisory' findings, created an assumption that the final judgement would also be against the Republic.[43]

While the court case was being argued, the accusations and counter-accusations continued at the UN, with Pretoria still adopting a more conciliatory attitude on Namibia than on other issues. In 1961, although it refused entry permits for the UN committee, it suggested personal visits by three past Presidents of the General Assembly. The suggestion was rejected by the Trusteeship Council which instead set up a new seven-nation committee, led by Mr Victorio Carpio of the Philippines and Dr Salvador Martinez de Alva of Mexico to whom Pretoria surprisingly granted visas. Their visit provided a comic interlude in an otherwise melancholy relationship. After their tour, Carpio and de Alva apparently agreed to a communiqué which was favourable to South Africa. It stated that 'in the places visited they had found no evidence and heard no allegations that there was a threat to international peace and security within South West Africa . . . or that the indigenous population was being exterminated'. Yet even as the communiqué was drafted there was confusion as Carpio was in bed said to be sick, and as soon as the two men left South Africa they recanted and issued another report which called for sanctions, and if necessary force, if the Republic did not change its policies.[44]

Despite the UN concern, the government continued to treat Namibia virtually as part of the Republic. In 1964 the Odendaal Commission presented a five-year development plan for Namibia, recommending the expenditure of R114.5m. and a roughly equal division of land between a 'white' area and ten black 'homelands' under local authorities responsible to Pretoria. To achieve this land would be purchased from whites, and about 30 per cent of the black population moved. Britain and the US warned that implementation of the proposals while the court case was unresolved would result in Liberia and Ethiopia applying for an injunction restraining South Africa and that would be backed up by UN action.[45] Verwoerd responded by saying that while he did not dispute the right of friendly governments to speculate, they did so on two false assumptions. First, that Pretoria was not taking account of the court case in assessing the Odendaal Report; and second, that if an interdict were granted, South Africa's behaviour would lead to Security Council action. At no time had the government indicated that it would challenge the Security Council. That cautious tone was also found in the government's White Paper on the Report, which accepted proposals for economic development but delayed a response on territorial arrangements. However, there was no doubt that the government looked favourably on the 'homelands' proposal. Verwoerd said the government was 'not forcing the policy of separate development on South West Africa – it was merely preserving the separate homelands, based on the historical differences'.[46] Indeed Pretoria's response to Odendaal reflected its prevailing policy of treating Namibia as part of the Republic without formalising the position.

In 1966 the government's immediate fears over Namibia were

removed. By the President's casting vote the International Court rejected the claims of Ethiopia and Liberia because, it was argued, these countries had no legal rights or interests in the matters before the Court. It was an extraordinary decision. After years of legal argument, it was a 'non-finding'. Nothing was said about the substantive issues; so in that sense Pretoria's policies were still as open to challenge. Rightly, however, Verwoerd hailed it as a 'major victory'[47] while on their part the militant opponents were infuriated. They had no doubt that their cause was just – they had no need of a court to tell them that – but legal steps had not provided the route to action. The result convinced some that 'It is better to be carried away by emotions than bogged down by legal sophistication',[48] and pushing aside the Court's findings, a resolution was rushed through the General Assembly, with only South Africa and Portugal voting against it, stating that the mandate for Namibia was terminated. A committee was appointed to recommend ways in which the local people could exercise self-determination. However, it was a resolution which bound nobody, and a UN Council and Commission for Namibia created by the Security Council was largely ineffective.

The anger of the African states at the Court's findings was part of a wider frustration. They had successfully used international organisations to institutionalise hostility against South Africa and to pressure the Western states. The Republic had been forced into ideological isolation, her diplomatic contacts restricted, and those which remained were strained. Yet this fell short of their objective which had been to mount a campaign to overthrow apartheid. The sanctions which had been imposed were at most inconvenient – even the arms ban was not fully implemented – and while the possibility of future action remained, the limitations of an international moral crusade had become clear. International organisations could move no further than their member states were prepared to go, and no governments (including black states) were prepared to support action against their perceived interests. For all the sound and fury at the General Assembly, the Security Council's recommendations and the findings of the International Court, Pretoria was weathering the storm.

6 THE GOVERNMENT'S RESPONSE

The government's response to the crisis of the early 1960s was dominated by the stern, authoritarian figure of the Prime Minister, Hendrik Verwoerd. Inspired by the belief that he was divinely chosen to lead a people who themselves were guided by God, on assuming the Premiership Verwoerd said: 'We, as believing rulers of a religious country, will seek strength and guidance in the future, as in the past, from Him who controls the destinies of Nations . . . In accordance with His will it was determined who should assume the leadership of the Government.'[1] He led the government with an absolute conviction of right, and while within white politics he faced criticism from the opposition and resentment from some colleagues for his authoritarian style there was no challenge to his position.

Verwoerd explained his views of political leadership in a private conversation with Macmillan in which Macmillan suggested that a government should remain in the mainstream of opinion, which often meant trimming one's sails and abandoning previous policies. In Macmillan's view a change of course was required by South Africa because it was heading against the stream of world opinion. He was expressing a British consensus view of politics, but Verwoerd's experience had been rooted in different soil. As a member of the National Party he had struggled to preserve and promote an Afrikaner identity against powerful opponents. Success had come from intransigence, from a refusal to compromise and from a dogmatic conviction of right. Privately Verwoerd found Macmillan's views 'repulsive'.[2] Publicly he commented: 'I said that I preferred to set a course for myself rather than be carried along willy-nilly by the stream; that I believed that in that way I would be able to exercise some influence over the course of history and that I would then be in a position to ensure fulfilment of the desire of that section of the Nation whose support I enjoy.'[3]

Verwoerd showed his resolution in face of the ferment of ideas the crisis produced among whites. The UP called for the end of apartheid;

the South African Chamber of Industries for 'a new approach based on consultation [between blacks and whites] as the key to a peaceful solution'; eleven members of the Dutch Reformed Churches published *Delayed Action* seeking a new outlook on race relations; an international church conference (the Cottesloe Conference) supported a major revision of racial policies.[4] The call for a new approach even spread to the government. At Humansdorp Paul Sauer, a senior minister, declared that 'the old book of South African history was closed at Sharpeville . . . Things will never be the same',[5] and three cabinet ministers (Sauer, Donges and Schoeman) supported the abolition of 'passes' for Africans. Yet nothing came of these proposals. The calls for change were met by strong 'right-wing' opposition, not least from Verwoerd. However, for a time Verwoerd's fate hung in the balance. In April 1960 a white man (David Pratt) fired two bullets into Verwoerd's head in an assassination attempt. Remarkably Verwoerd not only survived the attack but made a complete recovery. At first the attempt heightened the sense of crisis, but Verwoerd's personal courage and his remarkable recovery enhanced his reputation – forming 'a mystical bond' between him and the Afrikaner people and building respect among the English speakers. He used this to counter the alarm and the calls for reform. While still in hospital he sent a message to Sauer telling him to 'stand firm', and he wrote a major speech which Donges read for him in which he said that although recent events had given cause for reflection there was no reason to depart from existing policies. Indeed there was now an excellent opportunity to push forward quickly and thoroughly. He regretted the misinterpretation of apartheid at home and abroad, but it was the understanding and not the policy that must change.[6]

Verwoerd's reaction to the crisis was therefore not to shy away from apartheid but to apply it more thoroughly. He was convinced that the explanation for Sharpeville lay not in Pretoria's race policies but in subversive outside influences: liberalism, multiracialism, communism. Under his dominant influence speculation about a retreat disappeared. He told the NP that as national survival was at stake it must stand by its racial policies 'like walls of granite', and granite is the image that clings to Verwoerd – powerful, stark, unswerving, supremely confident in his own judgement.[7] Far from deterring him from his self-appointed task, the crisis had reinforced his resolution. He told his wife: 'If I cannot save the country I would rather resign. I will never be an accomplice to the destruction of our people by abandoning our policy.'[8] If few could match Verwoerd's determination and strength, most whites came to share his judgement that seeking international popularity would lead to 'the destruction of the white nation in South Africa'.[9] The government and the UP were at one in their common defence of the white state and its core values, and this revealed itself in views on foreign policy. Sir de Villiers Graaf, the UP leader, could not remember a substantial division with the government on foreign policy between the dispute over the Commonwealth and Rhodesia's Unilateral Declaration of Independence (UDI) in 1965.[10]

The government's increased strength among whites was confirmed in the election of October 1961. Before that the parliamentary opposition had split when a group of 'liberals' broke away to form the Progressive Party (PP) which favoured a sharing of power between the races on federal lines. In calling an election Verwoerd claimed that 'we are standing at the start of a new era', and fought on the interlocking themes of security and racial policies. Most whites, believing that security lay in following the government's tough lead, gave it a resounding vote of confidence. The NP increased its seats in the Assembly from 102 to 105, and for the first time won a majority of the votes cast. Among the opposition the UP regained ten of the eleven seats from which MPs had deserted to join the PP, leaving that party with only one member.[11]

REDEFINING NATION AND STATE

In consolidating apartheid Verwoerd advanced new concepts of 'nation' and 'state' for South Africa. Previously the NP had committed itself to promoting the Afrikaner nation and ensuring its control of the political structure. Ironically it was as these objectives were achieved that their limitations became clear. The search for Afrikaner dominance was within an exclusively white political system, but as that system was challenged the government was forced to defend it by seeking a broader white unity. The emphasis shifted from exclusive Afrikaner nationalism to inclusive white nationalism. Verwoerd claimed that this was possible because the new Republican status had removed external influences, but the real reason was the black challenge to white dominance. Campaigning in the election Verwoerd said: 'I see the Nationalist Party today ... not as an Afrikaans, or English, or Afrikaans–English party, whatever it may have been in the past. I see it as the party that stands for the preservation of the white man, of the white government in South Africa.'[12] Although the government now emphasised white unity the NP continued to govern as a predominantly Afrikaner party. Verwoerd broke new ground by appointing two English speaking cabinet ministers (Alfred Trollip and Frank Waring, who had defected from the UP) but overall the English speakers were being invited to join in the defence of the white state, not to have a full share in controlling it. The UP managed to retain the support of a majority of English speakers because of the continuing white social cleavages and the limits set on English speakers within the NP, but an increasing number of them voted NP in support of its tough approach to security and to keeping the black man in his place.

One indicator of the broader white nationalism was a change in immigration policy. As late as January 1959 Verwoerd had argued for tight controls and repeated the old accusations that the UP was trying to swamp Afrikanerdom. The crisis changed that. In 1960, for the first time since the Second World War, there was a net loss of whites. The government's old fears about the impact of immigrants quickly became subordinated to the need to strengthen the white community. Its suspicions of the British, of Mediterranean Europeans, of Roman Catholics and of Jews did not disappear, but they were less important than the new black challenge. Again Verwoerd gave a specious explanation, saying that the Republic had secured Afrikaner values and so allowed a new approach to immigration. However, the veil dropped in 1965 when he bluntly defended increased immigration by saying: 'Our motto is to maintain white supremacy for all time to come over our own people and our own country, by force if necessary.'[13] With that commitment a record number of white immigrants began to enter the country.

Alongside a white nation based on 'race', the government promoted the concept of black (Bantu) nations based on 'tribe'.[14] Pretoria's vision was of a multinational state containing one white and eight Bantu nations with whites in control of the state. There was to be no attempt to bring together the diverse peoples into a single South African nation based on loyalty to the state. The way forward was separation. In political terms this had the attraction of undermining the claims for majority rule because, as seen by the government, South Africa was not only a state with several nations, but one in which no one nation had a majority. Instead there were national minorities, each with its own identity, and each with the right to fashion its own destiny. In contrast the ANC called for a single nation and a single state with uniform rights for all. The government rejected that because it argued that there was no uniformity and never could be among diverse peoples. In the case of the Bantu nations, Pretoria recognised 'homelands' where Africans could develop separately and where they

92

Table 1. *South Africa's Population – 1960*

Total Population: 15,841,128

Government's 'national' groups		Population based on race	
Xhosa	3,432,000	Africans	10,807,809
Whites	3,067,638	Whites	3,067,638
Zulu	2,959,000	Coloureds	1,488,267
Coloureds	1,488,267	Asians	477,414
N. Sotho	1,122,000		
S. Sotho	1,089,000		
Tswana	863,000		
Asians	477,414		
Tsonga	366,000		
Swazi	301,000		

gained their political rights. Only those required for work would live in the white state, for which they required special permission, and they could never gain citizenship or political rights there. The great bulk of South Africa, roughly 87 per cent of the land surface, was reserved for whites, the Bantu nations were to share the remaining 13 per cent. While the land allocated to blacks was a reasonable cross section Pretoria had made little effort to promote development (investing less than R16m. between 1956 and 1961) and even the potentially fertile land was suffering the ravages of overcrowding and poor farming.

The political implications of Pretoria's policy are reflected in the different presentations that can be made of 1960 population statistics (see table 1).

In constitutional terms Verwoerd had taken an important step in 1959 when he introduced the Bantu Self Government Act which opened up the possibility of the Bantu nations developing towards self-government and even independence. The previous assumption that Africans would always remain politically subordinate within a white controlled South Africa had been restated earlier in 1959 by Dr W. W. M. Eiselen, who as Secretary of Bantu Administration had worked alongside Verwoerd in creating the apartheid structure. Eiselen wrote that the degree of autonomy granted to Africans would 'fall short of the actual surrender of sovereignty by the European trustees . . . The maintenance of White political supremacy over the country as a whole is a *sine qua non* for racial peace and economic

prosperity.'[15] Shortly afterwards Verwoerd introduced the new legislation, saying that the speed and extent of political progress would
depend on the wishes and the performance of the separate nations,
but 'if it is within the power of the Bantu and if the territories in which
he now lives can develop to full independence, it will develop that
way'.[16] The shift in Verwoerd's position is explained by his new
awareness as Prime Minister of international pressure, whereas previously in Native Affairs he had not been directly subjected to it. The
change came not from conviction, for he confessed that granting
independence to the Bantustans 'is not what we would have liked to
see. In the light of pressures being exerted on South Africa there is,
however, no doubt that eventually this will have to be done, thereby
buying for the white man his freedom and the right to retain domination in his own country.'[17] Verwoerd is said to have regretted
making that admission, which runs counter to his image, and on
another occasion he declared: 'The greater the pressure on us to make
concessions, the more emphatic we must be in refusing to do so.'[18]
Whatever the reason, the Transkei quickly took up Verwoerd's offer
and he personally helped in drafting a self-governing constitution
which was agreed in 1963.

Although the government gave increasing attention to the Bantustans, considerable uncertainty remained. Privately Verwoerd was said
to have regretted agreeing to independence, attributing the decision to
Muller's alarmist assessment of the international situation.[19] There
were also many whites, including party members, who were sceptical
of the ability of Africans to govern themselves, and thought that
Verwoerd's proposals were neither desirable nor practical. Nor were
the implications of the proposals clear. For every official statement
which recognised the possibility of Bantustans advancing to independence there was another saying that it would never happen. Verwoerd
himself was often ambiguous as he attempted to persuade the party
faithful that his proposals, although sounding new, were a direct
development of past policies. Yet he pushed ahead with renewed
purpose after a visit to South Africa by Dag Hammarskjold, the UN
Secretary General. Hammarskjold, who impressed Verwoerd, brought
home to him the strength of international feeling, and their meetings
may have persuaded Verwoerd to bring forward the date of Transkei's
self-government.[20] At home Verwoerd spelt out the message. Campaigning in 1961 he told white voters that they 'must realise that in the
end they could only rule over their own territory and over their own
people, and that they would have to learn to maintain friendly
relations with neighbouring states'.[21]

Alongside the internal aims of the Bantustan policy (the separation of the races; the provision of constitutional outlets for Africans; the creation of a socio-political framework for economic development) a substantial readjustment was implied in foreign policy perception. As the existing state was carved up to create new black states alongside the white controlled Republic, people and land which had been part of South Africa would become 'foreign', and the new black states would become a foreign policy concern. To his followers Verwoerd conveyed this as a message of hope. It was, he insisted, a practical and just outcome and would relieve international pressure as Pretoria was seen to offer its Bantu peoples the same opportunities as the imperial powers had offered their colonies. Jooste remembered a meeting at which Verwoerd outlined the plans to ambassadors and senior Foreign Service officials. They emerged elated, convinced that they had a policy that could be defended abroad because it offered justice to Africans.[22] However, at home white fears persisted and the UP closely questioned Verwoerd. Would not these black states become hotbeds of opposition to the Republic? Would they not provide bases for guerrilla fighters? Verwoerd recognised the dangers. The Bantustans might, he said, become Cubas or Zanzibars on the Republic's borders, and that 'may be dangerous – not only inconvenient but dangerous – but if three million whites have to live together in one State with four times as many of those same people who are liable to create a Cuba surely it is much more dangerous'.[23]

Lying on the Republic's borders the High Commission Territories already presented a similar situation, and as plans for the homelands advanced the British Territories became associated in Pretoria's eyes with its Bantustan policy. Although Verwoerd must have known that there was no chance of success, he appealed to Britain in 1963 to entrust Pretoria with responsibility for leading the Territories to independence within a broad scheme to consolidate and rationalise the separate black and white areas of South Africa. In this scheme the three Territories would take their place as black democratic states, 'but would be steered away from multiracialism'. Whites would still be needed to work in the Territories, but they would enjoy their political rights in South Africa in the same way as Africans from the Territories who worked in the Republic would have rights in their own countries.[24] Even when the British ignored the plea, Verwoerd's response reflected the changed approach. Instead of opposing independence for the Territories he said that they would benefit from it because Britain had subordinated their interests to its broader imperial aims, but now the inhabitants could concentrate on their own interests which were best served by co-operation with their neighbours and particularly South Africa.[25]

If the government was increasingly optimistic about its policy for Africans there was no such confidence about Coloureds and Indians. In their case it is easier to state the questions than to find any certainty in the replies. On what grounds could the Indians and the Coloureds be said to form separate nations? Where were the homelands in which they could develop separately? Dr A. L. Geyer (High Commissioner in London) confessed: 'When I think of the Coloureds my thoughts arrive at a dead end and I prefer not to go any further.' He chose to speak about Africans rather than Coloureds because 'in the case of the Africans I knew the answers'.[26] For the Nationalists the position of the Coloureds – the majority of whom spoke Afrikaans and many of whom had Afrikaner blood – was the most vulnerable aspect of apartheid. In the ferment of ideas of the early 1960s fresh suggestions emerged about their future. The South African Bureau of Racial Affairs (which had provided an intellectual backing for apartheid) debated bringing the Coloureds closer to the white community, and in July 1960 *Die Burger* suggested that Coloured voters should elect Coloured members to parliament. Although the motivation behind these suggestions may have been to persuade the Coloureds to help in defence of the existing white-dominated order by offering them a stake in it, the proposals were a clear departure from the past. Verwoerd would have none of them because they offended the principles of apartheid and dismissed these 'dramatic ideas' as a springboard for integration and biological assimilation. In June 1961 he repeated his opposition to a 'multiracial nation', and therefore to Coloured voters and Coloured MPs. Instead he reiterated the 'four parallel streams' policy (Whites, Coloureds, Asians and Bantu) in which the Coloureds and Asians would increasingly manage their own affairs within the white state, and the Africans in their homelands.[27]

Yet even Verwoerd felt uncertain about the Coloureds. He took the unusual step of summoning the party's Central Federal Council to gain its support on this issue, and at another time he mused about the possibility of political separation with economic interdependence and a 'state within a state' for Coloureds. However, these were only musings and despite the absence of a claim on the part of Indians and Coloureds for national status the government declared that they were separate racial groups aspiring to be nations. Referring to the Coloureds Verwoerd made clear his distinction between 'citizenship' and 'the components of a homogeneous nation', for while there was no doubt 'that the Coloureds are citizens of this country. There is just as little doubt they are not part of the homogeneous entity that we can describe here as "the nation".' He asserted that although the creation of the Republic had eliminated the old distinction between the English and Afrikaner so that they now formed a single nation, that did not imply further unification into a nation with Bantu and Coloureds.[28] However, although there was no advance for the Coloureds, the position of the Indians was made clearer. In the past there had been much talk of their repatriation as an 'alien' group, but in 1961 the Minister of the Interior declared that they were a permanent element of the population. 'We must realise', he said, 'that they are South African citizens and as such are entitled to the necessary attention and consideration.'[29]

THE ECONOMIC RESPONSE

The political crisis produced economic problems which Pretoria's militant opponents hoped to increase by persuading the UN to impose mandatory economic sanctions. The government could not ignore the threat and in addition to a propaganda drive emphasising South Africa's importance to the Western world, it started to store large oil reserves in disused mines. Even without sanctions there were difficulties. Already in 1959 there had been an economic downturn and a small outflow of foreign capital, but following Sharpeville that 'turned into a flood' as confidence plunged and investors pulled out. In 1960 there was a net capital outflow of R194m. (R148m. repatriation of foreign indirect investments) and the drain continued in the first part of 1961 with a further outflow of R45m. Between June 1960 and May 1961 the country's foreign exchange and gold reserves fell by more than a half (from R312m. to R153m.). The stock market suffered a sharp decline with the giant Anglo-American Company losing R100m. of its market value in a year.[30] These trends were first stemmed and then reversed through the efforts of the government and private companies, which led to the return of foreign confidence. This economic recovery provided the government with resources to meet the political and security threats.

The NP, which had come to power suspicious of foreign involvement in the economy, continued to underline the desirability of self-sufficiency but in government its views were modified as it recognised the importance of external economic links. Verwoerd, after stating that every country wanted to control its own economic destiny, acknowledged the foreign role in providing capital, technical knowledge and business skills. South Africa, he said, will 'continue to welcome participation of foreign investors . . . providing this does not conflict with the general principle of a country retaining control of its economic destiny'.[31] However, the immediate problem following Sharpeville was not to attract new investment but to check the outward flow of that already in the country. The government therefore increased interest rates; restricted credit; refused loan facilities if these led to repatriation of funds; and took out an IMF loan. In 1961 it imposed further controls to prevent South Africans from sending funds abroad and foreigners from remitting capital (but not interest) payments. Alongside these efforts were those of private companies which too sought to counter the outflow of funds by offering attractive investment terms and raising loans themselves. For example, Rand Selection Corporation, a branch of Anglo-American, raised a $30m. external loan which as a company it did not need but which helped the country's balance of payments. Together these measures saw South Africa through what was until then 'its most dangerous capital and foreign exchange crisis of the post-war era'.[32] Conscious of the private sector's contribution, Harry Oppenheimer of Anglo-American said: 'We have been able to use the credit and the overseas connections of our Group in a manner which has, I believe, been helpful to our country.'[33]

When the immediate crisis was over a cumulative process started whereby the revival of political confidence bolstered the economy which in turn further reinforced political confidence. Quickly the economic scene was transformed from one of gloom to 'one of the greatest waves of expansion that this country has experienced'.[34] From 1962 there was a marked upturn in world trade which South Africa could exploit because of the internal recovery which initially owed little to outside capital. However, once confidence was regained foreign capital poured into the country; the economy grew at more than 7 per cent per annum between 1963–5; GNP increased from R5,200m. in 1960 to R7,700m. in 1965; and the index of manufacturing production rose to 193 by 1966.[35] However, both government and business realised that the situation was volatile, that long term economic recovery would require sustained growth to remove the uncertainty generated by Sharpeville. Pretoria was also aware of the security and political implications of its economic circumstances. In 1964 Dr T. E. Donges, the Minister of Finance, stated that 'but for the soundness and strength of the economy, we should have been hard put to maintain ourselves, to protect the integrity of our land, and the independence of our people against the openly expressed aggressive designs of certain states'.[36]

The economic experience of the early 1960s underlined the Republic's integration into the Western international economy. In one sense this made her vulnerable, as the flight of capital had shown, and that was a message pressed home by the advocates of economic sanctions. However, in another sense, she gained strength because of her economic importance to the West and to her immediate African neighbours. Whatever their views of apartheid, economic partners, whether giants like the US or poor states like Malawi, had a stake in a prosperous South Africa. Pretoria never failed to stress that, or to stress that prosperity was built on political stability. The message was not lost, and the expansion of the economy strengthened and extended the Republic's international position. Her neighbours became increasingly dependent (especially Rhodesia following UDI) and internationally established ties with Britain and the US were reinforced by new ones, especially with Japan and West Germany. Between 1960 and 1966 South Africa's exports to Germany rose from R35m. to R150m. and to Japan from R30m. to R97m. There was also an important, if less spectacular, increase in trade with the rest of Africa. Between 1960 and 1967 imports from Africa rose from R77m. to R141m., and exports from R141m. to R223m. Britain remained the main source of foreign capital but investment became more widely spread. Although Pretoria failed to eliminate the view that investment in the Republic was 'risk capital', and therefore called for high returns, that could be met. In 1970, the *Wall Street Journal* reported that the South African investments of 260 American companies were their most profitable overseas investments, while a UN report described British capital earnings from South Africa as 'remarkable'. Between 1964 and 1966 Britain earned more from capital investment in South Africa than from any other part of the world.[37]

The government's role in economic management was a matter of dispute. The UP, with its close business associations, argued that success came despite the government's policies. There was some substance in this for Pretoria had made little effort to co-ordinate economic policy; it had often expressed hostility to private business; and its apartheid policies restricted the flow of labour, investment in black areas and the operation of a free market. However, the government did play an active part in the economic recovery. Indeed it could not fail to do so because it controlled large sectors of the 'mixed economy' and regulated the flow of labour. The revival was stimulated by both government and business, not through joint planning or close co-operation (although after Sharpeville Verwoerd established an Economic Advisory Council with representatives from government and business) but because it was in both their interests. That was clear in manufacturing industry where Pretoria encouraged self-sufficiency to stimulate the economy, promote exports, and make the Republic less vulnerable to external pressure. One example was motor manufacturing. By the early 1960s several foreign manufacturers were established in South Africa but they imported the bulk of their requirements. In 1961 the average imported content was 87.5 per cent. To reduce the foreign content, Pretoria in 1964 lifted restrictions on cars assembled in the Republic which contained a minimum proportion of 45 per cent locally manufactured parts, rising within three years to 55 per cent. The manufacturers therefore had the choice of pulling out, or facing severe import restrictions, or investing in their South African branches. Most chose the investment.

THE MILITARY RESPONSE

As vague fears of the past were replaced in the early 1960s by immediate dangers, Pretoria embarked on a programme of military expansion. J. J. Fouche, who replaced the inadequate Erasmus as Minister of Defence, gave three reasons for this: to preserve internal security, to support the West, and to counter military threats across the borders. On the first of these he spoke of internal disorders as the equivalent of war conditions, and mentioned plans that had been made if there were street fighting. Fouche's second reason was an echo of the old ambition to join a Western alliance against communism. We must, he said, 'have something decent to offer the West'. Finally there was the threat from new black states. Their capabilities and intentions were unknown, but in the climate of the day it seemed possible, if improbable, that they would attempt to take military action against the Republic. If they did it was assumed that they would have communist backing (in arms, training and subversion) whereas South Africa could not rely on the West. Pretoria was therefore consumed by uncertainty. Fouche in the same speech spoke disparagingly of ensuring that 'no insignificant little state' could bully the Republic, but also of the need for military power 'to stand on our own feet' against a potentially formidable foe.[38]

In its military preparations Pretoria trod a narrow path between alerting the whites and undermining their confidence. As Minister of Defence, Fouche tended to sound the alarm, and at one stage admitted that 'anything might happen'. As late as 1964 he was still speculating about the need to stand firm against military threats.[39] Verwoerd, on the other hand, compared military preparations with a man taking out an insurance policy, not expecting the worst but covering the unexpected. If that were the case the government was prepared to pay a high premium. Defence expenditure rose from 7 per cent of the total budget (R39.2m. from R602.8m.) in 1959–60 to 17 per cent (R213m. from R1,252m.) by 1966–7; in 1960 there were 11,500 men in the armed forces, by 1967 there were 42,000, the bulk of whom were conscripts. At first conscription was for three months by selective ballots, but the commitment was steadily increased to embrace all young white men for two years full-time service followed by reserve service. Fouche called on mothers to 'give up their sons in defence of their land'.[40] In addition the regular forces were increased from 9,000 in 1960 to 15,000 in 1964; reserve units were extended; the police were given military training; more school training corps were formed; and rifle and pistol clubs were expanded. (By 1964, 27,250 women were members of such clubs.) Fouche spoke of 'the formidable price we are called upon to pay for our protection against aggression'.[41]

The initial expansion of the forces was confined to whites. Fouche dismissed the idea that Africans might be recruited because 'it would clash with our way of life',[42] but characteristically there was ambivalence about the Coloureds. The government had disbanded the old Cape Coloured Corps in line with its apartheid principles, but in 1964 it reformed it as a non-combat unit. As in the government, the leaders of the armed forces were mainly Afrikaners, and they gained increasing influence as security concerns became more prominent. The full impact of this did not manifest itself until the 1980s, but the seeds were sown in the 1960s, and even in the early days social implications became clear as young whites entered military service and civilians were drawn into support services and arms manufacturing.[43] Although P. W. Botha, who in 1964 succeeded Fouche as Minister of Defence, dismissed UP criticism that young soldiers were being indoctrinated by the NP, he asserted that military training was more than teaching to kill. 'We must convince the youth of our country that through a spirit of *esprit de corps* and ruthless efficiency they must live for their country.' To achieve that they were taught 'civics and knowledge in regard to world trends, and knowledge of dangers threatening them, and knowledge of the cunning methods used by those people who want to subvert the free world'.[44]

Extra arms were required as well as extra men. Although since 1945 equipment had been purchased from Britain, the expenditure had been small and by the 1960s the equipment was inadequate in quality and quantity to meet the new demands. Pretoria therefore rapidly increased expenditure on arms (spending R660m. between 1960 and

1969) and looked not only to external suppliers but also to the domestic arms industry which gained in importance following the 1963 Security Council's arms ban. While that ban was not mandatory and external supplies continued to be received, it had an immediate impact, as P. W. Botha later admitted in relation to the navy, and was a warning for the future. However, the ban disappointed militant opponents because Pretoria was able to circumvent it. Anticipating difficulties it had already negotiated manufacturing licences from foreign firms – no less than 127 in 1961 – and even when the ban was in place some states ignored it, openly or covertly. As the ban was not mandatory the French and the British Conservative Government continued to supply arms for 'external' use: a distinction which critics said was meaningless. However, in 1964 British policy changed when the Labour Party gained power, leaving the French as Pretoria's principal arms supplier, and they enjoyed a virtual bonanza over the next decade with the sale of advanced aircraft, helicopters, armoured cars, anti-tank rockets and three submarines.

Even those who imposed the ban (including the US and Britain) continued to supply equipment which had dual civilian/military use and existing contracts were honoured. In Britain, after long agonising, the government decided to supply a squadron of Buccaneer fighter bombers which had been ordered under the Conservatives, while the US reserved the right 'to interpret this policy in the light of requirements for assuring the maintenance of international peace and security'.[45] Some governments either turned a blind eye or were unable to impose the ban. Italy, for instance, remained an important partner and undertook joint aircraft production, while others acted as 'middlemen' supplying arms manufactured elsewhere. These arms were reported to include British Centurion tanks from India and Spain, and anti-aircraft missiles from Jordan.[46] Not all Pretoria's covert efforts were successful. For example, the British Government blocked an attempt to purchase a £40m. ground to air missile system, but frequently South Africa did succeed because it was prepared to pay handsome premiums. The illicit arms trade cannot be quantified, but two examples illustrate its nature. In 1970 at the trial of six employees of Switzerland's largest arms company (Oerlikon-Buehrle) the accused admitted illegally exporting arms worth more than £4m. to South Africa, routing them through France for cover. (The court noted that the firm had also legally sent ninety heavy guns from its factory in Italy.) Another example came to light in the late 1970s when eleven Bell helicopters built in Italy under American licence were shipped to the Republic via Israel and Singapore.[47]

While an external trade continued in large, sophisticated arms, the greatest change was in the domestic arms industry, which had started during the war but was still small in 1960. That changed. While R315,000 was spent on arms manufacturing in 1960–1; by 1964–5 it had increased to R33m.[48] External decisions like the UN ban and the change in British policy became spurs to greater self-reliance. A new military/industrial structure was created – at first under the Arms Production Board with an initial budget of R100m. in 1964; then in 1968 it was reorganised into the Armaments Development and Production Corporation with powers over production and powers to enter agreements at home and abroad; and finally in 1977 it was further reorganised into Armscor (Armaments Corporation of South Africa) responsible for all phases of arms production and procurement. Drawing on capital and expertise from home and abroad Armscor became one of the country's major industrial enterprises and a major world manufacturer. Defence thereby came to involve not only soldiers but businessmen, industrialists, financiers and economists. Soon the government was triumphantly announcing the fruits of these efforts: the first automatic rifles in 1964; self-sufficiency in small arms production in 1965; the first Impala jet aircraft (made under Italian licences) in 1966; and by 1971 the first surface to air missiles (Cactus) and armoured cars (Eland).[49]

By the time Fouche retired in 1965 to be replaced by P. W. Botha as Minister of Defence there was greater confidence in the armed forces with their increased numbers, better equipment and training. In June 1963 Fouche still discussed the possibility of a conventional attack by black states, although he stressed their difficult long lines of communications and the strength of the Republic's forces.[50] A year later he dismissed such a possibility and endorsed a newspaper headline that: 'Black Africa has missed the bus. They are too late.' Yet Pretoria remained on guard, for as the fear of a conventional attack faded, so the threat from black nationalist guerrillas grew, and the forces' training became more orientated towards anti-guerrilla operations including urban fighting. Even as white South Africa entered a period of confidence the awareness of danger remained, but the confidence was more apparent. While previously Pretoria had refused to give details of military strength because it was unsure of itself, it became more open as confidence increased. In 1964 Verwoerd explained that although a powerful country like the US published her strength so that 'the world and possible opponents may know what they have to reckon with', for a small country like South Africa 'facing so many dangers, it would be folly to disclose information about defence forces and equipment'.[51] By the late 1960s the situation had so changed that Pretoria was very willing 'to lift the veil', as P. W. Botha put it. In 1969 an edition of an Information Department journal was devoted to explaining the strength of the armed forces and the country's strategic importance,[52] and an Afrikaner newspaper declared that 'the world respects a country which is militarily powerful'.[53] The days seemed far away when white South Africa 'lived with fear and anxiety'.

PART III

THE YEARS OF CONFIDENCE: 1965–1974

7 THE INTERNAL SETTING

On 6 September 1966 Verwoerd was assassinated as he was taking his seat in the House of Assembly. His assailant, Demetrio Tsafendas, a parliamentary messenger, was later found to be insane. As their new leader and the country's Prime Minister, the National Party chose Mr Balthazar Johannes (John) Vorster. Once again the party had turned to a man with a tough, 'right-wing' reputation. In Vorster's case this rested on his wartime record as a member of the anti-British 'Ossewabrandwag' (for which he had been interned) and his record in government as the Minister of Justice who had ruthlessly fought black nationalism.

The shock and uncertainty which followed the assassination soon disappeared, and the relative ease with which it was absorbed was a sign of confidence within the government and the white community. That was partly because Vorster quickly settled into the Premiership, but more because he inherited a strong position. By the mid 1960s white South Africa had overcome its most difficult immediate problems and moved into a period of confidence. Shortly before his death Verwoerd had called an election. The dominant issue for the white electorate was still security, for although at home the black nationalists had been suppressed there were disturbing events elsewhere in Africa – the collapse of white settler power in Algeria; military coups in Nigeria and Ghana; and the Rhodesian crisis on the Republic's own doorstep. At the election the government's message was that 'South Africa's future depends on a strong and determined government that will not surrender the rights of whites, while it deals honourably and justly with regard to the non-whites.' The way to ensure that, so the message went, was to create white unity and implement apartheid.[1] The UP countered by pointing to the dangers of the Bantustans – the potential Cubas on the borders as Sir de Villiers Graaf described them – but the government's message carried the day as the NP was returned with more seats than ever (NP 120; UP 39; PP 1).

During the campaign the NP sought increased support among English speakers, but it only had partial success, gaining about 16 per cent of their votes. Although the NP's power within the white political system had become impregnable, most English speakers remained alienated because of the party's Afrikaner origins and ethos and continued to support the UP, now reduced to an opposition of impotent fault finders.[2] Traces of the old communal bitterness persisted. When the UP introduced proposals to give sixteen parliamentary seats to representatives of Coloureds, Indians and Africans (the Indians and Africans to be represented by whites) the NP accused it of trying to undermine the Afrikaners by introducing a parliamentary block which would hold a balance between the white groups. P. W. Botha declared: 'There are elements, both inside and outside this House, that hate the Afrikaner.'[3] Yet there was considerable ambivalence among English speakers. Within the white community there was overwhelming support for the maintenance of white political dominance and a privileged white social order, and many English speakers as well as Afrikaners believed these were safe in the government's hands. The UP could afford 'the luxury' of opposition within a firmly defended structure. The common ground was reflected in shared policy approaches, especially in foreign policy. Vorster acknowledged this, speaking of 'drawing together', or 'toenadering', regularly discussing with Sirde Villiers Graaf 'the dangers that threaten us all'.

The government displayed its confidence. In 1968 Vorster declared: 'It seems as if it was only yesterday that supporters, as well as opponents . . . wondered what the future of the Republic would be. Now, after seven years, South Africans have the answer to most – if not all – of their questions. Doubts have gone and fears have vanished.'[4] Confidence was based on strength – economic and military power, white unity in defence of the existing order, the suppression of black nationalism and the ability to counter immediate challenges. Although the government warned against complacency, it gave confident signals. A senior civil servant commented: 'The outside world may not like us, but we have become so strong that, like Russia, we have to be accepted whether they like it or not.'[5] A government journal claimed that to South Africa's benefit 'realpolitik' had replaced ideology in world affairs. While during much of the post-war period 'ideology alienated men from their kith' and hard reality gave way 'to diffuse aspirations in determining political affiliations', now power and self-preservation had become the main criteria for international relations.[6]

Although there was white unity in defence of the political and social order, there were divisions on how that was best achieved and that was increasingly clear among Afrikaners. Even in Verwoerd's time a few dissatisfied 'right wingers' had broken away from the NP, but the real split came under Vorster. One of the issues was his leadership. In the contest following Verwoerd's death Vorster had been supported by 'the right', and outside the party he was criticised for his authoritarianism and inexperience. The *Rand Daily Mail* commented on his inexperience in 'the two most critical and most crucial areas of policy making' – race relations and foreign policy, whereas, the paper argued, 'Dr Verwoerd's great strength as a Prime Minister was precisely his complete command of race relations and foreign policy and the delicate interaction between the two.'[7] However, on those scores Vorster largely disproved his critics. He pushed ahead with apartheid through such legislation as the Prohibition of Political Interference Act (1968) which outlawed mixed race parties, and the Black States Constitutional Act (1971) which accelerated development of the Bantustans, and he became deeply involved in foreign policy. As a leader he was more relaxed and pragmatic than Verwoerd. In cabinet he acted as a chairman gathering the sense of the meeting rather than imposing his will. After meeting both men Chief Jonathan of Lesotho said that Vorster was 'a bit more realistic and practical' than Verwoerd, who had been 'a bit difficult, indeed very difficult' for he was a philosopher, 'and philosophers want you to accept their philosophy', while Vorster was more reasonable 'perhaps because he is a lawyer, and they are more amenable'.[8] However, the characteristics that helped to quell his early critics alienated Vorster from the 'right wing'. He was as committed as they were to apartheid and Afrikaner control of the government, but he was flexible in his methods – wooing English speakers; accepting some racial mixing in sport; and exchanging diplomats with black states. They were not.

The dissatisfaction with Vorster was part of a broader party split between 'verligtes' (enlightened) and 'verkramptes' (hard line). Within these categories were many differences of emphasis but broadly 'verkramptes' believed in the need for rigid racial discrimination and exclusive power to preserve the white (and particularly the Afrikaner) nation. The basis of their belief varied from gut feeling to theological argument but they had a common conviction that any concession endangered the whole edifice of apartheid. The 'verligtes' were also committed to preserving the white nation and state, but thought it necessary to dismantle parts of the old structure to defend more effectively its core; for if the whites were not prepared to be flexible and perhaps even to share power – and there were many views about what 'sharing' meant – they would face constant dangers. In brief, 'verligtes' believed that survival depended on a degree of change; 'verkramptes' that it depended on opposing change whatever the cost.[9]

The 'verkramptes' were led by Dr Albert Hertzog, who was dismissed from the cabinet by Vorster in 1968. In April 1969 Hertzog launched a dramatic parliamentary challenge in which he emphasised the differences within the white society which the government was seeking to bridge. The focal point, declared Hertzog, was that the whites, 'the civilized people . . . dare to rule as a minority'. Among the whites were two groups both with great but distinctive strengths. The Afrikaners 'are permeated by that great complex of principles called Calvinism; that code of moral, ethical and religious principles. They form part of our being, of our upbringing.' From this tradition they had developed values which recognised the diversity of creation, a love of freedom for their own people, and would stand firm against any who unlawfully challenged their authority. It was from these principles that 'the Calvinist Afrikaner, the Nationalist, makes such an ideal fighter and such a good soldier for white civilization'. The English speakers did not share this tradition; instead theirs was a 'liberalism' which is so deeply ingrained that they 'find it difficult to take action against those communistic and leftish movements when these movements make an attack upon them'. Indeed without the Calvinists the English would have collapsed before the challenge. It is the Calvinist, proclaimed Hertzog, who is 'the soldier', 'the champion' of his own and the English speakers' civilisation. For the future as in the past, it is on the Calvinists that the major reliance for the preservation of that civilisation must be placed.[10]

'Verkrampte' support was strongest in the Transvaal. It was there at the Provincial Party Congress of 1969 that the government sorted out the 'verkrampte' goats from the faithful NP sheep by asking for individually recorded votes in favour of four government policies: co-operation with English speakers; a vigorous immigration policy; improved relations with black states; acceptance of some racially mixed visiting sports teams. Although the 'verkramptes' were concerned about all these issues they bit the bullet on the first three and voted for government policies. However, on mixed sports teams, eighteen voted against the government's position. Following that confrontation there was a formal break and later in 1969 the most committed 'verkramptes' formed the Herstigte Nasionale Party (HNP) under Hertzog's leadership. The Afrikaner establishment, showing no mercy, forced HNP members out of other Afrikaner groups including the Broederbond under its Chairman Dr Andries Treurnicht.

Although the struggle among Afrikaners was fought over personalities and policies, its origins were partly in socio-economic divisions which had developed since 1948. The Afrikaners prided themselves on their unity, but the achievement of political power had led to a redistribution of economic and social rewards, and that combined with a period of rapid economic development had created class divisions. Afrikaners were no longer a society of farmers, blue collar workers and petty bourgeoisie. By 1970 only 8 per cent were still active on the land, 88 per cent were urbanised. Of these 27 per cent were blue collar but 65 per cent were white collar workers including many government bureaucrats. At the top of the ladder, alongside the governing elite, Afrikaner capitalists had established themselves in manufacturing, mining and banking.[11] Generally, but not exclusively, the 'verligtes' were drawn from the richer and better educated; the 'verkramptes' from the poorer and less educated and some whose position rested on traditional loyalties – in education, the church, bureaucracy and public services. At this stage many 'verkramptes' remained in the NP, including those in the professions, for the HNP breakaway reflected not just a division of principles but of class and it drew its main support from blue collar workers.

Government policies began to reflect the changed economic interests with less support for agriculture and white labour and more for capital. Vorster personally was mocked for his capitalist, golf-playing image, and his government sometimes tilted, but no more than tilted, towards 'verligte' views. More common was vacillation as it tried to satisfy both wings of the party. The situation was confused as new interests coexisted with the traditional values imprinted by a separate education system, the Dutch Reformed Church and the family (for government ministers and successful capitalists no less than blue collar workers).[12] The tensions were found both in individuals and in the whole party. All Nationalist governments have been haunted by the fear of being outflanked on 'the right', of being condemned for breaking 'volk' unity and abandoning traditional values. Vorster's was no exception, and when he called an early election in 1970 one of the aims was to crush the HNP and reassert the NP as the undisputed political voice of Afrikanerdom. Among Afrikaners the campaign was fought with the ferocity of a civil war, as NP supporters broke up HNP meetings and intimidated its supporters. The government's stated reasons for the election were to gain a mandate on five points: 'to maintain peace and order at all costs; to build a strong defence force against foreign incursion; to make the country's economic position unassailable; to ensure a permanent home for Whites; and to have a united English and Afrikaans-speaking White nation'.[13] To achieve these ends the government, conscious of the need to avoid further defections on 'the right', reiterated that apartheid would be vigorously pursued. In response the HNP called for rigid apartheid, Afrikaner pre-eminence, economic development limited by the availability of white labour; and it opposed mixed sport, black diplomats and immigration. In the event the HNP was heavily defeated. It won no seats and only gained 7.2 per cent of votes cast in the constituencies it contested. Vorster declared that the new party had been crushed.

In the Afrikaner turmoil there seemed to be a glimmer of hope for the UP. Taking advantage of the struggle, and accusing the government of inefficiency and arrogance, it regained ground for the first time since 1948. It won eight seats at the expense of the NP – all in constituencies which it had held until 1961. (NP 111; UP 47; PP 1.) However, the encouragement was short-lived. Soon the UP was caught in its own internal squabbles caused by policy differences and the frustration of continual opposition. 'Young Turks', calling for more reform and a vigorous opposition, challenged the 'Old Guard' and its 'toenadering' with the government. A bitter clash in 1973 saw Harry Schwarz oust the more senior and conservative Marais Steyn from the leadership in the Transvaal. Steyn immediately crossed the floor of the House to join the NP, and while nobody else followed him the UP's troubles persisted.

The UP's squabbles were advantageous for the government as it put increasing emphasis on the need for white unity in the face of communist dangers. Vorster repeatedly warned against 'The Red Menace' saying that 'we shall rise against it and oppose it with all the means at our disposal'.[14] In July 1970, P. W. Botha declared that 'we are being threatened by the global and overall strategy under the leadership of aggressive communism'. He claimed that it was not an onslaught against apartheid and for individual rights, rather: 'It is a communistic onslaught under the cloak of religion or freedom . . . and it is directed against stability, security and progress.' As the onslaught was total – including economic threats and student unrest as well as direct security issues – the response must be total. In that spirit he spoke of building better relations among whites (with greater respect for the Afrikaans language), good relations between black and white through separate development, and countering the hostility of the news media.[15] To emphasise its own unity and commitment the government used the UP, which was no threat, as a sounding board, accusing it of undermining the white position. When in 1973 Japie Basson criticised the Immorality and Mixed Marriages Act, Vorster retorted that there were two things the people (whites) demanded: 'Absolute assurance . . . that we shall continue to preserve the white identity', and the refusal to share sovereignty over their own people with others.[16] When Vorster called another election in April 1974, taking advantage of the UP's internal troubles, he emphasised the need for unity and to show to critics at home and abroad that there was a strong government in South Africa. The Prime Minister's calculations were well founded: the NP more than regained the ground lost in 1970, winning 123 seats against the UP's 41, but the 'liberal' PP increased its representation from 1 to 7 seats. However, the clear election message was that the government was secure in power and had a clear majority of whites behind it.

THE MACHINERY OF GOVERNMENT

Under Vorster foreign policy making became more complex and controversial involving not only the Prime Minister's office and the Department of Foreign Affairs, but the Department of Information, the Defence Forces and the intelligence services. Vorster retained Muller as Minister of Foreign Affairs, but while still respected he remained subordinate as Vorster increasingly acted as a 'super Foreign Minister'. In 1966 when Jooste retired, Brand Fourie (formerly Secretary of the Department of Information and Ambassador to Washington) was appointed Secretary of the Department of Foreign Affairs. Fourie was an immensely knowledgeable, hard-working official who gained great respect from those, including diplomats, who worked with him, but he was cautious and secretive, loath to delegate and any initiative he took was within established policy. He was admired by both Vorster and Muller, and Vorster sometimes worked directly with him, bypassing Muller.[17] Abroad the department's main activities were confined to the UN and the West. In 1966 there were only 22 diplomatic missions in the 122 UN member states, with no representation in communist states and diplomatic links in Africa confined to one state, Malawi. Even in the West where London, Washington, Paris and Bonn were the main posts, the determination to keep Pretoria at a distance was shown by Norway, Denmark, New Zealand and Japan who limited their links to consular representation.

If South African diplomats faced an emotional battering of criticism abroad, they faced increasing departmental rivalry at home. This was led by two powerful ministers – Dr C. P. (Connie) Mulder and P. W.

Botha. In August 1968 Mulder was appointed Minister of Information, greatly enhancing the status of a department which previously had worked under Foreign Affairs. In September 1972 Mulder selected as Department Secretary Eschel Rhoodie, a young, energetic, ambitious, flamboyant figure who had no background in formal diplomacy or the NP. Together Mulder and Rhoodie set out to transform South Africa's international position. The government, they argued, had been far too passive in projecting itself abroad. It should establish a much wider range of links and mount aggressive campaigns emphasising the country's strengths – its mineral wealth, technological achievements and continental power. This confident, aggressive approach gained Vorster's crucial support, and the department's budget for overt activities (such as propaganda, government publications and conferences) rose from R3.2m. in 1966 to R10.7m. in 1974. In addition it received substantial secret funds as it attempted to 'buy, bribe or bluff its way into the hearts and minds of the world'.[18] Among its many, sometimes bizarre, activities were secret funding of British and American politicians; financing research institutions; buying or attempting to buy control of Western newspapers; organising campaigns against hostile politicians; and secret African contacts. In 1974 the department's annual report spoke confidently of a distinct shift of opinion in South Africa's favour.

There were clashes between Foreign Affairs and Information. In public Mulder denied a dispute, but accepted that there were differences of approach. 'The Information people in every country', he said, 'are the people who are prepared to speak out loud in the political sphere, while Foreign Affairs on the purely diplomatic level acts correctly with protocol and acts on a different level.' He declared: 'My department will not remain on the defensive. We have now gone over to the offensive.'[19] Privately he and Rhoodie strongly criticised Foreign Affairs for being too cautious, for operating in too few countries and having too narrow a range of contacts within those countries, and even failing to give full support to government policies. Foreign Affairs countered by accusing Information of undermining years of conscientious diplomacy, of bringing the government into disrepute and of behaving as a law unto itself. In 1973 Vorster laid down operational guidelines for the two departments but they were ambiguous and the bureaucratic battles persisted. One of the most celebrated was in the Washington Embassy which led to the transfer of both the Ambassador, J. S. F. (Frikkie) Botha and J. J. Becker, a senior Information official.

The military also became increasingly prominent in foreign policy

114

making. This had started with the expansion of the forces in the early 1960s and although their budget did not increase significantly, from the mid 1960s military influence was prominent because of a new security situation, especially the border wars – in Namibia, Rhodesia, Mozambique and Angola. In responding to these situations foreign policy and military concerns overlapped, and P. W. Botha, the determined, aggressive Minister of Defence, ensured that the military had a prominent voice. In 1973 the Defence White Paper argued for a 'total strategy' in which military policy was determined by other policies, but they in turn 'cannot be developed properly unless they are sustained by a sound and adequate defence policy'.[20] The 1975 paper stated that a strong defence force removes weakness in foreign policy. The military were not therefore asking for a dominant voice but for involvement in a wider range of policy making than conventional security concerns, for they argued military action was not enough; 'hearts and minds' had to be won. They gave as an example the 'civic action' programme launched in Namibia in 1974 to counter SWAPO, which involved army teachers, doctors and agricultural specialists.

Another significant participant in the Pretoria power game was the Bureau of State Security (BOSS), an intelligence agency which in 1969 replaced the existing Republican Intelligence. BOSS's wide brief included the collection and evaluation of information that was a threat to the state, and the submission of intelligence estimates to the State Security Council. Intelligence gathering had become increasingly important as black nationalism moved into its revolutionary and international phase and anti-apartheid movements developed abroad. The government's view was that as its opponents had decided to operate unlawfully, and in the case of the black parties to wage an armed struggle, not only the collection of information but secret operations to counter the threat were fully justified.

There is limited and not always reliable information about the activities of the secret agencies, but certainly they were active abroad from the 1960s. The scope of the operations was steadily extended but it concentrated on two main targets – the refugee and guerrilla camps in the neighbouring black states, and the exiled black parties and their supporters in Europe. Infiltration into the camps became increasingly important as the danger posed by guerrilla fighters was recognised. Outside Africa the main initial effort was in London where the exiled parties and anti-apartheid groups were most active. In 1971, according to an *Observer* report, there were ten trained intelligence officers at the South African Embassy and twelve others operating elsewhere in London.[21] Added to these were part-time agents, like newspaper reporters and students, some of whom were given elaborate 'covers'. Gordon Winter, who wrote an extensive if not entirely reliable account of his experiences, underwent a staged imprisonment in South Africa as a government opponent before being deported to Britain in 1966 where he penetrated anti-apartheid groups.[22] Among examples of other agents' work Winter wrote of Hans Lombard, a newspaperman who, after befriending P. K. Leballo, the PAC leader, obtained a list of PAC members which was used to make arrests in South Africa. Some agents, like Jean Legrange, worked in anti-apartheid organisations – in her case as a voluntary helper for Christian Action and then in the office of the Defence and Aid Fund where she obtained valuable information and helped to plan the theft of confidential documents.[23] Other break-ins and thefts, some by agents and some by hired professionals, included the offices of the Anti-Apartheid Movement and Amnesty International. There were claims that BOSS agents were involved in trying to implicate Peter Hain in a bank robbery and in operations against politicians, such as Jeremy Thorpe and Harold Wilson.[24] BOSS was also said to be implicated in the murder of one of its own agents, Keith Wallace, who had clashed with General H. J. van den Burgh and threatened to expose BOSS's activities in Britain.[25] There can be no certainty of that, but later van den Burgh told a government inquiry: 'I have enough men to commit murder if I tell them to kill . . . I don't care who the prey is.'[26]

In undertaking intelligence and security work there was an overlap of functions which created tensions between individuals and departments, notably BOSS and the military. That was intensified by the personal position of van den Burgh, a rough tough man who, after becoming a close associate of Vorster during their wartime internment together, had cemented the friendship when he worked as Chief of Security Police during Vorster's time as Minister of Justice. The close relationship continued during Vorster's premiership. Van den Burgh became a power behind the throne – the leader of a powerful agency, Vorster's confidant and a policy maker in his own right.[27] The rivalries this created were noted by Ken Flower, a Rhodesian intelligence official. Flower admired van den Burgh's intelligence service, but noted that his access to Vorster and his erratic blunt character alienated him from his colleagues. In the foreign policy field van den Burgh allied himself with Rhoodie and Information and helped to set up African initiatives for Vorster, which was resented by Foreign Affairs. But the greatest antagonism was with the military and P. W. Botha in particular, with whom there was intense rivalry. Flower wrote of persistent internal jealousies which made it depressing 'to have to listen to "Boss" reviling against the Military, the Military berating "Boss", and . . . "Boss" railing against the Police – in short, almost everyone denigrating almost everyone else'.[28] The rivalries later led to conflicting policies in Mozambique and Rhodesia.[29]

BLACK MOVEMENTS

Inside South Africa the late 1960s and early 1970s were bleak years for black nationalism. The exiled ANC and PAC were building for the future (see chapter 9) but for the moment they were an irritant not a threat to Pretoria. Inside the country the major leaders were in prison or banned, the parties moribund, and among those who remained active there was a mood of 'realism' – an acceptance of the government's power and that a quick upheaval was not coming so that it was wise to gain what one could within the system. The most prominent and radical of the 'realists' was the Zulu leader Chief Gatsha Buthelezi who called for dialogue across the races to avoid alienating black youth and eventual violent confrontation. He said that after twenty-five years of NP rule 'I do not feel less of a "Kaffir" in 1973 than I did in 1948.' At a memorial service to Luthuli he repeated the cry of 'Freedom in our lifetime', and later called for the release of Mandela and other black nationalists, for while to whites they might appear to be 'subversive elements' to blacks they were heroes.[30]

In the absence of the established parties Black Consciousness emerged. This was in the 'Africanist' stream, influenced by black theology and black American writers, and it called for a reawakening of blacks to their values and dignity, arguing that prolonged sub-jugation by whites had led to black resignation to their own exploita-tion. That was to be changed.[31] It was not a single organisation, and ironically it was partly nurtured in apartheid policies as students from the exclusively black universities established by Pretoria to ensure racial purity organised themselves to advance black rights. The South African Students Organisation (SASO) was established in 1969 with Steve Biko as its first President. Black Consciousness did not direct its strongest early attacks against the advocates of apartheid but against white 'liberals' and 'leftists': 'that bunch of do-gooders' wrote Biko 'who argue that they are not responsible for white racism . . . who say that they have black souls wrapped in white skins', but in fact stifle and suppress blacks 'with whites doing all the talking and blacks the listening'.[32] Biko dismissed accusations that an exclusive black organi-sation was racist, arguing that blacks must develop their own identity and institutions before they could co-operate on the basis of mutual respect. At the 1972 conference SASO rejected co-operation with the 'realists' because that implied acceptance of government and white thinking, whereas the aim must be to create independent black psychological and cultural attitudes. Biko, commenting on the Bantustan leaders including Buthelezi, said that they were playing the white man's game, that black aspirations could not be achieved from a platform which is designed to oppress the blacks.[33] It was recognised that success in persuading blacks to rethink their position would be slow, but in seeking this all 'blacks' (including Coloureds and Indians) were welcomed.

Early responses to Black Consciousness were mixed. Initially the movement gained a warm, if short-lived welcome from advocates of apartheid. *Die Burger* saw it as a product of disillusionment with liberal doctrines and showed that 'non-whites do not want to be objects of white politics any longer, but desire to determine their future for themselves as people in their own right'.[34] Among blacks there were some who, despite SASO's denials, saw it as a new form of racism, and that view was strong among Coloureds and Indians who feared that they might exchange one form of racial domination for another. Despite these uncertainties Black Consciousness quickly gained ground among students, but when the leaders sought to extend its base they had mixed success. The search for a wider audience led in 1972 to the establishment of the Black Peoples' Convention (BPC), with similar objectives to SASO, but while it found support among young people in schools and churches, it never became a mass movement. After initial uncertainty the government moved strongly against the BPC. Early in 1973 there were serious black strikes in Durban which alarmed businessmen as well as the government by their scale and ferocity. Although the strikes were unconnected with a formal organisation, the government was determined to suppress all radical black activity and took the opportunity to ban SASO, the BPC, and their leaders.

THE BANTUSTANS

The Bantu homelands policy which had been charted by Verwoerd was linked to foreign policy in three ways. Two of these – the attempts to counter international criticism, and to externalise racial problems – were instituted in Verwoerd's time. The third was to try to use the Bantustans as the first link in a chain that led outwards, via contacts with neighbours, to the whole African continent. That had

118

been mentioned by Verwoerd in relation to the BLS states, but it was Vorster who pursued it. Although Vorster did not share Verwoerd's philosophical approach he was equally committed to apartheid. If we want peace, he declared in 1969, 'the development must not be towards each other, but away from each other'. In 1971 he told a by-election meeting that he had said to the Bantu leaders: 'Look we are different to you, and we have our land and you have your land, you will have no say over my land and my children. But what is more I am not prepared to integrate with them on any basis whatsoever. And this is also the view of the Black leaders. Indeed, anybody with self respect will take such a view whether Black or White.'[35] Vorster's government, having inherited the apartheid foundation, built on it with speed and thoroughness in a decade of major social engineering: with land transfers, heavy expenditure on industries bordering the homelands and the movement of vast numbers of Africans, often with considerable suffering. The dual purpose was to divide people on racial and tribal lines and to gain international acceptance of apartheid, for Pretoria saw it as the equivalent of decolonisation. 'We must', said Muller, 'view events in neighbouring states in the light of our internal relations . . . our policy is based on the self-determination of peoples . . . We hold no brief for colonisation in any form.'[36]

However, the Bantustan policy failed to satisfy critics. At home there was opposition from many blacks and doubts among whites, even government supporters. Many whites remained sceptical of Africans' ability to govern themselves and fearful of the security consequences if they were allowed to try. The government, immersed in its own doubts and surrounded by opposition from various directions, moved crabwise, making faltering progress, as it sought to counter its critics and reassure its followers. In April 1968 Vorster emphasised that Bantustans could not gain independence without negotiation and parliamentary approval. 'It is a question of negotiation', he said, depending 'on whether the parliament allows itself to be intimidated and shunted about.'[37] When P. W. Botha was questioned on the dangers of Bantustans supporting guerrillas and controlling coastlines, he snapped back his resentment at being asked such questions and said that the government would counter guerrillas by gaining the goodwill of the people; but then, on a harsher note, he said that the Bantustans were so dependent that they had no choice but 'to retain South Africa's friendship'. Finally he repeated Verwoerd's point that it was safer to have potential enemies outside the borders.[38] In 1969 M. C. Botha, the Minister of Bantu Administration, set out five tough 'determining factors' which would have to be met before

119

independence could be achieved,[39] and Dr P. Koornhof, the Deputy Minister, spoke of the need for Pretoria to control the Transkei coastline and coastal waters. The government, he said, would not be so irresponsible 'as to let the coastline cause any problem or danger for the country'.[40] Yet in more relaxed moments Vorster confirmed that Bantustans were welcome to approach parliament if they wanted independence, and Koornhof said that Pretoria meant 'real independence' with the prospects of UN membership.[41]

Despite such vacillation the government went ahead with homeland legislation. Since 1963 the Transkei had managed some of its own affairs, Pretoria retaining control of such services as security, foreign affairs, immigration, customs and banking. In 1971 the Bantu Homelands Act gave similar powers to Ciskei, Venda and Lebowa, and in 1974 further negotiations started for the Transkei when a joint South Africa/Transkei committee investigated arrangements for independence. Meanwhile the Bantu Laws Amendment Act of 1973 speeded up land consolidation and the consequent removal of people.

During this time there were attempts by Bantustan leaders to combine for mutual benefit and to bring pressure on Pretoria. In November 1973 when six leaders met at Umtata in the Transkei for their first 'summit' Buthelezi declared that the architects of apartheid would not have believed that their policy would be the base for black unity. An elated Matanzima stated: 'My dream has come true', and compared the meeting with a 'UN of black South Africa'.[42] At this and further meetings common ground was reached on opposition to the pass laws and influx control, support for a South African federation based on black and white homelands, and above all there was agreement that more land must be made available. Chief Mangope of Bophuthatswana spoke for all when he said: 'There must be a more fair and just sharing of the land . . . We reject outright the present attempts to make the 1936 Land Act the basis of settling the issue.'[43] All the leaders had substantial land claims to extend their areas and consolidate the fragmented pieces. They resolved to challenge Pretoria and there was talk of refusing independence if the land question was not settled. However, when they met Vorster in March 1974 and again in January 1975 (the first meetings of their kind) they gained nothing. The government agreed 'to consider' the points raised but stood fast against their main claims – the federal state, rights for blacks in white areas and the land question. On federation, which was being advocated by the UP as well as the black leaders, Vorster told parliament that it would mean abandoning white sovereignty. 'I am not prepared in respect of the whites', he said, 'to abdicate any part of their sovereignty to other people or nations.'[44]

The government was equally adamant in refusing more rights to blacks outside their homelands. M. C. Botha, the Minister of Bantu Affairs, stated that 'the Bantu are not here in the white areas because it is their natural and traditional area . . . [but] because of the work they want to do for the sake of personal earnings and to supplement the white lack of man power'. If there were no work there would be no place for them. 'The white area is the homeland of the whites; here the whites rule and here the whites have exclusive and sole control.'[45] Nor would Pretoria move on the land issue. M. C. Botha said that if the leaders wanted to link additional land to independence 'they will only have themselves to blame if their independence is retarded or comes to grief in the process'. Expressing the views of many whites, that all the land was in their gift, he told a National Party Conference: 'We as the givers must determine what land should be given and it is not for those who receive to point out what land they should have.'[46] Meanwhile a parliamentary committee, which tabled its report in 1975, opposed an addition to the total land available to Africans, but proposed greater consolidation for each homeland so that, for example, Bophuthatswana would consist of six rather than nineteen separate pieces; Lebowa five instead of fifteen; and most spectacular of all KwaZulu ten instead of one hundred and eighty-eight.[47] Although a programme of consolidation was much less than the Bantustan leaders had requested, even that involved heavy expenditure for the government in buying out existing land holders, and human suffering in the forced resettlement of Africans. Between April 1975 and February 1976 R57m. was spent on acquiring land, and according to the government's conservative estimate 231,000 Africans in the Transvaal and 132,000 in Natal were moved.

The parliamentary committee also revived security fears by favouring 'white' corridors between Venda and Rhodesia and along the KwaZulu coast between Richards Bay and St Lucia. The government was never allowed to forget such fears. In 1971, Vorster confirmed that the Bantustans could have their own defence departments, but added: 'It is an academic question which means absolutely nothing because there will be no need for these people to have such departments.'[48] Later he said that like the BLS states they 'are the luckiest people in the world as it is not necessary for them to spend a cent on defence . . . because they know they have nothing to fear from South Africa'.[49] In February 1974 P. W. Botha confirmed that he had been negotiating with Bantustans about their establishing armed forces, but he warned against recklessness in arming the Bantu as South Africa's history was full of tragedies. He said it would be foolish to announce a policy 'without being able to tell the country that there are guarantees and firm agreements'.[50]

Alongside Pretoria's opposition to their claims came divisions within the ranks of the Bantustan leaders. In part this came from policy differences – two refused to attend the first meeting because they opposed federation – and in part from different judgements. While, for example, Matanzima came to accept Pretoria's offer in full, Buthelezi believed that the homeland concept had been forced on them and they should resist complete separation. The greatest source of division, however, was the pursuit of separate interests which enabled the government to negotiate bilaterally on its own terms. Promises of solidarity came to nothing as each leader put loyalty to his own homeland first, especially in land claims which often infringed neighbouring Bantustans as well as white areas. Venda, for example, put in a claim for about one third of the Transvaal including parts of Bophuthatswana, Gazankulu and South Ndebele. In the Transkei, Matanzima demanded the creation of a greater Xhosaland to embrace not only the Transkei but the Ciskei, East Griqualand and the white areas between the Fish and Kei Rivers, including East London and numerous smaller towns. Both Pretoria and the Ciskei leaders immediately dismissed the claim, and in 1974 Matanzima dropped it. His small consolation was Pretoria's acceptance that the Transkei would absorb Port St John, a small coastal holiday resort. The fuss that surrounded the transfer of this 'white spot' indicates the severe constraints under which both sides worked. The government had resisted the transfer on two grounds: first, the opposition of the local whites, although there were only a few hundred of them; second, security fears, although the 'port' had not been used since the First World War, was on a wild stretch of coast, and would require major investment to bring it back into operation.

Despite the difficulties and doubts the decade saw the rapid implementation of the homelands policy – the ultimate flowering of grand apartheid. Alongside the new legislation, the consolidation of land and the movement of people, a Bantu Investment Bank was created, development funds were increased, subsidies were given to border industries and, departing from Verwoerdian purity, white investment was encouraged. Yet the main objectives were not achieved. Far from applauding Pretoria's initiative the international community was cool at best and bitterly hostile at worst. Far from equating the homelands with ex-colonial territories, critics dismissed them as puppets. Nothing, they argued, had changed – apartheid was still in place, while thousands of blacks had suffered from forced removal. The government probably anticipated that it would take time to win international acceptance, but more disturbing was the failure at home to reverse the flow of blacks into white areas. This was revealed in the 1970 census figures, despite the gloss Pretoria put on them. It pointed out that while in 1960 only 36.5 per cent of the African population lived in the homelands, by 1970 it had risen to 46.5 per cent. Yet those percentages masked the fact that the black population had grown so rapidly that the total number of blacks in white areas had increased from less than seven million in 1960 to close to eight million in 1970. They also masked the forced removals to the homelands; the failure to count the 'illegal' blacks in urban areas; and the redrawing of urban boundaries so that 300,000 blacks who had previously lived in 'white' areas now lived in 'black' areas without moving. The grand design simply was not working. The white urban areas continued to expand and draw economically active blacks to them; the homelands remained predominantly poor rural areas, further burdened by the forced dumping of the economically less active: the old, the children and the women.

8 THE AFRICAN SETTING

Rapid change in Africa continued as further decolonisation was accompanied by early signs of political and economic instability in some of the new states. Pretoria did not relish the turmoil and uncertainty. Its interests were served by stability and order, by an acceptance of the 'status quo' within and outside its borders, whereas it faced persistent uncertainty and change which it neither favoured nor entirely understood. However, with a confidence based upon strength at home it responded by setting out to achieve three main aims: to secure the white state; to foster and extend economic and technical links; and to gain acceptance as a leading continental power.

In the early 1960s black nationalism had gained such momentum that many inside and outside the Republic believed that it would quickly sweep across the entire continent. That did not happen because a bloc of white territories stood firm in southern Africa. Yet security remained a major concern for Pretoria. The government still believed there was an outside chance of a conventional attack, and although the threat receded the fear remained and was allied to the spread of communism. When in 1970 Botswana and Mauritius agreed to exchange diplomats with the USSR Vorster warned all neighbours (including the Bantustans) that South Africa would 'do the necessary' to protect itself if neighbours were used as communist springboards.[1] In 1971 P. W. Botha said that there were developments in Africa which did 'not bode well' and South Africa was vulnerable to air attack from hostile countries whose military capacity was enhanced by support from the USSR and China.[2]

However, the more immediate dangers came from black nationalist guerrillas and from psychological warfare intended 'to erode the national will'. In 1973 Botha identified these as the instruments used by the communists in a global campaign in which South Africa was a prime target. 'We are not', said Botha, 'arming ourselves against our Black and Coloured people – we are arming ourselves against the forces that are being built up against us under the guidance of Russia, China and their satellites.' He warned again of 'total onslaughts on the Free World, which means total war in every sphere', and castigated those who proposed new political dispensations in South Africa as unconscious dupes helping to undermine the state. He warned of a strategy based on the Chinese experience of first controlling the countryside (which in Africa meant dominating such countries as Zambia and Tanzania) before assaulting the industrialised areas.[3]

In defying black nationalism the government was joined by the Portuguese in Angola and Mozambique and the white Rhodesians. It was not a development that Pretoria had planned or particularly welcomed, but it recognised that its interests were best served by participating in the white regional bloc which emerged following Britain's colonial withdrawal. Pretoria had opposed that withdrawal but, with growing confidence in its own strength and increasing scepticism about that of the black states, it came to believe that black nationalism could be resisted at home and that new opportunities were opening up in Africa. The mood in Pretoria was far removed from the gloom of the early 1960s. Vorster asserted that the Republic was not just another African state but a leader in every sphere,[4] and in 1970 Muller triumphantly declared that 'over the ten years since Sharpeville the international climate has definitely taken a favourable turn'. The British withdrawal, he said, 'has brought about greater responsibility for South Africa as the most developed state in the continent', giving her the opportunity to take her 'rightful place in Africa'.[5]

To that end the government promoted the 'outward policy'. Its aims were to diversify diplomatic and trade links, to reduce political isolation and to demonstrate that South Africa could form new relationships. Initiatives were taken outside Africa with new missions established in Tokyo, Taipeh, Hong Kong and Wellington; and in Latin America, although Montevideo was the only new office, the Ambassador in Buenos Aires was accredited to Bolivia, and Paraguay and Chile. The main effort, however, was in Africa and especially southern Africa where the government identified two broad objectives: first, to promote peace based on co-operation and mutual respect; second, to further the material interests of all through shared economic and technical activities. There was, however, to be no interference in internal affairs or attempts to create common political positions. Among the whites who supported the policy there was a determination, sometimes bordering on missionary zeal, to show that they could work with black Africa and that they could lead where previously they had followed the colonial powers. Alongside the government private companies shared the sense of adventure in seeking opportunities for trade and investment. Yet, although African economic links were extended, they remained less important than those with the West, and in relative terms the African economic interests had to run hard to stand still.[6] This was a period of international expansion for South Africa's major companies, and none more so than Anglo-American which became a multinational giant with global interests. While the economic developments were important, the government's main objective was to gain security and political objectives by using the country's resources to project into Africa. Opponents recognised this. President Kaunda declared: 'Apartheid is on the offensive, the Boer trek is still on.'[7] The exiled ANC spoke of 'a spider's web carefully and systematically spun to ensnare weak African governments', while all the time Pretoria consolidated white rule, drew foreign support away from the liberation struggle and extended its internal rule over Africans through the Bantustans.[8]

Pretoria's African policy was built at three levels. First 'Greater South Africa', which was not a term used by Pretoria but captures its perception of a powerful white Republic surrounded by compliant black satellites – the Bantustans, South West Africa and the BLS states. Although there were clear constitutional and political differences between these territories they were all heavily dependent on South Africa. Second, a southern African bloc, which included Greater South Africa, Mozambique and Angola, and two of the members of the old Central African Federation – Rhodesia and Malawi. Third, the rest of Africa with which Pretoria's links were at best patchy. The government realised that success at one level would lead to success at others and ultimately influence its international position. Muller explained that the logical extension of recognising Bantu nations at home 'is that we should seek also to establish friendly relations and collaboration with the African states beyond our borders'[9] and later he claimed that the West's attitude was improving because of 'our fruitful co-operation in Africa . . . We must accept that our relations with the rest of the world are determined by our relations with African countries.'[10]

NAMIBIA

Namibia (whose international setting is discussed in the next chapter) continued to be treated as part of the Republic, but under external pressure Pretoria made concessions about its constitutional status. In 1967 Muller accepted that it was separate in international law,[11] and in November 1972 Vorster confirmed there was no intention to annex it.[12] In the following year, after discussions between the government and the UN Secretary General, Kurt Waldheim, an Advisory Council was established with representatives from all ethnic groups. However, Pretoria's continued grip on South West Africa was demonstrated by the introduction of apartheid, based on recommendations of the Odendaal Commission.[13] In May 1973, undeterred by criticism that it was ridiculous to talk of 'independence' for such poor, sparsely populated homelands, Pretoria proclaimed Ovamboland a self-governing area, and approved further capital investment as recommended by Odendaal.[14] At the same time Vorster assured the local whites that because of apartheid they could decide their own future. He told the SWA National Party in August 1973: 'Your future will not be decided in Pretoria; it will not be decided in the glass palaces of the United Nations. Your political future will be decided here by your own white representatives.'[15]

Yet progress inside the territory was not smooth. There were labour strikes in 1972 and 1973; the government had difficulty in filling black places on the Advisory Council; and in SWAPO (The South West Africa Peoples' Organisation) it faced a black nationalist opponent which had been formed in exile in the early 1960s and drew its main support in Ovamboland. There it succeeded in undermining the 'self-government' election for the legislature. (Of the fifty-four members twenty-one were elected, the rest were 'ex officio' or nominated.) Even the South African Broadcasting Corporation described the election as 'a farce', with few seats contested and few votes cast in those that were.[16] SWAPO also began infiltrating guerrilla fighters into Ovamboland in 1965–6 where clashes with government forces were the first in a prolonged and costly war. Like most guerrilla armies SWAPO made a faltering start and had difficulty finding recruits for guerrilla training in the USSR, China, Egypt, Ghana, Algeria and North Korea. Later, many of the guerrillas who penetrated into Namibia were either killed or captured, but SWAPO had its successes. Early in 1973, for example, it killed four policemen in an ambush; captured an ammunition dump; and shot down a government helicopter.[17] Yet neither side could secure victory. SWAPO was not strong enough to threaten the government, but Pretoria could not prevent guerrilla incursions and paid an increasing cost in countering them – in loss of life, resources, and international hostility.

BOTSWANA, LESOTHO AND SWAZILAND

The BLS states were among the last of the British colonies to gain independence – Botswana in September 1966; Lesotho October 1966; and Swaziland September 1968. All came under the control of 'moderate' or 'conservative' administrations. In Pretoria's eyes they were in a similar position to its own Bantustans and Verwoerd was tactless enough to say so. He added that while as colonies they could afford to be hostile because Britain would protect them, now they would have to acknowledge their dependence on South Africa. He argued that 'the one thing which really counts in international relations is common economic interest. So far as these Governments are concerned their political interests will be dominated by their economic interests.' The BLS states were acutely aware of the situation. President Khama of Botswana admitted that the 'economic links are virtually indissoluble'.[18] There were different levels of dependence, but all were to an extent 'prisoners of geography'. They shared a Customs Union with Pretoria and in 1969 a new customs agreement, which replaced the original 1910 arrangements, gave the BLS states a better deal by compensating them for the concentration of economic activity in the Republic. While under the old customs formula they would have received R6.5m. in 1969–70, now they received R17m. This was a major element in their revenue – ranging from 28 per cent of Botswana's budget to 53 per cent in Lesotho. *The Star* commented: 'This is the outward policy in action. We all want more of it.'[19] Yet even the development of their resources could serve to underline their dependence. In Botswana's case her economic prospects were greatly improved by large mineral finds in the 1960s, but it was South African capital and skilled manpower which played a major role in extracting and marketing the diamonds and copper-nickel. When Sir Seretse Khama opened the Orapa diamond mine in May 1972 alongside him stood Mr Harry Oppenheimer, Chairman of Anglo-American and De Beers which had a majority holding in the mine and marketed the diamonds.[20]

Only in part did BLS leaders accept Pretoria's assumption that 'political interests will be dominated by their economic interests'. They spoke of 'realistic' policies, of 'having to live with a powerful neighbour' and in response to Pretoria's warnings refused bases to guerrillas.[21] There were regular contacts between officials (and occasionally ministers) to manage the shared services, which usually went smoothly, but there were occasional upsets in these, as in 1972 when the BLS states objected to Pretoria devaluing the Rand without consultation, and in March 1975 Botswana announced its withdrawal from the Rand currency area. Nor were the BLS states fully compliant on political matters. Pretoria accused its neighbours of harbouring political refugees and terrorists, and on occasion took action. For example, in August 1966 the South Africans abducted John Pokela, the acting Secretary General of the PAC, from Lesotho and in February 1974 Botswana accused them of killing Abraham Tiro (an exiled student leader) with a parcel bomb. To Pretoria's disappointment economic dependence did not always lead to political acceptance. There was open criticism of apartheid by BLS leaders, whereas South Africa had anticipated silence at least and support at best. Yet Pretoria added to its difficulties by slighting the BLS states and failing to seize opportunities that opened up. It shied away from establishing diplomatic links probably from fear of white reaction at home, but publicly arguing that diplomatic relations were not necessary for friendship and that there were other ways of maintaining contacts such as 'telephone diplomacy'.

Of the three states Swaziland kept the lowest profile whereas Botswana's leader, Sir Seretse Khama, was openly critical. Addressing the General Assembly in 1970 he explained that although his country had no choice but 'to live and let live', that did not imply 'sacrificing our national interests and our fundamental principles. For we have made no secret of our detestation of apartheid.' He saw the development of a healthy non-racial democracy in Botswana as 'an effective and serious challenge to the credibility of South Africa's racial policies'.[22] Botswana kept Pretoria at arm's length by refusing to accept aid or exchange diplomats; granting asylum to political refugees; building a road link with Zambia at a crossing point which South Africa claimed as its own; and establishing links with the Soviet Union, which brought a stern warning from Vorster.[23]

Pretoria's relations with Lesotho were the most volatile. For several years Lesotho's acute economic dependence on the Republic was reflected in friendly political contacts. In 1967 Chief Jonathan, then a strong advocate of contact, was the first leader of a black state to visit Pretoria. In the early 1970s that changed. In part Pretoria brought this on its own head by its patronising attitude, as Vorster unconsciously revealed in reporting his first meeting with Jonathan. 'I have', said Vorster, 'offered him technical assistance, which he gladly accepted. I have offered him advice, which he gladly accepted.'[24] Pretoria failed to respond to Lesotho's request to exchange diplomats and dragged its feet over a proposed hydroelectric scheme (Oxbow) because it feared dependence for power and water on a potentially unreliable state.

Lesotho leaders later complained that for years they bore the brunt of international criticism by advocating contact while South Africa took them for granted. In response, however, Pretoria could point to Jonathan's unpredictable behaviour. After independence Pretoria gave aid and supported his regime, but in 1970 it criticised Jonathan for suspending an election when it became clear he was losing. That may have been a turning point. Whatever the reason, by 1972 Jonathan was criticising apartheid and advising others to boycott Pretoria. 'The opposition to racism', he said, 'is escalating to such a point where soon there will be no room for dialogue and the victims of the system will see violence as presenting the only chance of the attainment of equality and freedom.'[25] When belatedly Pretoria offered to exchange consuls Lesotho ignored it and instead revived claims for 'lost territories'. Vorster was incensed. 'For years', he said, 'we did him [Jonathan] only good; him personally and his government.' But now, said Vorster, he attacks us irresponsibly. He warned Jonathan to leave South Africa alone.[26] In April 1975 Vorster named Lesotho as an extremist state and said Jonathan and Lesotho's Minister of Foreign Affairs, J. R. L. Kotosokoane, were out of touch with the needs of their people because they promoted enmity between the two countries.[27]

THE SOUTHERN AFRICAN BLOC

The southern African bloc consisted of 'Greater South Africa', the Portuguese territories (Angola and Mozambique) and two of the old Central African Federation states – Rhodesia and Malawi. The position of Zambia, the third territory of the Federation, was ambivalent, for while it was forced to retain economic links with the bloc it adopted a hostile political stand and supported black guerrillas. The bloc was not formalised by treaty, nor was there a common ideology or political system; there were tensions as well as co-operation, and not all interests were shared, so that involvement in one set of relations did not imply involvement in all. However, the bloc was held together not only by common interests but by the commitment of the white members to white rule. The small black states did not share, but were unable to challenge, it. There was great disparity of size and wealth within the bloc, but South Africa's pre-eminence was clear. The Republic was a hub from which spokes extended across the region – economic, transport and geographical links, and also the immediate political and security concerns of the whites. The mix was reflected in Vorster's commitment 'to maintaining the closest economic and technological co-operation among all countries of the region . . . while each nation continues to retain its political autonomy, and therefore the right freely to choose its own racial, cultural and economic systems'.[28]

The region's economic links covered labour, transport, trade, investment, joint projects and aid. The employment opportunities in South African mines, farms and industry drew large numbers of unskilled and semi-skilled workers from neighbouring states, especially Mozambique, Malawi and Lesotho. To an extent there was mutual labour dependence, but it was not a balanced situation for some of the neighbours relied heavily on the money remitted home by their workers whereas South Africa had options. She demonstrated this in 1974–5 when a number of separate incidents curtailed the supply of external labour – Malawi suspended its quota following a fatal air crash; labour from Mozambique became uncertain after the Lisbon coup; and some Basotho workers were sent home following riots. The South African employers were fortunate that these problems arose when gold prices where rising rapidly so that the mines, the main employers of migratory labour, could offer higher wages. They were able to solve the problem by increasing the proportion of home recruited miners (including the Bantustans) from 22 per cent in 1972 to almost 60 per cent in 1976.

The regional transport system gave South Africa a pivotal position. All the newly independent black states and Rhodesia were land-locked and dependent, to a greater or lesser extent, on the Republic for major ports and the rail systems serving them – Cape Town, Durban and Port Elizabeth in the Republic, and Lourenco Marques in Mozambique (which served the Eastern Transvaal and Witwatersrand). Zambia's attempts to break the mould illustrate the strength of South Africa's position. Although Zambia had no direct border with the Republic, its main transport routes were to the south through Rhodesia, Mozambique and South Africa. Lusaka set out to break dependence on its white neighbours by creating alternative routes through Tanzania – an oil pipeline and a road built with Western aid and a railway built by China. President Kaunda made no secret of the political motives. Opening the pipeline in 1968 he said: 'It removes one of our greatest hardships in having to rely on hostile regimes which surround Zambia on three sides.' Later he described the railway as 'a political necessity. Even after Rhodesia wins majority rule, there will still be Mozambique and South Africa between us and the sea.'[29] Pretoria was equally concerned about the implications. P. W. Botha noted that the West had refused to support the railway because it did not make economic sense, but he said the Chinese had built it to move military supplies for 'an onslaught on southern Africa'.[30] The railway failed to match either the hopes or fears of the two sides. It was not used to support a military onslaught but it proved less effective than Zambia had anticipated, leaving her dependent on southern routes and, apart from periods of border closure, an average of a third to a half of her goods continued to pass that way.

Conscious of the potential of the transport situation the government engaged in 'transport diplomacy'. A major influence in this was J. G. H. Loubser (Manager of South African Railways and Harbours, 1970 to 1983). In his view transport links were 'the strongest and most effective counter-measure against isolation and the best way of achieving South Africa's potential wealth-creating and stabilising role in the subcontinent'. He identified three objectives: to promote stability in neighbouring states which would reduce hostility; to promote common interests which could lead to political co-operation with black neighbours; and (*sotto voce*) to provide a direct source of pressure if the two first objectives failed. Loubser was also keen to employ South Africa's skills and resources in encouraging development elsewhere in the region but, in line with the government's general approach, such aid would only be given if asked for and at a 'fair price'.[31]

The Republic had roughly six times as much trade with the rest of the world as with Africa, and yet in southern Africa her trade was 80 per cent of the region's total. The African market was of great importance to the manufacturing sector, and the export of such manufactured goods as chemicals, textiles and paper helped to give her a favourable trade balance, as did her increasing export trade in maize. (In 1970–1 she exported 250,000 metric tons, mainly to southern Africa.) As with other links there were differences in the volume of trade and its relative importance for her neighbours (see Table 2). Inevitably the BLS states were the most dependent – in 1968 the proportion of imports from South Africa were Botswana 92 per cent, Swaziland 91 per cent and Lesotho 84 per cent – but in volume terms South Africa's main markets were Rhodesia and Zambia, which took two thirds of the Republic's African exports. As shown in Table 2, political as well as economic considerations shaped the pattern of trade; with Zambia reducing her links, Malawi increasing hers and Rhodesia increasingly dependent as South Africa helped to circumvent international sanctions.

South African investment increased in Africa. By 1967 it stood at $1 billion and grew steadily, especially in southern Africa where the giant Anglo-American Company had large holdings in mining and land.

Table 2. *Proportion of imports from South Africa (per cent)*

	Malawi	Mozambique	Rhodesia	Zambia
1964	6.0	12.7	23.2	20.7
1965	5.3	10.5	23.0	19.7
1966	7.3	10.5	46.4	23.8
1967	7.7	11.3	51.5	23.6
1968	11.0	11.8	51.7	23.4
1969	14.2	15.1	55.5	22.4
1970	12.6	14.8	48.7	17.2
1971	10.6	14.9	45.0	14.8
1972	13.0	14.9	n.a.	14.6

Adrian Guelke, 'Africa as a Market for South African Goods', *Journal of Modern African Studies*, 12 (1) 1974.

Investment was linked to the 'outward policy'. For example, in 1965 the Industrial Development Corporation (IDC) announced a multi-million dollar loan for South African companies to construct sugar mills in Mozambique and Malawi.[32] The largest investments were in hydroelectrical and irrigation schemes. Two were undertaken with the Portuguese – one on the Cunene River, which divides Angola and Namibia, but the most spectacular was the Cahora Bassa dam on the Zambezi River near Tete in Mozambique. Planned as the largest dam in Africa at an estimated cost of R352m. (1969 prices) it was to provide power and to attract a million white settlers into irrigated areas of Mozambique's Zambezi Valley. For Pretoria, Cahora Bassa was a major example of the mutual benefits of regional co-operation. Together with French, West German and Italian companies a consortium (Zamco) was formed to construct the dam, funded by the four countries plus Portugal. Pretoria also agreed to take the bulk of the power although alternative sources could be generated at home. As with transport diplomacy such functional co-operation was seen by some as the bedrock of the 'outward policy'. Dr H. J. van Eck, Chairman of IDC, said: 'We can make electricity the most important single interlinking factor in Southern Africa. If we really want to help our neighbours these are the lines long which we must direct our thinking.'[33] However, Cabora Bassa was more than that. It was a political investment, offering immediate help to the Portuguese and giving South Africa a stake in Mozambique's future whoever governed it. The point was not lost on opponents. The OAU condemned the dam, President Kaunda campaigned against it, the FRELIMO vowed to destroy it. But FRELIMO did not carry out its threats perhaps because it realised the importance of the dam for Mozambique's future.

South Africa's regional strength was further illustrated by the provision of aid. The Republic gave aid: the black states received it. Although in international terms Pretoria's contribution was relatively small it increased sharply in the period between the mid 1960s and mid 1970s, although that is partly explained by the inclusion of aid to Bantustans.[34] Vorster, who criticised the West for using aid as a form of appeasement, declared: 'We do not believe in hand-outs, but rather in offering help in such a way that developing countries can with self-respect help themselves.'[35] Again policy reflected political and economic aims. Although Pretoria favoured technical co-operation, loans rather than grants, and bilateral rather than multilateral aid, it was flexible when it could see political advantage. Even small support was of value to poor neighbours. For example, early help was given to Lesotho to create a broadcasting service, to extend its electricity supply and to train its paramilitary police. Aid was also used to cement relations with Malawi where President Banda had adopted the view that: 'Being a good African does not mean cutting your economic throat.'[36] In 1967 Malawi signed new trade and labour agreements and gained support for two projects which were close to Banda's heart – a rail link to Ncala in Mozambique, and the building of a new capital at Lilongwe. Pretoria gave an R11m. grant for the railway and an R8m. 'soft loan' for Lilongwe. By the end of 1970 South Africa held 18 per cent of Malawi's public external debt, and alongside that was an increased private stake in such projects as the tourist industry and a fertiliser factory.[37]

Verwoerd and Vorster in their more expansive moods speculated about a Common Market and/or a Commonwealth in southern Africa. Each had its attractions. The Common Market would underline South Africa's economic strength; the Commonwealth suggested political co-operation between independent states with a clear leader. While the National Party had always resented Britain's leadership of the old Commonwealth, it savoured the prospect of displaying its own pre-eminence in southern Africa. In doing so Pretoria emphasised that it was ready to co-operate with other governments irrespective of their racial composition, and Verwoerd specifically made this point about the future of Rhodesia. Co-operation, he said, would be welcomed with a multiracial, or black, or white government 'whether in some form of organised economic interdependence according to the example of the European Economic Community, or whether for common political interests taking the Commonwealth as an example'.[38] However, in Rhodesia the issue became the defence of white rule and not the acceptance of a legitimate government irrespective of race.

RHODESIA – DIPLOMACY AND ECONOMIC SANCTIONS

The Rhodesian situation did not create the southern African bloc but it clarified it and defined its membership and the nature of the co-operation. To remain inside implied either supporting 'white' Rhodesia or at least abstaining from active hostility. For Pretoria the issue came to influence relations with the rest of Africa and the whole international community.

Following the break-up of the Federation a constitutional dispute arose between Britain, the sovereign authority, and the white Rhodesian Government which enjoyed a substantial degree of autonomy and control of its own armed forces. Britain pressed for progress towards majority rule whereas the Rhodesians were determined to retain white minority rule. As Verwoerd had indicated, the most satisfactory outcome of the dispute for Pretoria would have been a stable, internationally accepted Rhodesia prepared to co-operate with the Republic. Neither stability nor international acceptance were achieved because the Rhodesian Government illegally and unilaterally declared independence (UDI). Before taking the fateful step Ian Smith, the Rhodesian Prime Minister, recognising South Africa's critical regional role, visited Verwoerd. There are conflicting interpretations of the meeting. Pretoria's version is that Verwoerd listened politely but indicated that UDI would be unwise. Later Verwoerd said: 'I have offered advice to three Rhodesian premiers. The first two were wise enough to take it.'[39] A senior Rhodesian official confirmed that view, writing that: 'At no stage did those in power in South Africa encourage UDI; behind the scenes they did what they could to dissuade Ian Smith from such a rash act.'[40] Smith's memory is different. Recalling the meeting he claimed that although Verwoerd said it would be unfortunate if the problem were not resolved by negotiation, he recognised that there was a point of no return and said that without firm leadership all would be lost. According to Smith, Verwoerd did not advise either way but wished Rhodesia well whatever the decision. Smith claimed that there was no discussion of how the two countries would react if international sanctions were applied, although talks were taking place among officials. Smith left believing that if Rhodesia broke from Britain South Africa would at least be passive, but more probably sympathetic.[41] His view may have been influenced not only by his interpretation of the meeting with Verwoerd but the signing in 1964 of a new bilateral trade agreement lowering tariffs and giving South Africa an edge over competitors and a R5m. loan from Pretoria early in 1965 which Dr Donges, the Minister of Finance, said would both help a friend and South Africa's exports.

When UDI was declared in November 1965 Pretoria faced an unwelcome situation. The disadvantages were clear to the government if not to the white public, for it created regional instability and tension; brought economic sanctions to the doorstep; further soured international relations; and branded South Africa as the champion of a white bloc and, by inference, the main barrier to black nationalism. The situation was full of uncertainty and dangers. The British Government, which responded by imposing UN backed economic sanctions against Rhodesia, said that it did not intend to use force or extend sanctions to South Africa but that might change, and if it did Pretoria could not fall back on its usual legalistic defence. Whatever else might be said about UDI it was illegal. By supporting Rhodesia, Pretoria was furthering the illegal act and endangering its relations with Western states, especially Britain. Not surprisingly there was hesitation in Verwoerd's immediate response, but the government's position was soon clarified. A small committee in Foreign Affairs had been laying plans and had a draft statement ready for the Prime Minister. Verwoerd changed the style but not the substance of the response – that South Africa would not take sides and would retain normal relations with all the parties – and that became Formal Pretoria's position over the long years ahead.

Despite the drawbacks, and despite UP criticism that not enough was being done, Pretoria supported Rhodesia. While the government said it was uncommitted and urged a settlement, retaining normal relations was critical for Rhodesia. These comprised trade, transport, communication and banking links (including honouring Rhodesia's currency), and, as Verwoerd said, 'anyone will realise that maintaining regular relations, especially economic relations . . . means everything to a state which is isolated, as Rhodesia is today'.[42] Nor did 'regular relations' imply restricting contacts to their pre-UDI levels; instead businessmen were encouraged to seize whatever opportunities arose and the government started work on a new direct railway link over Beit Bridge. 'Sanctions busting' became a common and profitable activity, and although its full scale was kept secret it was substantial. For example in 1972 West Germany imported 273,300 metric tons of chrome from South Africa and Japan 719,600, but of this only 158,000 and 335,000 tons respectively had been mined in South Africa; the rest came from Rhodesia.[43]

The decision to support Rhodesia combined hard-headed calculation and 'gut reaction'. Although the government did not welcome UDI, once the step had been taken a new situation was created in which South Africa's interests were to ensure that a white government was not brought down either by economic sanctions or by black nationalism. Rhodesia became a cockpit for South Africa's own battles. Pretoria reasoned that if the threats to white rule succeeded in Rhodesia, South Africa would soon be on the list. 'Today Rhodesia', said Vorster, 'tomorrow some other state, and perhaps the day after South Africa herself.'[44] Both Verwoerd and Vorster opposed sanctions in principle and refused to impose them on Zambia when pressed to do so by 'right wingers' in the Republic. The business community, which largely shared the government's views, was active in sanctions breaking, but ensured that its interests and profits were protected. In the early days of sanctions, for example, many companies insisted on payment in advance or on delivery in Rhodesia.

Alongside the pursuit of immediate interests was a strong emotional response. White South Africans saw in the Rhodesians an image of themselves – a white minority determined to retain its identity and power in a black, potentially hostile continent. There was a surge of public support for the Rhodesians which no government could ignore. It was unthinkable to support sanctions not only in terms of immediate self-interest but also in terms of the values and premises of both white societies which government ministers shared. In his 1966 New Year message Verwoerd repeated that South Africa did not want to be involved, but 'it would be idle to hide that most South Africans are convinced that it would be neither just, advantageous nor wise to white or black in Rhodesia to hasten black government'. Conscious of Afrikaners who had settled in Rhodesia and of links between the white communities, he said: 'We have blood relations over the border. However others may feel or act towards their kith and kin, when their international interests are at stake, South Africans on the whole cannot cold-shoulder theirs.'[45]

In the years of sanctions that followed there were periods of concern, particularly when oil sanctions were imposed in December 1965 and the British blockaded the port of Beira in Mozambique, through which most of Rhodesia's oil had passed. Oil was South Africa's potential Achilles' heel, for none had been found in the Republic. The government had therefore invested in converting the country's abundant supply of coal into oil (the SASOL project) but it was still reliant on imports which came mainly from Iran. Pretoria's fear was that the British, under international pressure, and conscious that oil was being sent to Rhodesia via South Africa, might extend the sanctions to the Republic. Although Rhodesia's consumption of oil was only 7 per cent of South Africa's and therefore relatively easy to disguise, at first the government was cautious. The Secretary of Commerce told the oil companies that they should send only 'traditional' supplies, but as it became clear that British supervision was slack extra oil began to flow. At first it was private gifts of individual tankers but soon an elaborate system was developed under the cloak of a South African based firm, Freight Services Ltd. Oil was landed at Lourenco Marques and despatched into South Africa. Shortly after crossing the border it was turned back and consigned to Rhodesia as though it had originated in South Africa, but by mid 1966 even that charade was dropped. In 1967 10,796 railway tank cars were sent directly to Rhodesia in a trade that involved six major oil companies – Shell, BP, Mobil, Caltex, Sonarep and Total. Although sanctions were plainly undermined, the British, anxious to avoid a confrontation, averted their gaze.[46] The Johannesburg *Financial Mail* commented: 'There can be no greater blessing for South Africa – apart from the fact that Iran is well disposed – than that the oil business is still largely in the hands of international companies with no discernible leanings of excessive patriotism.'[47]

In the early years of UDI there was relative harmony between Pretoria and Salisbury as they combined against sanctions and black guerrillas. In the early 1970s signs of tension began to appear as the regional situation changed. If London found Smith a slippery opponent, Pretoria found him an obstinate ally. The most obvious clash came in 1973 when Smith, without consulting or informing Pretoria, closed the Zambian border in an attempt to counter Zambian support for guerrilla fighters. Although Vorster avoided public criticism, the closure, which endangered Pretoria's efforts to improve its links with black Africa and 'railway diplomacy', led to a clash in which Smith was forced to revoke his original decision. That demonstration of Pretoria's strength was further inducement for London to avoid a confrontation, and to hope that South Africa would help to pressure Smith into a settlement. The British hopes were false. Pretoria served as communication channel and favoured Anglo-Rhodesian negotiations (such as Smith's meetings with Wilson in 1966 and 1968, and the 1971 negotiation with the Conservative Government) but it did not play a direct part in the discussions and was not willing at that stage to force Smith's hand. The government was eager to find a Rhodesian settlement but within its own terms and not by exposing itself to 'right-wing' taunts that it was dancing to Britain's tune. In public Vorster said: 'I am neither prepared to twist Mr Smith's arm nor prepared to dictate to him', for to do so would be interference in Rhodesia's affairs.[48] In private he was tougher. He told Smith that despite criticism by 'wild boys of the right', he was determined to ensure a stable region. To achieve that settlements would have to be found in South West Africa and Rhodesia, and he added that 'Rhodesia could turn out to be the Achilles' heel of Southern Africa.'[49] For his part Smith later explained that he kept personal contacts with the South African Prime Ministers to a minimum to avoid exposing them.[50] For a time South Africa seemed to be enjoying the best of all worlds – proving sanctions ineffective (and profiting from it); underlining her regional leadership by playing a 'middleman' role; and fighting alongside the Rhodesians in a guerrilla war which they appeared to be winning.

THE GUERRILLA THREAT

In response to the guerrilla threat a white security group emerged comprising South Africa, Rhodesia and Portugal. South Africa had the greatest resources but was not dominant in the sense that the Portuguese in Mozambique, and even the Rhodesians (despite relying on South Africa for supplies and sanctions breaking) were determined to fight their own wars. The South Africans saw relatively little direct combat. Yet in Pretoria's eyes the guerrillas in Namibia, Mozambique and Rhodesia were directly linked to the communist-inspired assault in which South Africa was the final objective. Vorster declared: 'I know of no terrorism in southern Africa which, in the final analysis, is not directed against South Africa . . . The ultimate aim of all terrorists is to take South Africa away from us.'[51] He vowed that those who sought to attack the Republic would be hunted anywhere. The government did not underestimate the task ahead. In 1970 Mr P. C. Pelser, the Minister of Justice, said that there was a pool of 38,000–42,000 trained guerrillas in Zambia and Tanzania with more in the pipeline. To counter the threat a new Terrorism Act was passed (1967) and although expenditure on the armed forces did not rise sharply it increased steadily as they were trained and equipped for guerrilla warfare. Yet, as in the early 1960s, warnings of danger were matched by confident claims of Pretoria's ability to meet them. In 1966 P. W. Botha said the guerrillas 'are underestimating our determination and our military power; such attempts can only lead to the death of these people'. He warned those who gave help that although South Africa wanted peace, the price 'will be too high if it has to be maintained at the expense of our self-respect and freedom'.[52]

Military co-operation with Rhodesia started early in 1966 following an announcement by Oliver Tambo, President of the exiled ANC, and James Chikerema, Vice President of ZAPU, that their parties had formed a military alliance to march into Rhodesia 'as comrades-in-arms on a common route, each bound to its destination . . . [determined] to fight the common enemy to the finish'.[53] Initially it was planned that some ANC groups led by ZAPU guides would penetrate into South Africa while others would fight alongside ZAPU in Rhodesia. Pretoria responded immediately by offering paramilitary police to Rhodesia, police not troops being used to avoid the accusation of waging war in a foreign territory.[54] According to Smith, Vorster said that he wanted to counter the threat as far away as possible and the Zambezi was a better defensive line than the Limpopo. There were doubts among the Rhodesian military about accepting the offer because the South Africans were inexperienced in guerrilla warfare, but Smith readily agreed because of the political advantages. In response to international criticism Vorster said: 'We sent our policemen to Rhodesia to fight terrorists who were destined for South Africa. This action has nothing to do with the Rhodesian issue – all we are doing is pulling our own chestnuts out of the fire.'[55] In the years which followed, the size of the South African force steadily increased so that by 1974 it was estimated at more than 2,000. The bulk continued to be policemen, but military units were gradually moved north, including aircraft and helicopters, while training (including pilot training) was provided for Rhodesians in the Republic. Later some Rhodesians viewed the South African involvement as a mixed blessing because it gave Pretoria a lever to exert influence and they believed it 'was more use to South Africa than Rhodesia in that South Africa used Rhodesia as a training ground'.[56]

Between 1965 and 1974–5 the Rhodesian war fell roughly into three phases.[57] The first lasted until 1968. Initially few guerrillas entered the country and most who did were arrested. The earliest clashes (later mythologised as 'Chimurenga Day') came in 1966 when small ZANU bands fought government forces in encounters in which most of the guerrillas were killed or captured. However, the main fighting in this early phase came between August 1967 and July 1968 when three separate ZAPU/ANC units (each about 100 strong) penetrated from Zambia into the Wankie area. They failed to gain local support and suffered heavily in set piece engagements with Rhodesian and South

African forces. At the time ZAPU/ANC claimed success, but it was clear that they had been defeated as their nationalist rivals were quick to point out. A PAC pamphlet *Wankie Fiasco in Retrospect* stated: 'You cannot hope to gobble up a regular army all at once in a conventional war . . . It is unacceptable in theory and practice.' A ZANU newspaper criticised the ANC's involvement, saying that instead of fighting in Zimbabwe it should extend the enemy by fighting in South Africa. Yet ZANU and the PAC had little to boast about themselves. The PAC, riven by internal disputes, was so ineffective that in 1968 the OAU threatened to withdraw support unless it became active. It tried but failed. In co-operation with Coremo guerrillas, who were fighting the Portuguese, a PAC group entered Mozambique intending to blow up the Beira oil pipeline and penetrate into South Africa. It achieved nothing for it was intercepted by Portuguese troops who killed or captured most of the guerrillas.[58]

In the second phase, between 1968 and 1972, there was little activity. Defeat had undermined the nationalists' morale and led to fierce internal disputes about the strategy and the effectiveness of the existing leadership. Even the occasional raid could lead to bitter recriminations, as in January 1970 when South African police drove off an attack by ZAPU guerrillas on Fort Victoria. The strategic dispute reflected different supporters. The USSR, which backed the ANC and ZAPU, offered a good supply of weapons and although they favoured infiltration to gain local support they also trained for conventional attacks. China, which backed ZANU and the PAC, offered poorer equipment and gave patchy support (depending on its own internal struggles) but it drew on its experience to emphasise the need to politicise the local people and merge with them. The main success of that approach came later, but meanwhile both ZAPU and ZANU were in such disarray that they mounted few operations and the ANC/ZAPU alliance fell into disuse.

1971 saw the peak of white Rhodesian hopes. The war was under control, the economy was thriving and constitutional proposals favourable to the whites were initialled with the British Conservative Government. However, to the disappointment of the governments in London, Salisbury and Pretoria the proposals were not implemented because the Pearce Commission (sent by Britain to investigate the views of all Rhodesians) found that while the whites supported the proposals the blacks did not. Alongside that failure was the renewal of guerrilla activity. ZANU began to penetrate through Mozambique, seeking to avoid direct clashes with the security forces and attack only after the local population had been politicised, thereby denying intelligence to the authorities. The signal for renewed activity was an assault on a white farm on 21 December 1972. This took the government by surprise and its intelligence failure was further exposed by the decision to close the Zambian border in the mistaken belief that President Kaunda would respond by restricting guerrilla activity from his country to leave the Rhodesians free to concentrate on the Mozambique frontier. Kaunda was furious and took no action against the guerrillas. Vorster was equally furious. Three weeks later, under pressure from Pretoria, Smith lifted the ban saying that he had received assurances from Zambia, but his bluff was called when Kaunda refused .o reopen the Zambian side. On the military front the Rhodesians launched a major operation (Hurricane) but there were no easy victories this time. The campaign was slow and bitter as the ZANU guerrillas struck in small groups, refusing to present themselves as targets, and merging into the people.

The Rhodesians and South Africans became increasingly concerned about the situation inside Mozambique. There was co-operation with the Portuguese, and in 1973 Vorster privately lamented that millions of Rand had been spent supporting them, but this was limited by the Portuguese determination to act independently despite the worries of her allies about her strength and her strategy. Even when the war had turned against Portugal and Rhodesian forces were operating regularly in its territory and all three governments were considering a 'Zambezi Defence Line' (which implied pulling out of northern Mozambique), the Portuguese continued to claim that all was well and that they had no intention of abandoning the struggle. After a meeting between Smith and Caetano, the Portuguese President, Caetano said: 'Our timorous neighbours were more concerned over the situation in Mozambique than the Portuguese themselves who are well used to such a state of affairs and perfectly capable of coping with it.'[59] When the Portuguese Foreign Minister (Dr Rui Patricio) visited South Africa in March 1973 he reaffirmed that Portugal was capable of continuing the war indefinitely and saw no need for a military alliance with Rhodesia and South Africa because 'we don't like unnecessary alliances'.[60] Despite such reassurances Pretoria was actively considering how it would respond to a black government in Mozambique, or perhaps a white settler UDI.

Despite the uncertainties among the white government the guerrillas had not scored a decisive military victory either in Rhodesia or Mozambique, and by the end of 1973 Smith's government believed that once more it had the situation in hand. It estimated that only 145 guerrillas were still operating inside the country and that during the campaign 179 had been killed for the loss of 44 members of the security forces and 12 white civilians. In July 1974 a security report (which noted the part played by South African forces in holding the largely inactive Zambian border as well as giving backing to 'Hurricane') claimed that 75 per cent of the guerrilla leaders had been killed and the calibre of replacements was poor.[61]

DIALOGUE

Alongside the search for security Pretoria sought status in Africa: to be recognised as a major sovereign continental power. 'It is essential', said Vorster in 1969, 'that all independent states should be regarded and be treated as fully autonomous and of equal worth.' Yet Pretoria anticipated more than formal equality. 'We as Whites in South Africa', Vorster continued, 'have a special duty towards the whole of Africa.' To fulfil that duty friendly relations had to be established with black states, and 'to the extent that we establish the right relations with Africa, to that extent will our problems diminish in other parts of the world'. Vorster added a note of confidence: 'We are the only White people that are of Africa. I make bold to say: no-one understands the soul of Africa better than we do.'[62] To those ends Pretoria pursued a policy of dialogue, entailing contacts across the continent in a two-way flow of communication, including exchange visits of officials and ministers. For Pretoria dialogue developed from the 'outward policy', but a new element was added by the initiatives taken by black states. It was an attempt by both sides to come to terms with the Republic's continental position. 'South Africa', said D. J. de Villiers, a government backbencher, 'is an indissoluble part of Africa', and not 'an untouchable island in the sea of nations of Africa.'[63]

Dialogue was prominent in the late 1960s and early 1970s. It was a product of Pretoria's confidence and an acceptance of her strength by some black governments. In September 1970 Muller told parliament that the international climate had taken a favourable turn. 'We have', he said, 'come a difficult and long way since Sharpeville, but we can look back with gratitude for we have made remarkable progress under difficult circumstances.'[64] Dialogue included conventional diplomacy by Foreign Affairs, unconventional initiatives by the Department of Information and BOSS, and Vorster's own efforts. The internal rivalries accompanying this led to different interpretations of events. An admirer of Vorster declared that: 'He is opening up windows to the world quite fearlessly',[65] whereas Eschel Rhoodie, Secretary of Information, said that Vorster had to be carried 'kicking and screaming into

Africa'. Despite the squabbling there was a general commitment to enhance the Republic's status.

Dialogue started in southern Africa where it met with a mixed response. In Malawi President Banda chose co-operation – establishing diplomatic relations (the only black state to do so); signing trade and labour agreements; accepting aid and loans; and exchanging state visits. He gave two explanations for this. First, that it was in Malawi's immediate material interests; and second, that contact was the way to influence Pretoria. He said: 'If ever we are going to settle the problem of black and white in this part of Africa we have to start talking to each other.' He recognised that this might not produce quick results, 'but I honestly and strongly believe that in the end it is the only solution to our problem'.[66] He criticised those black states which continually attacked South Africa, because their protests were ineffective and because many of them had secret contacts, and viewed his critics with 'utter contempt' for 'while they are criticising me for trading with South Africa openly they themselves are trading secretly'.[67]

Although Pretoria was pleased with success in Malawi, it was a small country seen as a stepping stone to greater things. Zambia was an obvious target. She was regarded by Pretoria as a natural part of southern Africa with whom good relations would reinforce the bloc and enhance its own status while a hostile Zambia was a threat. The relationship proved to be complex and tense. An early opportunity had been missed when, after independence in 1964, President Kaunda said that although he strongly opposed apartheid, he favoured peaceful relations with Pretoria and suggested exchanging diplomats. There was no response. Years later Vorster said that Kaunda's proposal had only been a public statement, 'Countries do not exchange diplomats from platforms', and he pointed to Kaunda's unacceptable conditions and his failure to follow the public statement with an official approach. 'It remained a platform speech only.'[68] However, that was a limp excuse in 1971 when Pretoria was on the diplomatic offensive, eager to gain recognition. Had Kaunda made his offer then instead of in the days of Verwoerdian orthodoxy Pretoria would have leapt at the opening, but it had passed.

Following UDI, the scene was set for constant tugging and pulling between Lusaka and Pretoria: Zambia frustrated at its dependence on the white south, Pretoria angry that Zambia was not more compliant. Yet links were never completely cut because contact had advantages for both sides and South Africa refused to apply economic sanctions both on grounds of principle and immediate interest. Instead she

144

adopted a 'stick and carrot' approach, regularly offering friendship but also threatening to strike if Zambia harboured enemies. In 1968 Muller said that Kaunda knew that Pretoria was prepared to co-operate: 'It is high time he realised that he is sounding a discordant note in southern Africa where good neighbourliness is being practised.'[69] In 1970 Vorster said that if guerrillas 'take to flight we shall chase them and we shall do so right into the countries from which they come'. He warned Kaunda that if he gave support we 'will hit him so hard that he will never forget it'.[70]

In 1971 the relationship became strained when Vorster accused Kaunda of double dealing. He told parliament that Kaunda, while publicly criticising South Africa and those who co-operated with her, had initiated secret contacts. According to Vorster these started in April 1968 when Kaunda sent an envoy to South Africa for information and to deliver a letter. Vorster said that he had responded to criticism in the letter by saying that he had only threatened to attack Zambia if it supported guerrilla fighters, and that South Africa was also seeking to achieve human dignity and equal rights for all its people through apartheid. Vorster added that it was in everybody's interests to co-operate and concluded that Zambia 'holds the key to extension of this co-operation to all countries in southern Africa'. According to Vorster, following this first contact correspondence and visits continued during which Kaunda renounced violence against South Africa; accepted that it was not a colonial situation; explained that much of his public criticism was to satisfy particular audiences; and agreed in principle to a personal meeting. But whenever arrangements were made for the meeting he backed out, and while these contacts were taking place he continued to criticise. Kaunda, said Vorster, was opposed to dialogue and yet started a dialogue; opposed to trade and yet continued to trade; and he accused Pretoria of planning to attack Zambia yet privately admitted there were no plans. Despite this, said Vorster, the offer of co-operation remained open because the interests of the people of southern Africa were more important than the personal relations of leaders.[71] In response the Zambian Government admitted that there had been contact, but said that while Vorster had sent four emissaries to see Kaunda, no envoy had been sent to Pretoria, and it was South Africa which took the initiative in seeking meetings.

The ambivalence of Zambia's behaviour is explained by the inherent tension in her position: economic dependence on white neighbours matched by hatred of apartheid; overtures from Pretoria matched by opposition to contact by fellow black states like Tanzania; and internal political and economic problems. The African context within which Zambia operated increased the tension. That was exemplified in a meeting of East and Central African states in 1969 which issued the Lusaka Manifesto. The Manifesto (which was endorsed by the OAU and the UN) emphasised equal rights and human dignity, it criticised the white governments because they perpetuated racist rule, it recognised that there was a place for whites but no place for racism, and it called for a commitment to change rather than immediate change. In combating racism it said it was better 'to talk rather than kill', and 'if peaceful progress to emancipation were possible . . . we would urge our brothers in the resistance movements to use peaceful methods of struggle'. But if those in power blocked peaceful progress 'we have no choice but to give to the people of those territories all the support [including force] of which we are capable in their struggle against their oppressors'.[72]

The Manifesto was open to different interpretations. At first Muller welcomed its realism, but his attitude changed as that of the black states hardened. Shortly after the Lusaka meeting the Foreign Ministers of the group (with Malawi absenting herself) decided that, despite the Manifesto's hope, peaceful progress was not possible because the white governments had closed the door on that option. The 1970 Khartoum OAU summit meeting accepted this advice and rejected dialogue unless the objective was to gain legitimate rights for the oppressed and unless the liberation movements were involved in the process.[73] The prevailing mood at that meeting was that white minority rule could only be overthrown by force. Muller therefore concluded that while at first he had welcomed the positive aspects of the Manifesto 'there are certain parts which cannot be reconciled with these positive aspects'.[74]

However, the Khartoum decision to support the armed struggle was no longer the only view among black states. Some who concluded that contact was preferable to confrontation were prepared to pursue dialogue. Muller claimed in 1969: 'We are in direct contact with considerably more African governments than I am in a position to disclose at the moment.'[75] Encouraged by France, these included several Francophone states. In January 1970 President Tsiranana of Malagasy announced that despite opposition to apartheid his country would establish trade and social relations with South Africa. As in Malawi's case, Pretoria cemented the link with material support. In November 1970 Malagasy was given a loan of R2.3m. for airport improvements and export credit facilities for the tourist industry. In the same month when Muller visited Malagasy to finalise the negotiations he declared: 'This is not the end. It is a beginning. It is a milestone which will be followed by others.'[76] In 1972 the Chairman of the Tea and Coffee Association revealed that political considerations had influenced the import quotas agreed by the government – coffee 25 per cent from Angola, 18 per cent from Malagasy; tea 7 per cent from Malawi, 11 per cent from Mauritius (which acted as a clearing house for South African exports to Africa).[77]

Dialogue gained international attention in November 1970 when President Houphouet-Boigny of the Ivory Coast declared in its favour. 'We will not', he said, 'achieve the solution to the problem of apartheid in South Africa by resorting to force of arms. We must open talks with this country.'[78] Potentially this was a major breakthrough. At a press conference in March 1971 Vorster offered 'to hold meetings with African leaders anywhere', and, in contrast with the past said he would welcome discussing government policy with them, for he knew he could persuade them that South Africa was advancing on the right lines. 'I see', he said, 'a breath of fresh air stirring.'[79] Connie Mulder went on a ten-nation African tour, preaching that the whites were also Africans and had to be seen in the context of 'Africa for the Africans'.[80] But Pretoria's new enthusiasm was not shared by all. Lesotho had a particular sense of grievance. A spokesman said that for three years his country had been criticised by other black states for favouring contact, but once dialogue started the South Africans 'forgot about Lesotho. They were going to the Ivory Coast and elsewhere.'[81]

For a time Houphouet-Boigny was the main advocate of dialogue and gained support from leading figures like President Senghor of Senegal. Boigny raised the issue at the 1971 OAU summit. 'For seven years', he said, 'we have had nothing but grand and violent speeches, with tragic and sometimes ridiculous results. We cannot make threats without the means to apply them.' He and his supporters argued that sanctions had failed in Rhodesia, that direct black military action was impracticable and that the guerrillas had had little success. 'What we appear to be doing so far', said President Busia of Ghana, 'is to send our African brothers to slaughter.'[82] The advocates of dialogue concluded that it was only through contact, through demonstrating black men's abilities and by promoting peaceful change that racial barriers would be broken. But they faced formidable opponents. Dr Arikpo, Nigeria's Foreign Minister, said that unless Pretoria offered political freedom 'she must not expect peace with the Africans', and President Nyerere declared: 'If the right of self-determination does not exist for the blacks of southern Africa it does not exist for Tanzania.'[83] When the OAU voted, the advocates of dialogue were defeated by twenty-eight votes to six, with five abstentions and two absentees. Those who favoured dialogue were Gabon, Ivory Coast, Lesotho, Madagascar, Malawi and Mauritius. The abstainers were Dahomey, Niger, Swaziland, Togo and Upper Volta. The Central African Republic and Uganda were absent. Following the OAU decision the East and Central African Summit adopted the Mogadishu Declaration which affirmed that force was the only choice left in dealing with the white governments.

At the time the OAU vote and the Mogadishu Declaration were not seen as major set-backs. What was surprising was not that the vote had been lost but that it had taken place, and that several states had either favoured dialogue or abstained. The supporters assumed that time was on their side. Houphouet-Boigny declared that he would carry on, and sent a delegation to South Africa in October 1971. The Ivory Coast's Ambassador told the General Assembly that many black states favoured dialogue. Such assumptions proved false. When in April 1972 Houphouet-Boigny and Leopold Senghor sought further support there was no consensus even at a meeting of Francophone states, and they decided not to push the matter further. Senghor concluded that African attitudes to South Africa were hardening.[84] No attempt was made to raise the issue at the 1972 OAU summit at Rabat which Houphouet-Boigny failed to attend. The momentum which had grown so quickly disappeared equally quickly.

In formal terms the outcome of dialogue was sparse. By 1974 diplomatic representation in Africa was confined to Malawi (Ambassador), Rhodesia (Accredited Diplomatic Representative), and Angola and Mozambique (Consul Generals). Pretoria emphasised that formal relations failed to reflect the range of contacts, and Muller told parliament that in 1973–4 there had been confidential communications with twelve African states.[85] Indeed contacts (including trade and landing rights) with states like the Ivory Coast and Gabon continued. Yet these were small rewards and not the acceptance that Pretoria sought from the policy. Failure to gain recognition revealed the limits of dialogue. By late 1972 the government was admitting set-backs. When interviewed, Vorster agreed that there had not been much progress and said: 'I don't think the climate is very amenable at the moment.'[86] A gloomy Muller told parliament that dialogue had not gone as well as he had hoped. The effort would continue, but no one should underestimate the 'long steep hills ahead'.[87] The Department of Information's effort also continued. In 1973 it embarked on 'Operation Wooden Shoe' to sustain diplomatic relations with Francophone West Africa and open up air routes. Out of this came a dramatic meeting in May 1974 when Vorster, accompanied by Van den Bergh, Rhoodie and Brand Fourie, met Presidents Senghor and Houphouet-Boigny in the Ivory Coast. There was a further meeting in the Ivory Coast in September 1974, and in February 1975 Vorster had talks with President Tolbert in Liberia at which the South African leader said he was willing to withdraw troops from Rhodesia as soon as violence ended, and would not oppose independence for Namibia. However, as with earlier efforts these initiatives failed to fulfil their promises. Two months after his meeting with Vorster, President Tolbert was killed in a plane crash. Although in September 1975 Muller was still claiming that other leaders would follow Houphouet-Boigny and Banda there was no general revision of black opinion.[88]

The failure of dialogue was in part the product of circumstances, including the fragility of black governments and their individual leaders. Dialogue was hardly in train when two of its main black advocates – Presidents Tsiranana of Malagasy and Busia of Ghana – were overthrown and replaced by governments which opposed contact. And there were doubts both in South Africa and black states about the implications of contact. Some South African ministers were sceptical, and even those in favour were cautious. In 1967 Muller said that diplomats would not be exchanged unless the black states proved their 'bona fides' by promoting friendly relations with the Republic and not interfering in internal affairs.[89] Among the white public there was such unease about the social and political implications that when press photographs showed Vorster entertaining black leaders as equals the government had to assure its followers that no policy change was implied. While, therefore, Pretoria reaffirmed its commitment to dialogue, there was uncertainty about the terms, and that led to hesitant responses to approaches from black states, lost opportunities and unrealistic demands that 'local custom' (apartheid) should not be criticised.

On their side black leaders had to balance the advantages of links with a rich and powerful state against fears of adverse reactions at home and abroad, uncertainty of the treatment of their representatives and opposition to the principle of apartheid. In the end it was on the rock of principle that dialogue foundered. For Pretoria dialogue was a means of confirming South Africa's position and an opportunity to gain acceptance for apartheid. Vorster explained that contact did not mean abandoning apartheid; indeed his message to black leaders was that it was the only way forward. He claimed that on their part there 'has been a clear acceptance that we are of Africa . . . We do not interfere, nor do we permit anyone to interfere in our affairs . . . We, just like the other African states, are seeking understanding and peace.'[90] Vorster was deceiving himself if he believed that the black leaders accepted that message in full. It was most vigorously rejected by the radicals but it was unacceptable even to those who favoured dialogue. There were differences among them (Busia said dialogue and armed pressure were not incompatible; Banda that armed struggle would cause suffering without results; Senghor that there should be parallel dialogue among South Africans) but none saw it as an acceptance of apartheid. They saw dialogue as a means to gain change, not an endorsement of the 'status quo'. When the Ivory Coast's Minister of Information visited South Africa in September 1975 he spoke of South African racism as a 'poison on this African land'.[91] No black state could accept apartheid. Whether militant or moderate, they saw that it compulsorily segregated people according to race, and then discriminated against those who were black. That was a divide of principle which made it impossible for them to accept South Africa on Pretoria's terms.[92]

9 THE INTERNATIONAL SETTING

South Africa's international setting remained a patchwork of co-operation and bitter hostility. In the clamour of criticism and calls for boycotts it was easy to assume a picture of almost uniform animosity. However, there were activities, especially those related to the economy, in which South Africa operated largely unimpeded by criticism and the hostile rhetoric sometimes masked co-operation. Because the power of the black states was limited by their resources and internal political problems, their criticism was often stronger than their action, and they opposed apartheid not only to attack Pretoria but also to rally domestic support and consolidate the ranks of the Third World. 'If apartheid had not existed we should have had to invent it', said an Indian diplomat.[1] Yet the opposition persisted because behind the rhetoric was sincere hatred of apartheid. Nobody supported it – the opposition ranging from Western diplomatic remonstrance to backing for the armed struggle from black and communist states. Pressure on Pretoria persisted and intensified from governments, international organizations and non-government groups – some aiming to promote reform, others to promote revolution.

Neither Pretoria nor its militant opponents were entirely happy about the way the international dispute developed. The militants found that the Western states became more willing to criticise apartheid but would not endanger their economic or strategic interests, and without their active support there was little threat to Pretoria. Further, the international mood had changed. The prevailing view of the early 1960s, that the revolution was at hand, had disintegrated – black nationalism had been countered in South Africa, economic sanctions had not forced a resolution in Rhodesia, and the guerrilla wars were stalemated. The revised assumption was that although radical change would come it was not imminent. But Pretoria was also frustrated. It had achieved a great deal – increasing its electoral support, crushing black nationalism, circumventing Rhodesian sanctions, creating Bantustans and an economic boom – and yet it had failed to rid itself of the stigma of racism or improve its international status. Its hopes of transforming the situation on the foundation of the outward policy and dialogue were dashed. Instead of sweeping aside its critics it found itself trapped in trench warfare of accusation and counter-accusation. In its frustration it talked of establishing a new international role, of turning its back on the West and adopting a non-aligned stance, or of building a southern hemisphere alliance, but these ideas led nowhere.

BLACK NATIONALISTS IN EXILE

In the set-backs of the early 1960s most black nationalist leaders had been imprisoned or had fled the country. The ANC's newspaper *Sechaba* admitted that the arrests at Rivonia had 'smashed the very heart of the organisation'.[2] Small-scale activity continued, but it often consisted of no more than distributing leaflets. While in 1963 courts in the Eastern Cape had heard 1,096 cases against people accused of ANC and PAC membership, by 1965 this had dropped to 82.[3] Yet the government did not relax its vigil, and continued to bring to trial or to ban without trial those it accused of party membership. It recognised that black nationalism had been scotched not killed and that the parties were rebuilding themselves in exile. When there were signs of renewed activity in the early 1970s Brigadier P. J. Venter, Chief of the Security Police, warned that the ANC was moving 'trained terrorists with forged passports' in and out of the country and organising 'a subtle and large scale brainwashing' of youths.[4]

The nationalists' aim remained to gain power by overthrowing the white government but, having lost their domestic base, the talk was no longer of a quick victory but of a long and difficult struggle. Both the ANC and the PAC created external organisations. The ANC had sent Oliver Tambo abroad as early as 1960 to organise its external wing and help the international boycott campaign. At first the PAC, assuming that the government would be toppled quickly, established itself across the border in Lesotho, and it was not until 1964 that they followed the ANC by opening offices in London, Cairo, Accra and Dar es Salaam. In exile the parties passed through several phases. At first they were small and rudimentary organisations to support the internal movements, but when these internal movements were destroyed the exiles had to take the lead: preparing for guerrilla war; raising funds;

acting as diplomats to governments and international organisations; supporting anti-apartheid groups; and organising what aid they could for beleaguered members inside the Republic. In these tasks they faced the characteristic problems of exiles – infiltration by government informers; low morale; poor communications; internal disputes; a growing gulf between leaders and followers as the leaders became international figures; the absence of secure bases; and broken promises of support from others. Both parties faced similar problems, but attempts at reconciliation failed. Gradually, however, the exiles established themselves, gaining recognition from international bodies, backing from Western anti-apartheid groups, and military support from black and communist states.

In the late 1960s the exiles took stock of their situation. The PAC, which under Potlake Leballo's leadership had a particularly turbulent history, decided at a meeting in 1967 that more support should be given to the guerrilla war and to activities inside 'Azania' (South Africa) instead of 'aimless international diplomacy'.[5] The ANC met in April 1969 at Morogoro in Tanzania where it discussed party organisation; the role of non Africans and especially communist party members; and the conduct of the guerrilla war. Those attending included representatives of the South African Indian Congress, the Coloured Peoples' Congress and the Communist Party. Although Oliver Tambo urged delegates to 'cast their eyes southwards, to prepare to go home',[6] most attention was given to the problems of exile. After acrimonious debates four broad decisions were made. The first reasserted nationalist aims, giving primacy to the liberation of the African majority for 'the enemy is as aware as we that the side that wins the allegiance of the people wins the struggle'.[7] The second ensured African control of the party executive because 'the largest and most oppressed group' must bear the main liberation role. Third, greater effort would be directed to fostering relations with communist and Afro-Asian states, the opponents of imperialism and supporters of the liberation struggle, and less to the 'incorrigible' West. Finally, although the revolutionary struggle was 'in its infancy' with 'a long hard road ahead', the party committed itself to the armed struggle and the mobilisation of the people for revolution. With this in mind there was support for alliances with ZAPU, FRELIMO, SWAPO and MPLA, but there was no mention of the PAC or ZANU.[8]

In their search for international support the exiles found a powerful platform at the UN. In 1969 the General Assembly recognised the 'legitimacy' of the struggle of the 'oppressed people' of South Africa for self-determination and majority rule, and declared the ANC and

PAC the 'authentic representatives' of the majority. That was reassuring but Oliver Tambo recognised in 1972: 'We shall need to pay a great deal more attention to, and be more deeply involved in guiding and providing information for, the offensive against South African racists . . . Already there is much cause for worry.' He mentioned Pretoria's success in Malawi, Malagasy and French speaking West Africa, but finished on a note of optimism, claiming that 'if the blood-suckers in our country appear to be winning one or two new black co-suckers', the global campaign against racism and imperialism is gaining momentum year by year.[9] Tambo's public optimism and international awareness were evident again when he spoke in London in June 1974. He claimed that the stalemate following the Rivonia arrests was over, and that the whites of southern Africa were increasingly isolated as profound changes were reshaping mankind's destiny. The resounding victories of the people of Indo-China had buried the myth of colonial and racial superiority. In the course of the struggle 'we have come to know that our enemy resides not only in South Africa, but also in London, in Paris, in Washington and elsewhere'.[10] However, what Tambo did not admit was that despite the international activity the nationalists were largely inactive within South Africa. However, the ANC leaders had already recognised that new voices were being raised inside the Republic, including Black Consciousness, and decided that they should explore possible links.

INTERNATIONAL ECONOMIC RELATIONS

Between the mid 1960s and 1970s South Africa enjoyed impressive economic growth. The 'Financial Mail' spoke of 'The Fabulous Years'.[11] In 1970 Dr Diederichs, the Minister of Finance, pronounced the economy 'strong and virile'. There was a downturn in the early 1970s, with balance of payments and inflationary problems, but a sharp increase in the gold price stimulated renewed growth in 1973 and 1974. Meanwhile the debate about the political implications of economic activity continued. Leading businessmen, notably Harry Oppenheimer of Anglo-American, argued that growth undermined apartheid because expansion increased demand for black labour, broke the job colour bar and diverted wealth to blacks. In contrast Joe Slovo, a white communist ANC member, claimed that 'South Africa's most dramatic period of economic advance between 1967 and 1976 was also a period during which more was done than at any time during our history to implement the worst features of apartheid.'[12] The ANC came to link apartheid with capitalism and imperialism as Alfred Nzo, the Secretary General, explained: 'South African racists who cling to apartheid are an integral and key part of the sinister plot of exploitation by the imperialists on an international scale.'[13] What was not in dispute was that economic growth and the high profits offered in South Africa increased international contacts and interests: drawing in Western investments, trade and technology; attracting multinational companies; and extending the Republic's exports and overseas investments. Recognising the political importance of economic contacts Muller declared: 'The failure of the international vendetta against South Africa and the incapacity of the extremists to persuade the United Nations to use economic sanctions and force, should largely be attributed to the fact that South Africa is one of the twelve greatest trading nations in the world.'[14] In 1972 Vorster stated that 'each trade agreement, each bank loan, each new investment is another brick in the wall of our continued existence'.[15]

The calls for economic sanctions were ineffective because those who advocated them had few links with the Republic, while those that had, opposed sanctions. Yet the government was not complacent. To counter the sanctions threat it set out to increase self-reliance and reduce the country's vulnerability. Through the Defence Amendment Act and the Foreign Affairs Special Account, trade and investments were promoted but international partners could be shielded from adverse publicity by suppressing information. Strategic materials, including oil, were stockpiled, and strategic industries were promoted, such as the Iron and Steel Corporation (ISCOR), SASOL the coal to oil plants and Armscor the arms manufacturing company. Oliver Tambo concluded that: 'This enormous expenditure on arms and other weapons of war is only possible because of the thousands of millions of imperialist investment in the economy.'[16]

The strongest economic links were in southern Africa (see chapter 8) and with the West. In the West the traditional links with Britain flourished, while trade with the US, West Germany and Japan expanded quickly. For example trade with Japan which had totalled about $180m. in 1967 had risen spectacularly to more than $1,000m. by 1973. Britain remained the chief investor (with an average of £50m. per annum of new investment) but the US and West German stake increased. The Germans were the most active, increasing their investment from R70m. in 1965 to more than R1,000m. in 1970, while American investment which was R459m. in 1959 had grown to R741m. by 1969.[17] However, not all economic relations were smooth. The battle over gold prices continued, but with a decline in the strength of the dollar and increased demand for gold following the 1973–4 oil crisis the South Africans emerged in a strong position. Gold remained the Republic's single most important export, and its position strengthened on the free market. In 1971 the gold price, which had been fixed at $35 an ounce for forty years, was allowed to find its own value. By June 1972 it had reached $60 and by the end of 1974 it stood at $198. In 1973 96 per cent of gold production, worth R1,750m., was exported. Alongside gold the production of other minerals also increased reinforcing South Africa's links with Western industries.

Pretoria responded energetically to changing economic circumstances and promoted new links. When Britain's entry into the European Community in 1973 endangered traditional trading patterns (especially agricultural products) the government negotiated access agreements to EC markets, and within the spirit of 'the outward policy' made vigorous attempts to break new ground in the southern hemisphere – stretching from Australia and New Zealand across the southern oceans to South America. In 1966, after visiting South America, Muller said 'We must regard these people as our neighbours', and in 1967 Diederichs spoke of building a Southern Oceans trading bloc with Australia, New Zealand and South America.[18] However, Pretoria's enthusiasm was not matched by the other governments, and after meeting a visiting group of South Americans Muller said that 'there is no need for any unnatural or hasty attempts to force the pace in our relations with each other'.[19] Little progress followed.

Despite its successes South Africa could not escape the vagaries of the international economy, and in her case problems were compounded by political factors. That was underlined by the oil crisis.[20] The crisis, which started in 1972–3 with a sharp increase in prices, deepened following the October 1973 Arab/Israeli war. The Arab states cut 20 per cent of their production, increased prices further, placed an embargo on 'unfriendly' states and supported an OAU call for a total embargo of the white 'racist regimes'. Although South Africa could meet many of her energy needs from her own coal and hydroelectrical supplies she had no natural oil. Before the crisis oil supplies had come from Iran (38 per cent), Saudi Arabia (24 per cent), the Gulf States (20 per cent), and Iraq (18 per cent), while SASOL produced 7 per cent. In 1973 oil accounted for only 25 per cent of total energy requirements but it represented more than 80 per cent of transport needs. There was, therefore, great concern. The government reduced consumption by raising the price of petrol, imposing speed limits, closing filling stations in the evenings and weekends and calling for restraint, but the solution came in a new agreement with Iran for increased supplies. While the cost of the agreement was high it

156

was more than offset by the increased price of South Africa's own minerals as traders turned to gold as insurance against fluctuating currencies, and Western industrialists, alerted by the oil crisis to the vulnerability of strategic materials, stocked minerals. In January 1974 the government was able to announce that petrol rationing would not be necessary.

Diederichs' 1974 New Year economic survey was optimistic. He based it on the previous year's growth – domestic product 6 per cent; gross national product 8 per cent; and manufacturing production 9 per cent. He said that it would be misleading to suggest that South Africa had not been affected by adverse international developments because trade and investment were so important to her economy, but four factors had helped to overcome the problems – the recognition that South Africa stood 'on the threshold of a new phase of prosperity'; her limited reliance on oil for energy needs; the favourable climate for her manufacturers and exporters; and finally increased international demand for her natural resources.[21]

RELATIONS WITH BRITAIN

An uneasy relationship developed with Britain with areas of dispute (such as the arms ban and Rhodesia) but also of co-operation (economic contacts and ties of kith and kin). Britain remained the most important source of immigrants – of the 417,422 who entered South Africa between 1964 and 1973, 168,770 (40 per cent) were from Britain.[22] The contacts bred mutual awareness which was reflected in media attention and conflicting passions of admiration and anger on both sides. In Britain links with South Africa were the subject of public debate and political divisions, but they were not an election issue because the general public did not share the activists' concern and because the parties were unsure how voters would divide on the issue. For example, in the months before the announcement of the British 1970 election the media and the political parties were absorbed in the controversy surrounding touring South African sports teams, but that did not become an election issue, nor did the Conservative Party's openly stated pledge to resume arms sales. However, as soon as the Conservatives were returned to office the arms sales controversy leapt into the headlines.

Arms sales was a long standing issue between London and Pretoria. When the Labour Party was returned to office in 1964 it decided to impose the UN voluntary embargo. Pretoria was furious but impotent. In 1967, with the renewed closure of the Suez Canal and the build up of the Soviet fleet in the Indian Ocean, the South African Government re-emphasised the need for Western protection of the Cape route. As Britain was reducing its global commitments Pretoria accepted an increased role under the Simonstown Agreement whereby the Chief of the South African navy took 'a greater responsibility for the Cape route in time of war'.[23] Having accepted the additional task the government sought arms to fulfil it. P. W. Botha visited France, Portugal, West Germany and Britain, saying that 'South Africa is prepared to buy her needs where she can get them and we are prepared to pay for them.'[24]

In turning again to Britain (among others) the government had been encouraged by the Labour Government's continued supply of replacement parts and ammunition for existing equipment, and it knew of Britain's economic difficulties. It therefore tempted London with an extensive arms 'shopping list', and with the prospect of support in seeking a Rhodesian settlement. Alongside those carrots were the sticks of threatened withdrawal from the Simonstown Agreement, reductions in British imports and the removal of other defence co-operation such as overfly rights. After a prolonged and bitter cabinet debate Harold Wilson announced that Britain's ban would stand. Vorster indignantly responded that now that South Africa knew where she stood she would look at the Simonstown Agreement. He denied that the ban would undermine the country's defences and added that 'we shall not forget those friends who supply us now or when the storm clouds have passed'. Vorster said that Wilson would be mistaken to 'believe that co-operation can be carried on one-sidedly and that contractual relations, and the moral obligations which flow from them can be conveniently forgotten'.[25] In contrast with the Labour Government the Conservatives made clear that they favoured arms sales for external defence because it would benefit the British economy, help to defend the Cape route and fulfil obligations under the Simonstown Agreement. Therefore after winning the 1970 election the Conservatives began discussion with Pretoria but were immediately attacked by anti-apartheid groups and the Labour Party at home, and by Commonwealth leaders at the Singapore Conference. Under this pressure the new government, although confirming its legal obligation, restricted sales to Lynx helicopters for use by frigates.

However, Pretoria continued to hope for further military ties not only with Britain but with the West in general. In 1972 it announced plans for an expansion of the Simonstown base to take up to fifty warships, including nuclear submarines, far beyond the needs of the

South African navy, and to make available to the West facilities at the Silvermine intelligence gathering centre. Later, in 1978, Vorster repeated the old South African view that NATO was leaving its flank open. He said: 'You also have to look at the South Atlantic region and even further to the Indian Ocean.'[26]

Meanwhile, Pretoria was wary of all British Governments (how could it be otherwise after Macmillan's visit?) but the differences over arms sales reinforced its preference for the Conservatives. Vorster said he had 'a very high regard' for Edward Heath the Conservative leader,[27] whereas B. J. Schoeman, the Minister of Transport, with reference to the Labour Party, spoke of 'the abhorrent policy of socialism in that country and its spineless handling of trade unions'.[28] On its side many members of the Labour Party were AAM supporters, and anti-apartheid resolutions were a regular feature of party conferences. Yet, while there were differences, a change of government in Britain brought a tilt in policy rather than a major change because leaders on both sides recognised the limits within which they operated. The domestic and international criticism of ties with Pretoria were matched by economic interests. F. H. Y. Bamford, President of the South Africa–Britain Trade Association, said that if concentration were placed on economics many difficulties would be removed. 'The special relationship is by no means just good business: it is also a very good insurance policy. While Britain from time to time may be thought to be inimical to South Africa because of other pressures exerted on her, she nonetheless remains an ally because of her interests here.'[29] Even when it was known that Pretoria was undermining Rhodesian sanctions George Brown, the Labour Foreign Secretary, confirmed that 'Britain cannot and will not contemplate an economic war with South Africa.'[30] Personal relations also modified differences. Dr Carl de Wet, the Ambassador in London, said he had good relations with Wilson who was 'never devious and reasonably open', whereas he never felt at ease with Heath who was remote.[31]

Among non-governmental groups in Britain some, like the United Kingdom South Africa Trade Association, worked discreetly to foster contacts, and businessmen and trade delegations made regular visits. Critics also visited South Africa, including a Trade Union Delegation in 1974 which investigated working conditions and after a 'blunt but courteous discussion' with Vorster issued a mild statement offering support for the development of black unions. Most publicity was gained by the anti-apartheid campaigners – with rallies in Trafalgar Square, demonstrations against sports teams and protests at company meetings. The most effective campaigns followed revelations in 'The

Guardian' of low wages and poor conditions among the black employees of some British firms in South Africa.[32] A chain reaction started,
which drew in politicians, churchmen, the media, anti-apartheid
groups and culminated in the establishment of a Commons Select
Committee to investigate the reports. In this case the Committee was
refused permission to visit the Republic because, as Muller explained,
while relations between the British Government and companies were
not Pretoria's concern it was its concern if investigations were conducted in the Republic. He asked whether the same interest was being
shown in the practices of British companies elsewhere in the world.
Earlier Muller had stated that the government, although against
'excessive and reckless action', favoured improvements in labour
practices, the welfare of employees and narrowing the black/white
wage gap.[33] The Westminster Committee adopted a similar approach
recommending that British companies in the Republic should be
subject to agreed standards of practice. Although the British Government refused to make this compulsory (because it would be difficult to
police and it preferred company co-operation) in 1974 it introduced a
voluntary Code of Practice which was the first attempt to use business
companies as a source of pressure for reform.[34]

RELATIONS WITH THE US

The US Government paid increased attention to South Africa
from the late 1960s. There were a number of reasons for this: political
concerns (such as the Rhodesia dispute); growing American economic
involvement (in such areas as car manufacturing, petroleum and
computers); and global strategic issues (the 1967 closure of the Suez
Canal, the Soviet fleet in the Indian Ocean, overfly rights to Indo-
China, the region's mineral wealth and the establishment of a satellite
tracking station in the Republic). Yet southern Africa remained low on
the foreign policy agenda. Successive administrations acted on the
premise that the region was neither of vital interest nor an issue of
East/West confrontation. With the exception of Rhodesia, it offered
relative stability and was best left undisturbed by ignoring anti-
apartheid calls for action. However diplomatic relations, which were
cool and tense, were further eroded by a number of disputes which
although small in themselves underlined differences in values and
perceptions. These included Pretoria's refusal to lift colour bars for
visiting black American seamen; its anger at mixed race drinks parties
at the US Embassy; US criticism of apartheid at international gatherings; and the US role in introducing the 1963 UN arms ban.

The shifts in US policy were more of emphasis than direction and reflected changes in international circumstances and the American administration rather than changes in South Africa. For Pretoria the plurality of the US decision making process was frustrating. That was illustrated when President Johnson came to power following the assassination of President Kennedy. Kennedy's administration, which had adopted a 'liberal' stance on Africa, was critical of Pretoria but had avoided involvement. Johnson's administration, although ensnared in Vietnam, pursued policies which in Pretoria's eyes were contradictory. On the one hand there was economic and technical co-operation – including nuclear power, the establishment of a satellite tracking station, and investments – on the other diplomatic relations remained so cool that on leaving Washington after six years as South Africa's Ambassador, Chris Naude complained that he had met neither Presidents Kennedy nor Johnson other than at large social functions. At the UN there was open hostility when Arthur Golberg was the US Ambassador.[35] In October 1966, for example, Golberg supported a resolution opposing South African control in Namibia and in 1967 he voted in the General Assembly for termination of the mandate and described the introduction of Bantustans in Namibia as 'piecemeal annexation'. However, when George Ball succeeded Golberg in 1968 he adopted a conciliatory approach, seeing virtue in the Bantustan policy and dismissing boycotts as ineffective.

When President Nixon assumed power in 1969 the State Department continued to criticise apartheid, and William Rogers, the Secretary of State, said that although ties would not be cut with the 'rich, troubled land', the US would maintain the arms embargo, seek human rights and oppose Pretoria's administration of Namibia. Muller responded by saying that South Africa was striving for human rights no less than the US, but rights were not confined to political rights and could not be achieved without law and order.[36] More reassuring for Pretoria was the position of Dr Henry Kissinger, the National Security Adviser, who requested a report on southern Africa from the National Security Council.[37] The report (Memo 39 of 1969) concluded that there were no US 'vital security issues' in the region but apartheid could not be ignored because of international concern. So far US policy had tried to balance economic and strategic interests by keeping a political distance from the white regimes and their repressive racial policies. However, as there were different views about how this was best achieved the memo started by identifying US objectives. These were: to minimise the likelihood of conflict, to counter USSR and Chinese influence, to moderate racial policies, to improve the US's posture on racial issues and to protect economic and strategic interests. The memo concluded that US policy makers shared a number of assumptions, including the belief that black nationalism had been contained, and that the US could best stimulate change by contact with both black and white states. Based on these objectives and assumptions the report offered five policy options, ranging from closer co-operation with the whites states to dissociation.

Kissinger recommended acceptance of the second option which favoured contact with black and white states to encourage moderation and inter-state co-operation and reduce cross border violence. The option assumed that as 'the whites are here to stay' constructive change can only come about through contact; that black political rights could not be gained by violence; that the liberation movements were incapable of a serious challenge to Pretoria; that violence would only produce chaos and opportunities for communists; and that all states would be ready to co-operate with the US.[38] President Nixon endorsed the policy in speeches to Congress in which he reaffirmed the arms embargo and opposition to apartheid, but opposed isolating Pretoria. He considered 'the maintenance of contact and communication essential if the United States is to exert a constructive influence on South Africa'. Nor would America condone violence whether to enforce submission of the majority or to effect social change. He spoke of a 'sober hope' that economic development would undermine apartheid and that American companies would play a reforming role within this. Future progress, he said, depended on the US making her views known, and communication between the races.[39]

This softer approach to Pretoria led to a less rigorous application of the arms embargo (for example, the sale of computers and aircraft); trade and investment were encouraged through Export–Import Bank guarantees; the ban on imported Rhodesian chrome was lifted; there were visits in both directions by politicians and military leaders; 'all white' parties were held again at the US Embassy; and there was less criticism at the UN. However, the State Department was still committed to challenging apartheid and identified four areas (petty apartheid; urban blacks; the courts; and the Bantustans) in which reform could be furthered by contact. It also hoped that Bantustans, which had been set up to perpetuate apartheid, could be used to undermine it. It invited Buthelezi and Matanzima to the US, and in 1972 sent a team to explore the implications of investment in the territories.[40]

US policy was not without its internal critics. Following a visit to South Africa Charles Diggs, chairman of the House sub-committee on Africa, criticised US companies for 'forced labour situations which protect their huge margins of profit', and suggested an economic boycott. Anti-apartheid groups such as the American Committee on Africa tried to keep politicians informed of 'the course of the struggle for majority rule', and criticised the government for failing to understand that dialogue between the races was impossible under existing legal and constitutional structures.[41] A few labour unions took a stand. For example, mineworkers picketed the import of South African coal and sought an injunction against importing goods produced by 'indentured labour under penal sanctions'.[42] However, southern Africa did not feature prominently in domestic American politics.

In Pretoria the advent of the Nixon administration had been welcomed. The Department of Information was particularly enthusiastic. In May 1971 Mulder, after meeting Vice President Spiro Agnew, spoke of negotiating an agreement for American warships to use South African ports, and although nothing came of that Mulder kept up the contacts. In January 1974 on another US tour he met Vice President Ford, political leaders (including Ronald Reagan) and military officials. The department also promoted a range of other visitors, employed an American legal firm and public relations consultants, and in 1974 made $10m. available in an unsuccessful bid to buy the 'Washington Post' but it did acquire the 'Sacramento Union' through an agent.[43] Foreign Affairs characteristically gave a more cautious welcome to the warmer atmosphere. In May 1972 Muller told parliament that while the government was eager to promote good relations with the US there was a danger of falling victim to 'wishful thinking'. The Americans, he said, 'do not understand that we are a multi-racial country. They therefore do not accept the right to a separate nationhood of the Whites in South Africa, nor for that matter, of the Black nations', and they fail to appreciate that separate development offered 'human dignity' and 'national independence'. The Americans recognised that changes were taking place but they always pressed for more and 'the dividing line between persuasion and interference can be very flimsy'.[44] Despite such doubts there was deep concern when President Nixon fell from power in 1974. Vorster confessed that he had found it difficult to sleep after hearing the news. Nixon, he said, had rendered unquestionable service to the international community and with his resignation 'the curtain has fallen on one of the greatest tragedies of our time'.[45]

INTERNATIONAL SPORT

Controversy over sports links had started in the late 1950s and has continued ever since. The challenge to Pretoria's sports policies came from four main sources – anti-apartheid groups, international sports bodies, black states and non-racial sports groups at home, notably the South African Non-Racial Olympic Committee (SANROC). From early days South Africa was suspended from some organisations including the Federation of International Football Associations in 1961. Pretoria's response at that time was uncompromising. It reasserted apartheid principles, stating in 1962 that policy was based on the custom that 'Whites and Non-Whites should organise their sporting activities separately; there should be no inter-racial competitions; and the mixing of races in sports teams within the Republic and abroad should be avoided.'[46] That failed to halt the criticism and pressure mounted as anti-apartheid groups discovered that sports boycotts were among the most visible and effective protests against Pretoria and the white society. The campaigners gained public attention by exploiting the prominence of sportsmen, and increasingly they used pressure on sportsmen as a means of exerting pressure on Western governments.

Although these governments protested that sport was a private activity outside their responsibility, they soon discovered the high price of retaining links with South Africa and became increasingly reluctant to pay it. The scale and intensity of demonstrations against touring teams was illustrated by the 1971 Springbok rugby tour of Australia. Major clashes between the police and demonstrators led to more than 500 arrests. In Queensland a state of emergency was declared and trades unions called a 24 hour strike of over 100,000 workers. The tour was completed, but the Australians 'had seen their sporting arenas resembling military fortifications, guarded by miles of barbed wire and hundreds of police'. The total police bill was estimated by R1,600,000m.[47] There were similar disturbances during rugby tours of New Zealand and Britain, and while (as in Australia) opinion polls usually showed majorities in favour of sporting links with South Africa, the protesters were so effective that governments and sports bodies became reluctant to face the controversy, the disorder and the financial and political costs involved. In Australia, for example, the Cricket Board decided to cancel the 1971-2 South African visit because of the bitterness it would cause, the cost of policing and the pressures on the players.[48]

South African exiles played prominent parts in the campaigns.

SANROC, which had its origins in South Africa, became effective internationally when its chief organiser, Dennis Brutus, was forced into exile in London. Yet the exiles were few in number and they would have made little impact without the substantial sympathy and support they found. Peter Hain confessed that he was astonished at the size and persistence of support he found in Britain for campaigns against sporting links.[49] In the broader international setting the anti-apartheid groups and the black governments worked together. The groups provided information which the governments used at international gatherings to sponsor resolutions which usually were carried because the commitment of the black states to break links (sometimes for domestic reasons as well as international solidarity) was greater than that of the Western states to retain them. The anti-apartheid groups, armed with the legitimacy given by the resolutions, could then pressure governments and sporting authorities to comply. The case of Robin Jackman, the English cricketer, illustrates this. Jackman, who was called up as a replacement during a tour of the West Indies in 1981, was on a UN 'black list' of those who had played in South Africa which had been drawn up by SANROC and legitimised by the UN Special Committee on Apartheid. Anti-apartheid activists called on the West Indian authorities to ban Jackman, and when he joined the party in Guyana the government immediately announced its compliance with the UN resolution. The game in Guyana was cancelled and it was only after considerable uncertainty that the remainder of the tour was completed.

Those involved in the sports boycotts had different perceptions – governments from sporting bodies, sportsmen from officials and Western states from black states. Usually Western sporting bodies broke contact under protest, and when they did interpreted their action in narrow terms – to remove racism within the sport so that links could be restored – whereas for anti-apartheid groups the sports campaign was part of the drive against apartheid. The broader interpretation steadily gained ground during the 1970s. In 1981 when it was proposed to readmit South Africa to Test Match cricket because of improved integration in that sport, Father Trevor Huddleston, President of the AAM, wrote that South Africa 'must show the world that apartheid itself has been totally abolished in every sphere of life . . . Until such actions are taken South Africa must expect sport to be used as a political weapon.'[50] The campaign's effectiveness varied according to the influence of the black states. In rugby, for example, although demonstrators succeeded in preventing Springbok tours abroad, black states played little part in the game's organisation and rugby teams continued to visit the Republic. In contrast, in football and cricket in which black states played a prominent part, it became increasingly difficult for South Africa to retain links. From a combination of conviction and expediency the drift was to extend the bans.

Inside South Africa there was confusion and dispute both within and between the government and sporting bodies. That revealed itself in the D'Oliveira affair, which gained more attention than previous cases and spelt the end of South Africa's participation in international cricket. Basil D'Oliveira, a gifted Coloured cricketer, moved to England in 1960 because he could not play first class cricket in his own country. This dignified, apolitical man became the centre of controversy when the English team was selected to tour South Africa in 1968–9. D'Oliveira, who had played for England, was a strong candidate but was not chosen. There was an immediate outcry in which, fairly or unfairly, the English selectors were accused of fearing a confrontation with Pretoria. Then a member of the original party dropped out and D'Oliveira was chosen to replace him. Vorster responded by announcing that the English team would not be welcome. He declared that the Republic was 'not prepared to receive a team thrust on us by people whose interests are not the game but to gain political objectives which they do not attempt to hide'. Vorster claimed that the team was not that of the English selectors but the 'choice of the Anti-Apartheid Movement'.[51]

Vorster's intransigence in the D'Oliveira case was a reflection of the government's problems at home in handling sports policy. Some of its followers pressed for compromise to regain international contacts but many others opposed change, and the breakaway HNP had made sports segregation one of its main planks. Vorster was determined to avoid further splits. In the early months of 1970 when the government was fighting an election sporting blows rained on it from abroad – massive demonstrations in Britain and Ireland against the rugby team, a cricket tour to England cancelled, exclusion from the Davis Cup after refusing entry to the black American tennis star Arthur Ashe and finally exclusion from the Olympics. Conscious of 'right-wing' reactions Vorster declared that he would not bow to external pressure and would follow his predecessors' policies. Yet despite such assurances the government did move, but always too little and too late to gain international acceptance. It failed to find enough flexibility within an apartheid structure to satisfy external critics without breaking the principles on which that structure was built or losing the support of its followers. The changes it was prepared to make could never therefore satisfy the critics.

Each sport had its own story, but Pretoria's vain attempts to find a way between the Scylla of 'verkrampte' intransigence and the Charybdis of anti-apartheid criticism, can be traced in efforts to gain entry to the Olympic Games. In 1964, after prolonged negotiations, the Republic was banned from the Tokyo Olympics. The Olympic Committee (IOC) decided that a compromise proposed by the South African Olympic Committee – to send a mixed race team but to hold separate trials and make separate travel arrangements – contravened Olympic rules against racial discrimination. The government then announced that in any case it opposed sending a mixed race team. However, before the Mexico Olympics of 1968 its position changed. In April 1967 Vorster, following the straight and narrow road of Verwoerdian orthodoxy in relation to domestic sport, said that 'no mixed sport between whites and non-whites will be practised locally irrespective of the standards of proficiency of the participants', and even spectators would not be allowed to mix. However it was different when he turned to international sport. He accepted that for the Olympics, although the home trials would be separate, South Africa would be represented by a mixed race team travelling together, wearing the same uniform and selected by a mixed race committee.[52] Later in the year, based on these suggestions, a visiting IOC commission recommended re-entry, and much to the delight of whites and some black athletes a majority of IOC members supported the recommendation in a postal ballot. The joy soon turned to bitter resentment. Under the threat of a boycott by African, Asian and communist states, and of violent demonstrations against the South Africans, the IOC reversed its decision. Avery Bundage, the IOC President, explained: 'We thought the safety of the South African team and the success of the games was in grave doubt.' Vorster angrily retorted that if matters were arranged in this way 'it is not necessary for us to hold the Olympic Games; we should arrange tree climbing events for we are in the jungle'.[53]

Despite such disappointments government policy continued to change, although always within an apartheid framework. In 1971, reflecting the new face of apartheid, Vorster introduced the concept of 'multinational' as distinct from 'racial' sport, and then distinguished 'open' international events in which more than two countries were involved (such as the Olympics), and those with only two competing countries (such as cricket). He announced that mixed race teams would be tolerated in 'open' events but not others. In 1974 Dr P. G. J. Koornhof, the Minister of Sport, emphasised the advantages of 'sport with an individual national context', which recognised the national identity and gave individuals 'untrammelled opportunities' to climb to the top of their sport. He spoke of 300 years of separate development in sport and added: 'In a nutshell the policy of the Nationalist Government is one of multinational development, that each nation administers its sport separately at club, provincial and national levels.'[54] Pretoria also took initiatives to counter boycotts. In 1973, following a further Olympic rejection, it decided to organise the South African Games with wide international participation, but the games only served to show the gulf between the Republic and the rest of the sporting world. Most striking was the provision of separate white and black games with the black games a poor relation. New Zealand sent a team and some foreign individuals competed in the white games, but other sporting partners like Britain and Australia did not and the West German and Netherlands teams were withdrawn at the last minute.

THE UNITED NATIONS

As the sports campaigns illustrated, militant opponents continued to use international organisations to mobilise opposition against Pretoria. At the UN this became institutionalised with the establishment of the Special Committee on Apartheid in 1962 and the Unit on Apartheid in 1966. Reactions were predictable. Vorster declared: 'We do not consider ourselves bound by law created by Afro-Asians at will.'[55] In contrast the back states were inclined to believe that a General Assembly resolution created an obligation to act, whereas the Western powers and even the USSR were more circumspect. In 1964 the Special Committee on Apartheid failed to recruit to its ranks any permanent members of the Security Council or major trading nations.[56] In 1969, during an unsuccessful attempt to oust South Africa from the UN Conference on Trade and Development (UNCTAD), the US delegate, supported by the USSR, pointed to legal difficulties, but the militants accused him of bringing in 'logic and law' to confuse the committee who 'are going to do the right thing, whether it is legal or not'.[57]

There was a continuing debate in Pretoria about the pros and cons of UN membership. When the Republic was on the diplomatic offensive, seeking dialogue in Africa, the advantages were clear. In 1968 Muller explained that although the government was concerned at aspects of UN behaviour it recognised the organisation's importance and was no longer content simply to defend a position but would assert itself.[58] In the following year he described the UN as 'the best, the largest international forum where we can state our case in a positive and businesslike way', as the place 'where contacts can be made', and access gained to specialist agencies such as the World Bank and the International Atomic Energy Agency. He concluded that 'as long as we regard it in our interests, and as long as South Africa's honour is not impugned, we shall remain in the United Nations and co-operate'.[59] Yet frustrations also surfaced. Speaking in London in 1969 on his way home from a bruising UN session, Muller described the organisation as 'a mirror of the growing international disorder. Designed to uphold the rule of law and to advance a sense of order, it is itself in danger of becoming one of the agents of discord and strife.' Turning to Namibia he accused the UN of having no interest in the welfare of its people but simply of pursuing a vendetta and making 'its own laws as it goes along'. He wondered what strange perversity led people to concentrate on this while all around were 'threats to public order and peace itself'.[60]

In the early 1970s UN pressures intensified, and apartheid captured much of the General Assembly's attention. In 1972, nineteen of the fifty-one sessions of the Special Political Committee were devoted to it, and an increasing number of anti-apartheid resolutions were accepted without opposition. There were constant calls for sanctions, boycotts and the release of political prisoners. South Africa's credentials were challenged but were not immediately rejected by the necessary two-thirds majority and she continued to participate. However, in 1973 they were rejected and, although the Assembly's President still allowed the South Africans to speak, that changed in the following year when a new President ruled against South African participation. Incensed by this Pretoria withdrew its Ambassador ('Pik' Botha) and withheld part of its UN contributions. Yet, although Vorster had said that if the right to participate in the Assembly were denied the only option would be withdrawal 'for the sake of our self-respect',[61] and although in September 1974 Muller admitted that the picture was 'not rosy or encouraging',[62] membership was retained. Muller told parliament that the situation was under review but 'we want to stay in the organisation as long as it is practically possible', and explained that although it was not impossible to exercise full membership it would be a completely different situation if South Africa withdrew of its own volition.[63]

Several factors explain Pretoria's decision. First, there was more rhetoric than substance in UN criticism. Although the Republic suffered humiliation and frustration, the hostile verbal seeds often fell on stony ground. U Thant wrote in 1970 'with heavy heart' of the UN's ineffectiveness in eliminating apartheid – that 'continuing

169

affront to human dignity'. 'What is needed', he said, 'is the political will on the part of the member states to take effective measures which would induce South Africa to renounce its policies.'[64] Despite the General Assembly attacks and calls for boycotts and embargoes, a solid block of trading partners stood firm against economic sanctions and they included three permanent members of the Security Council whose approval was required for mandatory action.[65] The lack of action brought home the limitations of the moral crusade. Opposition to apartheid had been institutionalised, pressure maintained on the West, Pretoria isolated ideologically, but this fell short of the aims of militant critics who were reminded again that states, including those within their own ranks, were not prepared to act against their perceived interests. The second group of factors which persuaded Pretoria to retain membership lay in the UN itself. On the positive side Western states, defending the principle of universality, ensured that the Republic continued to participate in Security Council business. Therefore, while at home the government tarred the UN with a single brush, within the organisation itself it worked hard to retain Security Council links. It also participated in UN informal activities – explaining policies, retaining contacts with both friends and foes and using it as a listening post. On the negative side, a voluntary withdrawal would have given opponents an opportunity to challenge South Africa's sovereign status and perhaps fill her place with the ANC as a government in exile. Finally Pretoria was conscious that Namibia was under constant UN scrutiny.

NAMIBIA/SOUTH WEST AFRICA

Although South Africa was firmly in control of Namibia (still known as South West Africa in the Republic) the territory remained a focus for diplomatic and legal activity. Although, as previously noted (chapter 5), an immediate danger disappeared in 1966 when the International Court rejected the case brought by Ethiopia and Liberia, controversy continued. In 1968 the General Assembly declared that SWAPO guerrillas could not be tried under South African law because her writ did not run in Namibia, and that claim was advanced as a defence at a trial in the Republic. The court rejected it, convicted the guerrillas and sent them to prison.[66] The Security Council then condemned South Africa's defiance, and in 1969, with Britain and France abstaining, endorsed the Assembly's 1966 resolution calling on South Africa to withdraw and spoke of 'effective steps' if she did not comply, but the threats had no substance because the Western powers continued to oppose the use of economic sanctions or force. In 1970 the dispute returned to the International Court when the Security Council sought an advisory finding on Pretoria's defiance of yet another resolution declaring her occupation illegal (276 of 1970). As in the past, South Africa put up a vigorous defence and claimed title to the territory by right of conquest, by continuation of the sacred trust agreed in 1920, by long occupation and, most important, by the consent of the people who recognised the benefits of Pretoria's rule. Pretoria offered a referendum to test this but the UN refused. In June 1971 the Court found by thirteen votes to two that South Africa's presence was illegal and she should withdraw. Vorster rejected the finding, saying that the Court had been packed with opponents and the majority opinion was 'the result of political manoeuvring instead of objective jurisprudence'. It was South Africa's duty, he said, to promote the well being and progress of the people, and that duty would be carried out 'with a view to self-determination for all the population groups'.[67]

Despite rejecting the Court's findings the government still claimed that it sought an international agreement, and when the Security Council asked Dr Kurt Waldheim, the new Secretary General, to renew efforts to secure Namibia's independence, Pretoria agreed to co-operate. Waldheim visited Namibia in 1972 and had extensive talks with ministers and officials. He left saying that he favoured further discussions but recognised that disagreements remained over the interpretation of self-determination and independence; for while the UN favoured a single territory, Pretoria supported separate population groups. Contact continued through Waldheim's representative, Dr A. M. Escher, but like Waldheim he failed to break the impasse. The reality was that for all the UN resolutions, all the investigations and legal opinions, the situation had not changed. Pretoria controlled the territory and her power was not seriously challenged. While Vorster told Waldheim that he would co-operate in seeking eventual independence for Namibia, he also told parliament that the groups within the territory would have choice – whether they wanted a confederation, or a unitary state, or to opt out – and that South Africa would ensure how the choice was exercised.[68]

PART IV

REGIONAL UPHEAVAL AND SOWETO: 1974–1978

10 THE WATERSHED YEARS IN SOUTHERN AFRICA

COLLAPSE OF PORTUGUESE COLONIALISM

On the morning of 25 April 1974, as white South Africans were listening to the results of their general election, news came of a military coup in Lisbon. This dramatic event, completely unexpected by Pretoria, set in train developments which were to change the face of southern Africa and lead to the collapse of colonial and white domination of the subcontinent, except in South Africa itself and Namibia.

The guerrilla wars in Angola, Mozambique and Guinea Bissau had become increasingly costly for Portugal in human and material terms, and internationally had linked her with South Africa and Rhodesia in an 'unholy alliance' to halt the tide of black nationalism. However, the liberation movements were nowhere near achieving military victory against the Portuguese forces. It appeared that a stalemate had been reached with little chance of Portugal being displaced in the foreseeable future. That was the view not only in Pretoria but in most Western capitals, and yet there were indications in the early 1970s that the Portuguese commitment was weakening. Although the liberation movements had not gained military dominance, insurgency was spreading and threatening the security of Portuguese officials and civilians. The military effort needed to counter this had placed great pressures on Portugal, where by 1970 almost 40 per cent of the annual budget was being devoted to the military with 150,000 troops serving in the African territories and a death toll by 1972 of over 13,000 servicemen.[1]

As the old certainties of President Salazar's days disappeared and discontent grew with the emergence of left-wing groups, large scale emigration, sabotage incidents and dissatisfaction in the armed forces, the maintenance of colonial control was challenged. There was official talk of finding arrangements to give the territories more autonomy, which culminated in the publication of 'Portugal and the Future' by a leading military figure, General Antonio de Spinola, in which he maintained that a military solution in the colonies was impossible and argued for self-determination in a federal framework.[2] Spinola's views aroused widespread expectations of reform, but, while he went further than the government, he was not as radical as the younger military officers who organised the bloodless coup of 25 April. Nevertheless Spinola was appointed President of the new Junta of National Salvation. Although within three months he had abandoned his federalist approach and accepted the right of the African territories to full independence, Spinola was losing control not only of the younger left-wing officers but also of events in Mozambique where the avowedly Marxist FRELIMO was preparing to take over power, and in Angola where his efforts to form a provisional government from the three major liberation movements (FNLA, MPLA and UNITA) failed as the Moscow orientated MPLA gained control. In September Spinola resigned.

SOUTH AFRICA EXPOSED

Within a few months the political and security situation in southern Africa had thus changed fundamentally and the outlook for Pretoria had become threatening. The perception that regional stability could be maintained by the common interests and military strength of the white regimes was shattered. This forced a rethink of policy in Western capitals. In Washington, fear of growing Soviet influence led to an American involvement in the region, while in London there was recognition of the need for new initiatives to resolve the Rhodesian issue. But it was Pretoria that faced the immediate challenge on its borders. While the government had come to terms with the independence of small black states such as Malawi and the BLS states, the prospect of imminent independence for big and strategically important territories like Angola and Mozambique posed new problems. Political movements were coming into power which were ideologically hostile, which had succeeded through an armed struggle backed by communist powers, and which now posed security and political threats. Northern Namibia was open to penetration by SWAPO guerrillas from Angola and in the east the long Mozambique border was vulnerable to ANC and PAC penetration, both directly and via Rhodesia where the white regime was now in great danger. Among black South Africans, both at home and in exile, the common perception was that success had come from armed struggle. If force had triumphed against the Portuguese, could it not triumph against Pretoria?

The government now focused more sharply on regional problems. It had to deal directly with revolutionary black governments with no barrier between itself and the tide of political change which had moved through Africa and which had become more violent and revolutionary in southern Africa. The changes which followed the Portuguese coup also regenerated international interest in the region, and Pretoria would now be judged by the way it dealt with its immediate neighbours as well as by its internal policies. In these circumstances the government paid less attention to a policy of dialogue with countries further north in which it had tried to leapfrog the immediate unresolved problems of southern Africa. Now at short notice it had to fashion a new regional policy which would protect its political, security and economic interests.

IMPLICATIONS OF THE ENERGY CRISIS

Coinciding with this radical regional change were wider external developments, including the Middle East War of October 1973 and the resulting oil crisis, leading to sharp increases in energy costs with profound effects on the world economy. Although South Africa, with its abundant coal resources and its oil-from-coal process, was dependent on imported oil for only about 25 per cent of its energy requirements, the economy was seriously affected. Higher costs of imports, including oil, foreign exchange problems, and inflation contributed to depress the economy. As always, the price of gold was crucial. In the early seventies the gold price rose substantially after the fixed dollar price had been abandoned in 1971. By 1974 gold rose to a high of $198 an ounce, which served to push up the growth rate of the economy to 8.3 per cent by that year. But then decline set in, and by 1976 gold had dropped to $103 an ounce, with a growth rate of only 2.9 per cent in 1975, 1.3 per cent in 1976 and zero in 1977.[3] The downturn in the economies of the industrialised countries also served to reduce South Africa's earnings from its other mineral exports, further depressing the economy in the mid 1970s. In addition, South Africa faced an Arab oil embargo imposed in late 1973. However, although uncertainties remained, the supply of crude oil continued to be assured, particularly from Iran. It has been estimated that after the 1973 OPEC embargo until the overthrow of the Shah in 1979, almost 90 per cent of South Africa's oil imports originated in Iran.[4]

South Africa's established economic links with Iran developed strongly from 1974 as Iran continued to supply oil and South Africa in return sold iron ore, steel, cement, maize, sugar and other agricultural products. In mid 1974 an agreement was reached on co-operation in

177

the fields of nuclear energy, petroleum, mining and trade. This led in 1975 to the inclusion of coal and notably uranium in the list of South African exports, and to a tripartite agreement (South Africa, Iran and France) to build an oil refinery in South Africa. The Shah even suggested that a 'commonwealth' of non-communist nations bordering the Indian Ocean should be formed and should eventually include South Africa. This burgeoning special relationship, welcomed by Pretoria, which would have included growing military exchange, foundered with South Africa's domestic upheaval of 1976–7 and died with the Iranian revolution of 1979.

The effects of the energy crisis were more critical for the smaller economy of Rhodesia. In spite of sanctions, the Rhodesian economy reached a high point of growth in 1973–4. But the energy crisis and world recession did to the Rhodesian economy what sanctions had failed to do. Rhodesia was already paying a premium for oil; now the cost rocketed, while the world recession reduced Rhodesia's earnings from its exports, creating an acute foreign exchange problem. The energy crisis also had the indirect effect of alerting the West to potential threats to the availability of minerals from southern Africa. The Byrd Amendment in 1971 had exempted chrome and other 'strategic and critical materials' from the American ban on Rhodesian imports, but there were concerted efforts in 1973 and 1974 to persuade Congress to repeal the Amendment, to place the US 'on the right side' in southern Africa. The Assistant Secretary of State for African Affairs, Donald Easum, stated in December 1974 that it was 'a psychologically important moment . . . to return the United States to full compliance with UN resolutions, to encourage continued progress toward a peaceful solution in Rhodesia, and to help ensure long-range availability of Rhodesian minerals'.[5] Although the Byrd Amendment was not repealed until March 1977, the trend was now away from the argument that mineral supplies would be best assured by giving tacit support to white Rhodesia and, by implication, to South Africa.

Coinciding with the downturn in Rhodesia's economy was the prospect of a hostile FRELIMO regime in Mozambique. With the long common border (over 1,200 km.) and infiltration already taking place into north-east Rhodesia, it became clear in 1974 that Mozambique's independence would expose Rhodesia's eastern flank to even greater infiltration. Coupled with this expanded security threat was the threat to Rhodesia's access to the sea through the Mozambique ports of Beira and Lourenco Marques (Maputo). The outlook for Ian Smith's government was thus decisively changed for the worse by the combination of adverse developments. Although the Rhodesian Government was not under immediate threat, the deterioration in its prospects was bound to affect attitudes in Pretoria, Smith's last remaining friend, on whom he was now more than ever dependent.

MOZAMBIQUE

The immediate question for Vorster was how to react to the uncertain situation in Mozambique. The initial policy of the new Portuguese government under Spinola for a referendum or an election, in which all political movements would take part, was unacceptable to FRELIMO which demanded that independence first be guaranteed and that, as the only recognised and legitimate liberation movement, it already represented the people and was entitled to assume power. After fruitless attempts to negotiate an agreement on a more widely representative interim government, Portugal gave way. A FRELIMO-dominated transitional government was established in September 1974 with full independence promised for June 1975.

Meanwhile the economic and security situation within Mozambique had deteriorated, with smaller political groups attempting to oppose FRELIMO. No effective authority was being exercised by the Portuguese, disorder was spreading and anarchy threatened. Resistance came, in particular, from the white community and culminated in an abortive coup in Lourenco Marques in September by the white-dominated Movement for a Free Mozambique. Eighty-six people (twenty-seven of them whites) died in a week of violence in the city, and shops and homes were wrecked and looted.[6] Following the coup's failure and the establishment of the transitional government, a large-scale exodus of whites began. Some went back to Portugal, some to Rhodesia and many to South Africa.

The events in Mozambique had a traumatic impact on South Africans. Lourenco Marques and other coastal resorts had for many years been a playground for white holiday-makers. Businessmen were heavily involved in trade and investment, and the port of Lourenco Marques was important for the industries of the Witwatersrand and the agricultural producers and mines of the Eastern and Northern Transvaal. Contract workers from Mozambique, numbering approximately 120,000 in 1974, were employed in gold and other mines. The giant hydroelectric project at Cabora Bassa on the Zambezi River was nearing completion and its viability was based on Pretoria's agreement to purchase all the power generated in its initial years of operation. Despite these links and the country's geographical proxi-

179

mity, South Africans' knowledge of Mozambique beyond Lourenco Marques and the nearby coastal areas was limited and there was little contact with the people, black or white. Compared with the interchange with white Rhodesians, the difference was pronounced; most South Africans felt no common interest or common destiny with the Portuguese and their 'foreign' customs, language, religion and less rigid racial attitudes.

Yet the Portuguese presence had served as a barrier between white South Africa and the harsher political realities of Africa. Now the barrier was gone, disorder was evident, whites were fleeing and black nationalism – combined with Marxism and a menacing Soviet influence – was encroaching on South Africa's borders. The result was white apprehension and a negative reaction to the new rulers of Mozambique, previously regarded simply as 'terrorists'. Among many black South Africans there was a contrary reaction – equally disturbing for Pretoria – in which the overthrow of the Portuguese and the taking of power by FRELIMO were perceived as signs that the political liberation of South Africa itself was drawing closer. Given the limits on free expression, this black reaction was muted but it emerged publicly in a few pro-FRELIMO rallies by young blacks, in statements by community leaders, in comments in the press and in the adoption of the word 'viva' and even the phrase 'a luta continua' into black liberation slogans. Now, for the first time in sub-Saharan Africa, there was an example of liberation through the armed struggle. Black expectations included an assumption that an independent Mozambique, led by a new hero, Samora Machel, would aid their own liberation, at least by giving support and sanctuary to the ANC.

The security threat was to become a crucial factor for Vorster's government in future relations with Mozambique. Another, of more immediate concern, was the increased threat to Rhodesia, including its two best rail and road routes to the ports at Beira and Lourenco Marques, which carried 80 per cent of the country's exports. Initially the hostile rhetoric of FRELIMO strengthened the belief that an independent Mozambique would adopt a confrontational policy towards its white-ruled neighbours. However, after September 1974 the rhetoric of the transitional government was tempered by a recognition of the realities of its situation, particularly in regard to economic factors, such as the income from the use of the ports and the export of labour. Vorster responded positively, if cautiously. He made it clear that his government was willing to co-operate with the new state. 'Whoever takes over in Mozambique has a tough task ahead of him. It will require exceptional leadership. They have my sympathy and I wish them well.'[7] Vorster also stated that he was not concerned about the type of government which would be established, but only that it should be a good and stable one. He maintained that, while South Africa would defend itself if necessary, it would not interfere in Mozambique's internal affairs, and he stressed the importance of economic co-operation and the existing mutually beneficial links.

However, behind Vorster's confident 'cool statesmanship'[8] was an implied concern and even a veiled threat of a tougher reaction if there should be interference by Mozambique in South Africa's internal affairs. In view of the white perception of threat from a FRELIMO-controlled Mozambique, it was not surprising that there were policy differences within the government. P. W. Botha and the military establishment were sceptical of the co-operative approach advocated by Hilgard Muller and adopted by Vorster.[9] An alternative option would have been to use military and economic strength to try to prevent FRELIMO from becoming established in power and thus reduce the potential threat. There were later reports of pressure to support the white-led coup in Lourenco Marques in September 1974, and even that forces had been prepared for this purpose on the Transvaal border, without Vorster's knowledge. The action was only prevented by the discovery of the plan by van den Bergh who informed Vorster.[10] The policy of non-intervention was thus maintained, for the time being. Attempts to recruit mercenaries and to organise opposition to FRELIMO within South Africa among local Portuguese were stopped by the authorities.[11]

THE *DETENTE* POLICY AND RHODESIA

Pretoria's post-April 1974 policy towards Mozambique surprised and impressed outside governments, not least in southern Africa, and it formed the basis of a wider regional initiative which became known as *détente*. This policy differed from dialogue in two important respects: it was directed at more specific policy goals, and it was confined to southern Africa. *Détente* only survived for a little over a year, but it was a major effort by Vorster to pre-empt outside involvement in an unstable southern Africa and to avoid consequences 'too ghastly to contemplate' if negotiations on a settlement in Rhodesia failed.[12]

From President Kaunda's point of view the dire consequences of escalating confrontation were clear. Zambia was already burdened with adverse economic developments: the closure of the border with Rhodesia (since January 1973), which prevented the use of Zambia's most accessible port at Beira; severe disruptions of the Benguela Railroad; increased energy costs; and falling copper prices. In addition, Zambia was host to the two rival Zimbabwean nationalist movements and SWAPO. Apart from constantly having to intervene in factional squabbles within and between these movements, Kaunda was faced with an increasing number of armed men in Zambia who were not under his control, and with the threat of Rhodesian retaliatory strikes. He had previously also allowed FRELIMO to use Zambia, and he could now justifiably claim that his country had borne more than its share of the liberation struggles. The expectation of many blacks after the Portuguese collapse, that the neighbouring black states would simply proceed to step up support for the armed struggle in Rhodesia, was therefore premature. While these states wished to see the demise of the Smith regime, their ability to help the nationalists was limited by their own internal weaknesses. Assistance could only be given at great cost to themselves, and confrontation with Rhodesia raised the threat of a greater economic or military confrontation with South Africa which Zambia and Mozambique could ill afford. Encouraged by Vorster's initial non-confrontational response to change in Mozambique, Kaunda had every reason to seek an accommodation with Pretoria on Rhodesia, despite the acrimonious break-down in earlier attempts to establish contacts. The two leaders now had a mutual interest in achieving a settlement, and each let the other know through private links (including businessmen Tiny Rowland and Dr Marquard De Villiers of Lonrho) of his willingness to promote negotiations. Early in October 1974 official, but still secret, discussions began when Mark Chona, Kaunda's senior foreign affairs adviser, met in Pretoria with Vorster and Brand Fourie, the highly experienced diplomat and Secretary of Foreign Affairs who played a vital role in the ensuing *détente* negotiations. Further secret meetings were held in Lusaka and Pretoria, and van den Bergh was also involved as Vorster's envoy.

Kaunda's first concern was to persuade Vorster to agree in principle to withdraw the South African police from Rhodesia which would prove Vorster's commitment to a settlement and make it politically easier for Kaunda to work with him. Vorster required in return an assurance that South African 'terrorists' would not be allowed to move through Rhodesia from Zambia. It was agreed that to these ends a ceasefire between Smith's government and the Zimbabwean nationalists was needed. The aim would then be to move to negotiations on a new political structure for Rhodesia, requiring the release of political detainees and the unbanning of nationalist organisations. Kaunda's task was to obtain the co-operation of the nationalist leaders, Vorster's

182

to persuade or pressure Smith to play his part. The understanding between Kaunda and Vorster was that the negotiations would not be on the basis of immediate majority rule but rather of a five-year transition period.[13]

The first public disclosure of a new mood in southern Africa came in Vorster's address to the Senate on 23 October 1974 – a keynote speech on *détente*. 'Southern Africa', he said, 'is at the crossroads and should choose now between peace and escalating violence', adding that the cost of confrontation would be 'too high for southern Africa to pay'. He maintained that Rhodesia was the key to peace and argued that 'now is the time for all who have influence to bring it to bear on all parties concerned to find a durable, just and honourable solution'.[14] The timing and content of the speech were co-ordinated with Kaunda who three days later called it 'the voice of reason for which Africa and the rest of the world have waited for many years'. If Pretoria was ready to follow the way of peace, he said, then Africa would help.[15] The stage had thus been set, but the principal actors on each side of the Rhodesian drama still had to be persuaded to participate in what Mr Smith was subsequently to dismiss as the *détente* 'exercise'.

There followed for Vorster and Kaunda months of frustrating bargaining and cajoling. Although both sides were gradually dragged to direct negotiations, it became clear that neither Smith's government nor the nationalists, particularly ZANU, were enthusiastic about the envisaged settlement or even the ceasefire. Kaunda was faced with nationalist rivalry, not only between ZAPU and ZANU, but within ZANU which was undergoing leadership struggles both in its military wing, ZANLA, and its central organisation where Robert Mugabe was wresting the leadership from The Revd Ndabaningi Sithole. The divisions seriously complicated efforts to mould a unified front, especially as Kaunda and his fellow Presidents, Nyerere of Tanzania and Machel of Mozambique, were unaware of the ZANU power shift. Mugabe, who was suspicious of Vorster, antagonistic to Smith and unimpressed by Kaunda, was not committed to the *détente* proposals and had no serious interest in the negotiations. Later he said: 'We had decided to accept *détente* purely as a tactic to buy the time we needed to organise and intensify the armed struggle', and he maintained that the other black Rhodesian leaders were being led into a 'sell out'.[16] Following pressure from Kaunda, Nyerere and Machel, a united nationalist front was formed – which included ZANU, ZAPU, the internally based ANC (led by Bishop Abel Muzorewa) and Frolizi (a small group based in Lusaka) – under the umbrella of the ANC with Muzorewa as chairman. However, it made little impact as the separate movements continued on their own ways with ZANU in particular building up its strength in Mozambique.

Vorster's task was in a sense easier because he only had to deal with Smith's government and because he had strong cards to play in 'persuading' the Rhodesians to co-operate. Vorster, who had some doubts about Smith's political leadership, used economic and security pressures. Yet he had to tread warily. There was scepticism about *détente* among his own military advisers, including P. W. Botha, and there was still great sympathy for the Rhodesians among white South Africans, which Smith exploited. The latter said for instance, that 'appeasement is anathema to us' and that the Rhodesian war was to protect not only his country's frontiers, but also 'our kind of civilisation in the whole of southern Africa'.[17] In public, therefore, Vorster always maintained that he had advised but not pressured the Rhodesians, a view that was not shared by Smith who resented Vorster's *détente* policy which he saw a major shift from 'holding the line' with Rhodesia to accommodation of black Africa. Vorster, however, was determined to go ahead. In November 1974, while trying to convince Smith of the need to come to terms with the nationalists, he expressed confidence in gaining a regional agreement and said that in six months' time many would be surprised at South Africa's diplomatic position.[18] In December, when Smith was proving intransigent, Vorster spoke of the alternative to *détente* being 'too ghastly to contemplate', and at this stage he asked Smith to release the imprisoned black nationalist leaders so that they could participate in political activities, to agree to a cease-fire and to attend a constitutional conference. Smith was appalled. In his view he was being asked to release terrorists, but when Hilgard Muller personally came to Salisbury to discuss the situation Smith gave way without threats having to be made. Later Smith explained that he appreciated Pretoria's powerful position and did not want to alienate South Africa because it would have been against Rhodesia's interests to let the relationship deteriorate.[19]

An equally unpopular step among white Rhodesians was the phased withdrawal of South African police which went ahead although the cease-fire, of which it was to form a part, was never fully implemented. Smith saw this as a further breach of the previous undertaking that South Africa and Rhodesia would stand together against terrorism.[20] The consternation among Rhodesian whites was reflected by the Rhodesian 'Sunday Mail', which said 'Rhodesia is the first line against terrorism aimed at southern Africa, and the ultimate target is South Africa. It must be fought and defeated wherever it raises its ugly, murderous head, and we believe the majority of white

South Africans will be at least concerned, if not shocked, by the pull-out.'[21] For Vorster, however, the police withdrawal had more diplomatic than military significance. It was part of his search for a negotiated settlement, and South Africa continued to give support to Rhodesia with equipment and helicopter units which had greater military significance than the police.[22] Vorster's aim was not to cause the collapse of the Rhodesian whites, let alone to hand over power to radical black nationalists, but rather to negotiate a moderate, internationally acceptable government in which white Rhodesians would have a continuing part. Vorster and his advisers in Foreign Affairs and the Bureau for State Security believed that, as the UDI regime was no longer sustainable, South Africa's interests were best served by playing a role, and being *seen* to play a leading role, in establishing a moderate, black-led government.

Vorster's view that he was not abandoning Rhodesia but ensuring that it came to terms with its new situation, was not shared by Smith who believed that the military effort could be sustained and white rule maintained indefinitely. However, Vorster's determination appeared to bear fruit when Smith, albeit reluctantly, signed an agreement in Pretoria with Vorster and Mark Chona of Zambia which led to the Victoria Falls Conference in late August 1974. This was the dramatic culmination of *détente*. In a South African railway carriage, perched on the Victoria Falls bridge spanning the border between Zambia and Rhodesia, a Rhodesian delegation led by Smith tried to negotiate a settlement with the black nationalists. The attempt failed. Despite the presence of Vorster and Kaunda and all their efforts, no agreements were reached either between Smith and the nationalists or between the nationalists themselves. One potentially fatal flaw, even if agreement had been reached, was the absence of Mugabe who was in Mozambique, while the largely discredited Sithole led the ZANU delegation. However, even in Mugabe's absence there was no progress. Smith, who claimed that the nationalists failed to honour prior agreements and produced a 'bombshell' proposal for extended talks on different terms, also accused many of them of having consumed so much alcohol by the afternoon that they were incapable of negotiating.[23]

It can be argued that Vorster badly underestimated both the white Rhodesians' stubbornness and opposition to any form of majority rule, and the black nationalists' divisions and (particularly in ZANU's case) their unwillingness to compromise when they believed that they could achieve their ends through war. Yet it is equally clear that, given the constraints of Vorster's domestic circumstances and his personal views, *détente* was a bolder, better planned initiative than any previous regional policy pursued by Pretoria. It was taken in the confident mood of the early 1970s when both domestic and international pressures seemed ineffective. But now the government's fortunes began to decline as the impact of the Portuguese collapse made itself felt.

Détente did not die on the Victoria Falls bridge. The principal proponents, Vorster and Kaunda, both tried to keep it alive. But the momentum was lost, the façade of nationalist unity was broken, and Smith reverted to his defiant posture, dismissing the nationalist movements as ineffective and criticising interference from outside, including Pretoria. He nevertheless agreed to enter into negotiations with the ZAPU leader, Joshua Nkomo, who was the only nationalist leader to return to Rhodesia from Victoria Falls. The two sides were encouraged by Vorster and Kaunda, but their discussions in December and January 1976 came to nothing. Smith had advanced his position, under South African influence, to a form of 'power-sharing', with black/white parity of representation in parliament, while Nkomo was negotiating for majority rule, to which Smith remained adamantly opposed. At a meeting in Mozambique in early February Presidents Kaunda, Machel, Nyerere and Khama, leaders of what now became known as the Frontline States (FLS), concluded on the basis of advice from Nkomo that negotiations with Smith were unlikely to succeed and that there was no alternative now but to give full support to the armed struggle. Moreover, by this stage the focus of southern African attention had moved from Rhodesia to an even more critical and disruptive development, namely the civil war in Angola.

THE ANGOLAN WAR

Unlike Mozambique, there were three rival nationalist movements in Angola, each based in a different region of the country. General Spinola hoped to reach an agreement with all three and with the substantial local Portuguese community (numbering about 600,000), which would preserve close links with Portugal on a confederal basis. Angola was economically the most promising of Portugal's overseas territories, and its wealth of untapped mineral and agricultural resources made it potentially one of Africa's richest countries. These Portuguese hopes were not realised as a violent struggle for power developed.

Of the three liberation movements, the FNLA in the north, led by Holden Roberto, was the best trained and equipped, and it had the support of President Mobutu of Zaire plus assistance from the United

States and China. The MPLA, under the leadership of Augostinho Neto, drew support from the people in and around the capital, Luanda, and to the east among the Mbundu people, but it was less ethnically based than the other movements and, from its founding in 1956, it had attracted mestizos and intellectuals in Luanda. It was strongly supported by the Portuguese Communist Party (aligned with Moscow) and, after the exit of General Spinola, favoured by the new Portuguese rulers. Outside support, particularly with the supply of weapons, came from the Soviet Union, although this support had ceased prior to the Lisbon coup apparently because of Soviet frustration with the MPLA's factionalism and ineffectiveness. Aid was, however, resumed from about October 1974 and the contest for power developed.[24] The third movement, UNITA, was founded by Jonas Savimbi who broke away from the FNLA in 1964. It operated mainly in the south-east of Angola but it had considerable popular support among the largest tribal grouping, the Ovimbundu, who occupied the central highlands. Savimbi was also supported by many Portuguese whites because he argued – at least from 1974 – in favour of a mixed economy and stressed the need to keep the whites. On the other hand UNITA was ill-equipped, its forces were small, and it was receiving no significant outside assistance. It was favoured by Kenneth Kaunda and it was able to move across the border with Zambia. It also had links with some less militant African states, notably the Ivory Coast and Senegal, and sympathy from France. During the struggle against the Portuguese, and for a time after the Lisbon coup, UNITA assisted SWAPO in transit between Zambia and Namibia, although by the end of 1974 UNITA was distancing itself from SWAPO as Savimbi drew closer to Pretoria.[25]

Under pressure from the OAU and its Chairman, President Jomo Kenyatta of Kenya, the three nationalist leaders and Portugal signed the Alvor Agreement in January 1975. It recognised the three movements equally as 'the sole legitimate representatives of the people of Angola', set 11 November 1975 as independence day, and provided for an interim coalition government (including representatives of the three movements and Portugal) which would conduct elections prior to independence and begin forming a national army drawn from all three movements. But the Alvor Agreement failed. Fighting broke out between the FNLA and the MPLA and conditions deteriorated as most whites prepared to leave. A further agreement in June 1975, under Kenyatta's auspices, was also of no avail. No elections were held and the demoralised Portuguese authorities were unwilling or unable to do anything about the spreading civil war. On the eve of independence, 11 November, they simply sailed away, leaving the MPLA in control of Luanda and free to proclaim itself the government of the People's Republic of Angola.

However, the civil war continued, and what made it more serious in 1975–6 and reduced the chances of reconciliation and reconstruction was the involvement by outside powers, including both superpowers, Cuba and South Africa. There had been little, if any, superpower support for the movements in the months following the coup, although China, suspicious of MPLA ties with Moscow, gave aid to the FNLA in early 1974.[26] The US and the USSR at first supported the efforts of the OAU to find a 'democratic' solution involving all three movements, but by October 1974 the Soviet Union had re-started direct aid in weapons and funds to the MPLA to avoid 'being shut out politically after years of diplomatic and material involvement in the Angola cause'.[27] This aid proved to be crucial for the MPLA in securing its dominant position in Luanda, but it also provoked an American response. In January 1975 a covert US grant was made to the FNLA, but American support soon became widely known.[28] Fighting between the two movements in and around Luanda escalated, Soviet arms deliveries to the MPLA increased, and neither superpower used its influence to persuade its 'client' to observe the OAU-sponsored agreements.

Meanwhile UNITA, which was receiving no significant outside assistance, remained militarily weak, but it was found by an OAU Commission to have the greatest popular support in the country.[29] It had largely kept out of the fighting, placing its hopes in the proposed pre-independence elections. It was receiving political support from Kaunda who opposed the violence of the other two movements while he and President Mobutu of Zaire were also disturbed by the growing radicalisation of the liberation movements and specifically by the increasing involvement of the Soviet Union, to which Kaunda referred as 'a plundering tiger with its deadly cubs'.[30] Their practical concern was focused on the Benguela Railroad which carried their copper exports to the Angolan port of Lobito. As early as April 1975 Kaunda said that he was 'anxious to remove what he considered to be a tide sweeping the MPLA to victory', and later Henry Kissinger stated that Zambia and Zaire had turned to the United States to help prevent the Soviet Union becoming a dominant influence in the region.[31] Mobutu's support was mainly devoted to the FNLA,[32] but he also agreed to channel assistance to Savimbi through Zaire. Other African leaders, notably Presidents Houphouet-Boigny, Senghor and Nyerere were also concerned to prevent a Soviet-backed take-over by the

MPLA. The position of these African leaders significantly influenced Pretoria's approach to the Angolan War.

In the United States Angola was not an issue of public concern, but there was debate within the Ford Administration over whether to step up material help to the anti-MPLA forces.[33] The State Department's Bureau of African Affairs was opposed to greater involvement, arguing instead for diplomatic efforts in support of an African solution. Kissinger, on the other hand, saw Angola in global East/West terms, as a Soviet challenge to the United States which had to be stopped in the interest of *détente* between the superpowers: '[*Détente*] requires conscious restraint by both sides. If one side does not practise restraint, then the situation becomes inherently tense. We do not confuse the relaxation of tensions with permitting the Soviet Union to expand its sphere by military means. And that is the issue, for example, in Angola.'[34]

In June it was decided by the 'Forty Committee' of the National Security Council to provide military assistance to both the FNLA and UNITA.[35] The covert operation was conducted by the CIA operating from Kinshasa, Lusaka and Pretoria. Pretoria welcomed the American initiative which was fully in tune with Pretoria's own anti-communist thinking, and it served as another influence on the government's approach to Angola. The original American aim was to 'prop up' the FNLA and UNITA until independence and then to re-assess the situation.[36] In fact the operation continued into December, in spite of growing controversy in Washington, until the funds were cut off by Congress when it adopted the 'Clark Amendment' over Kissinger's strong opposition.

The third non-African country to become involved in Angola was Cuba, and it was the introduction of Cuban troops, combined with the supply of Soviet weapons, which decisively swung the war in the MPLA's favour by the end of 1975. The Cuban factor had a critical impact on Pretoria and remained a central issue in policy on both Angola and Namibia. While there was a close alignment of aims between the Soviet Union and Cuba, and while the Cubans could not operate in Angola without Soviet military co-operation and aid, Cuba to a great extent operated independently in its relations with the MPLA, emphasising always its role as a revolutionary Third World power. A pro-Cuban account maintains: 'Far from what has so often been said, it was an independent and sovereign act of Cuba. Only after the decision was made, and not before, was the Soviet Union informed.' But at the same time this account admits that 'Cuba was sure it could count on solidarity and material aid from the Soviet Union.'[37]

189

Cuba had been assisting the MPLA with military training since 1966, but it was not until May 1975 that Neto and the Cubans agreed that direct military assistance was urgently required.[38] However, apart from the presence of a few Cuban advisers by July,[39] no immediate action was taken as the Cubans were concerned about possible Portuguese reaction if they intervened before Angolan independence. Then, after appeals by the MPLA leadership, three Cuban troopships arrived in Luanda in early October carrying between 1,100 and 1,500 troops who set up four training camps for the MPLA army.[40] By this time the MPLA position had already improved in relation to the FNLA and UNITA with the help of Soviet weapons. Some observers were even saying by September that the MPLA had 'virtually won the civil war'.[41] However, it was during this period that the South African intervention began, in August 1975, injecting 'a new sense of urgency into Cuba's mission'.[42] The Cuban commitment was then rapidly and substantially increased.

SOUTH AFRICA'S ANGOLAN INTERVENTION

South Africa's intervention in Angola must be set in a context of the government's moves to promote *détente* through a Rhodesian settlement; its concern about relations with the West, especially the United States; and the continuing international dispute over Namibia. Before August 1975 South African military incursions into Angola from Namibia had been directed solely against SWAPO's presence in southern Angola. Condemned internationally and frowned upon by the Portuguese, these incursions were justified as pre-emptive or 'hot pursuit' raids of a defensive nature, but by 1975 the perceived security threat to Namibia was of growing concern, aggravated by increased SWAPO activity, and tension along the Angolan border with Ovamboland was heightened by incidents in July and August, including the assassination of the Ovambo Chief Minister, Filemon Elifas.

To assess the future prospects for Angola, Pretoria put out tentative feelers to the contending nationalist movements. For instance, in Europe in March 1975 an intelligence official met the UNITA leader, Jonas Savimbi, who soon afterwards appealed unsuccessfully for South African aid.[43] In May and July Daniel Chipenda, formerly a senior member of the MPLA, who had broken with Neto and joined forces with the FNLA, visited Windhoek and had secret talks with van den Bergh. Two months later he met P. W. Botha in Pretoria.[44] If Pretoria were to throw its weight behind one of the movements, the MPLA was excluded by its ideological commitment and links with the

Soviet Union, while the FNLA seemed the obvious choice in view of its anti-Soviet stance, its American backing and its support from Zaire. However UNITA, though militarily weak, had its main support in the south and could form a buffer between Namibia and a hostile Angolan government or, alternatively, cause trouble for South Africa by continuing to support SWAPO. UNITA's military weakness gave Pretoria an advantageous bargaining position and Savimbi was not slow in coming to South Africa for assistance when he realised how decisively the MPLA was being strengthened by Soviet aid.

Pretoria's initially cautious approach to the Angolan conflict was in part due to a concern (similar to that of the Cubans) not to offend Portugal and international opinion by interfering directly in what was still a Portuguese affair. South Africa's first step into the conflict in August was therefore taken simply to protect the joint Cunene River project at Calueque. Clashes between the MPLA and UNITA and harassment of workers at the dam site by the MPLA drew South African troops into Angola to occupy and defend the dam. Refugee camps were also set up inside Angola to control the flow of thousands of Portuguese and Angolans who were fleeing south to escape the conflict.

As the civil war moved to the south, with the MPLA dislodging UNITA from all the important coastal towns, Savimbi abandoned his conciliatory approach and on 21 August he issued a formal 'declaration of war' against the MPLA,[45] perhaps encouraged by the presence within Angola of South African forces. Although there is no evidence that Pretoria had specifically authorised the military to do more than protect the Cunene project and take necessary action against SWAPO, co-operation with UNITA and the FNLA was growing at this stage. The South African military agreed, for instance, to set up a training camp for UNITA and for Chipenda's section of the FNLA.[46] The South Africans were also encouraged because the Americans had at least decided to give UNITA material assistance, in addition to increased aid for the FNLA. South African intelligence services were in close contact with the CIA, whose covert operation began in earnest during August. Military equipment was flown to the two movements via Zaire and possibly via South Africa.[47] President Mobutu supported this operation. Kaunda was kept informed, although he may have believed that only funds to purchase weapons were involved and that American weapons would not be sent directly into Angola. He was in any case assured by the Americans that the aim of the operation was to promote a peaceful settlement between all three movements.[48]

This increased 'non-communist' activity was perceived by some elements in Pretoria as a legitimising factor for increased South African involvement. Vorster, however, was still reluctant to go beyond limited support to UNITA and the FNLA, plus co-operation with the CIA. Intense debate ensued within a restricted government circle while the Cabinet was not kept informed ot what was happening and was not involved in the decisions.[49] In June 1975 P. W. Botha presented to Vorster various options for further action in Angola, but no decision was taken for at least three months. Botha was in favour of South Africa playing an active role in Angola's future political course in order to counter the security threat and Soviet expansionism. The evidence of Soviet assistance to the MPLA and some Cuban support was used to bolster his argument and during the period of political indecision the military extended their operations far beyond the authorised defensive position on the Cunene near the border, on the basis of an instruction (agreed to by Vorster) that any attacker should be decisively driven off.

Hilgard Muller and Brand Fourie of Foreign Affairs favoured a 'hands off' approach, similar to that adopted towards Mozambique, but their voice in this case was less effective than that of Defence. The circumstances provided Botha with the opportunity to involve his department in foreign policy making, not simply in the military aspects, on the grounds that security considerations were paramount. Muller had to be content with sharing the foreign policy role, and in many of the decisions during the escalation of the Angolan intervention the Foreign Affairs Department had no say. Its 'religious adherence to the principle of non-interference in other countries' internal affairs was the very antithesis of the Defence Force's belief that South Africa should take a hand in shaping Angola's destiny'.[50] However, Foreign Affairs was not simply adhering blindly to a principle. It had practical reasons for caution, based on Pretoria's vulnerable international position, the confused situation in Angola and the lack of clear attainable political objectives which could be achieved by military intervention. These arguments served at least to delay Vorster's agreement to pursue a more active policy. For instance, he refused at first to respond positively to a personal appeal to intervene against the MPLA from Presidents Houphouet-Boigny and Senghor, partly because of opposition by Brand Fourie.[51]

However, it was probably van den Bergh's influence which contributed most to Vorster's hesitation. Van den Bergh was not opposed to *any* involvement in Angola against the MPLA, and BOSS was the main link with the CIA whose covert operation to aid the FNLA and UNITA it strongly supported. During this period BOSS co-operated closely with the CIA, whose agents in Pretoria felt that they had 'greater access [to BOSS representatives] than ever in agency history', although apparently they did not receive full information about South African activities in Angola.[52] (It subsequently emerged that CIA intelligence on Angola was inadequate and inaccurate,[53] which may help to explain South African miscalculations.) Van den Bergh was in favour of providing military hardware, logistic support and training to the anti-MPLA movements,[54] and of facilitating assistance from other countries, particularly the United States. Moreover, he wanted BOSS, rather than Military Intelligence or the Defence Force, to be the main instrument of South African involvement and influence. Van den Bergh was not therefore opposed to involvement in principle but was arguing for a clandestine operation, similar to the CIA's, rather than direct military intervention. His covert activities in support of the FNLA and UNITA in fact proceeded, escalating in step with the CIA's, but they did not prevent eventual direct military intervention.

The decision to become more deeply involved in Angola was taken by the beginning of October. Early that month South Africans helped UNITA forces to stop an MPLA advance on Nova Lisboa in central Angola, and then on 14 October a specially formed motorised strike force, code-named 'Zulu', entered Angola from Namibia. Led by South African officers and composed of Bushmen, an FNLA contingent loyal to Chipenda and a few Portuguese, the force was soon joined by South African armoured units. The combined column moved rapidly along the main road north-eastwards and then north up the coast towards Luanda, brushing aside MPLA resistance. UNITA forces and some FNLA units moved in behind the column which reached Lobito a few days before the independence date of 11 November. A further policy decision was now required of Vorster and his advisers: whether to continue the military operation or not. There is little doubt[55] that the decision to intervene directly in October included the compromise proviso (presumably to satisfy Vorster's more cautious advisers) that the military intervention would not continue once Angola was formally independent, whether or not a political settlement had been achieved. The intervention could thus be interpreted as a means of pressuring the MPLA to come to an agreement before independence. This did not happen. The MPLA leadership felt confident and strong, with increasing Cuban and Russian military assistance and with growing international political support, even though OAU support was still uncertain.

Having failed to achieve the political aim of limited military intervention, Vorster agreed to continue and even step up the operation, which meant that the MPLA's legitimacy as the government of Angola would not be recognised. The political aim remained the same, namely to enable UNITA and the FNLA to share in the government. Subsequent public statements, however, laid more emphasis on South Africa's own security concerns – Soviet and Cuban designs, threats to Namibia and to the Cunene River project – which were regarded as more defensible reasons for intervention.[56] In fact these concerns were the other side of the same coin, as it was the perceived security threats that dictated the need to prevent the MPLA taking sole power, or even to dislodge the MPLA altogether. The underlying, but unspoken, motive was thus to ensure a non-hostile, co-operative Angola, with Soviet influence eliminated, which would not threaten Pretoria's dominance in southern Africa, particularly in Namibia.

However, the government was still divided on the means of achieving this goal and even its feasibility. It thus lacked clarity of purpose as an uncertain Vorster decided to move into this more crucial phase of the Angolan venture. 'The very muddiness of South African policy on Angola is testimony that P. W. Botha alone did not have his way. The doves were able to confuse policy, and to them that represented a "victory" of sorts, given Defence's advantages.'[57] Yet Vorster was persuaded by events to back the military. First, the operation launched in October had been successful and the column had advanced further and more easily than expected.[58] Second, Jonas Savimbi appealed to Vorster to keep the South African forces in Angola at least until the OAU summit meeting could vote on Angola. Other African leaders supported this appeal,[59] which influenced Vorster, still in his *détente* mood. Third, Henry Kissinger and the CIA wanted to continue the battle, particularly as the MPLA now seemed militarily, and perhaps even politically, vulnerable. For the Americans, Pretoria's role was vital in keeping up the military pressure, and they made this known through CIA links.[60]

Success for the South African/UNITA/FNLA forces continued in November, particularly south of Luanda, but by the end of that month the tide was turning as Soviet weapons and an increasing number of Cuban troops told in the MPLA's favour. Early in November Castro committed many more Cubans, and an airlift of troops began (Operation Carlota), together with a Soviet airlift of weapons. By 11 November there were about 4,000 Cubans in Angola, rising to about 7,000 before the end of 1975 and to about 12,000 a month later.[61] Was the increased Cuban and Soviet commitment a response to Pretoria's intervention? Did the South Africans create, or at least aggravate, the threat which they aimed to prevent? There was undoubtedly some degree of cause and effect in these events, but South Africa was not the sole cause of the increased Cuban and Soviet commitment. The MPLA needed help against its opponents within Angola. 'It seems likely that the situation was more complex: that Moscow and Havana were already planning to give increased aid to the MPLA after 11 November, when the Luanda government could be given a measure of diplomatic recognition; the effect of the South African intervention was to lead them to step up their aid still more.'[62] Moscow could not afford the loss of prestige involved if Neto were to be abandoned in the face of American and South African pressure. The Russians and Cubans also realised that, with Pretoria now supporting the opposing side, they could increase their commitment to the MPLA without risking an overwhelming international reaction, especially from the rest of Africa. The political liability of having Pretoria as an ally was an important factor overlooked by Kissinger and the CIA and under-valued by the South Africans.

In December Vorster was again confronted with an agonising Angolan decision. The situation had changed drastically over the previous month. Although the South African/UNITA forces were less than 200 kms. south of Luanda, and had had successes in central Angola, their advance had been slowed by the Cuban-led MPLA resistance. In the north the FNLA had been pushed back in spite of American and some South African assistance. In addition, relations between UNITA and the FNLA were breaking down with actual fighting between UNITA units and the FNLA/Chipenda faction. Most important, there were no signs of increased Western or African support, but rather a shift in favour of the MPLA government. At the end of November Nigeria, which had only two weeks before denounced Soviet intervention, announced its recognition of the MPLA, giving Pretoria's intervention as the reason and alleging that there was an American–South African plot to destroy a 'sister African country'.[63] Several other African states followed suit. In these circumstances Savimbi attempted to distance his movement from South Africa, denying that he was receiving any significant assistance, criticising Pretoria's tactics and questioning the motives of Vorster's government in Angola.[64]

Then on 19 December came the decisive blow, when the American Senate voted by seventy-two to twenty-six to adopt the Clark Amendment prohibiting further aid to the Angolan opposition movements. The CIA's covert operation stopped. This caused deep resentment and a sense of betrayal in Pretoria and it led to Vorster's subsequent statement that the Americans would never be trusted again. The government was also faced with domestic political embarrassment, because full news of its military involvement in Angola, so long suppressed within South Africa, was now coming into the open. Nevertheless, in spite of these set-backs, the withdrawal was delayed, mainly because of a further appeal from Savimbi, supported by Kuanda. Savimbi met secretly with Vorster in Pretoria on 20 December and again in Windhoek early in January 1976. The special OAU summit (originally due to be held in December) was now scheduled for mid January and Vorster agreed that South African troops would remain in Angola until then. The Americans were pressing pro-Western African states to oppose recognition of the MPLA government, and there were hopes that a compromise calling for the withdrawal of all foreign forces could be reached. In the event the OAU meeting ended in deadlock, with twenty-two voting in favour of the recognition of the MPLA as the legitimate government and twenty-two against with two abstentions. But within two months most African states (forty-one out of forty-six) had granted recognition, Angola became a member of the OAU and UN and it joined the Southern African 'Frontline States'.

Within a few days of the OAU vote, senior South African officers told Savimbi, Roberto and Chipenda of the government's decision to withdraw. The Angolans protested that they would then be left with nothing other than 'bad names' from their association with Pretoria. The FNLA leaders – Chipenda in particular – were desperate, while Savimbi adopted a fatalistic attitude: 'If they want to leave us, they leave. If we have to die, let us die; this is our country; what can we do? We were not part of the arrangement when they came here, so we have no power to persuade them to stay. The one [presumably the US] who sent them in is sending them out, so we have to accept it.'[65]

The military withdrawal was completed early in March. Pretoria, politically humiliated by the failure of the Angolan intervention and embarrassed by having to disclose to its own people the extent of its secret involvement, was filled with resentment at what it regarded as Western betrayal. P. W. Botha told parliament that the intervention had been 'part of the involvement of the free world', but South Africa was 'not prepared to fight on behalf of the free world alone'. It would now, he said, 'defend with determination its own borders and those interests and borders we are responsible for'.[66]

NAMIBIA

While Vorster's *détente* policy in 1974–5 was primarily concerned with Rhodesia, he was aware that the long-unsettled Namibian
issue also stood in the way of *détente* in southern Africa and an
improvement in relations with the West. Although Kaunda was also
concerned mainly with Rhodesia, he made it clear that that was not the
only outstanding problem, and he even refused to characterise the
Rhodesian negotiations as *détente*. In the words of the Zambian
Foreign Minister: 'The minimum – I call them fundamental – changes
which could open the way to peace are South Africa's complete
disengagement in Rhodesia and the termination of her illegal occupation of Namibia. She must hand Namibia over to the United
Nations.'[67]

After the unsuccessful negotiations with Waldheim and Escher in
1972–3, the government tried to retain a 'two-track' policy of keeping
the door open for further talks with the UN to reduce international
pressure, while retaining its own constitutional plans for the Territory.
Separate development was thus implemented in terms of Act no. 20 of
1973, and in April of that year Ovambo ('homeland' of the Ovambo
people, nearly 50 per cent of the population) was declared a self-
governing area, with its own Legislative Council, while in May
Kavango (the neighbouring 'homeland', also on the border with
Angola) was raised to the same self-governing status. In June 1974 an
'ethnic army' for Ovambo was established under the control of the
South African Defence Force. In the second half of 1974 there was an
exodus of SWAPO members from Ovambo, which significantly
boosted SWAPO's potential for guerrilla activity. Between 1,500 and
2,000 had left by the end of October, reportedly fearing an increase in
repression by the Ovambo government.[68] At the same time Vorster
fulfilled an assurance given to Escher by establishing a multiracial
Advisory Council to advise on all issues of concern to the whole
Territory, including its future constitutional dispensation. But Vorster
did not deviate far from separate development; the members of the
Council were chosen on an ethnic group basis. After its first meeting in
March 1973 there were only two further meetings, in August 1973 and
September 1974, at which the 'homeland' leaders tended to concentrate on extensions to their authority and on proposals to remove
discriminatory measures which affected them, such as allowing
'prominent' blacks to stay in white hotels. Important black political
movements, such as SWAPO and SWANU, were not involved and the
Council therefore 'enjoyed little credibility among the majority of

Blacks in the Territory, nor in the international community. In terms of its composition and mandate the Advisory Council was fully compatible with the official ideology of ethnic fragmentation.'[69]

The Advisory Council did at least serve as the precursor of a more substantial initiative, the Turnhalle Constitutional Conference. Although still flawed by its ethnic group composition and the exclusion of national black political movements, the Turnhalle Conference during the next few years undermined the hope to which many Nationalist politicians were tenaciously clinging, that separate 'homeland' independence in Namibia would be feasible. Faced with increasing pressure from the UN and Western states, the changed southern African balance of forces and the requirements of *détente*, Vorster needed to show progress on Namibia, but the constraints of his own political beliefs and the potential reaction of his white electorate still applied. So the Turnhalle initiative was a compromise which it was hoped would impress international opinion but not arouse white fears about their future security.

With domestic political considerations in mind it was essential for the government that this initiative should be seen to come from the whites in South West Africa and not Pretoria. It was therefore the local National Party which first proposed in September 1974 that the time was opportune 'for the Whites in the Territory to take positive action to hold talks with members of other population groups with a view to reaching agreement as to the political future'. Although the party indicated a preference for separate development, it was willing to listen to other views 'so as to find a solution which will, to the greatest possible extent, enjoy the support of the various population groups of South West Africa and which will ensure security and prosperity'.[70] The party leader, A. H. du Plessis, was a minister in the South African cabinet, and he and his colleagues in Windhoek were undoubtedly following directions from Pretoria but their statement gave Vorster a political base to promote a constitutional conference. It took a full year of bargaining before the conference, with participants from all eleven ethnic groups, finally met in September 1975 in the historic, but specially renovated, Turnhalle in Windhoek. As the date was fixed before the Victoria Falls Conference and the escalation of Pretoria's involvement in Angola, the genesis of the Turnhalle Conference can be seen as part of Vorster's initiative to resolve southern African disputes, but always within the limits of the government's own political and security interests.

The Turnhalle Conference did not make an auspicious start – several SWAPO and other opposition leaders were arrested before it met –

and its legitimacy as a representative gathering was not widely recognised. Neither SWAPO nor other black nationalist parties was represented and there were disputes among the delegates who attended as to whether all of them were representative of their respective groups. SWAPO, which issued its own constitutional proposals in a 'Discussion Paper', dismissed the Turnhalle talks as 'meaningless' and *inter alia* accused the government of trying to 'present its divisive and tribalist scheme for our country . . . as somehow allowing for Namibia's independence as a single entity'.[71] There was no positive international response even from Western governments which, since the 1971 Advisory Opinion, had been aligning themselves with UN majority decisions, except on the question of sanctions. Cautious Western approval of Vorster's efforts to help with a Rhodesian settlement did not produce a more supportive attitude towards his Namibian initiatives. A unanimous Security Council resolution (no. 366 of 17 December 1974), instead of approving the Turnhalle idea, demanded South African compliance with UN decisions and the International Court's Advisory Opinion, as well as recognition by the government of 'the territorial integrity and unity of Namibia as a nation' – something the government was not yet ready to do.

At the first session of the Turnhalle Conference a Declaration of Intent was adopted without dissent, which committed the Conference to promoting human rights without discrimination on racial or other grounds and to drafting a constitution within three years. By implication this meant that the integrity of Namibia as one country would be maintained, but the Declaration also stated that 'mindful of the particular circumstances of each of our peoples' the participants intended 'to create a form of government which will ensure for every people the greatest possible say in its own affairs . . . with proper consideration of the interests of South West Africa as a whole'.[72] The Declaration still reflected the overriding influence of the whites, represented by the National Party with Pretoria in the background. Dirk Mudge, leader of the white delegation and the dominant figure at the Turnhalle, stated that one of the conditions for the success of the Conference was that the 'existence of separate ethnic groups must be recognised'.[73] Although none of the black groups wanted separate independence from the rest and the whites had given up pressing for that, the vested interests of all the delegates dictated that they should maintain as much autonomy for their respective ethnic governments as possible. This formed the basis of the Turnhalle's deliberations over the following two years. It was therefore dismissed by anti-South

African nationalist parties as an attempt by Pretoria to perpetuate its control by the manipulation of 'puppets' or 'stooges'. The international credibility of the Turnhalle was also undermined by Pretoria's continued implementation of the Odendaal Plan. For instance, the Rehoboth Gebied territory was granted self-government in early 1976, while separate education systems were being developed in each of the 'homelands' (similar to Bantu Education in South Africa).

It was not until mid 1976, with international pressure mounting, that a sense of urgency was injected into constitutional discussions. A constitutional committee, under the chairmanship of Dirk Mudge, concentrated on establishing an interim government representing the various groups which would draw up a constitution for an independent SWA/Namibia. In August it agreed *inter alia* that 31 December 1978 could, 'with reasonable safety', be set as the independence date, while it reaffirmed 'the interdependence of the different population groups and its strong desire to keep South West Africa a single unit', with 'a system of government, particularly in the central body, which will provide complete protection for minority groups'.[74] The agreement had been framed to retain National Party support, because, without it, Pretoria would not agree to an eventual constitution, and most whites believed the proposed interim government and subsequent independence would not threaten their political and economic position. Vorster's initial reaction seemed detached: 'It was the standpoint of the government through the years that the nations of South West Africa will decide on their own future. I assume the conference will contact the government on matters which have been decided, when they will receive the necessary attention.'[75] But this was a calculated attitude, designed to impress domestic and international opinion that the government was encouraging self-determination without interference. It was also intentionally noncommittal, because Vorster knew that there was not yet agreement on an acceptable formula on which to base the establishment of an interim government, let alone an independence constitution.

During this period differences surfaced among the National Party delegates, with Dirk Mudge leaning towards accommodating the frustrated expectations of many black and 'coloured' delegates. These divisions (which were to lead a year later to a break-away from the National Party, led by Mudge) upset Vorster who was not prepared to go further than his party and his own white constituency in South Africa would accept. In November 1976 he summoned the constitutional committee to Pretoria. Muller, Brand Fourie and Pik Botha (Ambassador to the US and UN) were present, as were ministers responsible for 'non-white' groups in the Territory. Significantly, P. W. Botha did not participate, and the main responsibility for Namibian negotiations was still firmly in the hands of Foreign Affairs. Vorster told the committee that, if it did not agree on an interim constitution, he would have to impose one, but, if the Turnhalle could agree on a draft constitution, he would put it through parliament without delay.[76]

Vorster's urgency was the product of growing international pressure, not simply from UN resolutions, but from Western governments which were now adopting a concerted approach on Namibia. He had hoped to present an agreed constitution as an alternative to the UN demands for South African withdrawal and a UN supervised process with SWAPO participation. This would, he hoped, reduce Western pressures and over time gain wider acceptance. These hopes were, however, not realistic in the mid seventies. International demands had advanced too far, and, if they were to be accommodated, neither the UN nor SWAPO could be excluded from the process. Moreover, during 1976 there was a hardening of international attitudes towards Pretoria because of Angola and the domestic upheaval within South Africa. Vorster and his advisers knew this but were prevented from going further by domestic constraints and perceived security needs. With these latter considerations paramount, the alternative to seeking international acceptance was to obtain an internal arrangement in Namibia which would secure the position of the whites and traditional black leaders. Many within the National Party, the government and significantly the military favoured this approach and were against a 'sell-out' at the expense of the white community. They also believed that the security of South West Africa and of South Africa itself required a strong military presence in the north of the Territory and in the Caprivi.

Yet the insistent voice of the West could not be ignored. The confidence which had marked almost ten years of Vorster's premiership was being eroded steadily, following failures in Angola and with détente. Defiantly Vorster said that South Africa would never trust the West again; it would 'go it alone' in defence of its own interests,[77] but his actions were not consistent with this posture. Discussions continued, in particular with the US, as Kissinger tried to recoup his losses in Angola by promoting diplomatic activity focusing on Rhodesia and Namibia. For the first time an American Secretary of State became personally involved in policy towards southern Africa. This was ironic in view of Kissinger's lack of interest in Africa prior to the Angolan affair, but it was the product of his geo-political view that southern

201

Africa was now a focal point in the East/West global struggle and a threat to superpower *détente*. Kissinger set out his aims in a speech in April 1976, significantly delivered in Lusaka during his first visit to the region. Kissinger's attention was primarily devoted to Rhodesia, and he engaged Vorster's close co-operation on that issue. But Namibia was next on Kissinger's list and in his Lusaka speech he endorsed UN decisions, called on Pretoria 'to permit all the people and groups of Namibia to express their views freely, under UN supervision, on the political future and constitutional structure of their country', and urged the government 'to announce a definite timetable acceptable to the world community for the achievement of self-determination'.[78]

Kissinger also obtained South African agreement to a seven-point proposal for Namibian independence. The core of the proposal was a constitutional conference in Geneva, with the UN participating as an observer. Pretoria would accept a constitution negotiated by the various internal and external parties, and the goal would be independence by 31 December 1978.[79] However SWAPO rejected Kissinger's proposal, regarding it as too favourable to Pretoria and the Turnhalle, and maintained that it would only attend a conference after prior commitments by South Africa to complete withdrawal and independence. The Turnhalle groups also opposed the conference proposal, suspecting that Pretoria, under American pressure, was preparing a separate deal with SWAPO.[80] So Kissinger's initiative on Namibia made no progress, although he subsequently secured from Vorster a private commitment to release a substantial number of political prisoners 'as a gesture of good faith'.[81]

Vorster continued to press the Turnhalle delegates to reach agreement, hoping that his willingness to co-operate with Kissinger on Namibia, as well as Rhodesia, might bring American support. However the Americans, the British and the French were now under pressure in the Security Council on both the apartheid and Namibian issues. In October 1976 the three Western powers again used their vetoes to counter an African-sponsored resolution calling for an arms embargo because 'the illegal occupation of Namibia and the war being waged there by South Africa constitutes a threat to international peace and security'. The Western powers were criticised for insensitivity to African aspirations, but the triple veto was probably preceded by an understanding with Vorster that he would not allow the Turnhalle to lead to unilateral independence and that the UN would have a role in the independence process with the Western powers acting as intermediaries.[82] In any case, whether or not there was such an understanding, the Turnhalle was running out of steam by the end of 1976 because of external pressures and internal disagreements. A renewed effort was made by the constitutional committee in early 1977, and in March a draft constitution for the interim government, defining the respective powers and functions of the three tiers, was accepted by the full Conference. But it was too close to the existing 'Bantustan' system to generate a positive response outside the Turnhalle itself and was never implemented.

By this stage the Turnhalle had been overtaken by the Western initiative which, following the election of President Jimmy Carter, was promoted by the group of five Western states (US, UK, France, West Germany and Canada) which were then members of the Security Council. The group, led by the US, based its initiative on Security Council resolution 385 of January 1976 which had been adopted with full Western support. Pretoria, succumbing to the mounting pressures, had to revert to the international track of its two-track policy. Vorster had in effect lost the initiative on Namibia, as he had on *détente*, and moreover he was now faced with a serious domestic racial crisis which aroused international opinion against his government as never before.

11 SOWETO – THE DOMESTIC AND REGIONAL IMPACT

On 16 June 1976 secondary pupils in Soweto – the vast black township on the edge of Johannesburg – marched in protest against the use of Afrikaans as a medium of instruction in their schools. Called out by the newly founded Soweto Students Representative Council they numbered about 12,000 when they reached Orlando West High School. There they met and clashed with the police. At first there were stones and missiles from the students, and tear gas, truncheons and warning shots from the police, but then the police fired into the crowd killing at least one youth, Hector Peterson. Rioting swept across Soweto with several deaths including those of two whites. The riots spread elsewhere, and five days after the first outbreak Jimmy Kruger, the Minister of Justice, announced that on the Witwatersrand alone there had been 130 deaths and 1,110 people injured; 33 Bantu Administration buildings, 27 Beer Halls and 90 schools had been burnt down (and opponents said he underestimated the losses).[1] In the months that followed there were similar risings across the Republic, with much loss of life and damage to property.

Two days after the Soweto rising Vorster met Henry Kissinger in West Germany. Following the Angola débâcle Kissinger was eager to minimise the advantage gained by the USSR and rebuild US relations in Africa. He had already toured black states and at Lusaka spoke of ushering in 'a new era of American policy' by collaborating with black states and supporting black majority rule. Turning to South Africa he said he hoped for an end to apartheid, 'based on the premise that within a reasonable time we shall see a clear evolution towards equality of opportunity and basic human rights for all South Africans'. However, his immediate concern was to find solutions to regional problems, notably Rhodesia and Namibia (see chapter 10 regarding Namibia). He challenged Pretoria to show good faith by using her influence 'to promote a rapid negotiated settlement for majority rule in Rhodesia'.[2] On his return to Washington from the African tour

Kissinger had confirmed that the US was 'prepared officially to acknowledge the current efforts to obtain a peaceful settlement' in Namibia (i.e. the Turnhalle talks organised by Pretoria). The meeting with Vorster was to pursue those issues.

These two events – the Soweto rising and the Vorster/Kissinger meeting – signalled a sharp change in South Africa's internal and international settings. Already Pretoria's ambitions in southern Africa had been thwarted by the collapse of Portuguese power, the advent of Marxist governments in Angola and Mozambique and the failure of military intervention in Angola. Now, inside the Republic, Soweto marked a revival of African political activity, led by 'a new breed of black man: radicalised and politicised youth'.[3] The black risings captured international attention and sympathy, and although they were not directly discussed at the meeting with Kissinger they formed a backcloth which weakened Vorster's position. The meeting marked the start of a direct US role in regional diplomacy. Although a global dimension had already been introduced into southern Africa through the fighting in Angola, the US had only been indirectly and covertly involved, but now as an active participant, the domestic and international interests of the world's most powerful state became superimposed on the region.

For Pretoria the years of confidence, already undermined by the Portuguese collapse, had finally been shattered by militant black school children at home and the intrusion of superpower politics. Once again there was an air of crisis: the government uncertain in its response to the new challenges; its black opponents confident that their hour was at hand. The government did not disguise the problems. The 1977 Defence White Paper called for a 'total strategy' to counter the 'total onslaught'. Opening parliament in 1977 the State President looked back on 1976 as 'a watershed year . . . characterised on the one hand by far-reaching developments on the international scene and on the other by the emergence within the Republic of elements who believe that the attainment of meaningful political rights for all our peoples is only possible by totally destroying, if need be through violence and bloodshed, the existing political, economic and social order'.[4] Vorster, no longer preaching dialogue and *détente*, warned of the need to stand alone in a hostile world.[5] The new Minister of Foreign Affairs, Pik Botha, spoke of summoning the Masada spirit – to fight 'to the point of death' – and while after Sharpeville Verwoerd had called on whites to stand like granite, Pik called on them to 'stand like a rock against the waves of the ocean until the tide ebbs, and then lift up one's head again and stand in full sunshine'.[6]

SOWETO AND THE BLACK MOVEMENTS

Although the immediate cause of the Soweto rising was dissatisfaction over Afrikaans as a teaching medium there was agreement on all sides that the risings had deeper causes, but there was sharp disagreement about what these were.[7] Black activists saw the risings as a witness to black power and an outburst against the injustice of apartheid; the government saw them as part of a communist-inspired revolution. Vorster, rejecting the view that the youths had acted spontaneously, saw a deliberate attempt by 'certain organizations and people' to 'bring about polarization between Whites and Blacks'.[8] Later he said that the continuation of such troubles must be expected: 'After all the communists have adopted this course and dare not deviate from it now.'[9] He also suspected that the risings had been timed to undermine his talks with Kissinger, and although he decided to go to Germany he did so emphasising that law and order at home had prime importance.

The risings continued throughout 1977, spreading unevenly across the country and drawing in Coloured and Indian students. In October 1977 an estimated 196,000 pupils were out of classes. More generally the risings regenerated black political activity with a renewed expectation of the imminent collapse of white power, and this time there were the inspirational examples of Angola and Mozambique. The protests started in schools and colleges where young *ad hoc* leaders emerged, and what organisation there was depended on students often in hastily arranged groups. Although there was sometimes confusion about aims and methods, the youths were intolerant of compromise and frequently refused to accept the authority of elders. 'They won't take anything we say', said Leonard Mosala, an old nationalist leader, 'because they think we have neglected them. We have failed to help them in their struggle for change in schools. They are now angry and prepared to fight.'[10]

The exiled parties and Black Consciousness probably played no direct part in organising the risings, and initially the ANC was as surprised as the government by events. Yet both Black Consciousness and the exiled parties (especially the ANC) were involved. Black Consciousness provided many of the ideas and attitudes which inspired the youths. Steve Biko, the Black Consciousness leader, when asked if he could point to support for the movement replied: 'In one word: Soweto! The boldness, dedication and sense of purpose, and clarity of analysis of the situation – all these things are a direct result of Black Consciousness ideas among the young in Soweto and

206

elsewhere.'[11] For its part the ANC became a symbol and a rallying point, and later provided a haven for the youths who fled the country.

Inside the Republic the risings revived black political activity which had been dormant since the early 1960s. In Soweto itself, although the government eventually gained control arresting many students and forcing others to flee, a Committee of Ten emerged, led by Dr Nthato Motlana, a contemporary of Mandela and Tambo in the ANC, and composed of older political activists who mediated between the students and the authorities. The churches were also active and threw up new leaders, notably Desmond Tutu. At the same time, Inkatha extended its activities. Although it claimed to be a national party Inkatha was predominantly a Zulu organisation led by Chief Gatsha Buthelezi, the Chief Minister of KwaZulu. It was committed against apartheid but advocated 'moderate' methods, calling for dialogue with the government and a national convention. It opposed withdrawal of foreign investment but favoured monitoring foreign companies. Because of its moderation Inkatha became unpopular with the radical youths, as Buthelezi discovered when he was forced from Robert Sobukwe's funeral.[12] Critics attacked Inkatha as a product of separate development but supporters pointed to its stand against the government and its success as a mass movement in bridging the gaps between rural and urban blacks, peasants and professionals. By August 1978 the fast growing Inkatha claimed 150,000 paid-up members.

The exiled ANC (and to a lesser extent PAC) were rejuvenated by the risings and by the injection of new blood from the youths who fled the country. In October 1976 about 3,000 political refugees were in neighbouring states with the number still rising.[13] Although Black Consciousness was established abroad, with a BPC secretariat in Botswana, its external presence was not strong, and the main beneficiaries of the refugees were the ANC and PAC.[14] An element of coercion may have been involved. For example, an Amnesty International investigation found that when refugees crossed the Botswana border the police gave them the choice of joining an exiled party or being returned to South Africa. Many of the refugees were subsequently sent for guerrilla training. In 1978 Brigadier Zietsman, Chief of Pretoria's Security Police, estimated that 4,000 (3,000 ANC, 1,000 PAC) were undergoing training in Angola, Mozambique, Libya and Tanzania.[15] However, the problems of reviving activities inside South Africa remained, and the change in circumstances did not heal the divisions between ANC and PAC. In July 1977 the ANC was declared 'the sole authentic representative of the people' at a Soviet orientated solidarity conference in Lisbon.[16] It was much the larger and better organised party and continued to grow. By the 1980s, backed by financial assistance from friendly governments and international organisations which amounted annually to about $100m., it was able to set up large training camps and to develop a bureaucracy at its headquarters in Lusaka of more than 150 administrators.[17]

Following Soweto the ANC had some immediate success in promoting political awareness through distributing the Freedom Charter, smuggling in funds via Swaziland and putting out feelers to other groups including Inkatha and Black Consciousness. Later it played down the Inkatha contacts and its early difficulties with Black Consciousness, proclaiming Motlana 'a patriot' and Buthelezi 'a betrayer of the struggle'.[18] It also increased guerrilla activities. In 1977 there were six explosions on railway lines, seven arms discoveries and some shootouts with the police. The higher level of activity continued in the following years, including attacks on police stations and other official buildings, and counter action by the government.[19] However, the period was more important for future preparations than immediate action. Between 1977 and 1979 Umkhonto concentrated on training new recruits, establishing communications and infiltration routes through Mozambique and Swaziland (until the Swazis clamped down in 1978), setting up arms caches and establishing a new cell organisation inside South Africa.[20] The new developments could not disguise the problems of exile. The youths complained that the leaders had 'lost touch', become bureaucratic and were too moderate. More radical than their predecessors, the Soweto generation revived debates about the conduct of the armed struggle, including the possibility of using terrorist tactics (which the leadership opposed). Some years later, at the 1985 Kabwe conference, a more militant approach was adopted, with greater prominence of Umkhonto and acceptance of 'a people's war', whereby those in training were seen as a potential officer corps to lead new recruits inside South Africa. In the early 1980s major successes were recorded in sabotage attacks on the Sasol plants, the Natref oil refinery and the Koeberg nuclear plant (which caused $40m. of damage). Yet divisions remained over the use of violence. While Tambo signed the Geneva Convention binding the ANC to avoid civilian targets and to humanitarian conduct, there were attacks which resulted in civilian casualties like the bomb which killed five people at a shopping centre in Natal in 1985.

The Soweto generation also raised questions about the ultimate goal of the struggle (was it simply to achieve majority rule or was that a step towards socialist reconstruction?) and the position in the party of 'non-blacks', and especially members of the SACP. This was a double debate, concerned with difference between the 'Africanists' and those favouring multiracialism, and the issue of communist membership. Communist links which had been useful in facilitating Soviet support and providing a network of international contacts, were now reinforced by the presence of Marxist governments in Angola and Mozambique which were soon visited by Vice President Podgorny of the USSR and President Castro of Cuba. A new military situation arose when Cuban troops and East European advisers and training camps were established in Angola, and guerrilla bases in Mozambique.[21] However, the presence of white and Asian communists in the ANC still created tension, and this was intensified by the arrival of Black Consciousness youths. In 1975 Tennyson Makiwane and seven other leading figures were expelled from the ANC for protesting at non-black interference, and branded as 'a clique based on the slogans of racialism, anti-ANC and anti-Communism'.[22] In 1980 Makiwane who had returned to the Transkei was assassinated.

The PAC had been plagued by internal rivalries and quarrels since Robert Sobukwe's imprisonment in 1961 and his subsequent banning. Sobukwe's death in 1978 led to further struggles from which Potlake Leballo, backed by the Swazi and Botswana authorities, temporarily emerged triumphant, but persistent internal conflict continued which absorbed the movement's energies at the expense of insurgency and diplomacy. There was a little PAC activity in South Africa between 1975 and 1977 as a small nucleus, led by Zephania Mothopeng, established cells in East London and Johannesburg, set up youth groups, and sent recruits through Swaziland for training in Libya and China. Three of the recruits were arrested when they returned in 1978 and an arms cache uncovered. However, there was little more to show, and in May 1979 Leballo's troubled leadership came to an end when he was overthrown by a discontented group who replaced him by a three-man presidential council. That ran into immediate difficulties when one of the triumverate, David Sibeko, was assassinated in Tanzania by followers of Leballo. The Tanzanian authorities arrested the plotters, and although Leballo continued to lead a small faction until his death in 1985 he had no real power. That passed first to Vusi Make and then, in 1981, to John Pokela. Under Pokela's leadership, and that of Johnson Mlambo who gained the chairmanship on Pokela's death in 1985, the PAC gradually overcame its internal problems and by the 1980s had built itself into a united and active, if small, movement. Led by the military wing (the Anzanian Peoples' Liberation Army) insurgency was revived inside the Republic; a vigorous diplomatic effort ensured continued recognition by the UN and the OAU and contacts with major Western states; and, perhaps most encouraging of all, the 'Africanist' philosophy continued to have considerable appeal, as was demonstrated inside South Africa by the formation in April 1978 of a movement close to the PAC, the Anzanian People's Organisation (AZAPO).[23]

While the PAC remained a small movement, the ANC grew in size and importance. It used the new situation to gain a higher international profile. After Soweto, as the best known and organised black party, it was courted by governments and anti-apartheid groups eager to demonstrate their opposition to Pretoria. Support for the armed struggle came from communist states, and limited financial and political backing came from the West – including Scandinavian governments, church groups, and socialist parties. On 26 October 1976 Oliver Tambo became the first black South African to address the UN General Assembly. He used the occasion to pay respect to the sacrifice of the black youths of Soweto. He saw the government's reaction, with its shooting of innocent people, not as an aberration but as the 'concrete expressions of the policy of the apartheid state', for South Africa was a colonial situation with its black people yet to be liberated. Vorster's regime, he said, was backed by international capitalism and could exist only 'because of the economic, military and political support it receives from the countries of Western Europe, from North America and Japan', and others who acted for the imperialists – Israel, Argentina, Taiwan and Iran. Calling for a mandatory arms ban and claiming that Western arms had killed the youths, Tambo said that the imperialists' aim was to further profits of the multinational companies. Yet, as events in Vietnam, Angola, Mozambique and Guinea-Bissau had shown, the imperialists and their lackies could not stop the forces of liberation. While imperialism associates 'its own survival on the survival of the white minority regime, the confrontation between the ANC . . . and the forces of imperialism led by the United States, cannot but grow sharper'.[24]

Tambo was voicing a commonly held view among black nationalists that the West and South Africa had an unwritten alliance to defend capitalism against progressive forces. According to this view, behind the cloud of Western rhetoric about democracy and social justice there was racism and exploitation. Although the West was diplomatically cool towards Pretoria, that masked its interest in exploiting the blacks of southern Africa while maintaining the Western dominated international economy. Thus while Pretoria perceived the ANC as the servant of communism the ANC saw Pretoria as the handmaiden of capitalism.[25]

THE GOVERNMENT'S RESPONSE

The government response to Soweto and its aftermath combined repression, enhanced security and reform. Vorster made clear that 'the government will not be intimidated and instructions have been given to maintain law and order at all costs'.[26] The military pressed the point that the total onslaught could only be defeated by political as well as military action. In September 1977 General Magnus Malan, Chief of the Defence Staff, declared that the country is 'involved in total war. The war is not only the area of the soldier. Everyone is involved and has a role to play.'[27] In this garrison-state mentality the government saw itself surrounded by dangers, the military gained a greater role in policy making and the white population was mobilised for defence of the state.[28] Before Soweto the 1975 White Paper had noted that the Portuguese withdrawal 'will undoubtedly encourage the radical elements in revolutionary organisations inside and outside [South Africa] and incite them to greater efforts. They regard Angola and Mozambique as new allies and potential new operational bases.' After Soweto, P. W. Botha warned a party congress that: 'We are moving more and more in the direction in which the state of Israel has already been since 1948, and that country spends more than 50 per cent of its budget on defence.'[29]

Security legislation was tightened by the Internal Security Amendment Act of 1976, which Jimmy Kruger said was aimed at communists, Black Power leaders, radical religious movements and those who were trying to organise revolution through black trades unions.[30] The power of the state was brought to bear in trials, bannings, detentions and prohibitions. By the end of 1976 1,000 persons (mainly youths) had been convicted under the Riotous Assembly Act, a further 3,000 were awaiting trial and more than 400 were detained under other security legislation. Widespread international criticism was heaped on Pretoria, particularly at the number of deaths among detainees. From March 1976 to November 1977 nineteen people were known to have died in custody. The most prominent was Steve Biko who died on 12 September after brutal police treatment. Biko's death, and the government's callous response, prompted a wave of bitter condemnation inside and outside South Africa. Over 15,000 people, including representatives of the major Western powers, attended Biko's funeral. However, undeterred by the criticism, the government continued its policy, and in a major sweep on 19 October placed at least fifty leading critics in preventive detention, including the Soweto Committee of Ten, black newspaper editors, leaders of the Black Peoples Convention (BPC), the Christian Institute and the Soweto Teachers Association.

The government's concern extended to border security. With increased guerrilla infiltration into the Republic and Namibia, the 1977 Defence White Paper concluded we are at war 'whether we wish to accept it or not'. In recognition of that white national service was extended, the military were given special powers in the border areas and cross border pursuits and raids were approved after the amendment of the Defence Act so that forces could operate not only 'in any part of the Republic of South Africa' but also 'in neighbouring states'.[31] In 1978 the military were empowered to enter private property within ten kilometres of the border and demolish or erect buildings for defence purposes without the consent of the owners. Steps were also taken to encourage white farmers to remain on the border and in 1979 new legislation gave rewards (including interest-free loans) to farmers who remained or returned to strategically important areas.[32] The vigilance and flexibility of the forces were improved by strengthening the navy's coastal surveillance and dividing the army between counter-insurgency and conventional forces.

As the strain on white manpower increased, so the forces turned to black volunteers who saw their first active service in Namibia. By late 1977 it was estimated that one in five of the forces fighting in Namibia was black (either South African regulars or local tribesmen). General Malan complimented them on their 'outstanding work', and in 1978 a full black battalion was in the Namibian operational area.[33] There was a similar story in the navy where, by 1979, Indians and Coloureds made up 20 per cent of the manpower.[34] The irony of these steps did not go unnoticed. 'They expect us to be "patriotic foreigners"', said Buthelezi, pointing out that while the government denied citizenship to blacks it recruited them for the forces.[35]

Alongside the repression and increased security the seeds of reform were planted. But it was reform within the apartheid framework. The government never tired of emphasising that developments would be based on multinationalism, and to that end the Transkei (1976) and Bophuthatswana (1977) were granted 'independence'. This full flowering of apartheid proved an anticlimax because international recognition was withheld. The chances of recognition had never been good, but following Soweto and Biko's death there was no hope, and not a single state recognised the homelands. Vorster was indignant.

He complained of double standards, accusing the West of refusing recognition because it was currying favour with black states, while the blacks refused because if they accepted it 'bang goes their whole argument of "one man, one vote"'.[36] On top of the international snubs Pretoria faced immediate disputes with the Bantustans' governments over land and citizenship. At Bophuthatswana's independence Chief Mangope, referring to the seven pieces into which his territory was divided, spoke of the Tswanas 'well-founded bitterness on the question of consolidation', and now of having 'greater independence' but not 'sovereignty'.[37] In April 1978 the Transkei even broke off diplomatic relations with South Africa following Pretoria's refusal to transfer Griqualand East.

Within the Republic there was some reform in hand at the time of Soweto – such as the Theron Commission examining the position of the Coloureds – but it was narrowly based and half-hearted. Soweto changed that. It shook the government into action partly to divert international criticism, but also from a recognition of underlying problems. Although the implementation of change took time the motivation for reform came in the wake of the black risings and can be attributed to them. There were divided views in the government and some early failures, such as the Community Council legislation of 1977, but more important in the longer term were first the Wiehahn and Riekert Commissions which were set up to examine the controversial field of black labour; and second a cabinet committee, chaired by P. W. Botha, which examined 'possible and desirable adjustments to the existing constitutional order'. (Black Africans were excluded because Pretoria believed they were catered for in Bantustans.)

THE GOVERNMENT RESPONSE AND WHITE POLITICS

Within the government two important steps were the appointment of a new Minister of Foreign Affairs, and the calling of an election. The ministerial change, which was unconnected with the crisis, came in April 1977 when Muller retired to be replaced by R. F. (Pik) Botha. Botha, who had been a professional diplomat (including service with the delegation at the International Court hearings on SWA/Namibia) had entered politics in 1970, and from the beginning had projected a 'verligte' image. He had been appointed Permanent Representative at the UN in September 1974, to which was added Ambassador to the US in 1975. Muller is said to have favoured Pik as his successor, despite their contrasting characters. Where Muller was quiet and self-effacing, Pik was assertive, ambitious and flamboyant.

He established himself as powerful public speaker, but attracted critics as well as admirers in the party and the department. Senior departmental officials were said to have divided themselves into a 'Pik group' and a 'Brand group' (after Brand Fourie the Secretary) and there was some resentment at the way Pik favoured young officials like Neil Van Heerden and J. A. Eksteen who had served with him in Washington. However, all the officials admired the way in which the new minister championed the department within the government and ensured its prominence in decision making and the public eye.[38]

The election, which was called by Vorster for 30 November 1977, came as a surprise in the sense that parliament had eighteen months to run, but such was the NP's grip on elections that they had become tools of government policy not competitions for power. The opposition offered no threat. The UP which had won forty-one seats in 1974 had disintegrated and its leader, Sir de Villiers Graff, retired. Some old members formed the New Republican Party (NRP), others joined the Progressives to form the Progressive Federal Party (PFP) and others the South African Party (SAP). On 'the right' the HNP again fielded candidates but was not a threat. Confident of victory, Vorster approached the election with a number of aims in mind. He wanted to consolidate white support against black demands; to take advantage of the opposition's disarray; to ensure solidarity in the government for his policies, including the reform proposals; and to counter external criticism and interference.

In the campaign the government played the patriotic card. 'All loyal and patriotic South Africans have a golden opportunity', said Connie Mulder, 'to show the world that it must not meddle in South Africa's affairs.' An editorial in 'Beeld' saw the election as an opportunity to show that 'the time has come to close our ranks against the outside world and the enemies in our midst'. For some it became the 'Anti-Jimmy Carter' election, as international criticism persisted and the US temporarily withdrew its Ambassador after the bannings and detentions in October, and in the wake of Biko's death most Western states supported a UN Security Council mandatory arms embargo. To that Pik Botha replied: 'We will resist with all the intensity of a nation that feels it is in a corner and has no choice.' That was confirmed by the election result which consolidated the government's hold on power. It went into the election with 117 seats from a total of 165. It emerged with 135, having gained 65.8 per cent of the votes cast, while the PFP, which became the largest opposition party, gained 17 per cent of the votes and 17 seats. 'The dominant feature of the election', wrote Midlane, 'was that of white unity within a garrison state.'[39] To underline the point further, in the following week a magistrate ruled that no criminal offence had been committed and no person could be held responsible for Biko's death.

SHIFTING SANDS IN SOUTHERN AFRICA

Pretoria's regional policy was in tatters. The white controlled bloc disintegrated after the Portuguese collapse, and Pretoria's attempt to impose its will in Angola by military power had failed. Following that and the installation of Marxist governments in Mozambique and Angola, immediate hopes of broad based regional cooperation disappeared. From the tatters a new policy emerged, but it was a reaction to adversity not the government's chosen path. The confidence had gone. In February 1977 a world-weary Muller admitted that South Africa had considerable international problems and few diplomatic links in Africa. He said that despite the government's efforts the Republic was still misunderstood and her policies criticised by 'distortion and emotional misuse of human rights'.[40] Vorster shared the gloom. Gone were hopes of transforming Pretoria's position in Africa, and while he claimed that initiatives continued, he admitted that 'some bridges had in fact collapsed' and events in Angola, South West Africa and Rhodesia were prejudicial. He spoke of having to stand alone, to weather a political onslaught. His boast was no longer of good relations with black neighbours but that Pretoria's power could not be ignored. What is important, he said, 'is the recognition throughout the entire world that South Africa has a role to play . . . and one cannot discuss the affairs of southern Africa without taking cognizance of the South African standpoint and without discussing the matter with South Africa. Accuse me of having failed in all respects, accuse me of being worthless and meaningless, but I claim the credit of having achieved this for South Africa.'[41]

As Vorster claimed, South Africa had considerable strength. Neighbours could not escape economic dependence and the political lever this gave to Pretoria. The Mozambique Government, for example, although strongly critical of apartheid and committed to Marxism and support for the ANC, decided to renew labour agreements, to encourage the use of the port at Maputo, asked for help in operating it, and in March 1977 began selling power from Cahora Bassa to South Africa. Of sanctions, the Foreign Minister, Joaquim Chissano, said 'we have to be realistic and recognize that we cannot do it ourselves'. The scale of economic interaction declined, partly from Mozambique's choice but also because of her internal problems. In 1977 South African traffic through Maputo was only 40 per cent of that for 1974, and while in 1975 120,000 workers had gone to the Republic, by 1978 it had dropped to 40,000.[42] Yet Pretoria came to appreciate that the political lever had limitations, that economic ties did not lead to broad-based regional co-operation. Its new approach was to try to counter external pressure by seeking settlements for regional problems piece by piece. If this were successful, it hoped that southern Africa would slip off the international agenda. Already Pretoria had been active in trying to gain settlements in Rhodesia and Namibia, and these efforts were now intensified, especially in Rhodesia. If a settlement could be found there with a 'moderate' government (black or white) which was prepared to co-operate with Pretoria, not only would international attention be diverted but the government's status at home and abroad would be enhanced as a regional power capable of playing a crucial broker's role.

THE SEARCH FOR A RHODESIAN SOLUTION

In his Lusaka speech in April 1976, Kissinger had stressed the US commitment to a rapid and just solution in Rhodesia, and had drawn attention to the role which South Africa could play in 'dedication to Africa' by using its influence in Salisbury to promote majority rule, as the independent black states were urging. Rhodesia was, therefore, high on the agenda of Vorster's meeting with Kissinger in June 1976. Following the failure at Victoria Falls the Rhodesian situation had deteriorated. Although the black nationalists remained divided, the war had intensified and, following Mozambique's closure of its border, Rhodesia became entirely dependent on South Africa for transport and for economic support to wage the war. Kissinger was eager to explore whether Vorster was prepared to separate the Republic's fate from that of Rhodesia. Smith had always argued that their futures lay together and that to accept the principle of majority rule for one would spell disaster for both. However, in 1975 Vorster had already authorised a secret Broederbond circular which recognised the inevitability and imminence of black rule in Rhodesia.[43] It was, therefore, Kissinger's view that prevailed. In Vorster's eyes the change in Mozambique made Rhodesia's position untenable, and her increasing reliance on raids into Mozambique and Zambia soured the regional atmosphere, undermining Pretoria's prospects of establishing relations with black states. Conscious of the Angolan débâcle and the severe domestic problems, Vorster was keen to stabilise the region and to avoid international isolation. Kissinger was prepared to help. He too wanted regional stability while enhancing US prestige by negotiating a Rhodesian settlement. He sought to persuade Vorster to 'deliver' Smith, while the Presidents of the Front Line States (FLS) would 'deliver' the nationalists. In return for Vorster's help the US would support anti-Marxist forces in Angola and reduce pressure on Namibia.

Vorster returned to South Africa ready to further Kissinger's plan, but before he acted the war entered a new phase. Rhodesia launched its largest raid yet against the Pungwe River camp in Mozambique. The Rhodesians saw it as a military triumph; Vorster as a political disaster – a dangerous escalation likely to spread conflict across the region and draw in outside powers as they had been drawn into Angola. Demonstrating his displeasure, Vorster immediately ended 'Operation Polo' (a secret arrangement to support Rhodesia's air force) and slowed the transport flow thereby reducing Rhodesia's capacity to fight. At the same time Muller announced support for Kissinger's initiative 'on the basis of majority rule'.[44] In the months that followed Vorster worked closely with Kissinger, who in turn worked with the British. After further discussions with Kissinger at Zurich in September 1976, Vorster (in contrast with Pretoria's post-Angola views) stated: 'America is the leader of the free world, and I am part and parcel of the free world, and therefore America is my leader.'[45]

On his return from Zurich Vorster first exerted great pressure on Smith at a secret meeting, and then arranged for Kissinger and Smith to meet in Pretoria. It was a blunt encounter. Smith felt bitter towards Vorster, for the Rhodesian leader believed he had been deceived, that Vorster had given an undertaking to defend Rhodesia.[46] However, Smith and the other Rhodesians were impressed by Kissinger. They found him well informed, sympathetic in style but tough and clear in his demands. Smith, who recognised that Kissinger was using British proposals, concluded that he was a channel for the British and Vorster was an agent for Kissinger. It was a formidable channel and a formidable agent. A 1976 Rhodesian intelligence report bluntly stated that the country 'was wholly dependent upon South Africa for military and economic survival', and recognised that 'the Republic is currently being subjected to formidable international pressure to coerce the Rhodesian Government to accept early majority rule'.[47]

Kissinger, who revealed that he knew Rhodesia's precarious situation from his own intelligence sources, made clear to Smith that he was not prepared to negotiate on principles. He presented the Rhodesians with an Anglo-American plan for majority rule in two years which he said had already been discussed with the FLS and endorsed by Vorster. Smith could take it or leave it, but if he refused Rhodesia would be unable to hold out for more than three or four months because South Africa would no longer offer support. Although Smith managed to modify arrangements for the two-year interim period – including retaining the Ministries of Defence and Law and Order in white hands – he had no choice but to accept the broad proposals. Ken Flower, head of Rhodesian Intelligence, concluded that: 'The South African political, economic and military arm-twisting, which had been growing steadily more painful, had finally proved too much for Smith, his government and his country to bear.'[48] Smith himself told Kissinger that: 'All I have to offer is my own head on a platter.'[49] After returning home, reporting to his colleagues and hearing from Kissinger (now in Dar es Salaam) that he believed the Frontline leaders would accept the terms, Smith made a dramatic radio broadcast in which he announced his government's acceptance of majority rule two years hence. For him it was a bitter moment. He still hoped to salvage something by working for a 'moderate' mixed race government, but his dream of indefinite white rule had gone. In contrast, hopes were high in London and Washington, and in Pretoria Vorster believed that his tough line had paid off.

Hopes were soon dashed, for Kissinger ran into problems with the black states. While the FLS leaders had supported an outline plan previously put to them by Kissinger they had not discussed its implementation, nor had they approved all the terms Kissinger had hammered out with Smith, in particular the composition of the Interim Government and control of security forces. They therefore refused to accept the scheme agreed with Smith. Some, including Nyerere and Mugabe, clearly favoured continuing the fight rather than settling. Kissinger, eager to gain agreement, had not made the situation entirely clear to Smith and Vorster in Pretoria, and after leaving South Africa his first message was optimistically based on an initial reaction from Nyerere who, said Kissinger, as chairman of the FLS, found the proposals 'an acceptable base for settlement of the Rhodesian question'. Kissinger did not mention that queries had been raised and agreement had yet to be given, and it was in ignorance of this that Smith made his broadcast. There was therefore a deep misunderstanding created by Kissinger's attempt to drive affairs on by 'tactical ambiguity'. Vorster and Smith believed that full agreement had been reached while the African leaders believed that the principle of majority rule had been accepted but its implementation had yet to be negotiated.[50] The distrust which had always surrounded the search for a Rhodesian settlement was compounded when the gulf of understanding became public with the black leaders' rejection of Smith's broadcast.

Although Kissinger soon departed from the scene when the Republicans lost the US Presidential election, the British tried to salvage the situation by convening a conference at Geneva. It was an unenviable task. Smith believed that the conference had been called to implement Kissinger's proposals while the nationalists saw the proposals merely as a basis for negotiation. There was even difficulty in persuading two of the principal figures to attend. Smith saw no point in going as he had already agreed Kissinger's proposals and would give no more, whereas Mugabe thought it pointless because he was committed to armed struggle. Eventually both attended because of pressure from their backers: from the FLS, and especially Mozambique, on Mugabe; from South Africa on Smith. Vorster's view was that there was little hope of success but that the US and Britain should see that Rhodesia was willing to implement a settlement while the nationalists were not. Vorster, now accepting that Smith had done what he could, restored full supplies to Rhodesia.

Despite the presence of Smith and Mugabe, the prolonged and bitter Geneva conference failed because of different interests, perceptions and lack of trust. During the conference the fighting had escalated as each side tried to enhance its bargaining position, and following the Geneva failure the war continued. But the situation could never be the same again. Although the whites temporarily remained in control, their political fate had been sealed. The developments which had ensured this were the Portuguese collapse, the intensified guerrilla war and Pretoria's recognition of Rhodesia's untenable position. Smith and his supporters only came to accept this under the joint pressure of Kissinger and Vorster, but after that the agenda changed. Majority rule was no longer in question: now it was how and when it would be achieved and who would form the new government. Faced by that Pretoria played a split role. On one hand it showed sympathy for the Rhodesians because it believed that Smith had genuinely tried for a settlement while the black nationalists had not, and because it distrusted the new US administration. On the other hand it held to the view that white rule could not continue. Vorster therefore encouraged an internal settlement based on majority rule, with whites retaining a prominent role in a government that would stay close to Pretoria. Vorster shared Smith's determination to prevent a take-over by 'extremists', in particular Mugabe and ZANU. To that end he restored financial and military support, and, on the advice of his own military leaders, accepted renewed Rhodesian raids into Mozambique.

External efforts to find a solution continued during 1977 and 1978. A new joint initiative was launched by Britain and the US through David Owen, the British Foreign Secretary, Cyrus Vance, the American Secretary of State, and Andrew Young, the US Ambassador to the UN. Owen and Young were two young men in a hurry, blessed with energy if not always discretion. At first the initiative was welcomed in Salisbury and Pretoria, but the British underestimated Smith's will to resist and overestimated the help that Vorster was now prepared to give. With Vorster keeping his distance, with the Anglo-American proposals failing to satisfy either Smith or the black nationalists, there was no settlement. Instead the ferocious war continued with increased suffering and loss, straining the Rhodesian economy, and making Zambia and Mozambique as well as Rhodesia into battle fields.

Inside Rhodesia Smith, reinforced by another sweeping white election victory in August 1977, tried to break the deadlock by recruiting black leaders for an internal settlement. Pretoria encouraged this and exerted pressure to ensure that leaders like Sithole were allowed into the country despite Rhodesian doubts. Smith even had secret talks with Nkomo, but they failed and served only to increase the bitterness between ZANU and ZAPU. Smith had more success with Muzorewa and Sithole, whom the British and Americans largely ignored and failed to invite to another abortive conference in Malta in January 1978, attended by Mugabe and Nkomo. Otherwise Muzorewa and Sithole had little in common. Muzorewa, had a large following, but was inexperienced and vacillating, whereas Sithole was a hardened politician but had few supporters after losing control of ZANU to Mugabe. Eventually Smith, Muzorewa, Sithole and a traditional ruler, Chief Chirau, signed the Salisbury Agreement in February 1978 which ushered in Zimbabwe–Rhodesia. The name reflected the pusillanimous compromise. Smith, however, claimed that it was based on Kissinger's principles, and announced elections for December to return a government based on majority rule but with a white controlling voice in security. The agreement was denounced by ZAPU, ZANU and the FLS, ignored by the US and Britain, but supported by Pretoria which hoped that the fighting would be greatly reduced and that the West would come to recognise the new constitution. Again hopes were dashed. The fighting continued, international recognition was withheld and a Rhodesian settlement remained as elusive as ever, leaving an unsettled region with continued dangers for South Africa.

NAMIBIA

There were similarities between Rhodesia and Namibia: both were long standing problems in which Pretoria was subjected to intense external pressure; there were bitter guerrilla wars; and the Western powers were active in seeking settlements. There were also clear differences. Unlike Rhodesia, Namibia was South Africa's direct responsibility. Moreover the government had already partly tied its hands. It had given pledges to the local whites based on the concept of separate national groups, and problems were increased by divisions within its own ranks. Foreign Affairs favoured diplomacy and restraint on cross-border raids; whereas the military believed in hitting the guerrillas in their Angolan bases. Like the Rhodesians, the military became increasingly wedded to the doctrine of cross-border strikes. Also there was little domestic political pressure to withdraw as military losses were limited and fighting was contained in the north of the Territory and in Angola, far from white farms and towns and from South Africa itself. In the two years from April 1975, 33 members of the Security Forces and 53 civilians (mostly black) were killed, with SWAPO losing 231.[51] The military had overwhelming support for their role from whites in Namibia and South Africa.

Pretoria pursued an ambivalent policy, shifting according to changing international pressures and its own internal balance of power. Personally Vorster kept his options open: whether to accept a UN settlement or impose one unilaterally, and if unilateral action were taken whether to retain direct control or grant 'independence' to a local administration. There was vacillation but also clear bench marks. First SWAPO must be kept out. Vorster was not, he said, prepared to hand over 'to the adventurer Nujoma and his Marxist SWAPO'. Second, the government would retain responsibility for security while it was the administering power. The security forces were there at local request, declared Vorster, 'and in accordance with the injunction which we have to protect the territory, an injunction which is inherently contained in the mandate itself'.[52] Third, he made clear that Walvis Bay would remain part of South Africa, and refused even to discuss the question. Finally, he said that change must be agreed by the various peoples of the Territory, based on the recognition of separate groups.[53]

Nevertheless, in 1977 Vorster had to take into account mounting international pressures, even the threat of sanctions, as a result of Soweto and the advent of the Carter Administration. A willingness to make some concessions on Namibia might help to reduce the

221

pressures and allow more time to deal with the pressing domestic crisis. This was essentially the enticement Kissinger had offered to engage Vorster's co-operation first on Rhodesia and then on Namibia, and Vorster was willing to continue negotiations on the latter issue, in spite of his bitter reaction to the Carter Administration. The Americans now sought the co-operation of Western allies in launching a new joint initiative through a 'Contact Group' of the five Western powers then members of the UN Security Council: the three permanent members – US, UK and France – plus Canada and West Germany. Formed early in 1977 by the new US Ambassador to the UN, Andrew Young, the Group was led by Young's deputy, Don McHenry, and during the next two years conducted the most intensive negotiations in the history of this dispute.[54] The Group talked not only to the South Africans and SWAPO, but also to the FLS whose support was essential if the negotiations were to succeed.

A set of initial proposals, based on Security Council resolution 385 (January 1976), was presented to Vorster in April 1977. It included elections under UN supervision, an orderly withdrawal of South African military forces, the release of political prisoners, the free return of exiles and the abandonment of the Turnhalle plans for an interim government. Vorster's approach was still ambivalent: he was not yet prepared to abandon the Turnhalle concept, which was strongly supported in a referendum of Namibian whites in May, yet he remained flexible enough to encourage the Contact Group. Even US Vice-President Mondale commented, after the generally unproductive meeting in Vienna with Vorster in late May, that on Namibia at least Pretoria was moving 'in a positive direction in certain important respects'.[55] South African perceptions of the security threat posed by SWAPO's communist links and by UN partiality to SWAPO were obstacles which would continue to block an agreement. Nevertheless progress was made during 1977.

The seriousness of Vorster's intention to maintain the momentum on the international track of his Namibian policy became clear in June, when he told a stunned parliament of a major policy shift whereby the government would introduce steps that could lead to Namibia's independence. Pretoria saw independence as a possible option, not yet as a commitment, but parliament agreed to the abolition of the representation of Namibian whites in Cape Town and provided for the appointment of an Administrator General.[56] Judge M. T. Steyn's appointment to this post in August marked the end of the Turnhalle experiment. While the diplomatic progress caused optimism in some quarters in South Africa, there were indications of dissatisfaction among the military. *Die Burger*, an NP paper closely linked to Defence Minister P. W. Botha, pointed out that the government, and especially Botha, had often made clear that the Defence Force would only withdraw when the 'nations concerned in the Territory' asked for its withdrawal. As long as they had this authority, the situation remained unchanged.[57] On the other side of the political spectrum, SWAPO leaders were also dissatisfied, especially with the West's acceptance of a South African Administrator General, arguing that it was 'the exclusive prerogative of the UN' to administer Namibia before elections.[58] But the FLS insisted that SWAPO must remain involved in the negotiations.

Although Pretoria maintained a hard line on security issues such as the size and role of the proposed UN military presence and withdrawal of South African forces, its resistance was weakening as a result of international reaction to events within the Republic, including the mandatory UN arms embargo. In April 1978, when the Contact Group presented its proposals, Vorster accepted them fairly quickly, with some reservations, while SWAPO argued that they favoured Pretoria. Efforts to persuade SWAPO to agree were endangered by the detention of nine of its executive members within Namibia, and the launching in early May of a major attack against SWAPO camps at Cassinga, 250 km. within Angola. That action (Operation Reindeer) was unanimously condemned by the Security Council. Nevertheless, the FLS persuaded SWAPO to rejoin the negotiations, and finally in mid July it indicated agreement. On 27 July the Security Council adopted resolution 431 (with the Soviet Union and Czechoslovakia abstaining), taking note of the Western 'proposal for a settlement' and requesting the Secretary General to submit recommendations for implementation and to appoint a Special Representative. The choice fell on Mr Martti Ahtisaari of Finland, who had previously held the post of UN Commissioner for Namibia.

The main elements in the Western proposal were: elections for a constituent assembly; a transitional period of seven months, during which the Administrator General would retain authority and organise the elections, working closely with the UN Special Representative who would have to be satisfied with the fairness of all measures; the creation of a UN Transition Assistance Group (UNTAG), with civilian and military sections; primary responsibility for law and order to remain with the existing police forces during the transition, but with their conduct monitored by UNTAG; all discriminatory legislation to be repealed, political prisoners or detainees to be released, and all Namibians outside to be permitted to return; a cease-fire to be observed by all parties, with the restriction of both South African and SWAPO armed forces to base and a phased withdrawal of all but 1,500 South African troops; and certification of the election results by the Special Representative, after which the constituent assembly would meet, with a new government installed and independence granted once the constitution was adopted.

At last it appeared that the interminable Namibian problem was on the point of settlement. It was not. The seeds of discord remained. Although Walvis Bay, the South African enclave, was not mentioned in the Western proposal, a separate resolution (432) was also adopted on 27 July, calling for the early integration of Walvis Bay into Namibia (but not necessarily before independence). This decision was a compromise to meet SWAPO's concerns and to obtain the necessary support for resolution 431, but Pretoria reacted furiously against it, and although it reiterated its acceptance in principle of the Western proposal, doubts and mistrust were again becoming evident. These were compounded by disputes over the interim arrangements, with Pretoria suspicious that the UN was attempting to take control rather than monitor the situation.

The Secretary General's plan for implementing the Western proposal was submitted at the end of August,[59] and later approved in Resolution 435. Pretoria claimed that it contained deviations from the original proposal which it had accepted in 'final and definitive form' with regard to the role of UNTAG and the Special Representative. The cabinet, chaired by P. W. Botha in the absence of the ailing Vorster, rejected Kurt Waldheim's plan. Botha told an NP Congress that the government would 'not allow a SWAPO take-over in South West Africa',[60] which clearly he believed would happen if the UN were allowed to play a significant role. Security concerns were therefore again becoming stronger, and the case of diplomacy and compromise was weakening as the level of international pressure fell during 1978. Domestic disturbances had subsided and the government felt more secure, with international attention diverted by conflicts in Lebanon and Iran. The shock of the arms embargo had largely passed and the threat of further sanctions appeared groundless, while in Rhodesia the internal settlement appeared at this stage to be working. The pressing need to make concessions on Namibia was receding.

When Vorster announced his resignation on 20 September, he confirmed the intention to go ahead with elections in Namibia in December, to elect a constituent assembly which would be able to decide whether to draw up its own constitution or to accept the UN 435 plan. This was a clear rebuff of the UN and the Contact Group.

12 SOWETO – THE INTERNATIONAL IMPACT

Since the collapse of Portuguese colonial rule the superpowers had increasingly been drawn into southern Africa, and both sides took Soweto as a sign of profound change. The Soviet Union and its allies had long given military and diplomatic support to 'the liberation movements' in which the USSR favoured the ANC because of its links with the pro-soviet SACP, and because of the Republic's large working class. Indeed the ANC/SACP alliance was taken as a model for all Africa in a Freedom Manifesto published in Moscow in 1978.[1] Soviet support also continued for ZAPU in Rhodesia and SWAPO in Namibia. In SWAPO's case the USSR had consistently given military and material aid and recognised it as the people's sole legitimate representative. At the UN the USSR consistently opposed South Africa and accused the West of supporting her. The pattern continued as the Contact Group sought a settlement, which the Soviets said would install a puppet pro-Western regime.

Alongside continuing support for the liberation struggles, the emergence of Marxist governments opened up new opportunities for the communist bloc. This was best illustrated in Angola where the MPLA Government became dependent on Soviet aid and Cuban troops. In the eyes of most black states the South African invasion had legitimised the USSR's role and the Soviet Government was able to consolidate this in 1976 by signing a Treaty of Friendship and Co-operation which, while accepting Angola's non-aligned status, gave economic and military aid without committing Moscow to much. A relationship also developed with Mozambique where USSR support of the victorious FRELIMO led in March 1977 to another Treaty of Friendship which too emphasised 'unbreakable friendship', stressed the importance of military co-operation and agreed mutual support if there were a threat to peace, but again did not heavily commit

Moscow. However, Mozambique invoked that clause in February 1981 following a South African raid on ANC offices in Maputo. Two Soviet warships, *en route* East, called in the port and the Soviet Ambassador stated that: 'We are not threatening anyone, but if anyone attacks our friends we will give an appropriate response.'[2] Another indication of increased Soviet awareness was the appointment of a leading African expert Vasily Solodonikov as Ambassador to Zambia where he was in a key position to monitor regional developments.

Pretoria, which had always identified communism as its main external threat, now found the enemy at the gate. Regional developments between 1974 and 1976 had reinforced fears of a communist plan for southern Africa to include domination of the sea lanes, control of mineral supplies and the overthrow of white power. The developments also served to reinforce Pretoria's self-image as a bastion of the West standing firmly, if often alone, against the communist threat. It infuriated the government that the major Western powers either failed to understand the situation or were too timid to act. In January 1978 P. W. Botha said that there was 'unprecedented intervention on the part of the super powers . . . South Africa is experiencing the full onslaught of Marxism and it must not be doubted that the Republic enjoys a high priority in the onslaught by Moscow . . . However, South Africa is also experiencing double standards on the part of certain Western bodies in their behaviour to her. They are doing this in an attempt to pay a ransom to the bear whose hunger must be satisfied.'[3] Such fears were shared by some 'right-wing' Western groups who saw the USSR 'helping history along' in its progress to communist domination, and like Pretoria they feared that the West lacked the will to take a stand.[4] Within this context Pretoria both expressed concern and noted its limitations. P. W. Botha described his country as 'a medium sized power' whose objectives were to defend its own frontiers and coasts and give what help it could to defend the sea routes, but because of resource limitations 'we cannot defy a great power. Nor is that our policy.'[5]

Yet, while global politics and the actions of the superpowers intruded more obviously into South Africa's foreign policy setting, neither southern Africa nor the South African issue at international gatherings was high among USSR or US priorities. In both cases their degree of concern had increased and they would take what advantage they could of the situation and counter perceived dangers, but their main interests and commitments were elsewhere. Nor did Pretoria's concern at communist expansion lead to greater contacts with the communist powers. They were seen as the major enemy but one with whom there was little day to day contact. The picture was different with the West.

WESTERN CONTACTS

The Western states with strong South African links – Britain, US, West Germany, France – came under intense international pressure following Soweto, and they too joined the chorus of condemnation. 'We face in South Africa', said David Owen, 'the greatest challenge to our universal policy on human rights . . . the evil of institutionalised racism.'[6] But radical critics wanted more than condemnation; they wanted action. They pointed to the example of the Scandinavian governments which gave support to the ANC and urged the major Western states to follow suit and to impose mandatory economic sanctions. Some Western governments also faced strong pressures at home – as anti-apartheid groups, churches, opposition parties and students demanded the end of South African ties; and the media exposed the brutality and inhumanity of apartheid. The domestic pressure varied considerably. At one end of the spectrum the British Government faced established, well-organised anti-apartheid bodies, whereas there was little pressure in Japan. Although the West failed to satisfy the critics' demands, they did take further steps against Pretoria; reducing sporting links and introducing codes of conduct and eventually a mandatory arms ban. Vorster was bitter. In his 1977 New Year address he said that the West had 'lost its will to take a firm stand against the increasing [communist] menace'. With Angola in mind he concluded that if 'a Communist onslaught should be made against South Africa, directly or under camouflage, South Africa will have to face it alone, and certain countries which profess to be anti-Communist will even refuse to sell [us] arms'.[7]

Yet, while restrictions were imposed, some contacts flourished, especially economic, and others were in dispute. These included sport which continued to capture attention inside as well as outside South Africa. At its 1976 Congress the NP approved competition between clubs of different races but not the establishment of mixed race clubs, and the Minister, Piet Koornhof, confirmed that sports policy would never be allowed to threaten the separate identity of the racial groups.[8] At an international level, although links remained, the tide continued to run against the Republic. In 1976, for example, the International Amateur Athletics Association and the International Football Federation suspended South Africa. In the following year Commonwealth members signed the Gleneagles Agreement by which each government agreed to discourage sporting contacts (in accordance with its own laws) because these contacts might encourage a belief that apartheid was condoned.[9] For South Africans the implications were felt most keenly in reduced contacts with Britain, Australia and New Zealand.

A major thrust of Western policy became the attempt to use economic contacts as levers for reform. In 1974 Britain had introduced its Code of Practice and in the wake of Soweto further codes were introduced. In contrast with the demands to isolate Pretoria (through disinvestment and sanctions) this approach assumed that economic contacts could be used to promote reform, first in the workplace and then leading to broader social and political change. In September 1977 Britain proposed a European Community code for firms of member states. 'The Code of Conduct' was agreed shortly before a major UN anti-apartheid meeting in Nigeria and was intended both to promote reform and to forestall criticism of Community inactivity. In parallel with the European move, an American initiative was under way. In March 1977, after Secretary of State Vance had met business-men and church leaders, the Revd Leon Sullivan published guidelines for US companies. In July 1978 he set them out in the 'Sullivan Principles'. Unlike the EC code, which was sponsored by govern-ments, this rested on agreements with companies. However, both Code and Principles were met by opposition and scepticism. Some businessmen complained of political interference and problems of implementation, but the sharpest reaction came from radical critics who dismissed them as cover for Western capitalist exploitation. In Pretoria, except for a touch of exasperation at foreign interference, the response was low-key, based on a view that the codes might bring reform to the workplace but were not a political threat.[10]

1977 saw a clear change in the West's position at the UN. Previously, the permanent members of the Security Council had vetoed man-datory action against Pretoria (which could only be invoked if inter-national peace and security were threatened under Chapter VIII of the Charter). However, in October 1977 they proposed a six-month mandatory arms ban, arguing that the acquisition of arms by South Africa now constituted a threat to peace. The African Council members responded by proposing full mandatory sanctions, and although the West vetoed this they conceded that the arms ban should be indefinite and supported a resolution calling for the release of political prisoners and the abolition of the homelands policy. The Council then instructed all states to cease the supply of arms.[11] In taking this step the West was responding to the outcry against the

October detentions and Steve Biko's death. Shortly before these events David Owen had told an AAM delegation that the British Government would not support a mandatory arms ban. Yet so great was the shock of Biko's death and Pretoria's callous response that Britain had to demonstrate its repugnance and supported the ban.[12]

Despite the absence of sanctions the South African economy suffered. As in previous crises business confidence was undermined, foreign capital withdrawn and reinvestment declined. A 1977 UN report showed that foreign firms had cut by half reinvestment of earnings in their South African operations. Disinvestment campaigns were launched, notably in the US where churches and universities were in the forefront. In response Pretoria took counter measures – lifting restrictions on foreign investment, stockpiling essential goods, threatening to play 'the mineral card' and urging foreign firms to keep faith. Chris Heunis, Minister of Economic Affairs, called on firms to persuade their governments that anti-South African measures were counter-productive, and he had the consolation that the major Western states refused to impose mandatory economic sanctions. There were several reasons for this. One was disillusionment over Rhodesian sanctions. Others were concern that Afrikaner intransigence might increase; scepticism about effective implementation; hopes that economic contacts would bring change; fear about the adverse effects on neighbouring states and black South Africans; and worry about the impact at home. Among Western states attitudes to sanctions were influenced by self-interest. In relative terms Britain's stake was still greater than any other. In 1975, Britain had 10 per cent of its total foreign investment in South Africa, whereas the US had 1.5 per cent and West Germany 1.1 per cent, and while 1,200 British firms were represented there the West Germans had 350 and the US 335.[13] The British Labour Government warned that: 'Prudent businessmen and prudent investors no less than the British government should be taking a hard look at their South African connections. We stand to lose more than most if things go wrong.'[14] Yet, in taking a hard look, businessmen, and not only those from Britain, soon began to recover confidence. As in the past the economic impact of the political crisis was relatively short-lived, for as Pretoria regained its security grip the Western business community regained its appetite for involvement.

Profit was certainly one of the motives for continued contact, but so was concern about the supply of vital resources. Alerted by the 1973–4 OPEC oil shock there was special concern about southern Africa's minerals. Among these chrome provides an example of the issues at stake. Between 1970 and 1980 the world trade in chrome doubled as industrial demand increased. There was no easy substitute, and although supplies were plentiful in the main production areas (Soviet Union and southern Africa – Rhodesia and South Africa) chrome had become 'critical' for Western economies. South Africa was an attractive supplier because of its relatively low labour costs, its investment in research, its reliability and its sound infrastructure. Added to that, by 1977 the international chrome market was in confusion when Soviet supplies became erratic and the US repealed the Byrd Amendment (by which the US had continued to import Rhodesian chrome). In that situation South Africa, which in 1978 produced 35 per cent of the world's chrome and 52 per cent of ferrochrome, was of key importance. In 1977–8 the Republic supplied 50 per cent of the EEC's chrome (70 per cent in Britain's case) and 48 per cent of the US's. Pretoria was alert to the situation. Although the industry was in private hands the government provided a supportive framework and services, and it influenced the market by its taxation, transport and credit policies. At this time more precise government steps included the establishment of a Minerals Policy Committee composed of senior government officials and personnel from the private sector, and the appointment of specialised mineral officials to consular posts abroad.[15] On their side, Western businessmen were not slow to voice their fears about a possible interruption of supplies because of UN sanctions or South African reprisals or communist resource denial.

South Africa's minerals were especially important to Japan with its booming industries but limited natural resources. Until the 1960s bilateral trade had been small, but then it increased rapidly ($179m. in 1962, $552m. in 1968, and $1,822m. by 1976). The Japanese, who needed both fuel and industrial minerals, had signed a uranium contract with the Rossing Mine in December 1973 and later started to import coal. On the industrial side they became major importers of platinum, chrome, manganese, cobalt and vanadium, and in return sold motor vehicles, electrical goods and high technology including some used in the Sasol plants. The economic contacts continued to grow even after Soweto, but Japan was reasonably successful in projecting an anti-apartheid image and keeping economics and politics apart by restricting diplomatic contacts to an exchange of Consuls, and banning investment by her citizens. However, the image masked extensive economic links, which were handled through the Consuls, while the restriction on investments was circumvented by using overseas branches of firms, locally franchised partners and Bantustans. There was international criticism but the Japanese escaped lightly because there was little anti-apartheid activity at home, and the small protest groups were outmatched by those favouring contact, such as the Nippon Club of South Africa.[16]

RELATIONS WITH THE US

The more active role of the US reflected not only regional and global concerns but increased awareness at home where anti-apartheid groups became active. While Pretoria welcomed the idea of involving the major anti-communist power, in practice the relationship was frequently strained, as had been shown in Angola. Looking back at that bitter experience P. W. Botha said 'we were ruthlessly left in the lurch', and he countered complaints about Pretoria's continuing involvement by recalling a time when 'American aircraft offloaded arms at military positions and bases [in Angola] which were held by South African troops.'[17] The plurality of US policy making, with its eye on domestic interests, continued to confuse and irritate the government, and US involvement often left Pretoria responding to developments not shaping them. However, the bitterness was not directed personally at Kissinger. His 'realpolitik' approach was welcomed because Pretoria also sought regional stability, the defence of Western interests and a counter to communist expansion. Kissinger also avoided moral posturing and expressed sympathy for the white position. Pik Botha recounted how he said that 'the whites have an historic right to be in this country, that our problems are immensely more complicated than those of Rhodesia and South West Africa and therefore the solutions need not be all the same'.[18] There was also a shared belief that the best approach was to isolate and solve particular problems. In Kissinger's view, the most pressing was not apartheid but Rhodesia, followed by Namibia. With tenacity and imagination he hoped that solutions could be hammered out, and in that spirit Pretoria helped him. 'We leaned over backwards', said Pik Botha, 'to act constructively in an attempt to find peaceful solutions to the problems of southern Africa.'[19]

Kissinger turned to southern Africa late in his period of office, and in the short time available to him his efforts failed. At the beginning of 1977 a new US administration came to power. Jimmy Carter, the President, had already promised 'unequivocal and concrete support for majority rule in South Africa', which must have alarmed Pretoria, but at first Vorster was cautious. When asked if he was worried about the new administration he replied it was 'more a question of wondering than worrying'.[20] The wondering persisted as different voices still came out of Washington and the worrying soon started. Pik Botha spoke of 'a great about face in the USA's attitude towards South Africa'.[21] The language and aims of 'realpolitik' were replaced by those of 'human rights', and the isolation of issues was abandoned in favour of facing the core problem of racial discrimination. 'Our policies', said Cyrus Vance, the Secretary of State, 'must reflect our national values. Our deep belief in human rights . . . means making our best effort peacefully to promote racial justice in southern Africa.'[22] While Kissinger had been criticised for concentrating on short-term aims at the expense of the deep-seated racial issues which were the root of the region's problems, the new administration was criticised for seeking long-term aims which it could not achieve, and thereby losing influence in Pretoria which could have been used for more limited objectives.

The change and the diversity was signalled in Carter's appointments. Among the most important were those to the UN, where initially much of southern African policy was shaped. Andrew Young, a black civil rights worker, was made US representative. With his deputy, Don McHenry (also a black politician) he set the pace and direction of policy: emphasising human rights; setting the Republic in an African rather than a global context; and showing himself to be committed to ending apartheid. Young alienated Pretoria by branding it a 'racist illegitimate' regime and compounded his sins by saying that the US was prepared to work with Marxist governments, and the Cubans in Angola were a stabilising force. Visiting Africa in February 1977 Young assured the black states and liberation movements that the US supported majority rule, and he called on Pretoria to pressure Smith into an agreement. In March 1977 a US 'Declaration on Southern Africa' was delivered to Vorster, calling for the elimination of apartheid, equal rights for all, an end to the illegal occupation of Namibia and compliance with the UN sanctions against Rhodesia.[23] The change in the US approach was not only rhetorical. After tightening the voluntary arms embargo, withdrawing some bank loans and credit facilities and supporting the Sullivan Principles, the US played a prominent part in promoting the UN mandatory arms ban.

Yet there were more conciliatory voices in Washington. When Anthony Lake, a State Department official, outlined policy assumptions, although he concluded that Kissinger had failed, he saw Pretoria becoming more 'enlightened' not from US influence but because of pressure from blacks at home and in neighbouring territories. Unlike Young, he concluded that the US could not force change in South Africa and should 'set clear limits on the scope of our relations'.[24] In July 1977 Cyrus Vance himself tried to lower the temperature by seeking to persuade rather than threaten. He said that America had limited influence and could not dictate terms, and like Kissinger he argued that her best role was as a bridge between the white and black states. However, he repeated the point that progress had to be made there against racism if a long-term settlement were to be achieved.[25]

The South Africans, who were more conscious of the verbal attacks than the conciliatory speeches, were especially furious with Walter Mondale, the US Vice President. Mondale met Vorster in Vienna in May 1977. During the meeting he made clear that the US would not reduce pressure against apartheid in return for help on Rhodesia or Namibia. In that case, responded Vorster, there would be no help from Pretoria. The meeting with Mondale was unsatisfactory, but worse followed at a press conference where Mondale said the US 'cannot accept, let alone defend, governments that reject the basic principles of full human rights'. He warned that the perpetuation of an unjust society would encourage Soviet expansion, and without progress to end discrimination relations between the US and Pretoria would be strained, nor would the US intervene to save Pretoria from the tragic consequences of its policies. Questioned on political participation, he stated: 'Every citizen should have the right to vote and every vote should be equally weighed.' It was a statement which white South Africans never forgot or forgave. Vorster responded immediately saying that, although South Africa wanted good relations with the US, the whites were not prepared to share political power in their own territory, for to share power would be to lose it. He said he had the right to expect others to appreciate the complex issues involved and his government's efforts to do justice to all.[26]

At home, Vorster was less circumspect. Speaking at a Foreign Affairs banquet he accused the US of embarking on a course that would lead to regional anarchy. The result would be the same as a Marxist revolution, for while the American approach was 'strangulation with finesse' the Marxist was 'death by brute force'.[27] Pik Botha was equally blunt. He asserted that 'neither Mr Carter nor Mr Mondale has a monopoly on morality', and described Mondale's behaviour as 'superficial and noisy'. After noting that South Africa had fought alongside the US and had never relied on her economically, he accused Washington of misunderstanding southern Africa. If South Africa was to avoid confrontation with the US it was best to be blunt 'to bring it to its senses'.[28] A number of explanations were suggested for US behaviour. Vorster said that the basic mistake was 'to equate the situation and the position of the American Negro with the South African Black', whereas the situations were quite different. Unlike the American blacks, who had lost their own language and culture, South Africa's blacks had distinctive languages and cultures in a multinational not a multiracial society.[29] Pik Botha added that the Americans assumed that as the Third World and the Soviet bloc would become increasingly dependent on Western technology it was pointless to confront the USSR everywhere. Thus South Africa's anti-communism 'is not necessarily regarded as a virtue by the USA any longer', for it believed that the USSR would over-extend itself in Africa. While, said Pik, that might be reassuring for Americans, it was not for Africans who would suffer if the assumption were false. He further argued that the US, disillusioned after Watergate, 'has made human rights an important, if not the main pillar of its foreign policy', and in domestic politics Carter was dependent on the black electoral support. He concluded that the US had decided that good relations with South Africa were against its interests and had committed itself to majority rule on a false understanding of human rights, which deprived the whites of the right to govern themselves and to be themselves.[30]

Despite the disputes with Pretoria the Carter Administration was not the darling of the radicals. Washington's aim was to gain change by peaceful steps, not by armed struggle. Nor did it want to withdraw American business from the Republic, but rather to use it for change. As President elect Carter had suggested that 'our businessmen can be a constructive force in achieving racial justice within South Africa', and Andrew Young repeated the point in January 1977, saying that the time was ripe for non-violent change via the market place – a transformation 'better than any other so-called revolutionary system going'. It was in this spirit that the US opposed mandatory economic sanctions.[31] Furthermore the characteristic pluralism of the US Government ensured that there were those in the administration who were more concerned with East/West rivalry than human rights in southern Africa, and their voice was increasingly heard as the administration lost momentum especially after the Iranian revolution in 1979.

DEFEATING THE ARMS EMBARGO

The mandatory arms ban was a blow to Pretoria. Despite the expanding domestic arms industry there was still reliance on external sources for large and sophisticated items. In April 1977, before the mandatory ban was imposed, P. W. Botha announced that 43 per cent

234

of current defence hardware was purchased externally, but he explained that this figure dropped to 25 per cent if naval vessels (mainly from France) were excluded.[32] Following the ban some suppliers withdrew, including France which announced that it would not deliver two corvettes and two submarines already under construction. Despite such set-backs Pretoria was determined to ensure that its forces were well equipped and had no compunction in undermining the UN ban because it regarded the ban as illegal, and because it saw itself in a battle for survival. 'If we do not understand that we are in a struggle for survival', said P. W. Botha, 'we will not be able to make the sacrifices that are necessary.'[33] Pretoria, which was already well versed in circumventing the 1963 voluntary ban, developed further an already well established pattern. This included trading with governments which were prepared to ignore the UN; increasing domestic arms production; and making secret deals with private manufacturers and dealers.

The South Africans were tenacious in their search for arms. Despite the secrecy which surrounded the search, enough evidence emerged to show that a wide range of sources was tapped. Some governments (including Italy, Taiwan and Israel) could not or would not impose the ban, and even communist states were probably involved. Between 1976 and 1981 there were reports that five large consignments of arms arrived from Bulgaria, each worth between $8m. and $20m.[34] Alongside the deals with governments were those with private companies. One concerned a new 155 mm. gun. The search for improved artillery had started after the South Africans had been outgunned by the Cubans in Angola. The solution came in a deal with an American company, Space Research Corporation of Vermont, which covered its tracks by using 'paper chases' and shipping arrangements through Canada, Antigua and Spain. A US Senate committee later uncovered the deal whereby between 1976 and 1978 the company delivered 60,000 shells and at least four guns with the technology to produce more. As the weapons were mainly supplied from army stores the committee not surprisingly concluded that several US agencies were at fault and the monitoring of arms sales was inadequate.[35] Late in 1978 P. W. Botha, by then Prime Minister, triumphantly announced the development of new 155 mm. artillery and shells. Although Botha denied that the technology had been smuggled from the US, Armscor had succeeded in refining the American system into advanced battlefield artillery.

Armscor became a corner-stone of South Africa's security arrangements. It was already well established when the mandatory ban was imposed, and following that it expanded rapidly through its own enterprise, through covert deals and through the continued manufacture of foreign arms under licence. For example, when the French announced the embargo on the warships they also explained that they could not prevent the manufacture of arms for which licences and blueprints had been sold – including Mirage aircraft, Panhard armoured cars and anti-aircraft missiles. The expansion of Armscor, which became one of the largest financial and manufacturing undertakings in the Republic, was a joint government and private venture promoted by P. W. Botha as Defence Minister. In 1977 he called a meeting at the Rand Afrikaans University which was a '"take-off point" in the military–industrial complex'.[36] It reinforced links between civil and military interests and incorporated part of the business elite into the military realm.[37] Substantial contracts were placed throughout the private sector and many workers became dependent, directly and indirectly, on the arms industry. In 1978 Armscor itself directly employed 19,000 people, and that grew to 29,000 by 1981. As a result of the activity South Africa was not only able to match its own needs in many weapons but became an arms exporter.

RELATIONS WITH ISRAEL

The arms ban illustrated that South Africa was an international pariah, a member of 'the league of the desperate', which also included Israel. In these circumstances the two states combined to share economic and military strengths, to reduce psychological isolation and to limit their dependence on others. Before the 1970s there was a long-standing but equivocal relationship between the two which had been subjected to contradictory pulls: the sympathy of South Africa's Jews for Israel, matched by Israel's suspicion of Pretoria's racist policies; and economic links (including an important trade in diamonds) matched by diplomatic coolness as Israel sought influence in black Africa. Even when the two states moved closer in the 1970s it was a relationship of convenience not affection. They drew together as enemies marshalled on their borders and they shared the humiliation of 'pariah' status. In the General Assembly they were both condemned as 'racist', Zionism was bracketed with apartheid, the PLO and ANC were supported as liberation movements, after the 1973 Arab/Israeli war the Arabs denied oil to South Africa and black African states broke ties with Israel. In contrast, during the war Pretoria had supplied Israel with spare parts for weapons, and South Africa's Jews gave substantial financial support.

With characteristic panache the Information Department took the initiative. Its 'Operation David' envisaged Israel and South Africa standing together as pillars of the Free World in two vital but volatile regions and, on a more prosaic scale, Mulder argued that links with Israel might improve relations with the US. Foreign Affairs was more cautious, pointing to Israel's attempts to woo black Africa and the danger of permanently antagonising the Arab states. Vorster also had personal doubts, fearing that his wartime record might make him unacceptable to the Israelis. Despite this the Information Department pushed ahead. Rhoodie made fourteen trips to Israel in two years and following a secret visit with Mulder in June 1975 the Israelis sent an invitation to Vorster. After some hestitation he went in April 1976, taking with him Muller and Brand Fourie of Foreign Affairs, not Mulder and Rhoodie. Orthodox diplomacy took over 'when the trumpets sounded and the guards of honour stepped to the front'.[38] If nothing else the visit was important in demonstrating mutual support among 'pariahs', but there was more to it than that. On his return, Vorster spoke of 'co-operation between middle-rank countries', and outlined agreements that had been reached – encouragement of investment, scientific and industrial activities, combined projects using Israeli manpower and South African minerals, and joint ministerial committees to foster co-operation.[39]

The fruits of co-operation soon appeared. There was a significant increase in trade. In 1970 Israel had exported goods worth $10.7m. to South Africa and imported $10.2m.; by 1980 the respective figures were $80m. and $117m.[40] A joint steel project was developed, imports of South African coal reduced Israel's reliance on oil and intelligence agencies exchanged information. During his visit Vorster suggested joint arms production and asked for Israel's help (either directly or as a channel) in obtaining naval vessels, fighter aircraft and counter-insurgency equipment. He received a warm response as Israel soon supplied refurbished tanks and three Reshof class missile-carrying boats (armed with Italian guns and Israeli Gabriel missiles) and agreed that Armscor could manufacture another nine boats and missiles. For its part Pretoria provided improved tank armour. There were also exchanges of military personnel and Israeli advisers helped plan the Republic's border defences.[41] In their public statements neither Vorster nor the Israelis mentioned the arms deals, but they became especially important for Pretoria after Soweto and the arms ban, and continued at least until 1987 when US pressure on Israel may have brought them to an end. Before that it was estimated that Pretoria had purchased several hundred million dollars worth of arms, including advanced navigational and electronic equipment which enabled the South Africans to improve their aircraft to evade Soviet air defence systems supplied to Angola, and to convert two Boeing 707 in-flight refuelling tankers which greatly extended the range of Pretoria's air power.[42]

SOUTH AFRICA AND NUCLEAR POWER

Israel co-operated with South Africa in the development of a nuclear industry, and along with Taiwan may have helped in the development and testing of nuclear weapons. The nuclear co-operation with Israel, which included trips by leading scientists, started in the 1960s, and Vorster's visit may have extended it to include an exchange of Israeli technology for South African uranium and the use of South African territory to test nuclear bombs. In the case of Taiwan the co-operation came later. When the Taiwan Premier visited South Africa in March 1980 he visited Pelindaba and signed an agreement to buy uranium. On P. W. Botha's return visit to Taiwan in October of that year he spoke of an exchange of know-how and information and said that military matters had been discussed, although they may not have included nuclear weapons.[43]

Pretoria was always keen to participate in nuclear developments and the arms ban increased its determination. As one of the world's main sources of uranium, South Africa had been involved in the nuclear industry from its early days. The uranium came both as a by-product of the gold industry and from direct mining, notably at the Rossing mine in Namibia, owned by the British company Rio Tinto Zinc. The early trade was with Britain and the US, with whom long-term agreements were signed to supply uranium. However, the growth of the international nuclear power industry was slower than anticipated, and South Africa's uranium production which had reached 6,400 tons in 1959 fell in the 1960s and 70s and only reached 6,000 tons again in 1980. Yet the Republic's importance as a uranium producer was reflected first in its continuing trade (the US imported $450m. worth between 1953 and 1971) and second its membership (along with Australia, France and Canada but excluding the US) of a cartel, the 'Société d'Etudes et de Recherches d'Uranium', which was formed in 1972 and succeeded in raising the price of uranium from $7 a pound in 1972 to $20 a pound in 1976.[44] Inevitably criticism arose of Pretoria's role in nuclear affairs and pressure was exerted against it at the International Atomic Energy Agency (IAEA). Despite Western arguments that it was easier to influence and check the activities of those states which were inside the organisation, the Republic lost her seat on the Board of Governors in 1977 and two years later, in a move similar to that in the UN General Assembly, a majority of members rejected her credentials at the IAEA's General Conference.

Pretoria was not content merely to mine and sell uranium but set out to create its own nuclear power industry. As early as 1946 Smuts appointed a Uranium Research Committee, and in 1949 the Atomic Energy Board was established. By July 1963 a nuclear research station had been built at Pelindaba; in 1970 Vorster announced that a new technique for enriching uranium was being developed; and in 1974 it was decided to construct a commercial light-water reactor at Koeberg near Cape Town. Although South African scientists made substantial contributions to these developments, they could not have achieved them without considerable international help. This came from several sources and in several forms, including the exchange of scientists and information, and the sale of plant and enriched uranium. At first the US was the main partner, importing uranium in return for technology and enriched uranium. In 1957 a twenty-year agreement was signed which included co-operation in research and the exchange of scientists and students, and when South Africa built a small research reactor (SAFARI I) in 1962 the technology and fuel were supplied by America. Despite increasing anti-apartheid protests the contacts continued: for example in 1973 the Foxboro Company sold two computers for the Pelindaba enrichment plant. In 1976 Dr A. J. A. Roux, President of the South African Atomic Energy Board, said that most of the equipment at Pelindaba was from the US and although South Africa had its own nuclear philosophy it 'owes much to the thinking of American scientists'.[45]

There was, however, increasing tension in the US nuclear relationship. Inside America opposition came from anti-apartheid groups and from those who were concerned at Pretoria's failure to sign the Non-Proliferation Treaty (NPT), while in contrast support continued from those with commercial interests and others who believed that influence could best be exerted by technical co-operation. By the early 1970s Washington was moving cautiously because of the political division at home. The government continued to supply fuel rods for South Africa's plants but avoided publicity and refused to co-operate in an advanced enrichment process. Undeterred, Pretoria announced in 1974 plans for a large enrichment plant which would produce mainly for export.[46] When in 1976 General Electric of the US applied to export $2 billion worth of nuclear plant for Koeberg, the Ford Administration was ready to agree, but after critical Senate hearings and threats to cut export credit guarantees the deal was cancelled.[47]

Pretoria therefore turned elsewhere. In the case of the Koeberg plant a French consortium won the major contract, and by early 1978 more than 100 South African technicians were in France training to operate the reactors. By 1985, despite ANC sabotage which delayed the work, they were in operation. Koeberg was done openly, with French leaders denying that the reactors could contribute to South Africa's nuclear weapons capability, for the spent fuel would be sent to France for reprocessing whereas, they argued, there was danger from the unguarded enrichment plant. In that case there was secret collaboration, notably with West Germany and Israel, which helped Pretoria to gain its much desired enrichment process. Mordechai Vananu, an Israeli technician, exposed his country's links while the collaboration with Germany was uncovered when anti-apartheid activists obtained copies of secret papers from the South African Embassy in Bonn.[48] Vorster claimed the new process as South Africa's own, but it was another example of the adaptation and development of foreign technology to the Republic's requirements by South African scientists. The scale of the new process was much smaller than the original proposal and was designed simply to supply South Africa's own reactors, but it gave Pretoria the degree of independence it wanted. In April 1981, immediately before the election, the government announced that enriched uranium elements had been produced. Although the enrichment was much lower than originally planned it was sufficient to produce weapons grade enriched uranium.[49]

One way of interpreting the external dimension of South Africa's nuclear industry is simply to see it as an aspect of peaceful economic and technological co-operation. However, other considerations come into play. One is that nuclear contacts can be used as bargaining counters. For example in 1976, while Kissinger was trying to reach regional agreements, James Blake, a senior official, told a US Senate hearing that the sale of nuclear facilities to Pretoria would help to maintain contacts and Kissinger's current efforts. When questioned he agreed that the sales might help to 'bring about a solution with Ian Smith in Rhodesia or in Namibia'.[50] Later, when the Carter Administration was eager to persuade Pretoria to sign the NPT, the South Africans, knowing the high value the US placed on it, pushed up their price. They said they would sign the treaty only if Washington would guarantee long-term supplies of uranium fuel for Koeberg, enriched uranium for the SAFARI research reactor, and non-sensitive technology for Valindaba. There was even speculation that Pretoria was trying to negotiate a US 'nuclear umbrella' as an incentive to abandon its own nuclear weapons. The Americans did not agree and the South Africans did not sign.

The concern which sets the nuclear industry apart from others is over nuclear weapons. Behind the negotiations of the 1970s was the nagging fear that Pretoria was developing its own bomb. Some governments took this more calmly than others. When France was chided for supplying the Koeberg reactors the Prime Minister, Raymond Barre, stated that South Africa 'already had a nuclear military capability and the reactors add nothing to that'.[51] Elsewhere there was more concern. As Pretoria had not signed the NPT there was consternation in August 1977 when Soviet, and later American, satellites discovered what appeared to be a nuclear test platform in the Kalahari Desert. Although Pretoria denied that a test was planned, there was hectic diplomatic activity with pleas and warnings to South Africa not to test a bomb for itself or for anybody else. No bomb was tested. Perhaps the South Africans ran into technical difficulties, but more probably diplomatic pressure told, especially from France who threatened to pull out of Koeberg if a test went ahead. Pretoria's responses were ambiguous. Connie Mulder, while denying posses-sion of nuclear weapons, said that if attacked no rules would apply and South Africa would use all means at her disposal, 'whatever they may be'.[52] Vorster, furious at the international pressure, said that if 'these things continue, the time will arrive when South Africa will have no option, small as it is, to say to the world, "So far and no further; do your damndest if you wish"'. Earlier, in 1976, he had said: 'We are only interested in the peaceful application of nuclear power', but added: 'We can enrich uranium. We have the capability, and we did not sign the nuclear Non-Proliferation Treaty.'[53] Later, in 1980, a senior official, Commander H. F. Nel, was reported to have said that 'it would be shortsighted of South Africa not to develop nuclear weapons if other African countries did so'.[54]

There was further international concern and much confusion in September 1979, and again in December 1980, when satellites picked up signals which might have indicated nuclear explosions in the southern oceans. In both cases, despite strong denials, there was suspicion that South Africa had tested weapons either for herself or in collaboration with Israel and Taiwan. However, the evidence was ambiguous and the concern was not simply about Pretoria's action (if indeed there had been action) but about the uncertainty which surrounded the detection of nuclear explosions. The outcome of the Kalahari and southern ocean incidents was therefore to stimulate

241

international concern, but not to provide firm evidence that the Republic had nuclear weapons. Yet, even if she did not possess them already, it was generally accepted that she had the capacity to produce them and an ability to deliver either via aircraft, small rockets, or, for tactical weapons, her 155 mm. artillery.

In 1988 Pik Botha refuelled international speculation in a statement that went as far as any previous government pronouncement. 'We have', he said, 'the capability to make one [a bomb] . . . We have the capability to do so should we want to.'[55] He was speaking in Vienna after talks with the US, Soviet and British officials about South Africa signing the NPT. The meeting followed a move in 1987, initiated by Nigeria, to expel Pretoria from the IAEA because of its refusal to sign the treaty. This was resisted by the major powers (including the USSR) because they were eager to keep South Africa in the organisation so that they could monitor developments and exert pressure on her to sign the NPT. Pretoria was unlikely to do that without major concessions.

Speculation about 'the bomb' was enough to raise the question of motivation. Why would Pretoria consider developing nuclear weapons? One answer was deterrence. In 1981 South African officials explained their country's reluctance to sign the NPT because it might 'set the minds of our would-be attackers at rest, allowing them to proceed freely with their plans against us'.[56] However, nuclear weapons (even tactical ones) seem inappropriate to counter the two immediate and obvious threats – guerrilla fighters and urban insurrection. Even guerrilla bases in neighbouring territories, or capitals such as Lusaka and Maputo, are unlikely targets, and nuclear weapons within South Africa's own townships are not an option. Also the threat of an attack by black conventional forces seems highly improbable, as does an assault by the major powers, with or without nuclear weapons. Nuclear weapons therefore appear inappropriate to match the threats facing the Republic. However, military planners may have reached different conclusions. Taking worst case scenarios to cover many years ahead, and recognising the long lead time required to develop nuclear weapons and delivery systems, the planners may have assumed a continuing deterioration of the military situation which could leave South Africa facing conventional assault and/or concentrations of guerrilla forces and/or superpower threats. In such situations (so this argument might go) nuclear weapons, including tactical weapons, might be a useful deterrent. In a world of uncertainty, in which Pretoria cannot even rely on those it regards as allies, it might be wise to hedge all bets against uncertainty.

While such military reasons may have been important, it seems as likely that nuclear weapons may have been developed for the intangibles that are associated with them – prestige, reassurances at home, a political lever on other states, and a demonstration of power and technical ability. They would increase bargaining power by showing the West that Pretoria is prepared and able to 'go it alone'. Each time the US has approached the South Africans to sign the NPT they have demanded concessions. For example, in June 1978 they asked for the resumption of deliveries of enriched uranium for their research reactor and the power stations, assured technology for the enrichment plant and US support to reinstate South Africa on the Board of Governors of the IAEA.[57] Again there was no agreement and no signature. Pretoria may also believe that it benefits from the uncertainty that surrounds nuclear weapons. One explanation of the 1977 Kalahari incident is that Pretoria simply intended to outwit the superpowers by pretending to prepare a test. That sounds unlikely, but the argument is that as nobody could be sure the effect is the same, because others have to assume the worst. If South Africa has nuclear weapons some riveting questions arise – In what circumstances, if ever, would they be used? Against whom? With what effect? The uncertainty may be compounded in South Africa's case by the references that have been made to 'the Masada spirit'. Would an Afrikaner government choose to go down fighting, using all its resources, including nuclear weapons, rather than surrender power? However unlikely that may appear, if such uncertainty can be induced in the minds of friends and foes, the government may believe that its search for status and security is enhanced by the possession of nuclear weapons.

PART V

DOMESTIC REFORM AND REGIONAL POWER: 1978–1984

13 THE ADVENT OF P. W. BOTHA AND THE RETURN OF CONFIDENCE

THE CHANGE IN LEADERSHIP

P. W. Botha became Prime Minister on 28 September 1978 after an internal Party struggle filled with suspicion and intrigue. The week between the announcement of Vorster's resignation and the election of a new National Party leader saw the most intense lobbying by the main contenders in the Party's history. The intrigue revolved mainly around the Information scandal (the extent of which was not yet publicly known) and the role in that affair of one of the main contenders for the premiership, Dr Connie Mulder. As leader of the NP in the Transvaal, Mulder had a strong political base and, if it had not been for questions about his responsibility for the Department of Information, his position as 'crown prince' to Vorster would have been unchallengeable. In the event, he came close to election by the Party caucus, winning seventy-two votes in the first ballot to P. W. Botha's seventy-eight and Pik Botha's twenty-two. The latter then withdrew in favour of P. W. Botha who won in the second ballot with ninety-eight votes to Mulder's seventy-four.[1]

P. W. Botha's election as leader in these dramatic and divisive circumstances, and his automatic appointment as Prime Minister, marked a significant break with the Vorster years. Very different in personality and style from his predecessor, he quickly set his stamp on the tone and even substance of policy and the management of government affairs, domestic and foreign. Essentially a Party man, Botha had started his working life as a Party organiser. He had risen through the ranks to be elected to parliament in 1953, to join Dr Verwoerd's cabinet in 1961 and to become Leader of the NP in the Cape Province in 1966. He had been Minister of Defence since 1966 and it was his experience in that portfolio which was to have the greatest influence on his leadership, particularly in the conduct of foreign policy.

South African foreign policy has always become closely identified with the person of the Prime Minister (and later State President). Policy concepts or initiatives, whether they originated with him or not, have tended to be closely associated with the current leader. This was particularly true of Vorster's 'outward', 'dialogue' and *détente* policies. Botha proved to be no exception, even though he had a high-profile Foreign Minister in Pik Botha. His name thus became associated with the concepts of a 'total national strategy', a 'constellation' of southern African states and, in domestic policy (but with foreign policy implications), with 'reform'.[2] Botha's years as Defence Minister gave him more exposure to foreign policy issues than Vorster had had in his Police portfolio. But they had had a common concern with security matters, and both came into office, following periods of internal disturbance and external threats, with reputations for toughness, ability to resist pressure, strident anti-communism and complete intolerance of militant black nationalism. In both cases they continued to rely heavily on key senior officers from their former Departments: van den Bergh in Vorster's case; and General Magnus Malan, Chief of the Defence Force, and other Generals in the case of Botha.

Botha, however, went much further than Vorster in relating his previous experience to his role as Prime Minister. His Defence experience led him, first, to believe that government could be more efficiently managed, that the structures for planning and decision-making could be made more effective and that the cumbersome bureaucracy could be rationalised. Second, he had developed, more than any previous leader, a clear-cut, almost dogmatic, view of the world in military–strategic and geo-political terms, in which the contest between the 'free world' and communism was dominant, and South Africa a target of communist expansionism. Third, Botha brought with him the belief that reform was needed, not only of policy-making, but also of the political system. The motivation for this was not ideological – i.e. it did not stem from doubts about the basic approach of apartheid – rather it was based on practical concerns about the security and survival of the whites as a group; about the need to avoid meeting a growing external threat from a weak and divided internal base; and about the need for a more manageable and more controllable political system. Reform in his view would expose and eliminate the 'extreme' and subversive elements, particularly those aligned to the external, communist-inspired threat, by bringing 'moderates' of all groups behind a common cause. Botha's reforms were thus related to the other aspects of his approach to government: the need for efficient management and for a 'total national strategy'.

EXPOSURE OF THE INFORMATION AFFAIR

After assuming office, Botha was faced immediately with cleansing the Augean stables of Information Department activities. In his first statement as party leader, he promised a 'clean and honest administration' – an obvious reference to the deception and irregularities of the Information affair, although the public was not yet aware of the extent of clandestine operations or even that their threatened disclosure had played a decisive role in Botha's election. He clearly did not at first intend to open up the affair to public scrutiny or expose the bitter divisions within the government, but he failed to prevent exposure because of the courage and determination of a Supreme Court Judge and of some newspaper editors and journalists.

In early November 1978 Judge Anton Mostert refused Botha's demand that he should not disclose information from an official investigation into exchange control contraventions. Mostert's release of this information, which he said was his contribution to a 'clean administration',[3] confirmed public suspicions, denied by the government, that the pro-government daily newspaper, The Citizen, had been founded with secret government funds controlled by Dr Eschel Rhoodie, Secretary of Information. Botha then moved quickly to contain the potential damage to the government and his own reputation. He appointed a Commission, headed by Judge Rudolph Erasmus, to report on the possible misuse of public funds, and he formally closed down Mostert's investigation. Botha also summoned Parliament to a special session in December to debate the Erasmus Commission's report, and he requested Mulder, still Minister of Information, to resign. At the same time he threatened action against the press if it continued to report on the Information affair now that a Commission had been appointed. He was accused by the Opposition and the English press of attempting a 'cover-up'. The Rand Daily Mail editorialised: 'It must be a desperate government to do such desperate things. Desperate to limit the disclosure of damaging facts in this appalling scandal, and to conceal from the public just how far its ramifications go.'[4]

Botha was clearly trying to limit the damage of Mulder's and Rhoodie's many and various secret activities, particularly those in other countries. He was also concerned that the blame should fall on certain individuals and not himself and the government as a whole.

Rhoodie subsequently maintained that a political 'consensus' was formulated by Botha that three men – Mulder, van den Bergh and Rhoodie – bore all the responsibility, whereas seven ministers in Botha's government 'either knew of, shared in the decision-making process or actually participated, personally, in secret operations'.[5] In the case of Botha himself, the Erasmus Commission cleared him of complicity and found that, although the secret operations had been financed from the Special Defence Account, 'It went against his grain [as Defence Minister] to have to pretend to Parliament' that all these funds were being spent on Defence activities.[6] Rhoodie called this a 'whitewash'. He maintained that Botha was involved (with Vorster and Finance Minister Horwood) in the original decision to establish the secret fund, and that Botha must have known how the money from his Special Account was being used; if not, he was negligent and irresponsible.[7]

To achieve public acceptance of his 'consensus', Botha focused on the 'irregularities' in the use of public funds, which was the task given to the Erasmus Commission, rather than on the merits or otherwise of the secret projects. The Commission concluded in its first report (December 1978) that there were 'irrefutable indications of large-scale irregularities and exploitation' of the Information Department's secret fund, including possible theft and fraud, 'through which the State suffered great losses'.[8] It recommended that criminal proceedings be considered against Rhoodie and his close associates.[9] The Commission also strongly criticised Mulder for *inter alia* incompetence and negligence,[10] and van den Bergh was condemned as unscrupulous, as considering himself beyond the law and as using 'his office and his personal friendship with Vorster to try and himself influence the course of events in South Africa'.[11] Van den Bergh had undoubted power and influence on State policy under Vorster, but the extent to which he had manipulated Vorster is open to question. He had also used his position to curb Botha's power and attempted to prevent the latter from becoming Prime Minister. It was not surprising, therefore, that Botha regarded him as an enemy, and he resigned his BOSS post the day Botha became Prime Minister.

In its first report the Erasmus Commission largely exonerated Vorster who had by then become State President. But in a later report it concluded that Vorster had known of, and been involved in, more of the decisions on clandestine activities than he had previously admitted. On 4 June 1979 Vorster resigned as State President, with his reputation and authority destroyed even within his own Party.[12] The Erasmus Commission thus served Botha's purpose of fixing the responsibility for the scandal on three key actors, all of whom were political opponents of Botha, and for good measure it discredited Vorster who had opposed Botha's accession to power as Prime Minister. Pik Botha emerged unscathed with his public reputation enhanced. Although his Department had opposed attempts by the Defence Department to increase its influence on foreign policy decisions, and although he was himself a political rival of P. W. Botha, Foreign Affairs had also opposed Rhoodie's activities abroad, which it regarded as interference in its domain and ultimately counterproductive. In the crisis of September 1978 Pik Botha took sides against Mulder and Rhoodie and provided P. W. Botha with the crucial votes he needed in the caucus. The new Prime Minister, therefore, was politically indebted to him, but the personal antipathies and departmental rivalries did not disappear.

Nor was the ghost of the Information scandal easily laid. Questions remained about the government's responsibility for clandestine operations behind the back of parliament, and particularly about the means employed, including widespread deception, in foreign countries. Although the Department of Information was closed down and its legitimate functions (even within South Africa) taken over by Foreign Affairs, and although most of the clandestine operations (details of which were gradually exposed by the press and Rhoodie himself) were ended, the Information affair was another serious blow to Pretoria's international position, following the Angola fiasco and the Soweto crisis. The secret Information project was originally conceived by Rhoodie and approved by the government as a response to South Africa's growing isolation. The outcome instead was a further weakening of the government's credibility and its ability to counter that isolation. However, Botha was still determined to use his position as the new leader to restore confidence in his government at home and abroad.

POLICY-MAKING AND THE STATE SECURITY COUNCIL

Botha took steps to create a more efficient management system, including the rationalisation of civil service departments and the establishment of permanent Cabinet Committees, each dealing with a defined area of government responsibility.[13] The centrepiece was the State Security Council (SSC) which was the chief Cabinet Committee and undoubtedly the most powerful, chaired by the Prime Minister himself. It had a status different from, and above, the other

Committees, as it was the only one established by legislation, namely the Security Intelligence and State Security Act, no. 64 of 1972. Under Vorster the SSC had met on an *ad hoc* basis and dealt with strictly security matters in terms of a narrow definition of its 1972 brief, namely to advise the government on the formulation and implementation 'of national policy and strategy in relation to the security of the Republic'. Botha took this existing institution, instructed it to meet regularly, and widened its responsibilities to include all matters related to security, including foreign policy – and not simply those aspects of foreign policy directly linked to security considerations. For Botha security was the central and overriding issue which must determine foreign policy, so that defence policy was not a handmaiden of foreign policy, but rather an equal, or even senior, partner. The SSC was used to integrate defence and foreign policies into one strategy for the security of the state against externally based threats. Many aspects of domestic affairs were also gradually embraced by the SSC and integrated into the security-orientated national strategy, or 'total national strategy'.

The need for better policy co-ordination and more efficient decision-taking and implementation was clear after Vorster's unco-ordinated and often *ad hoc* approach. Especially in his last years in office – even though an aura of power still surrounded him – Vorster lost his sense of direction and his overall control of affairs. The lack of co-ordination and control was reflected in the Angolan débâcle of 1975–6, and Magnus Malan later commented (in 1980, after becoming Defence Minister) that the war 'focused the attention on the urgent necessity for the State Security Council to play a much fuller role in the national security of the Republic than hitherto'.[14] This weakness in Vorster's regime, including his tendency to rely on a few close associates rather than institutions of government, was reflected in the Information scandal. 'The scandal itself grew out of a slovenly administrative and decisional style, marked by departmental autonomy and debilitating interdepartmental political competition.'[15] Change therefore had to come, but there was more to Botha's security management system than simply the restoration of efficient government. 'To be sure, there is a good deal of rationalisation in these measures and efficiency has its own rewards. But underlying these changes is a widely held belief that the Prime Minister is clearing the decks for action – not merely for fighting a war with violent opponents of the regime, but for fashioning significant political changes in order to outflank those opponents.'[16]

Formally the SSC had only an advisory role, but in fact it had great power derived from its membership and the degree to which the

Prime Minister relied on it. In addition to the Prime Minister as Chairman, the Ministers of Defence, Foreign Affairs, Justice and Police (later renamed Law and Order), plus the senior cabinet minister (if not one of the four named), were members, and by co-option certain key ministers attended SSC meetings regularly, including the Ministers of Finance and of Constitutional Development and Planning. Senior civil servants from relevant Departments and the chiefs of the Defence Force, Police and Intelligence Service were members. Botha also established a permanent SSC Secretariat, headed by a senior military officer.

Although government spokesmen maintained – correctly in a *de jure* sense – that the SSC, like other Cabinet Committees, had no executive authority and that its recommendations were subject to Cabinet approval, there were grey areas involving sensitive security, intelligence and foreign policy matters, where the SSC in practice was effectively the decision-making body. There was, for instance, an important difference between it and other Cabinet Committees, in that it was exempt from the rule that all their decisions be circulated as appendices to cabinet minutes and thus be subject to confirmation by the full Cabinet.[17] In any case, given the strength of SSC membership, particularly at ministerial level, and of its supporting bureaucracy, it was highly unlikely that any agreement reached in the SSC would be turned down by the full Cabinet. While the Prime Minister (and later the State President) continued to use this institution and invest it with his authority, it was bound to occupy the central policy-making position.

This development therefore marked a significant change from the Vorster era, when the SSC 'was clearly subordinate to the Cabinet, politically as well as legally',[18] and it affected foreign policy issues. It was a question not only of a more co-ordinated policy-making process, but also of a clearer thrust and direction in policy decisions now based primarily on security considerations. This did not mean, however, that the authority of the Prime Minister was being reduced. If anything, it was enhanced by the new structures which depended on Botha. Moreover it was his perception of how best to meet the security needs of the country, which formed the basis and motivation of the operations of the SSC.

TOTAL ONSLAUGHT AND THE TOTAL NATIONAL STRATEGY

The concept of the Total National Strategy (TNS) reflected Botha's view of security as the critical consideration in foreign and domestic policies. The development of the SSC and other aspects of his security management system must be seen in that context. Although TNS only emerged clearly as the basis of government policies after Botha became Prime Minister, the term had been used (at first simply as 'total strategy') in public statements from the early seventies. It was the response to a perceived 'total onslaught' on South Africa, communist-inspired and orchestrated from Moscow, but to which other 'hostile' elements contributed, wittingly or unwittingly. According to General Malan, 'the total onslaught is an ideologically motivated struggle and the aim is the implacable and unconditional imposition of the aggressor's will on the target state. The aim is therefore also total, not only in terms of the ideology, but also as regards the political, social, economic and technological areas.' The enemy, said Malan, applied the whole range of measures it possessed (coercive, persuasive or incentive) and, apart from military action, this included political, diplomatic, religious, psychological, cultural/social and sports activities. In the case of South Africa, the aim was 'the overthrow of the present constitutional order and its replacement by a subject communist-oriented black government'.[19]

The 'total onslaught', as perceived by Pretoria, was directed against the 'free Western world' of which South Africa was a particular target, because of its strategic location, mineral wealth, highly developed infrastructure and strong economy; and because it posed a major obstacle to Soviet attempts to gain control of Africa. As a direct military attack would be 'too expensive', an indirect strategy was employed, including economic boycotts and psychological propaganda. It was further argued that 'it is . . . logical to expect that the communists will concentrate on the non-white section of the population in creating an internal revolutionary climate', and that the SACP, the ANC and the PAC were the major vehicles for promoting these designs, assisted by neighbouring black states (especially those with Marxist governments), the OAU, the UN, Western church groups and anti-apartheid movements. From time to time Western governments were included, usually from frustration with Western actions on southern African issues. In March 1979, for instance, Botha gave Parliament a list of cases where 'South Africa had been left in the lurch' and promises had been broken. In 1980 Malan gave his view of Western policy as designed to force the government to abdicate, as in the case of Rhodesia. He then stated: 'It can therefore justifiably be claimed that the Western powers make themselves available as handymen of the communists and they are indirectly contributing to the destruction of capitalism and the establishment of world communism.' Sanctions by

Western states were seen as part of the onslaught and as contributing to the work of Moscow.

Events in southern Africa gave a sharper edge to official statements on the perceived threat from Moscow. For instance, in a typical statement, Lieut. Gen. C. L. Viljoen, Head of the Army (and later to become Chief of the Defence Force), said in September 1976 that, whatever the outcome of regional diplomatic initiatives, Russia would try to stretch a communist belt across Africa to isolate South Africa. There was little doubt, he said, that Russia aimed to gain control over the Republic's raw materials and economic riches, and over the strategic position on the routes between Europe and the East. Russia's determination had been demonstrated by its campaign in Angola where it had obtained a permanent base to act against South Africa, Zaire and Zambia. In the east, said Viljoen, there was a permanent communist stronghold in Mozambique, from which the so-called liberation movements could move against Rhodesia.[20]

Given the all-embracing nature of the total onslaught concept, it followed that the response should be equally all-embracing. In parliament in March 1980 Botha argued that there was only one way of withstanding this onslaught 'and that is to establish a total national strategy'.[21] In the 1977 *White Paper on Defence* TNS had been defined as 'the comprehensive plan to utilise all the means available to a state, according to an integrated pattern, in order to achieve the national aims within the framework of the specific policies. A total national strategy is, therefore, not confined to a particular sphere, but is applicable at all levels and to all functions of the state structure.'[22] This theory, as with the theory of a total onslaught, was considered by its authors to have universal application and not to be derived only from South Africa's particular circumstances. The theory was based on strategic studies by Western writers who had moved military thinking away from a narrow definition of strategy to a wider, all-inclusive, concept.[23] 'In practically every respect, the fascination with a co-ordinated "total national strategy," and consequently with the deepening involvement of the defense establishment in multifaceted aspects of civilian life, as well as in defense concerns, grows quite logically from the strategic thinking now identified with top-level SADF personnel. These views are increasingly popular in the National Party and with its voting constituents.'[24]

Botha had clearly been converted to the theory, but it now remained for him to implement it in South Africa. The utilisation of all the available means of the state was to be affected by the establishment of what was known as the national security management system, with the SSC at its centre, supported by the other Cabinet Committees and various related structures, including a number of 'joint management centres' whose task would be to implement and monitor national security strategies at regional and local levels.[25] The active involvement of the private sector was also seen as a necessary complement to the government's efforts.

THE TWELVE-POINT PLAN AND DOMESTIC REFORM

The shock of Soweto had brought home to the government the need for domestic policy changes to reduce both internal and external pressures. 'Reform' was increasingly used in political parlance, but uncertainty prevailed over its nature and degree. There was growing recognition of the need to devote more resources to black education, to upgrade employment and living conditions for black workers, to improve labour relations structures and to remove discriminatory measures in the social field (so called 'petty' apartheid). There were the beginnings of reform in these spheres before Botha became Prime Minister, but the political system, within which the social and economic changes were to take place, remained unaffected. Faced with 'right-wing' resistance Vorster had hesitated in his response to the Soweto crisis. Botha on the other hand was prepared to embark on the road of domestic reform, provided it was effectively managed and controlled. He was not burdened with the paralysing fear of further dividing the Afrikaners, as Vorster had been after the HNP breakaway. Reform would in Botha's view broaden his political base to include a significant proportion of the English-speakers, particularly the business sector where he had already, as Defence Minister, found a readiness to co-operate. His version of reform would, he believed, also enable him to gain support from Coloured, Asian and even some black leaders, without affecting the political dominance of whites. Such co-operation and support was necessary if the TNS were to be employed effectively. In this approach he had the backing of his senior Defence Department advisers.

Botha's policy framework was best expressed in the 'twelve-point plan' which he presented in August 1979 before an NP Congress in Durban as the answer to the total onslaught.[26] There was no alternative for South Africa, he later maintained in parliament. While he insisted that the plan did not constitute a change in policy, rather a 'reaffirmation of the basic principles of the National Party',[27] the emphasis was at least different. The plan, which outlined a co-ordinated strategy including the broad lines of both domestic and foreign policy, set the agenda for Botha's premiership and gave a new sense of direction for his government and party after the uncertainties of the past few years. As such it was a landmark statement of principles which were pursued fairly consistently during the following years.

Most of the twelve-point plan dealt with domestic issues. Although the word 'reform' was not used, there were pointers to two areas where the government would subsequently focus its reform initiatives. One was the relationship between whites, Coloureds and Indians (point 4), where Botha referred to the 'division of powers' between these three groups in 'a system of consultation and co-responsibility so far as common interests are concerned'. This principle was to lead to the new Constitution eventually implemented in 1984, with its concept of 'own affairs' for each group and 'general affairs' covering common interests. This principle was supplemented by another (point 5), which stated that 'where at all possible each population group should have its own schools and live in its own community', and that the acceptance of this principle was 'fundamental to social contentment'. There was to be no deviation from these 'fundamental' tenets of NP policy (separate 'group areas' and separate educational systems), even for the Coloured and Indian groups in a new dispensation with the whites.

Reform would also be pursued in the social and economic spheres, and Botha stated (point 6) that he was 'in favour of removing hurtful and unnecessary discriminatory measures'. The use of 'unnecessary' of course implied that some discriminatory measures (such as separate schools, hospitals and residential areas) would still be necessary, an implication reinforced by his statement that he was *not* in favour of 'compulsory integration' or of 'endangering my own people's right to self-determination'. Perhaps more significant for reform were the two principles dealing with economic affairs. The principle which recognised 'economic interdependence' within South Africa and the need for 'the properly planned utilisation of manpower' (point 7), and the principle emphasising 'the maintenance of free enterprise as the basis of our economic and financial policy' (point 12) reflected a theme which had emerged clearly during Botha's first year in office, namely his advocacy of the free enterprise system, coupled with his courtship of the private sector. Responding to calls from business leaders, Afrikaans and English, Botha looked for ways to remove the constraints of apartheid on the operation of market forces. In contrast to Vorster, who had come to distrust the business community, Botha wanted to involve it in national strategy. Shortly after announcing his twelve-point plan, he invited business leaders to a conference at the Carlton Hotel in Johannesburg, which was widely welcomed in the business community and the English press as evidence of a commitment to reform. In the event that impressive array of business leaders was overawed by the occasion and did not use the opportunity to press their own views on the government. Subsequently many of them complained about the meagre results of the conference and what they saw as Botha's attempt to co-opt them to his side.

Where Botha's government did move significantly in economic reform was in its positive reaction to the reports of the Wiehahn and Riekert Commissions which had been appointed in Vorster's time and which made far-reaching recommendations affecting black trade unions and the mobility of black labour (see chapter 14). The government came to accept the arguments of the Commissions and of business leaders that the economy required a more efficient use of black manpower. The government had come to recognise 'that in order to generate growth and accumulate capital, it has to service the manufacturing sector and provide it with a stable and contented labour force, which will have to be drawn increasingly from the black population'.[28] Neither the government nor the business community could have anticipated in 1979 what profound political effects the implementation of Wiehahn and Riekert proposals would subsequently have, particularly the granting of legal recognition and protection to black trade unions. But the die was cast, and the economic restraints on blacks and whites were beginning to come off, in the interests of the freer operation of market forces.

The moves towards a *rapprochement* with the business community were also a product of Botha's Defence experience, where both sides had co-operated in the development of the arms industry. Particularly since the UN Security Council's mandatory arms embargo of November 1977, the government needed to obtain the co-operation of key industrial sectors, while for industrialists there was the obvious incentive of more and bigger contracts from Armscor for the manufacture of weapons and related material. Most of Armscor's production was contracted out to the private sector, and in its establishment and development leading industrialists played a vital role as advisers to Botha and as members of the Armscor board. This relationship has been described as a 'lower-order version' of the 'military–industrial complex'.[29]

258

THE TWELVE-POINT PLAN AND FOREIGN POLICY

Botha also sought the co-operation of business leaders, although less successfully, in creating a 'constellation' of southern African states (CONSAS). His reference in the twelve-point plan to the 'striving of a peaceful constellation of southern African states with respect for each other's cultures, traditions and ideals' (point 8) linked domestic and regional policies. The regional dimension was further emphasised in his reference to 'a policy of neutrality in the conflict between superpowers, with priority given to southern African interests' (point 10).

The constellation concept had cropped up in Vorster's day, and its roots went back even further to include Verwoerd's idea of a 'commonwealth',[30] but after Botha's accession it assumed a clearer form as a means of institutionalising South Africa's regional relationships. In its most ambitious form the constellation was envisaged as embracing the neighbouring black-ruled states of Botswana, Lesotho and Swaziland, plus SWA/Namibia and Rhodesia, together with South Africa and those 'homelands' granted independence by the government. Pik Botha presented this as the government's regional goal, and he added that the member countries would not only expand existing economic links but would also develop 'a common approach in the security field . . . and even the political field'.[31] This official optimism in 1979 was based on assumptions which at the time gave the government new confidence, but which in the longer term proved ill-founded. The first assumption related to the future political course of SWA/Namibia and Rhodesia. In both cases Western settlement initiatives had so far been unproductive, whereas internal political developments, backed by Pretoria, looked decidedly hopeful: in December 1978 the Democratic Turnhalle Alliance (DTA) had won an overwhelming victory in territory-wide elections with a high percentage poll, in spite of an official SWAPO boycott, and in Rhodesia in April 1979 Bishop Abel Muzorewa's United African National Council (UANC) won a similar victory in an election which followed a constitutional agreement from which Mugabe's ZANU and Nkomo's ZAPU were excluded. Pretoria was encouraged by these events to assume that viable majority-supported political alternatives to the militant 'marxist' movements had been found in both countries which could therefore be expected to be co-operative in the future. Moreover, they would constitute with South Africa the strong central triangle of the constellation to which the weaker countries of the region would be attracted, primarily by economic necessity. It was further assumed that the weaker countries would come to share the anti-marxist stance of the central triangle, and that different domestic political systems would not prevent co-operation even to the extent that the 'independent' homelands would eventually be accepted as members. The government's security concerns would thus hopefully be met in the creation of this 'power bloc' as a bastion against further Soviet encroachment, with the additional hope that legitimacy would be gained for apartheid.[32] (Angola and Mozambique were not included in the constellation vision, but the possibility of their eventual participation was not excluded.)

Directly related to confidence about the feasibility of a constellation was the growing attitude of detachment from the West, an attitude fuelled by the perceived hostile policies of the Carter Administration and British Labour Government. In March 1979 Pik Botha told the Swiss–South African Association in Zurich that South Africa would have to consider seriously 'the desirability of adopting a neutral position in the struggle between East and West'. He linked this neutrality option with the government's regional ambitions by stating that South Africa should commit itself solely to the 'security and advancement of our own southern African region' and to the establishment of 'a sub-continental solidarity which could form the basis for co-operation in important spheres of life'.[33] The neutrality 'threat' was a reflection of a continuing love–hate dualism in Pretoria's fluctuating relations with the West,[34] and vehement criticisms of the West could be seen simply as reactions to Western actions which offended the government. After the Angolan intervention of 1975–6, and particularly from the time of P. W. Botha's accession to power, the anti-Western theme became more pronounced and more consistent, while policies in southern Africa became much less responsive to Western persuasion or even threats. Although the neutrality option was vague in definition and even naive, Pik Botha's Zurich speech and P. W. Botha's speech in Durban served as a warning of what was to come. It was also a clear indication that in future the government would pursue its regional goals as ends in themselves, dictated primarily by security considerations, and not as means to gain wider acceptability in the West. The old adage that for South Africa 'the road to the West runs through Africa' was no longer as relevant as it had been at the time of Vorster's 'outward' and 'dialogue' policies.

That P. W. Botha intended the inclusion in his twelve-point plan of the neutrality principle, coupled with the emphasis on regional interests, to indicate a shift in foreign policy is apparent from his explanatory statement referring to five 'strategic options' (but not all mutually exclusive), three of which he appeared to favour. The first option was 'to follow our natural instincts and align ourselves unreservedly with the West, on the side of democracy against communism'. This course could not be maintained because the reciprocity required was lacking, and he repeated various criticisms of the West for taking South Africa for granted, interfering in domestic policies, even adopting a 'threatening posture' and 'rejecting our economic and military potential as a partner'. The second option was 'qualified neutrality or neutralism' which he favoured, although he neither provided a clear definition of what this option would mean in practice nor recognised the distinction between 'neutrality' and 'neutralism' (the former being a position in which a country remains 'uninvolved in international disputes or armed conflict' and the latter being a 'militant variant' of non-alignment).[35] Probably Botha was not attempting to outline a specific policy with his neutral option, but rather was setting a general direction in political relations with the West and asserting Pretoria's independence from any undue Western influence on domestic and regional policies.

His third strategic option was 'the opposite one to alliance with the West', and he said any overtures from the Soviet Union 'would require objective assessment in the same way as overtures from any other quarter'. It was surprising, even bizarre, that Botha even included this, in view of Pretoria's consistent anti-communist and anti-Soviet stance, and in the same speech he stated that South Africa would have to help 'to counter foreign intervention and especially communism far north of its present borders'. No doubt he simply intended to reinforce his implied threat to the West, and in fact his fourth option 'would be to avoid any sort of commitment to any of the major powers and to seek to develop an alliance with other middle-rank powers whose political philosophies have something in common with ours'. This 'pariah' option,[36] a banding together with other politically unpopular states, was pursued by strengthening relations – economic, political and military – with Taiwan and Israel, plus, to a lesser extent, Chile and even Paraguay, although it would be an exaggeration to call this an 'alliance'. The fifth option, a repetition of point 8 of the twelve-point plan, was 'to look to our hinterland and concentrate on our relations with Africa, in particular with our immediate region'. This was linked to the vague idea of neutrality in wider international relations, but given substance by the proposed constellation of states.

The constellation concept, however, did not flourish and soon became confined simply to South Africa and its satellite 'homeland' states. Botswana, Lesotho and Swaziland made it clear that they would not consider joining while Pretoria adhered to its racial policies, Namibia did not achieve the anticipated independence, and the final nail in the constellation coffin came with the transformation of Rhodesia into Zimbabwe early in 1980. In 1979 a new British Government, led by Margaret Thatcher, came to power, determined to end the long Rhodesian dispute. It was fortunate in its timing. Although neither the Rhodesian forces nor the black nationalists had been defeated in the field, both sides were feeling more sharply than ever the heavy costs of the prolonged war, and even more noticeably their main backers – Zambia and Mozambique for the black nationalists, and South Africa for the Rhodesians – were utterly weary of the war and its costs, and weary of the constant disturbance of the region. Building on this situation the British called a conference at Lancaster House in London, chaired by Lord Carrington, the Foreign Secretary, who, by skilful diplomacy and constant pressure on the antagonists, hammered out a settlement. Pretoria kept in close touch during the negotiations, including visits to London by Pik Botha, and urged the delegations led by Smith and by Muzorewa to work for a settlement. When eventually the settlement was agreed, with a fresh election in which the exiled black nationalists would compete, Pretoria gave strong support to Muzorewa, including substantial financial backing during the election campaign. The South African hope was that Muzorewa would win an outright victory, but even if that were not the outcome they were confident, and none more so than Pik Botha, that it would be a split decision in which power could be shared between Nkomo and Muzorewa. The worst outcome would be victory for Mugabe who, in Pretoria's eyes, was a hard-line Marxist and a terrorist. To the shock and consternation of Pretoria the election in 1980 produced 'the worst outcome'. Robert Mugabe became the first Prime Minister of independent Zimbabwe.

After that the word 'constellation' soon dropped out of general use. Even before the end of 1979 Botha was pulling back. He told the business leaders at the Carlton Conference in November that this concept did not 'primarily denote a formal organisation, but rather a grouping of states with common interests', and he admitted that political realities made it impossible 'for the present, to establish common consultative structures and secretariats'. In mid 1980 he commented: 'It is true that a number of centrifugal forces, not the least of which are of a political nature, are at present working against closer development co-operation between South Africa and its neighbours.'[37] The plan for such structures and secretariats was not abandoned as far as relations between South Africa and the 'homeland' states were concerned, and it was later vigorously pursued with the emphasis on economic development, but with security considerations also a major factor. A 'summit' meeting of the heads of government of South Africa, Transkei, Bophuthatswana and Venda in Pretoria in July 1980 agreed *inter alia* on a declaration to promote free enterprise and to encourage private investment in their respective territories. Botha sought the co-operation of the private sector, and the promotion of the free enterprise system was a central theme in relevant official state-ments and development planning. 'The emphasis on the role of the private sector fits in with the South African idea of presenting the constellation as an incomparably better alternative to the "Marxist order"; South Africa is in effect trying to promote a counter-ideology based on free enterprise.'[38] The final point of the twelve-point plan stated, that 'the maintenance of free enterprise' was 'the basis of our economic and financial policy'.

Finally, in regard to the twelve-point plan, Botha's overriding and interlinked concerns with security and the effective management of government reappeared. Point 9 referred to 'South Africa's firm determination to defend itself against interference from outside in every possible way'. He then continued: 'We are better able tonight to defend South Africa militarily than ever before in the country's history. And I want to warn those who think that we practise our politics from a position of weakness: We are not speaking from a position of weakness, we are speaking from a position of decency. If they want to test us, our strength, we will hit back for the sake of South Africa's self-respect.' In point 11, Botha laid down as a basic principle of his government 'the maintenance of effective decision-making by the State', and, significantly, he then stated that this rested on a 'strong Defence Force to guarantee orderly government as well as efficient, clean administration'.

If the government under Botha found a new sense of direction and a new thrust, as the result of his firm hand at the helm and the appearance of a more co-ordinated system of policy-making, this did not mean that problems were disappearing. While domestically there was an impression of greater normality with the economy reviving, the trends in the region at the beginning of the 1980s were not all favourable. No progress had been made in Namibia towards an acceptable independence agreement, and in Rhodesia/Zimbabwe events had taken their unexpected and, for Pretoria, unwelcome turn. Nevertheless, Botha was prepared to react with confidence and strength even against these unpropitious developments, because he felt he could handle the situation.

NAMIBIA

The day after Botha became Prime Minister the UN Security Council adopted resolution 435, approving the Secretary General's plan for the implementation of the Contact Group's settlement proposal and calling on Pretoria 'forthwith to co-operate'. This was done in spite of a hardening of Pretoria's position on Namibia and specifically the government's complaints about 'deviations' from the Western proposal. With Botha in charge, it was predictable that the harder line would be reinforced, because security considerations now weighed more heavily than diplomatic. The Western powers thus recognised that they were threatened with a major obstacle at this late stage in the negotiations. Cyrus Vance viewed Botha as 'a determined opponent of concessions on Namibia', and his advisers urged him to support limited sanctions aimed at obtaining agreement to implement resolution 435. Carter and the NSC concluded that, if there were no positive moves by Pretoria, the time had come for direct pressure. The other four Western Foreign Ministers were then persuaded that a list of possible punitive measures should be prepared, although some scepticism was expressed to his colleagues by David Owen.[39] It was agreed, however, that a major diplomatic effort should first be made in a visit by the five Foreign Ministers to Pretoria in mid October. Although this visit underlined the urgency and seriousness of the crisis over Namibia, the timing was not propitious. Botha had been less than a month in office, and he was preoccupied with the burgeoning Information scandal and with asserting his authority. He was not in a mood for concessions and, according to Vance, the talks with him and Pik Botha were 'extremely difficult'.

Vance brought a personal letter from Carter which *inter alia* invited Botha to visit Washington to discuss how South Africa's international standing could be improved, provided the government reversed its position on resolution 435. Although neither this offer nor the offer of the Western five to attempt to modify some of the provisions in the UN plan caused any substantial shift by Botha, the door to further negotiations was not closed. He agreed that the government would use its best efforts to persuade those elected in the unilateral December elections 'seriously to consider ways and means of achieving international negotiations through the good offices of the Special Representative and the Administrator General'.[40] The Foreign Ministers did not threaten Botha with sanctions, and subsequently they continued to resist demands for sanctions at the UN. Carter, at a meeting with Pik Botha in Washington at the end of November, warned that failure to implement the UN plan 'would inevitably lead to sanctions' and run the risk of increased Soviet involvement, but the five powers were not of one mind on how to exert appropriate pressure on Pretoria with the strongest opposition to sanctions coming from Britain, even under a Labour Government. Instead they tried simply to ensure that the negotiations continued.

The elections in early December resulted in a high percentage poll, in spite of the non-participation of SWAPO and some other smaller parties. The Democratic Turnhalle Alliance (DTA), formed by several parties and groups which had participated in the Turnhalle Conference, won forty-one of the fifty seats in the new constituent assembly. The results greatly encouraged Pretoria in its belief that a viable political force, with majority support and favourably disposed to South Africa, could be developed to counter the militant influence of SWAPO. Although questions were raised about the results, particularly regarding possible coercion used by the military and white employers to achieve the high percentage poll, and although no international recognition was forthcoming, the internal track of the government's Namibian policy was strengthened and the incentive to make international concessions significantly reduced. In May 1979 the constituent assembly was converted into a National Assembly with limited legislative powers, but not including the power to change the international status of the Territory. All legislation still required the assent of the Administrator General.

Meanwhile the Contact Group continued to seek an agreement on the implementation of 435. As Vance later commented: 'I was determined that we should leave no stone unturned in preventing the negotiations from collapsing, leaving no option to the Africans but intensified conflict and greater dependence on Soviet and Cuban military assistance.'[41] In further talks with SWAPO and Pretoria the Group made various new and modified proposals, including one for a demilitarised zone along the Namibia–Angola border to deal with South African concern about SWAPO bases in Angola. But the Group failed to resolve the outstanding issues and new ones were raised as time passed. Although exchanges continued throughout the last two years of the Carter Administration, the negotiations were in effect stalemated.

Meanwhile within Namibia the internal track was pursued, and the process of strengthening the DTA-dominated National Assembly continued during 1979 and 1980, including steps to increase the number of local recruits to the armed forces and central bureaucracy. In July 1980 the powers of the National Assembly were enhanced by the establishment of a Council of Ministers with executive authority. Control over the South West Africa Territory Force (SWATF) and the Police was then handed over to this 'cabinet'. At the same time intensified military action was taken against SWAPO which suffered increasingly heavy losses in southern Angola and northern Namibia.

In January 1981 the Carter Administration made a final attempt to achieve a breakthrough with resolution 435, before giving way that month to the Reagan Administration. A 'pre-implementation conference' was held in Geneva, attended by SWAPO and various internal parties, including the DTA, and chaired by Brian Urquhart, Under Secretary-General of the UN. Although the internal parties were formally present as part of the South African delegation, headed by Brand Fourie, the DTA claimed to be there in its own right. No commitments were given by the South Africans or the internal parties, and there was never any realistic hope that the conference would produce positive results. It served as a public relations exercise for the DTA and a useful delaying device for Pretoria which was not looking forward to the effects of the change in Washington. Clear indications came from the incoming Administration, including Reagan's Secretary of State, Gen. Alexander Haig, that there would be a policy shift closer to Pretoria's position on Namibia, and British Prime Minister Thatcher was strongly inclined to align herself with Reagan's policies.[42] Moreover, the independence of Zimbabwe in April 1980 had drastically changed the regional context and had caused Pretoria to reassess the outlook in southern Africa. Security was now clearly the overriding factor in regional policies, including policy towards Namibia. Any international settlement which contained a perceived security risk, such as a SWAPO government in Windhoek, had become less likely than before.

14 ASSERTION OF REGIONAL POWER AND CONSTRUCTIVE ENGAGEMENT

EFFECTS OF ZIMBABWE'S INDEPENDENCE ON
REGIONAL POLICY

The South African government was not invited to Zimbabwe's independence celebrations on 18 April 1980. Instead, among the foreign dignitaries in Salisbury (soon renamed Harare) were representatives of the PAC, ANC and SWAPO. This dramatised the transformation in Pretoria's relationship with its strongest and closest neighbour. For most whites the links with Rhodesia were stronger than those with South Africa's own 'colony' of South West Africa. The dramatic change from Rhodesia under Smith to Zimbabwe under Mugabe therefore had a traumatic impact. While blacks were encouraged, whites felt threatened. Many whites were even reluctant to accept the election as a true reflection of opinion, making much of the stories of intimidation during the campaign. The government's reaction reflected this feeling of mistrust and threat, and Mugabe's victory lent weight to those who emphasised the 'total onslaught'. The influence of the military on policy was thus strengthened, while diplomacy was discredited by the view that all the efforts to promote a Rhodesian settlement had in the end produced a highly unfavourable outcome.

Pik Botha's vision of a constellation of states south of the Zambezi and Cunene Rivers, based on the mistaken expectation that Muzorewa would succeed, had been punctured by the new Zimbabwe north of the Limpopo River. In a greatly reduced form the constellation concept was applied in the relationship between Pretoria and the homeland states, but the word 'constellation' itself quickly disappeared from use. In contrast all the other independent states of the region, plus Tanzania, formed a loose economic association in the Southern

African Development Co-ordination Conference (SADCC), launched in April 1980 on the eve of Zimbabwe's independence. With seven of SADCC's nine members dependent on trade and transport links with South Africa, its formation was motivated in part by a desire to reduce this dependence and counter Pretoria's regional ambitions. In practice SADCC only made slow progress in reducing the economic dependence of its members on their powerful neighbour.[1]

For Pretoria this economic dependence continued to be a means of threatening or actually exerting pressure on neighbours, and economic strength would now be combined with military superiority to assert the Republic's regional dominance. From this viewpoint the diplomatic approach of accepting the need to co-exist with ideologically opposed governments and bargaining over differences (as Vorster had tried in his *détente* approach of 1974–5) had only allowed further strengthening of the 'enemy' forces. The view that 'the gun and the maize train will speak louder than a hundred speeches at the United Nations'[2] thus gained ground and came to dominate policy decisions in the State Security Council. Diplomacy, conducted by Foreign Affairs, continued to play a role in this assertive regional policy, but mainly in the form of coercive diplomacy, i.e. with the threat of force or economic measures behind it.[3]

Coercive diplomacy had already been used in dealing with Ian Smith, but in the view of many in Pretoria it had then been used against the wrong side. Now Zimbabwe was subjected to pressures. Early in 1981, after President Mugabe had voiced strong anti-apartheid sentiments and called for sanctions against South Africa, Pretoria recalled 25 locomotives and 150 railway technicians from Zimbabwe leaving that country's railway system in disarray, and shortly afterwards threatened that it would not renew a preferential trade agreement. The situation eased when Chester Crocker, the US Assistant Secretary of State, persuaded Mugabe to modify his rhetoric and allow contact at official level and warned Pretoria against destabilising Zimbabwe. Pretoria itself also used diplomatic contacts with neighbours to reduce pressures from the West over a policy which was increasingly perceived internationally as one of regional 'destabilisation'. The diplomatic approach reached its highpoint, after strong American encouragement, with the Nkomati Accord with Mozambique in March 1984, but even in that case coercion was an essential ingredient. The two strands of regional policy were thus brought together more effectively under P. W. Botha. Although differences between Foreign Affairs and the military persisted, they did not affect the self-confidence with which Botha responded to the changes in

Zimbabwe, in spite of the apparent political set-back for his government.

The response in Namibia was to adopt a harder line in the negotiations under resolution 435. The lesson of Zimbabwe, as interpreted by Pretoria, was that an internationally monitored election would probably – contrary to previous expectations – result in a SWAPO victory which was unacceptable after the 'loss' of Zimbabwe. Therefore it was necessary to gain time, firstly to inflict military damage on SWAPO which would reduce its political standing. In Zimbabwe the mistake, it was now felt, had been to hold elections while ZANU's military activities were expanding so that it could threaten that, if it did not win, it would continue the war. Military operations against SWAPO were stepped up, including strikes into Angola. In June, while discussions were going on with the UN Secretary General and the Contact Group, government forces launched attacks into Angola. Operation 'Smokeshell' lasted into July and, according to Angolan sources, inflicted many casualties and considerable damage, on Angolans as well as SWAPO.[4] There was suspicion that these actions were intended, *inter alia*, to halt the UN peace initiative and assist UNITA.[5] After July South African forces operated almost continuously within Angola. Secondly, time was needed to strengthen the internal parties in the DTA to make them a viable alternative to SWAPO. On 1 July the authority of the DTA was accordingly enhanced by establishing a Council of Ministers with executive powers, drawn from the National Assembly. Over the next two months they were given responsibility for the SWA Territorial Force (although it still remained under Pretoria's operational command) and for the Police.

These steps, together with increasing aid for UNITA (which in the second half of 1980 began a thrust northwards within Angola), formed a new co-ordinated strategy to demonstrate Pretoria's determination not to capitulate to hostile forces. Compromise, which was considered to have led to the set-backs in Mozambique and Zimbabwe, was now out. Nevertheless, to counter Western pressures the door to international negotiations was not closed, and talks with the Western five continued through 1980 with the abortive Geneva Conference of January 1981 as the only result.

MOZAMBIQUE AND THE MNR

Pretoria's actions in Mozambique provided a clear case of the assertion of military influence on policy and the abandonment of the principle of non-intervention in the domestic affairs of other states.

269

This principle had already been breached in Angola during Vorster's time, but it could at least be argued in that case that several outside powers had become involved before South Africa, and that UNITA, as a recognised liberation movement, was being denied its right to a share of power. In Mozambique, Pretoria supported an internal rebellion against a regime which it had recognised as legitimate. The involvement began in a small way soon after P. W. Botha became Prime Minister, but the decision to intervene substantially came in reaction to events in Zimbabwe.

The trends in Mozambique since independence had caused concern to Pretoria, namely: the close links with the USSR and the Eastern bloc; attempts to implement socialist policies; support given to Rhodesian insurgents; provocative anti-apartheid rhetoric; and particularly the use after 1976–7 of Mozambique as a corridor for ANC infiltration. To the proponents of total onslaught Mozambique was a part of that Soviet-inspired conspiracy and posed an obvious security threat. Yet Vorster had maintained his pragmatic policy of co-existence which, while it included warnings to Machel, allowed the mutually beneficial economic links to be maintained. The humiliating lesson of Angola also made him cautious about another intervention. When the head of the Rhodesian Central Intelligence Organisation (CIO), Ken Flower, approached him to support a dissident anti-FRELIMO movement within Mozambique, Vorster refused on the grounds that it would be contrary to his policy of *détente*.[6]

Flower and the CIO had brought together dissident Mozambicans to establish the Mozambique National Resistance (MNR or RENAMO). 'The objectives of the MNR', Flower said subsequently, 'were essentially to provide the opportunity for Rhodesia to deal with ZANLA (the military wing of ZANU) in Mozambique without doing so directly, and to perpetuate or create instability in areas of Mozambique.'[7] Initially based and trained inside Rhodesia, the MNR had grown by 1978 to about 500 men with a base also inside Mozambique. When P. W. Botha became Prime Minister, the CIO obtained limited South African support for the MNR during 1979 in the form of supplies for the training base[8] provided through Military Intelligence which had now moved into a more influential position.[9] During this period of Muzorewa's government there was close liaison between the South African and Rhodesian military, including sabotage operations in Mozambique.[10] When a military delegation, headed by Gen. Malan, visited Salisbury in March 1979, Flower concluded: 'Essentially, the attitudes the South Africans were promoting were that military influence would now dominate their domestic and foreign policies.'[11]

Before Zimbabwe's independence, therefore, the clandestine connection between the South African Defence Force and the Rhodesian-created MNR had been made. Prior to the pre-independence elections the military chiefs had agreed to contingency plans, in case Mugabe won, for Rhodesian units which might be subject to reprisals, including those involved with the training and direction of the MNR, to be moved to South Africa. When the election results were announced the plans were hastily implemented with the knowledge of the British Governor and his advisers, and 'the MNR was transferred lock, stock and barrel' across the Limpopo.[12] The transfer included the staff and equipment of the MNR radio station, 'Voz da Africa Livre', which claimed to be inside Mozambique, but which had in fact been operated in Rhodesia by the CIO.[13]

Pretoria now had the option of simply giving asylum to those MNR personnel and Rhodesians who wanted it and in effect ending support for resistance activities inside Mozambique, but instead it decided to use the organisation for its own ends. From the limited role played since 1979, the Defence Force now moved covertly to develop a much bigger and more effective operation than the Rhodesians had envisaged. Recruits trained in the Transvaal were infiltrated into Mozambique; supplies, including arms and ammunition, were delivered by air and sea; directions were given to the MNR commanders on the conduct of the insurgency; logistic and communications assistance was provided; and a secret radio station was maintained in the Transvaal to broadcast MNR propaganda into Mozambique. Recruits were not hard to find inside Mozambique because of deteriorating economic conditions and spreading dissatisfaction with the government's incompetence and its socialist policies. Within a year MNR numbers had greatly increased, with one estimate (possibly exaggerated) giving its total strength as 10,000,[14] whereas it had probably been under 2,000 at independence, according to CIO estimates.[15] From being an irritant, the MNR thus became a real threat to Machel's government. As administrative control broke down in many rural areas, with the government unable to provide adequate security against MNR attacks, economic development became all but impossible and popular disaffection increased, further benefiting the MNR. In April 1981 the leader of the MNR, Alfonso Dhlakama, predicted the overthrow of Machel by 1985 and promised that food shortages would then end because supplies would come from South Africa.[16]

As Pretoria's involvement with the MNR was not officially admitted, there was no explanation of the purpose. Subsequently, after Nkomati (see below), previous support for the MNR was

271

acknowledged, but even then neither the purpose nor the extent of the involvement were divulged. It seems clear that the decisions to promote the MNR were set in the context of the total onslaught concept, the reaction to Mugabe's victory and the shift under Botha to the greater use of military strength. The fact that MNR activities caused greater instability, thus weakening the Frelimo government, led to the widely-held conclusion that Pretoria had embarked on a regional policy of 'destabilisation'. However, this can be misleading if it is assumed that the policy was simply a defensive one of creating a buffer of unstable countries.[17] Instability and deprivation on the borders could not provide a buffer of security, but rather a source of insecurity as the military were aware. The aggravation of instability – which already existed in Mozambique for economic and other reasons – was not therefore an end in itself; it was a convenient and temporary means to other ends for Pretoria, whose own interests were affected by the instability, for example loss of power from Cahora Bassa and sabotage of the railroad carrying exports to Maputo. Such losses could, however, be regarded from the destabiliser's viewpoint as an unfortunate but temporary necessity if he had a political objective beyond the instability. 'Essentially, he wishes to promote (or force) profound political changes in the target state . . . At the very least, the destabilizer demands a fundamental shift or reorientation in the target state's policy vis-à-vis the destabilizer.'[18]

Pretoria may thus initially have hoped for a collapse of the Frelimo government, its replacement by a regime favourably inclined to Pretoria and stability restored with South African assistance. Direct intervention was not feasible because of international reaction and probable domestic opposition after the experience of the Angolan war, and the MNR offered the opportunity of operating through a surrogate force. If this was the intention, it was a serious miscalculation. Certainly there was later (1984–5) an attempt to bring the MNR into a joint government with FRELIMO and so to end the war with a more 'moderate' government indebted to Pretoria, but even this limited political objective was not attainable.

A more specific objective was a change in Maputo's policy towards the ANC. Warnings on this score had been directed at Machel's government since Vorster's time, and in February 1980 a diplomatic note threatened action if Mozambique did not stop supporting ANC 'territories'. The Mozambique Foreign Minister, Joaquim Chissano, indicated that he was aware of this concern: 'I am convinced that the conditions of the struggle in South Africa differ very much from those in Zimbabwe. So we cannot think about the same type of assistance given to the South African ANC as given to the PF.'[19] However, he added that the assistance given to the PF 'was not calculated in advance', but was rather given 'according to the needs of the struggle in Zimbabwe'. That was not reassuring for Pretoria and the military continued to believe that real pressures, as distinct from diplomatic warnings, were needed to restrain Maputo. The weakness in the case for using the MNR for this purpose was that disorder might make it harder for the Maputo government to control ANC use of its territory, but in 1980 the extent of eventual MNR disruption was probably not envisaged. In any case, the effects of the MNR insurgency were to prove an important ingredient in the coercive diplomacy which led to the Nkomati Accord and Machel's undertakings on the ANC. Supporters of the MNR in Pretoria may therefore have felt that their actions were vindicated; the offer to remove the military pressure could now be used as an inducement for Frelimo to come to terms.

Another objective of Pretoria, which evolved during the MNR operation, was to maintain the dependence of other regional states. Mozambique's geographic position gave it a vital importance for the four land-locked countries – Swaziland, Zimbabwe, Malawi and Zambia – which had used its railroads and ports as their most economic routes. Zimbabwe was particularly vulnerable, as the Rhodesian experience had shown when the closure of Mozambique's borders in 1976 had forced it into complete dependence on South African routes. After independence, traffic reverted to previous patterns and at the beginning of 1983 54 per cent of Zimbabwe's traffic was passing through the Mozambique ports of Beira and Maputo. However, as MNR sabotage, inefficiency and economic decline took their toll, Zimbabwe had to revert to South African routes so that by the end of 1983 only about 30 per cent was using Mozambique routes, and by 1986 this figure was reduced to less than 10 per cent.[20] Swaziland likewise had no alternative to South Africa when its outlet to Maputo was disrupted, while Malawi was particularly hard hit because it had no alternative rail routes at all, and the growing conflict in Mozambique necessitated the use of road transport on long, slow routes to South Africa. Zambia had two alternatives to South Africa, but one – the Benguela railroad – was also closed by UNITA, and the other – the Tazara railroad – had limited capacity. In consequence, by late 1983 40 per cent of Zambia's exports and 70 per cent of its imports were dependent on South African routes. For Mozambique, the loss of this traffic deprived it of considerable revenue in foreign currency. Whether or not it was Pretoria's intention in sponsoring the MNR, the increased dependence of several countries was the result.

273

Probably there were originally no defined political aims behind a decision taken on military grounds (and in the heat of the reaction to change in Zimbabwe) to give covert support to the MNR. However, once the project began, its apparent military 'success' encouraged greater commitment and attracted support from right-wing sources abroad, including wealthy Portuguese who had previously lived in Mozambique. The lack of clear ideological direction or political cohesiveness led to divisions and rivalries in the MNR and increasing banditry, so that the South African sponsors lost effective overall control. Ken Flower commented that, after he had handed it over, the MNR 'seemed to go from strength to strength, and I began to wonder whether we had created a monster that was now beyond control'.[21]

FROM CARTER TO REAGAN: CONSTRUCTIVE ENGAGEMENT

Pretoria's shift to a harder line regional policy and the radical change in Zimbabwe occurred during a Presidential election year in the US. The subsequent defeat of Carter by Ronald Reagan led to a change in US southern African policy. Carter's hopes of succeeding where Kissinger had failed had made little progress, for although the Rhodesian conflict had been resolved, the process had been started by Kissinger and completed by the British. Carter's contribution had been to maintain sanctions against Muzorewa's government, in spite of considerable domestic pressure to lift them. While the American-led initiative on Namibia had by 1978 apparently brought a settlement closer, the remainder of Carter's term saw no progress towards implementing the 435 plan for independence. On South Africa itself, US attempts to promote change during Carter's last two years were confined mainly to rhetoric which antagonised Pretoria, while failing to satisfy black expectations.

There was a realisation in Washington that the ability of the US to influence events was more limited than was thought in 1977. A difference of approach also emerged between the State Department, under Cyrus Vance, and the National Security Council staff, led by Zbigniew Brzezinski. The latter was more concerned about Eastern bloc 'meddling' than the State Department which, he felt, 'took an excessively benign view of the Soviet and Cuban penetration of Africa, underestimating its strategic implications'. He argued that blacks must be convinced that the US was serious about promoting majority rule, while whites must be convinced that there was a future for them, 'particularly by opposing the Soviets and Cubans and insisting the

Africans join us in that opposition. The whites had to believe that serious social change did not automatically mean a Marxist revolution.' Brzezinski concluded: 'We were failing to deliver enough to satisfy the black Africans and yet at the same time we were frightening the whites into unshakeable intransigence.'[22] In the latter part of his term these views 'eventually struck a chord with Carter himself'.[23] The resignation of Andrew Young in mid 1979 and of Cyrus Vance in April 1980 contributed to an increase of Brzezinski's influence, and Carter's preoccupation with Iran, Afghanistan and other issues facing his beleaguered Presidency also reduced attention to South Africa. In his own account of his years in office Carter does not even discuss the South African issue.[24]

For Congress and the US public, South Africa was no longer in the limelight. Opinion surveys indicated a consistently low level of public concern, except when critical events attracted media attention. A poll in 1979 found that only 18 per cent of the public had ever heard of apartheid.[25] Nevertheless, domestic pressures had begun to influence relations with South Africa in the seventies and would increasingly do so in the eighties. These pressures came from activist groups in the churches, universities, labour unions and the black community, and they were directed mainly at American corporations. Student demonstrations against investment in South Africa were held across the country in the late seventies, and the issue was raised at shareholder meetings. In 1980 alone thirty-seven corporations faced shareholder resolutions from minority groups on employment practices, sales, loans and investment in South Africa.[26] Although demands for disinvestment were strongly resisted because of the attractive rates of return and the belief in South Africa's economic potential, the 'hassle factor' was growing for chief executives. One response was the 1977 Sullivan Principles, endorsed by 130 corporations by early 1980[27] (still less than half of those involved). Within South Africa the US business presence had great importance. Although total US direct investment was much less than that of the UK, loans by US banks, estimated at $1.7 billion in mid 1979, constituted 22 per cent of all foreign loans, and in 1979 the US was South Africa's top trading partner, with 19 per cent of the Republic's foreign trade.[28] After the initial controversy, the role of American and European companies in promoting change in employment practices had generally come to be accepted and a similar code had been adopted by local businessmen. In 1979 the Wiehahn Commission recognised the importance of this influence and commented that the presence of multinationals in a country 'creates a conduit through which strong influences and pressure can be exerted on that country's policies and practices'.[29] However, foreign companies had no influence beyond the workplace, and their inability to effect political change meant that the disinvestment campaign continued and would gather strength if conditions in South Africa should worsen again.

Reagan's victory over Carter in November 1980 was welcomed in Pretoria because of his conservative position and his tough anti-communist record and rhetoric. Past years had shown that the level of US interest in southern Africa was not sustained or consistent and was dependent on developments elsewhere in the world or within the US. Nevertheless the expectation now was that the US would adopt a stronger line against Soviet 'expansionism' and would be more tolerant of Pretoria's position on Namibia. There were right-wing Republicans, notably Senator Jesse Helms, who supported Pretoria as a bulwark against communism. They were backed by fast-growing movements of the 'New Right', which believed that they had been responsible for Reagan's election and expected his active opposition to Third World Marxist regimes. In this global view South Africa deserved support as an ally against Moscow, and Reagan's instinctive sympathy for this view was reflected in the 'Reagan Doctrine'. It also had great appeal in Pretoria, and contacts were fostered with the conservative right in Washington in expectation of a major shift in American policy. Botha's confidence that this government would now be freer to pursue its regional and domestic reform policies had already been strengthened by the Conservative victory in the UK in 1979. The international climate, at least in the West, thus seemed more propitious than it had for many years.

These expectations were not fully satisfied. American policies to southern Africa did not consistently follow the line of the Reagan Doctrine, because apartheid distinguished this region from others. Also there were differing views within the Administration and between it and elements in Congress. Southern Africa therefore continued to be treated as a region which could not always be dealt with in the context of the East/West struggle, but the balance changed. Carter's policy, mainly informed by regionalist thinking, was criticised 'for being insensitive to the need to protect US national interests and America's position of power within the global system'.[30] With Reagan the balance swung towards the globalists, and an impression developed among US Democrats and in the black community, as well as among blacks in southern Africa, that the US had become an ally of P. W. Botha. The unpopularity of the Reagan Administration among blacks throughout southern Africa became a notable feature of relations. Soviet analysts and official spokesmen were quick to draw attention to what they perceived as the interconnection between Reagan's 'global offensive' and Botha's 'regional offensive' and refusal to withdraw from Namibia. Washington was accused of seeking to preserve the apartheid regime as a 'reliable ally'.[31]

That US policy stopped short of the full globalist position was partly the result of Reagan's choice of Dr Chester Crocker, an academic, as Assistant Secretary of State for African Affairs. The choice of Crocker was influenced by a major article he published in 1980,[32] where he used the term 'constructive engagement' which soon became the accepted definition of the new southern Africa policy. Crocker argued for the strengthening of a 'centrist consensus' on policy to South Africa, which he said had foundered in 'a fog of stereotypes and polarized perceptions' about a country which 'operates as a magnet for one-dimensional minds'. In his view the global/regional choice was a false one; both dimensions had to be taken into account in a great power's foreign policy. This implied a rejection of the simple globalist East/West confrontational approach, and of operating 'on the basis of a Marxist/non-Marxist litmus test in the choice of regional partners', or of choosing 'between aligning ourselves with black or white, since our interests cross racial lines'. This apparent impartiality resulted in virulent opposition to his appointment from the conservative right, and Helms held up the Senate's confirmation for nine months in 1981. In Pretoria, too, there was considerable suspicion. When he accompanied the Deputy Secretary of State, William Clark, on a visit in 1981, the South Africans attempted to exclude him from some of the high-level talks.[33] These suspicions were fed partly by the views of right wingers and partly by Crocker's rejection of Pretoria's claim to be of great economic and strategic importance to the West. Instead he argued for political change within South Africa and for Western involvement in promoting the process through appropriate pressures and informed encouragement. He had previously said that 'the days of "business as usual" with South Africa are gone, and so are the days when US rhetorical opposition to apartheid was contradicted by a covert co-operation with South Africa'.[34]

On the other hand, Crocker's view of South African domestic political developments was optimistic, and this provided the basic thrust of constructive engagement. The opportunity existed 'for the first time in decades' for 'meaningful evolutionary change'. Crocker presented an image of a South Africa under P. W. Botha where 'grand apartheid' and its architects had been rejected by many Afrikaners; where social apartheid had been recognised as offensive; where Botha

277

was committed to controlled change towards a new dispensation; and where a freer economy was showing 'a potential for sustained growth that could undergird change toward a more equitable order'. While he recognised that a more pessimistic image could be presented because suppression and discrimination were still much in evidence, he was an optimist and did not expect the current 'official promises to be followed by paralysis'. In these circumstances constructive engagement focused attention on the process of change, not simply on the ultimate goal of an end to apartheid. In the past the US had 'forfeited significant influence over South Africa through our lack of appreciation of internal South African dynamics' and through 'an inflated notion of American power'. 'Since the power to coerce Pretoria is not in American hands, the limited influence available should be husbanded for specific application to concrete issues of change.' The US should favour 'sustained and orderly change' and 'align itself with particular processes, change agents, and political forces in concrete cases'.

sequent willingness of the Reagan Administration to support the limited steps in Botha's reform process, and its readiness to meet regularly with South African leaders, attracted criticism from those who felt that Botha's reforms, far from abandoning white domination, were a means of modernising the basic structures of apartheid. The impression grew that the Reagan Administration, although it took a public stand against apartheid, was more concerned to avoid offending Pretoria and the whites than to take account of 'the needs, the politics and the passions of the black majority'.[35] The critics saw constructive engagement as 'all carrot and no stick'. It was not only the apparent faith in Botha's reform, but also the influence of the globalist view of South Africa's strategic importance – a view which the President and Secretary of State Haig shared and which Crocker had to take into account in formulating policy. In a briefing for Haig, before the May 1981 meetings with Pik Botha, Crocker spoke of 'shared strategic concerns in southern Africa, our recognition that the government of P. W. Botha represents a unique opportunity for domestic change, and willingness of the Reagan Administration to deal realistically with South Africa'.[36] The 'shared strategic concerns' no doubt related to the Soviet threat and to Crocker's belief that Western credibility depended on 'adopting a strong line against the principle of introducing external combat forces into the region'. With this approach Crocker hoped to mollify the hawks in Washington and gain Pretoria's co-operation in reducing regional conflict, which a supportive position on Botha's reform policies might help to achieve.

Constructive engagement, in Crocker's conception, was a policy for southern Africa as a whole. Crocker saw a 'window of opportunity' in southern Africa, because he considered that 'most of the region's governments are in pragmatic hands'. The Soviet position in the region had been weakened by Mugabe's policy in Zimbabwe (where Moscow had not yet in early 1981 been able to establish an Embassy), and he saw the conflicts in Namibia and Angola as 'tantalizingly close to some resolution' which would 'further erode [the] Soviet position'. As with South Africa itself, Crocker thus approached the region's problems optimistically and hoped to help create 'a regional climate conducive to compromise and accommodation in the face of concerted attempts to discredit evolutionary change'. Thus the underlying purpose of Western engagement in the region was the need to ensure 'that South Africans are permitted to build their own future'. However, the 'regional climate' did not develop as favourably as Crocker had hoped, and Zimbabwe, for instance, proved difficult from a Western view on South Africa and other international issues, in spite of Mugabe's perceived pragmatism.

CONSTRUCTIVE ENGAGEMENT AND NAMIBIA/ANGOLA

Namibia presented the first test of constructive engagement. The US accepted resolution 435 as the basis for achieving independence, but Crocker felt that the negotiations had reached an impasse. Therefore, as Pretoria was a 'key factor', it was necessary to consider additional 'steps which would make it possible for the government to take a decision that would lead to Namibia's independence'.[37] After his exploratory discussions in April with Pik Botha and the Frontline States, the Contact Group agreed that progress 'would be enhanced by measures aimed at giving greater confidence to all of the parties on the future of an independent Namibia'.[38] It was addressing mainly Pretoria's fears which Crocker wanted to allay. Further discussions between Pik Botha and Haig in Washington, when Botha also met President Reagan, were followed in June by the visit to South Africa and Namibia by Clark and Crocker.

The June visit was a turning point in the Namibian issue. The Americans were keen to achieve a settlement which would provide a foreign policy success, but they recognised that Pretoria was under no military pressure to leave Namibia and that it would only do so if its concerns were addressed.[39] During Pik Botha's visit to Washington it had emerged that Pretoria would not accept a SWAPO victory leading to Soviet/Cuban forces and influence in Namibia.[40] While the Americans agreed that the Soviets and Cubans in Angola presented a threat, they believed that a Namibian settlement would reduce that threat and make possible Angolan agreement to a Cuban withdrawal. However, Clark now indicated a willingness to reverse the US position and put the Cuban issue first, i.e. to require agreement on Cuban withdrawal before a Namibian settlement. In this attempt to satisfy Pretoria's fears, the Cuban linkage to the Namibian issue was born. Although Cuban withdrawal only emerged later as a South African/US pre-condition for Namibian independence, it was the discussions with Clark, who was politically close to Reagan, that gave P. W. Botha and his military advisers greater confidence in their approach to the Namibian and Angolan issues, and in US support.

This confidence was demonstrated in late August when Pretoria launched one of its biggest operations, 'Protea', into Angola's Cunene Province. Armoured and infantry columns with air support advanced up to 250 km. against resistance from both SWAPO and Angolan forces (but not Cubans), and vast amounts of military equipment were captured. About 450 SWAPO members and Angolans were reported killed, and South African forces lost 14 men. In addition, four Russians were reported killed and one Russian military adviser captured.[41] The operation occurred shortly before a UN General Assembly session on Namibia and when the Contact Group was co-ordinating its approach to new negotiations. International condemnation rained down, including criticism from Britain, Germany and France, but the US government was cautious. Although dissociating itself from the operation, it referred to the context of SWAPO incursions into Namibia plus Cuban and Soviet military involvement, adding that 'this incident underscored the need for urgent movement towards a negotiated Namibian settlement'.[42] In the Security Council a resolution seeking to condemn Pretoria was vetoed by the US, while France supported it and Britain abstained. Although the members of the Contact Group were divided, they continued negotiations, and American tolerance kept the South Africans involved too.

In the south-east of Angola UNITA continued to build its strength. In May 1981 it repulsed a major MPLA and Cuban attempt to recapture the town of Mavinga, held by UNITA since September 1980. Savimbi still denied military co-operation with South Africa, claiming that Pretoria mistrusted him, but he acknowledged that relations were good along the Namibian border, over which he obtained fuel and non-military supplies, traded for diamonds, ivory and other produce.[43] At the time of Operation Protea in August UNITA was engaged in its own offensive, and this increasing military pressure on the MPLA on two fronts, whether co-ordinated or not, led to a reinforcement of Cuban troops from about 10,000 in September to between 12,000 and 15,000 by end of the year.[44] Constructive engagement raised UNITA's hopes. Savimbi was invited to Washington in December 1981 where Haig assured him of help with funds and Crocker briefed him on US plans for parallel peace settlements in Namibia and Angola, including negotiations between the MPLA and UNITA.[45] Savimbi was willing to co-operate to retain US support. The MPLA government, under military and economic pressure, wanted US diplomatic recognition and aid, and so it also signalled its co-operation in early 1982 by initiating tentative contacts with UNITA and announcing its agreement to a Cuban withdrawal once Namibia was independent and South African troops were withdrawn.

The negotiations on Namibia continued, in spite of Operation Protea, with Crocker taking the initiative on behalf of the Contact Group. By early 1982 new Western proposals on constitutional principles had generally been accepted by the parties, who also agreed that adoption of the independence constitution would require a two-thirds majority of all members of the constituent assembly elected in terms of resolution 435.[46] These served as confidence-building steps for Pretoria and the internal parties in Namibia, raising new hopes of early implementation of 435. However, in spite of much diplomatic activity, various compromise proposals and even a meeting between P. W. Botha and Kaunda (their first) on the Botswana/South Africa border in March, there was no agreement on an electoral system for the constituent assembly. In June Crocker proposed putting this aside while the parties moved to a second phase of the new Western initiative, namely the mechanics of transition to independence. Then at the end of June P. W. Botha suddenly announced that South Africa was ready to accept this second phase and proceed to phase three, which in Crocker's schedule would be the actual implementation of resolution 435. But Botha also laid down conditions, the most important of which was the withdrawal of Cuban forces from Angola.

Botha thus for the first time brought the Cuban issue into the open as a specific South African pre-condition. The Western powers knew that it had become a stumbling block and had tried to obtain South African agreement by compromising with Botha on other issues. Angola and the Cuban presence had become increasingly linked with Namibia in Crocker's negotiating strategy, but the UN's 435 plans had no Cuban link and the other parties, including the other four Western powers, were not prepared now to accept it. They felt that it was only raised now because all other obstacles had been overcome and Pretoria was still opposed to independence. The Americans had in fact given the South Africans the opening to raise the issue and now strongly supported their position.[47]

As the major issue was now the Cuban link, and as the Contact Group as a whole was not involved with this, the Group's role receded. (In December 1983 the French withdrew, citing lack of progress in the negotiations.) It was now left to Crocker to find a formula acceptable to the Angolans, which would satisfy the South African/US pre-condition. The dilemma for the Angolans, however, was that although the Cubans were required as protection against UNITA, the South African 'threat' was needed to justify internationally the Cuban presence. For Pretoria the Cubans provided a convenient symbol of the total onslaught and a reason for delaying Namibian independence. However, if the Cubans left, UNITA's position would greatly improve and this would also suit Pretoria's policy. UNITA, therefore, was part of the equation once the Cuban link with Namibia was made, as Washington and Pretoria knew. A State Department official said in June 1982 that there could be no *regional* solution to the Namibian problem, without taking into account the interests of all the parties, including those in conflict with the MPLA.[48] In November Pik Botha reiterated in Washington the Cuban pre-condition but added that the future of UNITA in Angolan politics would also have to be decided.[49] In Angola the war continued, with UNITA expanding its guerrilla activities northwards.

US diplomatic efforts included a visit to seven African states by Vice-President Bush in November 1982. In December and January Angolan/South African meetings, facilitated by the Americans, were held in Cape Verde, which discussed the ending of the conflict on the Angolan/Namibian border. The talks produced neither immediate results, nor agreement on the larger issues of Namibian independence, the Cuban presence and UNITA. They did nevertheless open lines of communication between the two governments which were used in the future, and they laid the basis for an important agreement in early 1984.

Meanwhile, in Namibia the fruitless search for a viable internal government continued. Personal and political differences and the lack of popular support eroded the credibility of the DTA-dominated National Assembly and Minister's Council. In February 1982 an important component of the DTA, the Ovambo group led by Peter Kalangula (who was the DTA's President), left complaining of its ethnic composition. He formed a new non-ethnic party which was still supported mainly by Ovambos. In March the all-white National Party withdrew from the Assembly, arguing that the latter no longer represented all ethnic groups. Pretoria during this period paid more attention to the international track, but was still concerned to maintain its internal track as a viable alternative. In November 1982 P. W. Botha visited Windhoek accompanied by the Foreign and Defence Ministers. Botha had effectively taken over South West African affairs from the Foreign Minister who had played a central role under Vorster, and now the military had more influence on decisions. The meetings in Windhoek were marked by acrimonious exchanges with Dirk Mudge, the DTA leader. He opposed the powers granted to second-tier ethnic authorities, because these authorities were costly and had become obstacles to national unity and the removal of discrimination. For Pretoria, however, the maintenance of separate ethnic authorities was still a cardinal principle of policy.

In January 1983 the DTA withdrew from the National Assembly, with Mudge stating that he had learned 'that everything the South African government does in Namibia is in the interests of the ruling party in South Africa'.[50] The Assembly was dissolved and all central legislative and executive authority reverted to the Administrator General. During 1983 attempts were again made to form a broad anti-SWAPO coalition, and the Administrator General's discussions with political parties eventually led to the formation in August of the Multi-Party Conference. However, it was not until the first half of 1985 that sufficient agreement was reached in this body for Botha to try again to form an internal government at national level for the Territory.

REFORM AND REACTION

The greater 'fluidity and pragmatism' which Crocker saw in domestic white politics were a product both of growing international and regional pressures and of forces within South Africa. The influential American scholar, Samuel P. Huntington, argued in 1981 that it was 'likely that a minority-dominated hierarchical ethnic system in South Africa will become increasingly difficult to maintain', because of increasing external opposition, the need for skilled black workers and the social and economic mobilisation of blacks who will 'become increasingly opposed to a system which effectively excludes them from political power'. This did not mean, said Huntington, that revolution was imminent, but that within 'the next decade or two' a combination of these three factors was likely to create a crisis 'that will only be resolved by fundamental change of that system'. For Huntington reform meant fundamental institutional change which he felt could be achieved given 'some small amount of luck and a large amount of political talent'.[51] However, it is questionable that P. W. Botha's conception of reform ever amounted to fundamental change rather than an adaptation of the existing political system, as indicated by his oft-quoted phrase 'adapt or die'. He viewed reform as part of the national strategy to counter the total onslaught, and he failed to appreciate the strength of internal forces which were opposed to apartheid and not prepared to accept simply a reform of that system.

This problem of differing perceptions also affected international attitudes. Western governments – notably those in Washington, London and Bonn – welcomed Botha's reform policy but chose to view it as a process which would lead to full black political participation. These expectations went much further than anything promised or intended by Botha, for whom reform did not mean moving away from the basic National Party political philosophy. Reform supporters in South Africa and abroad often claimed that the government had to operate by 'stealth' to avoid white reaction to changes, and that there was more in the pipeline than was indicated in public. However, the product did not fulfil this expectation. While conservative whites were increasingly alienated by government changes, black political opinion was unimpressed, and resistance grew. International attitudes in turn became more sceptical.

The re-emergence of black resistance had been demonstrated by Soweto. But the mobilisation of blacks during the seventies was most evident in labour relations and the growth of black trade unionism, despite legislation which denied blacks the right to strike or even access to industrial conciliation procedures. Illegal strikes, particularly in 1973, and continuing labour unrest, combined with the growing need for more skilled workers than the white community alone could provide, caused a reappraisal of attitudes to black workers among business leaders. Increasing pressure on international companies at home and the adoption of codes of conduct also played a part. These internal and external pressures could not be ignored by the government, and as a result two commissions were set up by Vorster in 1977 to examine issues related to black labour.

One commission, chaired by Professor Nic Wiehahn, examined industrial relations. In 1979 it found (in the first of six reports) in favour of recognising black trade unions, but controversy surrounded the resulting legislation. While black unions could register and be recognised under the law, they objected to the strict controls imposed on them, the failure of government to recognise mixed (black/white) unions, and the exclusion of migrant workers. However, the refusal of unions to register under the new legislation and the upsurge of labour unrest in 1980 persuaded Labour Minister Fanie Botha, a strong advocate of reform, to introduce legislative amendments. By 1982 the position was thus more tolerable to the unions, whose numerical strength was increasing, and there was a significant increase in recognition agreements between unions and companies.[52] These were the product also of a growing awareness among employers of the need for sound industrial relations as the ability of the black unions to disrupt the economy became clearer. The other commission, chaired by Dr P. J. Rieckert, examined the mobility of black labour. Its report in 1979 recommended *inter alia* measures to improve mobility of labour in urban areas, including a relaxation of influx control, but even its limited proposals ran into official opposition. Despite criticism by the private sector of the harmful effects of influx control,[53] and the bitter feelings of blacks about one of the most hated aspects of apartheid, it was several years before the government ameliorated influx control and then in July 1986 abolished it.

Labour negotiations were complicated by the political orientation of many unions and by the competition for members between unions of differing political persuasions. Many union leaders also saw in the apartheid system a 'racist' alliance between government and capitalism. However, the post-Wiehahn labour dispensation brought this force into the open as one of the most important dynamics in the changing South Africa. In spite of growing frustration among employers about political motivation in many disputes they were opposed to government interference and pointed out that, with blacks excluded from participation in government, they were bound to seek political expression through organised labour. The government was constrained from turning the clock back by the attitude of the corporate sector, by fear of violent disruption of the economy by black workers and by concern about international reaction. Financial and training support was coming from trade union sources in Europe and North America for emergent labour organisations, and the possibility of concerted boycott actions posed a potential threat to external trade. Moreover, the changes in labour legislation were being 'sold' abroad as a prime example of the genuineness of the government's reform policy, and they were accepted as such by Western governments and by international companies which were fighting off disinvestment pressure.

At the same time the government faced pressures to curb the

285

unions. Groups of white workers, particularly the white miners' union, were incensed by the new laws and resistance spread to other traditional NP supporters. 'The resistance was understandable. For decades, the National Party had told its supporters that job reservation and curbs on African unionism guaranteed white survival; they became articles of faith to party voters. Now they were told to unlearn years of conditioning and accept new ways of ensuring white supremacy.'[54] Instead of acting against the black unions by changing the law, the government moved against their leaders. In 1981 and in 1982 many unionists were detained and the police also intervened in strikes to break up union meetings and demonstrations, often in spite of the protests of employers. A case in early 1982, which aroused widespread local and foreign protests, was the death in detention of a young white doctor, Neil Aggett, who was secretary of a black union. The controversy surrounding Aggett's death attracted attention to the unions and to brutal police action.

The white worker reaction was one factor in the split in the NP in 1982 and the formation of the Conservative Party.[55] A swing to the right in traditional NP constituencies was already discernible in the 1981 general election and was attributed to reaction against P. W. Botha's reform. The overall share of the vote received by the HNP rose from 3.3 per cent in 1977 to 14.1 per cent, and the National Conservative Party (NCP), formed by Connie Mulder, received 2.5 per cent in its first election. In straight contests between the NP and HNP, the HNP's share of votes rose from 8 per cent in 1977 to 29 per cent, although it did not win any seats. Within the NP itself there was a strengthening of the right wing among MPs elected in the Transvaal[56] where Dr Andries Treurnicht was the leader. At the same time on the left there was a limited swing to the PFP which increased its seats from seventeen to twenty-six, taking votes from both the NP and the small New Republic Party (NRP). The PFP's gains were ascribed to some dissatisfaction among English-speakers with the slow pace of reform, concern about the economy and reaction to the emerging divisions in Afrikaner Nationalist ranks.

Concern about the slowness of reform was evident in the business community. When P. W. Botha called a second conference with business leaders in Cape Town in November 1981, the 'Good Hope Conference', businessmen refrained from a confrontational approach, but they raised issues they felt needed more urgent attention. Harry Oppenheimer, Chairman of Anglo-American, referred to a 'sense of disillusionment' over the results of the 1979 Carlton Conference, with the government unwilling or unable to act on the facts of the situation, except in the field of industrial relations. He added that, unless the government devised an acceptable political dispensation for the blacks, their growing industrial power would be used for political purposes with disruptive effects on the economy. He and other leaders also referred to the mobility of labour, black education and black housing as matters requiring urgent action.[57]

Education was the subject of another investigation launched in 1980 and chaired by Professor J. P. de Lange. The de Lange Committee's wide-ranging report, tabled in Parliament in October 1981, dealt with education from pre-school to tertiary levels, laying special emphasis on technical education in view of the skilled manpower needs of the country. Some of its recommendations challenged established government policy and practice, and it firmly rejected racial differences as ground for discrimination in the allocation of resources.[58] While the government's interim response accepted many of the report's recommendations, separate departments and systems for the various groups were retained.[59] Two years later a government White Paper again endorsed the concept of separate education systems, but accepted the need for a central department to deal with macro-policy and for a racially mixed advisory Council for Education. This received a mixed reception, with some members of the original Committee again expressing disappointment and de Lange himself commenting that 'change in education is a notoriously slow process'.[60]

The proposed and actual reforms in the labour and education fields illustrate a pattern of expectations aroused by the government's willingness to launch investigations in critical problem areas, followed by disappointment with the degree of change implemented. Reaction from the right against change and from the increasingly militant left against 'cosmetic' measures constrained the government. Nevertheless, P. W. Botha pursued 'step by step' reform, as part of his total strategy, while maintaining NP policy of group identity and self-determination. In the early eighties he was gaining ground at home and abroad. Western governments, particularly in Washington and London, encouraged him, and at the Good Hope Conference he commented that South Africa's position was stronger economically and militarily, and 'relations with the USA and some other countries are also characterised by greater realism'.[61] The main focus of external and domestic attention, however, was on questions of political change and constitutional reform. These raised the greatest expectations, but they also led to the strongest reaction from right and left and eventually to South Africa's worst domestic and international crisis.

THE 1983 CONSTITUTION AND NEW DIVISIONS

As with the labour reforms, the constitutional reform process had started under Vorster and his 1977 proposals were in 1979 presented in the form of a draft Bill. Still lacking agreement with Coloured and Indian leaders, the government referred the Bill to a commission headed by Mr Alwyn Schlebusch, Minister of the Interior. In 1980 the Commission recommended, and parliament approved, the abolition of the Senate and the creation of a President's Council of sixty members drawn from the white, Coloured and Asian communities, but excluding blacks. The Council, duly established at the end of 1980, was to advise the government on draft legislation and other matters of public interest, but its main purpose was to propose new constitutional dispensation. It was also intended to consult a separate council of black South Africans, but the blacks themselves, including even homeland leaders, refused to participate in such an arrangement. A constitutional committee was formed under the chairmanship of a former political scientist, Dr Denis Worrall, which presented a report with new constitutional proposals in 1982.[62]

The Worrall Report kept within the parameters of government policy on group differentiation but based its arguments on models applicable to plural societies, such as Arend Lijphart's.[63] He had introduced the concept of 'consociational democracy' by which identifiable groups could reach decisions on the basis of consensus rather than confrontation, while having control over their own affairs, i.e. 'segmental autonomy'. This meant a departure from the Westminster system. The Worrall Report, however, deviated significantly from Lijphart's prescription, particularly in the exclusion of the majority from representation. In Lijphart's view this was its 'gravest weakness' and 'not only unconsociational but also undemocratic'.[64] While the Worrall Report advocated a confederal relationship with the black 'states' (homelands), it asserted that 'a single political system in South Africa which includes blacks on an unqualified majoritarian or consociational basis could not function as a successful democracy in current or foreseeable circumstances'.[65] This was in fact never an option for a committee seeking acceptance from an NP government, but the result was to make its proposals unacceptable to the vast majority of South Africans, except the whites. Differences with the responsible minister, Chris Heunis, led to Worrall's departure to Australia as Ambassador, and the Committee then issued a second report in late 1982 which satisfied some particular concerns of

288

the government. After a Constitution Bill had passed through parliament it was submitted to a referendum of white voters in November 1983.

The proposed new constitution provided, firstly, for one parliament with three legislative chambers (instead of three separate parliaments as in the 1977 plan): a House of Assembly for whites, a House of Representatives for Coloureds, and a House of Delegates for Indians elected on separate ethnic rolls. Second, there would be an Executive State President (combining the two existing offices of non-executive State President and Prime Minister) indirectly elected by a college of MPs from the three Houses in a ratio of 4:2:1. As the majority party in each House would elect all the representatives from that House, the majority party in the white House would have a majority in the electoral college. Third, each House would be responsible for 'own affairs' legislation of its community, for example, culture, education and hospitals, while 'general affairs' legislation would pass through all three Houses. This distinction between 'own' and 'general' affairs was central to the new constitutional concept. Fourth, the President would appoint a cabinet drawn from MPs. He would have to consult the cabinet, but not necessarily follow its recommendations. For each House there would a Ministers' Council to deal with 'own' affairs. Fifth, a system of joint committees of the three Houses was established, to which draft legislation on 'general' matters would be referred and where it was intended that consensus should be reached. Sixth, the President's Council, with members elected by the three Houses and a minority appointed by the State President, would continue to be advisory, but its role would have particular importance in resolving a deadlock between the three Houses.

Before the proposed Constitution was submitted to parliament, the National Party split. The growing resistance to Botha's reforms and his leadership came to a head early in 1982. Botha had used the term 'healthy power-sharing' with particular reference to the Coloured people. His words had been carefully chosen: 'For us the concept of consultation and co-responsibility is a healthy form of power-sharing, without undermining the principle of self-determination. Therefore we prefer the term co-responsibility.'[66] Nevertheless, Treurnicht objected to this concept as being utterly foreign to Nationalist philosophy. With twenty-one other members of the NP caucus, he refused to support a motion expressing full confidence in the Prime Minister and his interpretation of Party policy. However, the dissidents did not resign from the Party and in early March Treurnicht was expelled by the Party's executive in the Transvaal. The initiative was taken by

F. W. de Klerk who replaced Treurnicht as Transvaal leader. Later the same month Treurnicht launched the Conservative Party (CP) which absorbed the New Conservative Party but not the HNP. The latter was still wedded to hard-line Verwoerdian apartheid, whereas Treurnicht had adapted to the Vorster policies contained in the 1977 constitutional proposals. Vorster even emerged briefly from retirement to support Treurnicht. The former Nationalist MPs who had joined the CP now formed a separate opposition group in parliament, and the new party mobilised white opposition to the proposed constitution in an active campaign before the referendum on 2 November 1983.

On the left of the government the PFP, led by Dr F. van Zyl Slabbert, also attacked the new constitution. It objected to entrenchment of ethnic divisions, the exclusion of blacks and the great powers of the Executive President. It found itself campaigning alongside the CP for a 'no' vote, although for different reasons (except on the State President's powers). The association with the CP affected many of the PFP's supporters, as did the widely-held belief among English-speakers that Botha was at least taking a step in the right direction of sharing power and he should be encouraged. The ability of the PFP to get its message across was hampered by the fact that important sections of the English press, normally opposed to the government, campaigned strongly for a 'yes' vote. Both the CP and the PFP suffered from 'an unprecedented propaganda onslaught on the electorate by the government, both through full-page advertisements in all the country's national and local newspapers, and full use of SABC television'.[67] In addition, the Afrikaans government-supporting press refused to accept advertisements advocating a 'no' vote. In the event the referendum produced a substantial two-thirds majority in favour of the new constitution, with the bulk of the opposition coming from conservatives. English-speakers, including most business leaders, gave their support, believing either that further changes involving the blacks would follow, or that their security and privileged status would best be maintained by Botha and his policies. Those who favoured further change refused to heed the warnings of black leaders that the constitution would entrench white power, in particular the power of the NP which would be strengthened by its co-opted allies, and that moves towards participation of blacks would become more difficult.

Black leaders, including the moderate Buthelezi and his Inkatha movement, reacted bitterly to the referendum results. This black reaction was more serious than the reaction from the right. The latter had even helped Botha internationally where the West gave him credit for standing firm against his right wing to the extent of splitting his

Party. White support for a change away from undiluted white rule was seen as a positive indication that South Africa was moving away from apartheid. Crocker acknowledged it as 'a step in the right direction'. However, black resistance was fuelled by Botha's success and the disregard of whites and the West for black majority views. In August 1983 the United Democratic Front (UDF) had been launched at a mass rally in Cape Town, specifically in reaction to the government's constitutional proposals. Dr Allan Boesak, a minister in the Coloured branch of the Dutch Reformed Church and recently elected President of the World Alliance of Reformed Churches, was a leading figure in the movement. The UDF was not a political party and its membership was drawn from many existing organisations mostly at local level, including educational, religious and social groups, trade unions and even sports clubs. But its leadership identified with the goals of the ANC and it accepted the 1955 Freedom Charter as its basic document. It grew rapidly at grass roots level throughout the country and by March 1984 was said to have over 600 affiliated organisations with a membership of over 2 million spanning all classes and races.[68]

Meanwhile the ANC itself was stepping up its activities, both externally and within South Africa. Thousands of young blacks, supporters of the BPC, who had left the country clandestinely after the 1976–7 uprising, had joined the ANC and some the PAC. The ANC recruits were trained at camps in various countries, including Tanzania and Angola, and they started to filter back into South Africa. According to government figures the number of sabotage incidents increased from twelve and nineteen in 1979 and 1980 respectively, to fifty-five in 1981.[69] While in 1982 the number dropped to thirty-nine, it increased again in 1983 to fifty-five.[70] Not included in these figures were incidents in Transkei and Ciskei. The targets included police stations, electric power stations and railroads, fuel storage tanks at a Sasol plant in 1980 (with considerable damage caused), the military base at Voortrekkerhoogte in 1981 (with little damage from a rocket), the Koeberg nuclear power station where two bomb explosions occurred in December 1982, and another Sasol plant in 1983 (with minor damage). In August 1981 Defence Minister Malan said that the revolutionary threat had reached an extremely dangerous phase,[71] but another view was that the attacks were intended 'to inspire confidence among the dominated population rather than terror within the white community'.[72] In any case, they raised the profile of the ANC and drew more attention to it from all quarters than it had received since the early sixties. The widening support for the ANC's political aims among blacks, including the Coloured and Indian communities, was also reflected in the expanding membership of the UDF.

The Coloured and Indian groups were not asked to express their views on the new constitution in a referendum. Recognising the strength of opposition within these groups, Pretoria decided that there would simply be two general elections in August 1984 to chose their representatives. (The white House of Assembly, elected in 1981, simply had its term extended for five years to that it would run concurrently with the terms of the other two Houses. This saved the government from facing the CP too soon in a general election.) The denial of a referendum further strengthened resentment within the two groups and boosted the UDF's standing, and it joined the Transvaal and Natal Indian Congresses in a campaign to persuade potential voters to abstain. The weeks running up to the two elections in August and early September were highly disturbed, especially among Coloureds in the Cape, with increasing incidents of violence as UDF supporters clashed with parties participating in the elections and with the police. The eventual percentage polls were low in both elections: 29.6 per cent for the House of Representatives (Coloureds) and 20.2 per cent for the House of Delegates (Indians).[73]

In these rather unpropitious circumstances the new constitution came into effect at the beginning of September 1984, the tricameral parliament was launched, and P. W. Botha was duly elected the first Executive State President. During the first half of 1984, however, there had been other surprising developments in southern Africa which had enhanced P. W. Botha's image domestically and internationally, and by the time he became State President he appeared to be at the peak of his power and prestige.

BREAKTHROUGH FOR CONSTRUCTIVE ENGAGEMENT

Encouraged by constitutional developments, Crocker redoubled his diplomatic efforts to resolve the regional conflicts. To all appearances the conflicts between Pretoria and its neighbours were escalating, and within the Republic the ANC was more active, provoking counter-action by the military. In May 1983, within a few days of a car-bomb blast in the centre of Pretoria killing seventeen people, an air strike was launched on ANC targets on the outskirts of Maputo in which the South Africa Defence Force claimed forty-one ANC members and seventeen Frelimo soldiers died. Previously, in January 1981, South African troops had raided ANC houses in the Matola suburb of Maputo, and in September 1982 they attacked others in Maseru, capital of Lesotho. There was also a smaller commando raid in Maputo in October 1983. These attacks drew condemnation both from within the region and internationally, but Pretoria maintained that they were justified because the ANC was being allowed to use neighbouring territory for incursions into South Africa. In contrast, the international perception was that these raids were only part of an aggressive regional policy of destabilisation which included also the military action in Angola and covert support for the MNR, UNITA, dissidents in the Matabeleland Province of Zimbabwe and even for the Lesotho Liberation Army (LLA).

By the end of 1982 there had been eight known large-scale South African operations in Angola, and in December 1983–January 1984 Operation Askari involved some of the heaviest fighting ever.[74] Much stiffer opposition from the Angolans was encountered than previously and Pretoria's statements referred to the presence of Cubans, although, as in all past incidents since 1976, Cuban troops were not deployed against South African forces.[75] The diplomatic links which Crocker had fostered were nevertheless maintained and the South African and Angolan governments agreed to a meeting in Lusaka in February, with Crocker and Kaunda acting as mediators. The costliness of Operation Askari to both sides may have influenced them to seek at least a limited agreement to reduce the chances of further confrontation but the earlier diplomatic exchanges had prepared the ground. Pretoria was represented in Lusaka by Pik Botha and Gen. Magnus Malan, and the meeting demonstrated the ascendancy during this period of the diplomatic approach, although Malan's presence was a reminder of the continuing coercive element. The agreement reached on 16 February provided for a ceasefire, the withdrawal of South African forces from Angola and the establishment of an Angolan/South African joint monitoring commission (JMC). It was envisaged that the Angolan forces would be responsible for ensuring that southern Angola would not be used by SWAPO for incursions into Namibia, and the JMC was expected not only to monitor the South African disengagement but also to 'detect, investigate and report any alleged violations of the commitment of the parties'.[76] But very soon disputes arose over Pretoria's claims that SWAPO was being allowed to infiltrate into Namibia. As a result the withdrawal slowed down and the process, expected to last only a few months, dragged on for over a year.

For the time being, however, the Americans, who saw the agreement as one step towards the eventual goal of Cuban withdrawal and Namibian independence, were satisfied that they had helped to create a better climate of trust between Pretoria and Luanda. Then within a month a more dramatic agreement was achieved, also with Crocker's assistance, between Mozambique and South Africa. The Nkomati Accord was signed by Presidents Machel and Botha on 16 March at a highly publicised ceremony near the border (the Nkomati River) between the two countries. The two governments undertook 'to respect each other's sovereignty and independence, and in fulfilment of this fundamental obligation, to refrain from interfering in the internal affairs of the other'. More specifically, they agreed not to allow their respective territories to be used by organisations of individuals planning 'to commit acts of violence, terrorism or aggression' against the other party. The Accord went on to specify in detail the various types of acts which the two parties undertook to prevent or eliminate.[77]

The negotiations that led to Nkomati had been going on for some months. Crocker had been trying to improve American relations with Mozambique to reduce Soviet involvement and improve the US's image in the region. His aim was to end conflict with South Africa and restore Mozambican stability. In June the American Under Secretary of State for Political Affairs (and Crocker's immediate superior), Laurence Eagleburger, spoke of a 'coherent regional strategy' in southern Africa and committed the US to the problems of the region, sending a signal to Pretoria that Western interests were involved in the other countries. With reference to Mozambique, he said that the US had 'pressed for dialogue' between South Africa and that country, and 'an end to cross-border violence'.[78] The dialogue had in fact started at ministerial talks in December 1982 and May 1983, but little progress was made until December 1983 when the two sides met in Swaziland. Further meetings followed until finally, in Cape Town in early March 1984, a draft agreement was accepted. While the South Africans would have preferred all ANC personnel to be removed from Mozambique, they eventually accepted that a non-military office with limited staff could be maintained in Maputo. Pretoria, it was understood, would end all its support for the MNR. Although neither of the organisations was mentioned by name in the Accord, these understandings were its basis and raison d'être. There was also an understanding, important to Machel, that Pretoria would promote economic assistance to Mozambique, including an increase in the number of migrant workers from Mozambique employed in South Africa, mainly on the mines. Their number had decreased very considerably since independence, but it increased after 1984 (see tables in Appendix). It was expected that there would also be American aid.

There is no doubt that the influence of the Reagan Administration was important in persuading the parties, particularly Pretoria, to come to an agreement. On the South African side the role of Pik Botha's diplomacy was a crucial ingredient, both within the government, where the military hard-liners had to be persuaded or out-manoeuvred, and with the Mozambicans. However, apart from the immediate circumstances, it had been one of the long-time aims of Pretoria, since Vorster's days, to obtain non-aggression pacts with neighbour states. P. W. Botha had said at the 1981 Good Hope Conference: 'The South African government has time and again stressed its willingness to sign non-aggression pacts with neighbouring countries as well as treaties that will prevent states in Southern Africa from making their territory available for use as bases for hostile action against one another.'[79] After the public signing of the Nkomati Accord, it was revealed that a similar security agreement had been reached secretly with Swaziland in 1982.[80]

The initial ANC reaction to Nkomati was bitter. An official statement accused Pretoria of having undertaken a frantic diplomatic, political and propaganda counter-offensive with the aim of isolating the ANC and compelling the independent countries to act as South African agents in emasculating the organisation. Oliver Tambo himself expressed more understanding for Machel's predicament, saying that, as Pretoria had decided to destroy Mozambique, the Maputo leadership 'was forced to decide between life and death'.[81] However, in Western capitals the Nkomati Accord was welcomed. Following the Lusaka Agreement, it appeared to indicate that Botha's government had changed its regional policy and that the era of destabilisation was over. Others saw it at least as indicating a new approach, in which diplomacy and negotiations had been added to the pressures which had previously been dominant; i.e. a 'thump and talk' approach.[82] For the Reagan Administration it was a reward for the long efforts of constructive engagement and for the risk of working closely with Pretoria.

The euphoria over Nkomati and the sudden bloom of *détente* in the region did not last long; by the end of the year they were fading, together with the hopes for political progress within South Africa. But for the few brief months of this false spring P. W. Botha was able to savour what amounted to a diplomatic triumph, after the years of pariah status. On the basis of the cautiously positive Western reaction to the new constitution and of the positive view of regional developments in early 1984, Botha was able to undertake a tour of West European capitals in June (and there were strong rumours that a visit to Washington would come later). Not since the days of General

Smuts before the National Party came to power was a South African Prime Minister able to embark on such an extensive series of official visits to countries overseas. It appeared to some that South Africa was at last beginning to emerge from political isolation.

PART VI

RENEWED CHALLENGE AND RESPONSE 1984–1988

15 DOMESTIC AND INTERNATIONAL CRISIS AND PRETORIA'S RESPONSE

On 31 August 1984, in his last public address before becoming State President, P. W. Botha confidently predicted that 1984 would be seen as 'a watershed year in the affairs of South and southern Africa'. He referred to 'developments of great significance' in the region where 'the diplomatic and political scene . . . has acquired a new image, a new vitality', with relationships based on 'a new recognition of realities' and South Africa emerging 'as a regional power willing to play a positive role in the normalisation of relations and the settlement of disputes'. He also referred to domestic constitutional achievements and the beginning of 'the implementation of concepts and structures on which we can pin our hopes for a better and more prosperous future for this country'. All these events, he said, had reinforced his 'confidence in the future'.[1]

Botha had reasons for confidence. In southern Africa his tough policy had produced two security accords plus the agreement with Angola, had contained the perceived threat from Zimbabwe, and had asserted Pretoria's regional strength. Moreover, the major Western powers had approved of the security agreements, if not of the cross-border military actions which had helped to bring them about. Domestically, his socio-economic and constitutional reforms were going ahead with general Western approval, and his political base had been widened by growing support from English speaking whites and by the co-option of the other two minority groups into the new constitutional system. Botha believed that he was on the road to a significant improvement in South Africa's international position. This confidence – almost euphoria among the government's reform supporters – was not destined to last. The signs of the trouble, which over

299

the next two years was to plunge the country into another crisis more severe than that of 1976–7, were already there in mid 1984.

The growth of the UDF was one sign. The fact that the UDF was not banned, in spite of its ANC sympathies, was a reflection of the government's confidence, greater tolerance of opposition and concern about international opinion. But the growth of the UDF, plus the opposition of Azapo and Inkatha, clearly demonstrated that the constitution was unacceptable to black political opinion. They saw it as an attempt to exclude black Africans from power for all time and leave the white group dominant. The impending implementation of the new constitution mobilised opposition, and the low polls in the Indian and Coloured elections indicated that its credibility and legitimacy were challenged even before it came into effect.

In the region, too, there were signs by mid 1984 that the Nkomati Accord was not producing stability. The Accord was not welcomed in the region (except for Swaziland) and was not viewed as an example to follow. In Angola the Lusaka Agreement immediately ran into problems preventing the early withdrawal of South African troops. Nevertheless, constructive engagement was still pursued and Western governments remained hopeful.

SEEKING SUPPORT IN EUROPE

P. W. Botha's tour of Europe in June 1984 indicated, however, that difficulties remained with the West. The tour, which was undertaken in a mood of great expectations, was the culmination of Botha's period of achievement. The Johannesburg *Sunday Times* wrote that it would 'help South Africa feel a little less like the world's polecat' and that it was important that 'South Africa's gestures towards domestic reform and its very real progress towards peace on the borders are beginning to bear the first small fruits of recognition.'[2] In parliament Botha was praised by his own party and complimented by the PFP,[3] and on the eve of departure Botha himself claimed that South Africa could become the 'spiritual link' between the 'old world and developing Africa'.[4]

The high expectations evinced a degree of self-deception.[5] This was a product of the isolation from widely and strongly held Western views, even in conservative circles, about the immorality and the political and economic impracticability of apartheid as it remained in the new constitution. Further it took insufficient account of domestic pressures on Western governments (dismissed, for example, as 'the storm-troopers of the British left')[6] and other foreign policy interests affected by links with South Africa. Portugal was the only country where Botha was received as an official state visitor. His warm reception by the socialist Prime Minister, Mario Soares, reflected a swing in Portugal from the left to the centre and was influenced by the presence of a large Portuguese-speaking community in South Africa (estimated at 600,000, forming a substantial minority among whites). There were common concerns in Mozambique, including Cahora Bassa, for which Portugal retained responsibility for debt servicing and maintenance, while no revenue was being received because of disruption of supply by MNR sabotage. The resuscitation of the dam was high on the agenda and later led to further negotiations with Maputo. In addition, Lisbon wanted stability in Mozambique and Angola to increase its trade while the Nkomati Accord had shifted Pretoria's policy to the diplomatic track.

The rest of the European odyssey was more difficult. Botha did not receive the anticipated acclaim as a reformer and regional peacemaker, and everywhere the focus of attention was on ending apartheid. Although Botha was given opportunities long denied South African leaders to explain his policies, there was no breakthrough. Instead he was pressed to move further. In Switzerland the government's approach was low-key, emphasising the private nature of the visit to address businessmen and bankers – as important to Botha in any case as any official talks. In France, where Botha laid the foundation stone of a memorial to South Africans killed in the two world wars, the government ignored the visit.

It was the visits to Britain and West Germany which were the most important. Given the domestic criticism which these governments endured, in meeting him they were concerned to clarify their continued opposition to apartheid. Botha's brief visit to Britain, the first by a South African Premier since Verwoerd led his country out of the Commonwealth in 1961, was confined to a five-hour meeting with Mrs Thatcher at Chequers. Meanwhile in London 15,000 people demonstrated against apartheid. The 'candid' Chequers talks were comprehensive, including Namibia, assistance to other southern African states, the Gleneagles sports agreement, the arms embargo, the ANC presence in Britain and primarily Pretoria's domestic policies. Thatcher was frank in her criticism of black exclusion from parliament and forced removals to 'homelands'. She raised Mandela's release, made clear she would not close the ANC office in London, and reaffirmed support for the arms embargo. Botha was equally determined in his defence of his reforms and it was only on Namibia that there was agreement on the need for progress towards independence and the withdrawal of troops. Nevertheless Botha was pleased that the meeting had taken place and said he did not regard Thatcher's criticism as 'unnecessary interference'. For her part Thatcher defended the meeting as part of a process 'for the sorts of changes we all want to see in southern Africa', and claimed that Botha now understood clearly where Britain stood on the major issues.[7]

The time in Germany was less hurried, with a visit to West Berlin and talks with businessmen added to the official meeting in Bonn, but it too was controversial. The talks with Chancellor Kohl were frank but easier than those with Thatcher, but there was confrontation with Dr Vogel, the Social Democratic leader, and later an unproductive meeting with the Austrian Chancellor in Vienna. In contrast the last stop in Rome went better. The Prime Minister, Bettino Craxi, was cordial, and Botha had a half-hour audience with the Pope. The Vatican reiterated its opposition to apartheid, but Pik Botha maintained that while the Pope had expressed concern at certain elements of government policy, this 'gave us the opportunity to explain South Africa's objectives', and he added that here had been a positive reaction to internal reforms and regional peace initiatives.[8]

In sum the tour was seen as a success by Botha and by most whites, if only because it had been possible. Botha himself said that he had 'warned the West that a new approach to southern Africa was needed'.[9] However, the substantive results were minimal and the discussions, especially in Britain and Germany, had a sobering effect. Although Thatcher and Kohl gave him the benefit of the doubt on the direction of reform, they made clear that there was still a long road ahead which must include political rights for blacks in central government. Pretoria anticipated further visits to African states and the US but events in the second half of 1984 prevented that. However, one tangible result was the opening of a direct line between Botha and Thatcher, based on mutual respect which developed between them at Chequers, and letters were exchanged at critical times ahead.

This personal link and the wider relationship with Britain were severely strained within months of the tour by two events which attracted wide publicity. In mid September six UDF leaders sought asylum in the British Consulate in Durban to avoid police detention and to publicise their cause. With Pretoria demanding their eviction and the British refusing to comply, the issue dragged on for nearly three months until the six eventually agreed to come out with an agreement that they would not immediately be detained. The strain this issue caused was greatly aggravated by Pretoria's decision to retaliate by not allowing four South Africans to return to Britain in

October to stand trial in Coventry on charges of attempting to break the arms embargo. After their earlier indictment the court had permitted them to return to South Africa pending their trial, but only after it had accepted an official South African undertaking that they would come back for the trial. Pik Botha's public linking of the 'Coventry Four' with the 'Durban Six' was seen in Britain as no more than an excuse for preventing a trial which would have embarrassed Pretoria and revealed how it was circumventing the arms embargo. In any case the decision damaged South Africa's international credibility and left a scar on relations with Britain. The controversy surrounding these events occurred against the background of ominous developments for Pretoria as black unrest destroyed the image of reform and stability Botha had tried to project.

THE UPSURGE OF VIOLENCE AND THE BLACK MOVEMENTS

For years the vast and expanding black townships had been relatively quiet. However, sporadic disturbances and school boycotts had continued, and by 1984 the UDF was mobilising support, as grievances built up into an eruption which was greater even than Soweto of 1976 and lasted for two years. As well as the persistent problems of apartheid, an underlying cause was economic decline and increasing unemployment. For two years there had been no growth and, although a mini-boom early in 1984 produced a growth rate of 4.5 per cent for the year as a whole, it was not sustained. Inflation was over 13 per cent, and official measures causing high interest rates gave a shock to an economy already slowing down. There was no prospect that the economy would grow at the steady 5 per cent required to absorb new black job-seekers, including an increasing number who had enjoyed better educational facilities. The Department of Manpower warned that 2.4 million people would be unemployed by 1987. The rise in the cost of living also played its part. Although average black earnings doubled between 1979 and 1983, inflation had eroded them and they were still substantially lower than average white earnings (R310 as against R1,210). Following increases in the price of maize in 1984, black consumer bodies said that such increases in 'the most essential foodstuff for people in the lower bracket would make African poverty unbearable'.[10] The economic decline was general, but it was particularly severe in the Eastern Cape and, while in 1976–7 the main disturbances were on the Witwatersrand, now the Eastern Cape was prominent. Another difference from the previous crisis was the

303

spread of unrest to small rural towns and here, too, there was a link with unemployment which had become higher in rural areas than in the big urban townships.

Within this context of economic hardship and opposition to constitutional change, the spark which set off serious disturbances was rent increases by the new local Councils in the Vaal Triangle (southern Transvaal and northern Free State). The Councils, which the government said would give blacks a say in running their own affairs, enjoyed little legitimacy and were challenged by the UDF and the National Forum (a black consciousness group linked to AZAPO and opposed to the UDF). Protest meetings were held and on 3 September 1984 an estimated 60 per cent of workers and most school children in the Vaal Triangle stayed at home. Violent clashes followed, and during September sixty people were killed, thousands were arrested and detained and property damage amounted to about R30m.[11] The protests and violence spread to the East Rand, Soweto, townships near Pretoria, the Eastern Cape and finally the Western Cape, and they became so serious that from October the Defence Force was called into townships to support the police.

In November the largest ever stayaway was organised by trade unions, student groups and the UDF in the Transvaal, with demands ranging from scrapping the rent increases to the release of all political prisoners. The government ascribed the success of the stayaways to intimidation, and Buthelezi and black consciousness groups separately accused the organisers of intimidation against fellow blacks. Nevertheless the high participation, especially in unionised factories, frightened the business community which questioned the detention of union officials as jeopardising industrial peace. International criticism, alerted by dramatic television coverage, also mounted, but P. W. Botha responded by asking whether the government should sit still when it had proof that the Communist Party was involved and that violence and revolution were being promoted.[12]

By the end of 1984 'unrest' had become a euphemism for a country in turmoil, and the violence continued to escalate throughout 1985. A major difference from 1976–7 was the presence of effective black organisations to articulate grievances and mobilise resistance: the trade unions, the UDF, AZAPO and Inkatha. All opposed the government's constitutional reforms, but the UDF and AZAPO also challenged the legitimacy of 'the system' and made targets of its institutions and officials. Inkatha opposed the government but was not prepared to back the militancy of the UDF and AZAPO, and initially maintained relative calm in its areas. Such was the scale of the protests elsewhere, however, and such the degree of international support, that the belief grew that the black movements could make the country ungovernable.

While the black movements operating inside the country directly challenged the government, the main symbol of black resistance remained the ANC. Although it could not operate openly, had few active guerrillas in the country and probably played little part in the township risings, its 'armed propaganda' had been effective. At major protest meetings it was the ANC colours, its leaders and its songs which bore witness of the struggle. In 1983 the pattern of ANC activity had persisted with low intensity military moves and counter-moves. The most serious incidents took place in May when the ANC set off a bomb outside a Defence Force building in Pretoria killing 19 people in the street and injuring 215, and the government retaliated by raiding an ANC centre near Maputo, killing 41 ANC members and 17 Mozambique citizens. 1984 was a mixed year for the ANC. Although its leaders tried to brush aside the importance of the Nkomati Accord, it was a blow. The Mozambique authorities not only forbade military bases but raided ANC houses in Maputo, expelling 200 members and restricting the ANC to a small diplomatic mission. Nor could the ANC easily find other bases on the border. The Zimbabwe, Botswana and Lesotho governments were sympathetic but fearful of Pretoria's reaction, while the Swaziland government was not even sympathetic. Yet the ANC continued to infiltrate some guerrillas into the Republic who succeeded in attacking government and business targets and in training youths in simple guerrilla skills. But most significant was the increased public attention. By 1985 the ANC's prestige had risen so sharply that many whites were said to favour some form of negotiation with it.

In exile the ANC re-examined its position. Eager to increase its activities inside the country, it declared 1985 as 'Year of the Cadre' and called a major conference at Kabwe in Zambia in June where the main topics were military strategy, the role of workers and underground organisation. Unlike the Morogoro conference in 1969, the mood was said to be self-confident and united. On military strategy it was agreed that attacks might include some 'soft targets' (i.e. civilians, such as prominent government supporters, state witnesses and border area farmers), and that a 'people's war' should be waged. The people's war involved a change of direction from attacks on economic and strategic installations to mass participation and military action to undermine state administration. The people were no longer to be spectators but should involve themselves by supporting the cadres, disrupting work, establishing local authorities and resigning from government posts. 'The doors of the houses of our people should be open to our cadres. Everybody . . . has a role to play.' On the organisational side, a larger National Executive was formed, comprising most of the old executive but bringing in younger, more radical elements. In its political aims the conference rejected dialogue with the government – unless apartheid were to be totally dismantled – reaffirmed support for economic sanctions and disinvestment, called for efforts to work with the PAC and for trade union unity to mount an industrial campaign that would bring the government to its knees.[13] This euphoric talk was based on a gross underestimation of the state's power and the government's willingness to use it. 'We as oppressed and struggling masses have power and we can use it the way we like . . . We can determine the future of this country's economy' and the stayaway had shown that 'we have power in our hands . . . that we can bring the machinery of this country to a standstill'.[14]

Although the government did not deny the need for further reform, it viewed the actions of the UDF and AZAPO as part of a communist and ANC-inspired effort to make the country ungovernable and ripe for revolution. 'Revolutionary onslaught' came to replace the 'total onslaught' as the official description of the threat facing the country. As the conflict spread and intensified during 1985 and 1986 the government attempted both to suppress it by tough security action, and to defuse it by further piecemeal reform. International criticism mounted against the forceful suppression of black protest as unprecedented media coverage – especially television pictures of violence and confrontations in black townships – caused mounting public reaction in Western countries. Pressure on governments to take action increased sharply, notably in the US where the racial dimension of the South African conflict touched a sensitive nerve. The European Community (EC) tried, but failed, to adopt a common approach. Denmark, the Netherlands, Belgium and France favoured imposing economic sanctions, while Britain, Germany and Portugal were opposed (in Britain's case despite the Commonwealth whose members increasingly favoured sanctions and for whom South Africa was still a prime concern).

THE CHALLENGE TO CONSTRUCTIVE ENGAGEMENT

In November 1984 the award of the Nobel Peace Prize to Bishop Desmond Tutu, an outspoken critic of apartheid, drew worldwide attention to the Bishop himself and to the unrest within South

Africa. Tutu's vigorous criticisms of apartheid made the greatest impression in the US where ironically Reagan's overwhelming re-election in early November had provoked the anti-apartheid lobbies into renewed activity. South Africa had not been a significant issue in the election, but constructive engagement had been opposed by the Democratic candidate, Walter Mondale, and it was an issue on which Democrats felt public opinion could be mobilised against the Administration. The campaign was spearheaded by the black American organisation, TransAfrica, led by Randall Robinson, who argued that the 'long-range interests of the United States lie in accommodation and identification with the black majority that will inevitably inherit South African society'.[15] TransAfrica concentrated on universities, state and city governments, churches and companies, and in Washington it became an active and vocal lobby for disinvestment and sanctions legislation by the Congress. A Senator commented: 'It was not a Congressman, a Senator or a President who brought the matter of South Africa to the attention of the American people. It was a citizen, Randall Robinson.'[16] A longer established organisation, the African–American Institute based in New York, with strong links to the corporate sector, major foundations and universities, was not a militant lobbying organisation like TransAfrica, but it brought American politicians and opinion-formers together with prominent Africans and introduced ANC leaders to business circles in the United States.

Against that background the television pictures of violence in South Africa and Tutu's Nobel award 'sparked across America a prairie fire of anti-apartheid protest'.[17] The most dramatic protests were daily demonstrations outside the South African Embassy in Washington which started on 21 November with a sit-in inside Ambassador Brand Fourie's office by Randall Robinson and two other black Americans who were arrested and spent the night in jail. By March 1985 2,000 people, Democrats and Republicans, many of them prominent and newsworthy, had been arrested but charges were not pursued against them. Robinson called his campaign the 'Free South Africa Movement', although it was directed primarily against the Reagan Administration and focused on Congress where support for sanctions legislation grew, led by the Black Caucus. Robinson did not conceal his resentment that the Reagan Administration had 'almost entirely shut out Blacks',[18] and he also said: 'It's not only a protest against South Africa, it's a kind of rejuvenation of ourselves.'[19] Bishop Tutu lent his weight by telling black Americans to 'get your act together' and pressure Reagan to support black South Africans.[20]

Reagan and the State Department remained firmly opposed to sanctions and disinvestment, but they could not ignore the vociferous campaign. In December Reagan invited Bishop Tutu to the White House, an invitation which Tutu ascribed to the President's need to respond to the pressures because Reagan, he said, had not previously been enthusiastic for a meeting, and he was surprised that it turned out to be more than a formal picture-taking session.[21] The President also spoke out publicly saying that there were 'occasions when quiet diplomacy was not enough'. He called on Pretoria to 'reach out to its black majority by ending the forced removal of Blacks from their communities and the detention without trial and lengthy imprisonment of black leaders'. Such actions can 'only comfort those whose vision of South Africa's future is one of polarization, violence and the final extinction of any hope for peaceful, democratic government'. Peaceful change could only come through effective dialogue between whites and blacks, 'a dialogue sustained by adherence to democratic values and a belief in governments based on the consent of the governed'.[22]

Reagan's critical words and his inclusion of South Africa in a list of countries where human rights were violated shocked Pretoria. Although P. W. Botha responded by accusing the US of interfering in domestic affairs, there was serious concern about the direction the tide was flowing. The changed mood in Congress was reflected particularly in a letter which thirty-five conservative members addressed to Ambassador Fourie in December, indicating in effect that they were no longer prepared to stand against the adoption of sanctions. Crocker for his part maintained that constructive engagement would still be pursued, but 'we are going to need the help of people in South Africa who are committed to constructive change . . . that moves beyond some of the limited steps that we have seen to date'.[23] However, as violence escalated during 1985 and as Congress moved to adopt a sanctions bill, constructive engagement became less and less of a viable policy.

THE GOVERNMENT'S RESPONSE

Botha was aware of the growing threat of sanctions and disinvestment. Business leaders, who took this threat even more seriously, became increasingly outspoken on the need for meaningful reform. When Senator Edward Kennedy, a prominent sanctions advocate, visited South Africa in January 1985 at the invitation of Bishop Tutu supported by the UDF (but opposed by AZAPO which wanted no contact with American capitalists, and Inkatha which opposed sanctions), businessmen emphasised the need for change in an attempt to counter the influence on him from those in favour of sanctions. When Botha opened the first full session of the new tricameral parliament later in January he promised further reforms, including: an informal, non-statutory, forum in which the government would discuss constitutional issues with black leaders; possible freehold rights for blacks in urban areas to replace the existing ninety-nine-year leasehold scheme (in itself a significant earlier reform); clarification of the issue of black citizenship (blacks had been deprived of South African citizenship when their ethnic 'homelands' had been declared independent); steps to eliminate 'negative and discriminatory' aspects of influx control; and a re-examination of the problems of black removals. This speech was welcomed in the West, with a White House spokesman calling it 'a clear statement of intent to address the major outstanding issues of constructive change affecting the black majority', and even the usually critical *Guardian* in Britain commented that 'Botha finally took the "step in the right direction" yesterday which some observers mistakenly discerned in last year's constitutional changes.'[24]

Within South Africa, however, there were no plaudits from the militant black organisations. The UDF and AZAPO saw Botha's promises as falling far short of their aims and as an attempt to divide urban blacks from those in the homelands. 'Only a constitution based on the will and full participation of all South Africans can be the basis for a lasting peace' said a UDF spokesman, and AZAPO maintained that it would be satisfied with nothing less than 'repossession of the land'.[25] Buthelezi also rejected the idea of participating in the non-statutory forum, saying that it would be 'like co-operating in our own political suicide'.[26] On the other hand, most whites viewed Botha's speech as heralding a significant departure from apartheid. In a highly critical reaction Treurnicht said that the government had 'finally scrapped separate development', and there was reportedly concern even in NP ranks that Botha had gone too far. In contrast, the positive reaction of other whites was expressed in the comment of a leading editor: 'It is no exaggeration to say that it was the most important, constructive statement on race policy since Dr Verwoerd codified hardline apartheid in the 50s and sent South Africa down a dead-end street that imperilled security at home and wrecked our reputation abroad.'[27]

Thus, once again, Botha had aroused expectations among reform-minded whites and in Western governments. However, in domestic politics he had again fallen between two stools: his suggested reforms were 'enough to estrange more hardline Whites, but too vague and tentative to impress black nationalists'. In the final analysis, too, Botha's January speech was long on references to the problems but short on the specifics of how to deal with them. As Dr Motlana commented, 'he didn't commit himself to anything' and there was still no 'real declaration of intent' on which black leaders would be willing to negotiate.[28] Fear of right-wing reaction and black unwillingness to consider negotiations on Botha's terms thus inhibited reform steps, and by the end of the parliamentary session in June little had been done to give effect to the expectations of January. For example, although Minister Gerrit Viljoen announced in February a suspension of *forced* removals, partly because of international pressure, no guarantee was given that 'compulsory resettlement' would be abandoned where it was required to consolidate homelands or to deal with squatter problems.[29] A concrete reform step, which it was hoped would make an impression abroad, was the repeal of the legislation prohibiting mixed racial marriages and sexual intercourse across the colour line. The repeal of these notorious racial laws was controversial in the white community with the CP strongly opposed, but among blacks it made little impression. 'We are not interested in the repeal of these laws; we want effective participation in the running of our country', said Dr Motlana.[30]

The new tricameral parliament's first working session did not therefore inspire confidence that the participation of Coloureds and Indians would satisfy the demands for change, and the two new Houses were no nearer achieving legitimacy in their respective communities. The White House, with its NP majority, still dictated the substance and pace of reform, and the other two Houses had little to show for their efforts except the repeal of the Mixed Marriages and Immorality (Section 16) Acts. Moreover, the inclusion of the Coloured and Indian majority leaders, the Revd. Alan Hendrickse and Mr Amichand Rajbansi, in Botha's cabinet (but without portfolios) exposed them to accusations of complicity in government security measures.

International attention was focused instead on the township disturbances and the measures to quell them. The violence reached a peak in the Eastern Cape on 21 March (the 25th anniversary of Sharpeville), when police fired on a crowd marching from the Langa township of Uitenhage to a funeral, which had been prohibited by the police, killing twenty and injuring twenty-seven. Botha responded to the outcry by appointing a one-man judicial commission (Judge Donald

Kannemeyer) to investigate the incident, whose report in June concluded *inter alia* that the attitude to funerals of people who had died from police action should be urgently reviewed. With most public gatherings banned, these funerals had become major occasions when large crowds showed 'solidarity with and support for the cause for which the deceased are thought to have died', and the atmosphere was always 'highly emotive'.[31] The judge also criticised the police for not being properly equipped to handle riots so as to avoid loss of life.

The conflict continued. By the end of June 1985 there had been over 400 deaths since the start of the disturbances in September. On 20 July Botha declared a state of emergency in thirty-six magisterial districts because 'the ordinary law of the land is inadequate . . . to maintain public order'.[32] Almost all the affected districts were in the Eastern Cape and the PWV region of Transvaal, but in October the emergency was extended to districts in the Western Cape. Botha argued that it was 'essential that the situation be normalised in such a way that the climate for continued dialogue, in the interest of all people in the constitutional, economic and social fields is ensured'.[33] But it was probably intended more as a show of strength to counter the widespread impression, at home and abroad, that the government was critically threatened by black resistance and that the collapse of white power was within sight. It was also needed in the white political context to counter the accusation from the right that the government was too weak in its response to black militancy. Pretoria was, however, conscious of the effect on international attitudes of the use of emergency regulations giving even wider powers to the security forces. Detention without trial was particularly controversial. The official figure of detentions under the Internal Security Act during 1985 was 2,436, but an additional 7,361 were detained for varying periods under emergency regulations after 20 July.[34] (The total number of detentions in 1985 alone exceeded the numbers detained during each of the Sharpeville and Soweto crises.) The deterioration of the situation, culminating in the partial state of emergency, fuelled the pressure on Western governments to impose economic sanctions, and on internal companies and banks to disengage. At the same time Pretoria's actions in southern Africa were also disturbing these relations.

REGIONAL TENSIONS

Policy towards neighbouring states continued to be closely linked to the domestic conflict by Pretoria's overriding security concerns and specifically its attitude to the ANC and SWAPO, with their presence across borders and their links with the Soviet Union. It was not surprising, therefore, that the domestic security deterioration strengthened the 'hawks' on regional policy, who saw the border threat as a direct cause of the domestic revolt and were determined not to relax against that threat. The counter argument that regional concessions, for example on Namibia or Angola, would help to reduce international pressure at a time of domestic crisis, carried little weight. Regional policy continued to include a variety of ingredients – diplomatic contacts, economic co-operation, 'railway diplomacy' – but the exercise of military strength became increasingly prominent. It was also increasingly in Pretoria's interests to emphasise that South Africa was the dominant regional power, and that international punitive action would have a deleterious impact on the whole of southern Africa, threatening the economic health and stability of all the black neighbours.

No progress had been made towards the implementation of the 435 independence plan for Namibia. Crocker's efforts to resolve the Cuban linkage problem through contacts with the Angolans and South Africans had not borne fruit. In mid June 1985 Botha launched another internal government for the Territory – the Transitional Government of National Unity (TGNU) – based on the Multi-Party Conference (established in August 1983 to bring together non-SWAPO parties). Provision was made for an executive and a legislative authority (National Assembly), and the new government was given all powers previously exercised by the Administrator General (AG), although strong reserve powers remained with the AG and the State President. So the reins were still in Pretoria's hands and Botha insisted that nothing would be done 'irreconcilable with the international settlement plan as long as there are realistic prospects of bringing about the genuine withdrawal of Cuban troops from Angola'. This did not allay Western concern because Botha added that, if it became clear that there was no real prospect of achieving this goal, all parties would obviously have to reconsider how internationally acceptable independence might best be attained in the light of prevailing circumstances.[35] Moreover Pretoria, acting unilaterally, made provision in the June proclamation for a Constitutional Council, with members drawn from the National Assembly, to draft a constitution for Namibia.

The Western powers refused to recognise the TGNU which mounted its own international lobbying campaign. Its main problems after 1985, however, related to the achievement of legitimacy within the Territory and to its relations with Pretoria. On the one hand, differences between the participating parties themselves (which included the white Nationalists) and between them and the non-participating parties (including the internal SWAPO and parties based in the Ovambo and Damara ethnic groups) severely limited the TGNU's popular support. On the other hand, the efforts of a majority in the Assembly and Constitutional Council to move away from the ethnic group structure of government (as reflected in their draft constitution published in 1987), ran into the powerful opposition from the white ethnic authority and P. W. Botha himself. By the beginning of 1988, therefore, the TGNU was threatened with collapse or dissolution, amounting to yet another set-back for Pretoria's efforts to construct a viable internal government. For Botha and the military, however, a viable political alternative to SWAPO was still the aim. In the meantime they believed that the military emasculation of SWAPO in Angola and a campaign 'to win hearts and minds' in the north would reduce SWAPO's political support. The prospects for independence were in any case remote, while Namibia's future remained linked to the outcome of the Angolan conflict.

The South African troop withdrawal from Angola, in terms of the Lusaka Agreement, was at last completed in April 1985, although Pretoria maintained the Agreement was still being violated by SWAPO incursions while Luanda argued that the withdrawal had not ended South African support for UNITA. Then, on 21 May in the Cabinda enclave in the far north of Angola, two South African soldiers were killed and one was captured by Angolan forces. Malan said that a small force had been on a reconnaissance mission to find ANC and SWAPO training camps, but the captured South African officer stated that the force had intended to sabotage oil storage tanks of the American corporation Gulf Oil. If it had succeeded – which would have been a severe blow to the Angolan economy – UNITA would have claimed the credit. This 'admission' was politically embarrassing for Pretoria, and it caused Luanda to break off the negotiating contacts which had followed the Lusaka Agreement. It also influenced Castro to increase the number of Cuban troops in Angola from an estimated 25,000 to 31,000 by the end of 1985.[36]

From the end of June 1985 South African forces regularly crossed into Angola to attack SWAPO and to help UNITA. The pre-Lusaka situation had thus been restored and one of the successes of constructive engagement nullified. At the same time US policy shifted towards active support for UNITA in the context of the Reagan Doctrine. In July Congress agreed to repeal the Clark Amendment (1975) which had banned US aid to Angolan rebel movements, opening the way for military aid to UNITA. This shift exposed a contradiction in Washington's policy, with one strand promoting negotiations, stability and peace in the region, reflected in Nkomati, and the other promoting violent conflict by military and political support for one side in a civil war. The justification for aiding UNITA lay in the increased supply by the Soviet Union of more sophisticated weapons to the MPLA, as well as the increased number of Cubans. The US thus became engaged in a classic case of military escalation, with each side arguing that it had to match the increased force available to the other. Moreover, the US actions had the effect of encouraging Pretoria, which could again argue that it was on the side of the West in the struggle against communism. Support for UNITA now became more open.

In September Malan explained the three major military considerations in Angola: 'limited military action' against SWAPO; 'moral, material and humanitarian aid' to UNITA; and resisting the build-up of sophisticated Soviet military material. On SWAPO he was categoric that action would be taken against it and its supply lines because, contrary to the Lusaka Agreement, SWAPO was rebuilding its bases. On the third point Malan maintained that the 'flood' of military equipment and its sophisticated nature (estimated by him as worth $10 billion in the five years up to 1982) were much more than needed to cope with South African actions against SWAPO and with UNITA's guerrilla campaign. He asked therefore whether this was not a 'prepositioning of military equipment to be used, ultimately, against South Africa', and claimed 'that the Russians want to develop a firm, stabilised base in Angola and then use the equipment and the personnel positioned there wherever necessary in the sub-continent'. He continued: 'If you look at our (South African) massive reserves of strategic minerals, don't you ask yourself whether this mineral treasure house is not the cherry on top of the African cake? . . . The Communists want a black–white polarisation in South Africa so that they can attack our country with conventional military forces, knowing that not a single country in the world will lift a finger to help South Africa, because they (the Communists) would be acting against "those white racists".' He referred to UNITA as a 'potent anti-communist force' which would be lost to the West if the marxist forces were allowed to wipe it out.[37] P. W. Botha himself called on the US and other African countries to join in trying to rid the region of foreign troops. 'Say to the Cubans "go home", and say to the Russians "go home", and the minute this happens, I will be prepared to settle all our military forces inside South Africa.' If the Russians and Cubans were allowed to succeed in Angola, he said, the next target would be South West Africa, followed by Botswana and then South Africa.[38]

These statements were made about the time of the biggest offensive ever against UNITA by Angolan forces. It began in August but, after initial successes, was halted at the end of September. In a major battle both the MPLA and UNITA suffered heavy casualties, and the MPLA lost considerable quantities of Soviet-made equipment. Luanda maintained that these losses were the result of South African air and artillery attacks, but Savimbi retorted: 'We did not need South African assistance, we did not request it, and South Africa was not prepared to give it.'[39] Similar denials came from Pretoria, but it was widely believed 'that the SA Air Force had gone into action on UNITA's behalf at Mavinga and that the SADF's 32 battalion was there on the ground with radar-guided G-5 and G-6 artillery'.[40] The covert military involvement and Botha's and Malan's commitment to UNITA reflected their concern about this specific threat and their determination not to relax Pretoria's firm regional posture.

Washington's influence was limited by its policy contradictions. On the one hand, Crocker dissociated the Administration from Pretoria's actions and in October 1985 the US voted for the unanimous Security Council resolution condemning Pretoria for 'its latest premeditated and unprovoked aggression' against Angola, just as it had joined in the condemnations over the Cabinda incident. On the other hand, Reagan favoured supporting UNITA although he announced, surprisingly, that he preferred to provide *covert* aid. By the beginning of 1986 the CIA was organising the supply of Stinger shoulder-fired ground-to-air missiles and other equipment to UNITA, and Savimbi made a well-publicised visit to the US. Washington thus joined Pretoria in backing UNITA, countering Soviet and Cuban support for the MPLA, but American policy remained confused. Public criticism of Pretoria was maintained during 1986 when South African forces were again active in the south and south-east of Angola, although Luanda still perceived the US as tacitly supporting South African 'aggression'. In August and September, South African assistance to UNITA again helped to prevent a renewed Angolan/Cuban push towards Jamba, UNITA's main base.

Another front where tensions increased in 1985 was on the Botswana border. On 14 June the SADF launched a cross-border attack on houses and offices in Gaborone – the first operation of its kind in Botswana and, apart from Cabinda, the first anywhere since the Nkomati Accord. Gen. Constand Viljoen maintained that the object was to disrupt the 'nerve-centre' of ANC infiltration which had been moved to Botswana. Twelve people were killed in the raid, some ANC financial records and other documents were captured, but little

315

military equipment. According to Gaborone those killed were three Botswana nationals (including a six-year-old child), a Dutch national and eight South African refugees, of whom only five had any connection with the ANC, and none had belonged to Umkhonto we Sizwe. The raid was justified by some in South Africa as a retaliation for a bomb attack on two Coloured MPs in Cape Town a few days before, as well as previous violent incidents which Pik Botha said had been launched from Botswana, and as a pre-emptive move against ANC actions around the Soweto anniversary of 16 June. Even PFP spokesmen in parliament hesitated to criticise this action, reflecting the overwhelming support of whites for the SADF and its cross-border operations.[41] In contrast, black opinion was sharply critical. The *Sowetan* referred to the raid as 'despicable' and an 'extraordinary tragedy and cock-up, that seems to have the same hamhandedness of the generals who blew the Cabinda affair'. In criticising the SADF the *Sowetan* also sympathised with Foreign Affairs which had 'to spend anxious days getting this country out of a mess'.[42] The senior black editor, Percy Qoboza, wrote: 'Mere words cannot describe our people's anger, horror and disgust at the actions of the SADF in Gaborone . . . A mission of death by South Africans to kill South Africans.'[43]

International reaction to the raid was universally critical and provided further ammunition to those demanding strong action against Pretoria. US Ambassador Herman Nickel was recalled to Washington for consultations, and the State Department issued a strong denunciation. While Reagan himself was less critical, he expressed doubt about Pretoria's claims that the raid was aimed at ANC 'terrorists' and was not rather a general act of coercion against Botswana. British and West European reaction was equally critical, while the UN Security Council unanimously condemned the raid, granted $14m. to Botswana to improve security and upgrade facilities for screening and accommodating South African refugees, and demanded that Pretoria pay 'full and adequate compensation' to Botswana. Pretoria's reaction was adamant that the policy was not to destabilise but 'to prevent the build-up of any hostile terrorists – or of conventional forces – in neighbouring states, which may pose a threat'.[44]

1985 also saw a deterioration in relations with Mozambique. Allegations persisted that assistance to the MNR from elements in the SADF and private South African sources was continuing, in spite of denials from both Malan and Pik Botha. In April the latter told parliament that all aid had stopped after Nkomati. Admitting there had previously been aid (because Maputo had aided the ANC), he said it no longer served the country's interests to have the MNR blowing up Cahora Bassa power lines or threatening Maputo harbour, and he added that the MNR 'must stop its violence . . . In any event it cannot achieve decisive military victory.' Malan declared the border area 'restricted airspace' to prevent private interests from aiding the rebels, and he announced that an investigation had revealed five possible MNR 'sympathisers' in SADF units. To avoid further suspicion of collaboration, certain units with Portuguese-speaking members were to be moved. Pretoria's credibility, however, received a severe blow in September when diaries found at a captured MNR base at Gorongoza in central Mozambique revealed recent South African contacts. The Vaz diaries (named after their author) revealed *inter alia* flights to the Gorongoza base with military and medical supplies, and three visits by the Deputy Foreign Minister, Louis Nel. Pik Botha and Malan did not deny the contacts but claimed they were only 'technical' violations of Nkomati and were all – particularly Nel's visits – aimed at bringing together the two sides in the war. Pik Botha admitted he did not even know of one of Nel's visits, giving rise to speculation that the Defence Force had been acting without Foreign Affairs' knowledge. Although Maputo did not renounce the Nkomati Accord, relations with Pretoria were badly soured and the joint security committee (set up to monitor violations) was suspended.[45]

The first half of 1986 saw a gradual easing of the tension between the two governments. Pik Botha, for instance, visited Maputo in March, and later there was agreement to set up a joint liaison committee with talk of resuscitating the joint security committee. But in October the death of Samora Machel in an air crash a few hundred metres inside South Africa inflamed all the Mozambican suspicions and antagonisms. It was widely believed that South African security forces had somehow caused the crash, for instance by luring the aircraft off its course by a decoy radio beacon. Although the investigating commission, appointed by Pretoria in terms of international aviation law, rejected this allegation and blamed the Soviet crew for not following the correct procedures, the suspicions did not disappear. Neither the Soviet Union nor Mozambique accepted these findings which were made public in July 1987.

In spite of these severe set-backs, labour, transport, trade and energy links continued. The apparent contradictions in the relationship were illustrated by South Africa granting a loan of R3m. in May 1987 for upgrading of Maputo harbour, whereas in the following month Malan referred to the Mozambique government as 'Marxist lackeys'.[46] In these circumstances Nkomati remained a fragile agreement, but neither side wanted to end it and thus appear to be encouraging further conflict. For Mozambique, too, the Accord had at least stopped overt SADF attacks (as distinct from covert aid to the MNR). The new President (previously Foreign Minister), Joaquim Chissano, therefore adopted a pragmatic attitude, criticising Pretoria for not observing the Accord, but declaring Mozambique's continued support for it and willingness to avoid confrontation.

Meanwhile relations with Lesotho were also strained. Apart from Prime Minister Jonathan's frequent criticisms of apartheid, the main problems were Pretoria's concern about the presence of the ANC and Lesotho's counter-allegations of SADF assistance to the dissident Lesotho National Liberation Army (LNLA). Pretoria wanted a security agreement, but Jonathan refused, and matters came to a head in December 1985 when nine people were killed in a commando-type raid on houses in Maseru. Pretoria denied involvement, but eye-witnesses confirmed that whites speaking Afrikaans were responsible. As with the Botswana raid, there was controversy over whether those killed were ANC members or refugees, but it appeared that at least three were Lesotho nationals. Despite renewed international reaction Pretoria exerted further pressure on Lesotho in January 1986 by imposing a partial blockade which almost immediately caused food and other shortages. The use of this coercion was preceded and accompanied by intense diplomatic efforts to convince Jonathan to act against the ANC and to accept a security agreement. Pik Botha attempted to use coercive diplomacy as an alternative to military action, and he sought the help of the US and UK to convey to Jonathan the seriousness of the situation. Given its geographic and economic vulnerability, Lesotho quickly agreed to talks on security where it was made clear that nothing less than the 'elimination' of the ANC from Lesotho would satisfy Pretoria.[47] Before these talks reached a conclusion Jonathan's government was overthrown in a military coup – the first in southern Africa. A military council, headed by Maj. Gen. Justin Lekhanya, took control with apparent acceptance by the king. The new government quickly airlifted ANC members out of Lesotho, and procedures at the border posts returned to normal.

While there was no evidence of Pretoria's involvement in the coup (for popular dissatisfaction with Jonathan had been growing), there was no doubt that it was precipitated by the pressures exerted on the border. In his first public address Lekhanya supported 'peaceful coexistence and good neighbourliness', and he cricitised politicians who had damaged relations with South Africa.[48] Although the new rulers were not mere puppets, and communist embassies, for instance, were not closed, relations with Pretoria became more co-operative on security and economic matters. Most significant was the signing in October 1986, after years of vacillation by Pretoria, of the agreement on the R4 billion Highlands Water Scheme (previously Oxbow). This immense project was to be developed in stages over the next three decades to supply water to the PWV region and provide a major source of revenue and employment for Lesotho.

The always uneasy, but relatively stable, relationship with Zimbabwe was disturbed towards the end of 1985 by a series of landmine explosions in the northern Transvaal which the military maintained were brought across the Zimbabwe border by the ANC. When Pik Botha threatened that suspects would be pursued into Zimbabwe, Harare reiterated that it had not and would not allow ANC bases on its territory. Although Malan foresaw a potential Namibian/Angolan border situation, this did not happen, because the relatively short border was more easily secured and the Zimbabwe forces were more capable of preventing infiltration into South Africa. On the South Africa side extensive security measures had been introduced after 1980 and further steps to protect the farmers were taken in late 1985 and 1986, including extensions to an electrified border fence, better alarm systems and more weapons for families of farmers. A particular problem was the low occupancy of farms – about 50 per cent were unoccupied (more as a result of persistent drought than of any security threat) – and efforts were made to remedy this by economic assistance. Political relations remained strained but, although Mugabe consisten-tly refused contact at ministerial level, trade and transport links continued and trade missions performing consular services were maintained in Harare and Johannesburg. These functional links were, however, more seriously threatened as tensions increased in 1986 and 1987.

Relations with Swaziland were relatively free of tensions but not always smooth. The secret security agreement signed in February 1982 had been followed within a few months by Pretoria's announcement of a plan to cede to Swaziland two pieces of territory claimed as part of 'Greater Swaziland': the Kangwane 'homeland' (created for ethnic Swazis in South Africa) and Ngwavuma which was part of the Kwazulu 'homeland' and inhabited by both Swazis and Zulus (which would give Swaziland access to the coast at Khosi Bay). This announcement was met by amazement and opposition in South Africa, not least from Buthelezi and the Chief Minister of Kangwane, Enos Mabuza, neither of whom had been consulted. The cession plan had clear potential advantages for Pretoria: it would have legitimised the ethnic group approach, making 'Greater Swaziland' the independent Swazi 'homeland' of the region and disposing of nearly one million black South African citizens; and it would have extended the buffer zone along Mozambique's southern border. However, as a result of the opposition, successful legal action by Buthelezi and Mabuza, the death of King Sobhuza later in 1982 and the uncertain outcome of a commission of inquiry, the plan was abandoned in mid 1984.

Despite that set-back relations were maintained. Economic co-operation continued, and in early 1986 a new rail link from the Eastern Transvaal was opened. The Swazi government made clear that it would not support sanctions, and there were indications that South African businessmen viewed Swaziland as a useful back door for evading trade embargoes.[49] P. W. Botha attended the coronation of the new king in April 1986 (with several other African leaders, including Machel and Kaunda), making Swaziland the only independent African state which he had been able to visit. The 1982 security agreement led to close police liaison, and tough action, including frequent deportations, was taken by the Swazis against ANC members. However, there were a number of allegations of clandestine South African raids, notably in December 1986 when two people were killed and four abducted to South Africa. Responsibility was by implication admitted by Pretoria. Although the Swazi government protested, nothing changed. Economic dependence and the military threat were powerful constraints on Swaziland, as they were on the other BLS states, and only Botswana was able to assert a degree of political independence.

REACTION TO RUBICON

In mid 1985 South African foreign relations were at a low ebb with strong Western criticism of domestic and regional policy. A British minister, Malcolm Rifkind, commented that Pretoria seemed 'almost suicidally determined to alienate even those who wish the best for that country'.[50] The EC Foreign Ministers, faced with growing calls for sanctions, sent a strong statement in late July calling for an end to the emergency regulations and the release of detainees. This was followed by the recall of all the Ambassadors for consultations and the despatch of three Foreign Ministers (Netherlands, Italy and Luxemburg) to convey EC views to Pretoria. Australia also recalled its Ambassador, Canada announced a package of mild sanctions and France banned further investment, while the Security Council approved a resolution recommending sanctions by all UN members (non-mandatory), with only the US and UK abstaining. In the US the Congress moved closer to the adoption of sanctions legislation. Crocker said everything possible was being done 'to sustain constructive engagement', but the Cabinda and Gaborone incidents 'had damaged South Africa's credibility', and the 'real story of reform' had been 'overwhelmed by the stories of repression, police killings, black-on-black violence' and Pretoria's 'self-destructive' regional acts.[51]

Faced with this situation Pik Botha's public rhetoric was defiant. He referred to the 'agitators of violence' and 'supporters of Marxist doctrine' who were stirring up international emotions to 'break the country with economic sanctions' and to end the process of peaceful change. He declared that the top priority of the government was to restore order, and it would not yield to international pressures.[52] However, at the same time, Botha was working to persuade Western governments that reform was continuing. Attention was focused on P. W. Botha's forthcoming addresses to the annual NP provincial congresses, the first in Durban on 15 August. Pik Botha travelled to Europe to brief senior British, German and US officials on measures the President would announce in Durban, including common citizenship for all South Africans and a relaxation of the pass laws, although, he said, common citizenship would not mean political rights for black Africans in a unitary state, and the emergency would not be lifted. Robert McFarlane (Reagan's National Security Adviser) and Crocker were encouraged by what they heard, and the White House press spokesman said that the South Africans 'are taking into consideration the views of the US government and of other countries'.[53] The Japanese Foreign Ministry was also briefed beforehand by a senior official from Pretoria.

Such was the unprecedented interest in the Durban speech that it was transmitted live by major TV networks in the US, Britain and Germany, giving P. W. Botha a vast international audience: an opportunity never previously accorded a South African leader. Given the high expectations it was almost inevitable that the speech would be an anti-climax, but it was worse than that. There was deep international disillusionment and disbelief. Botha promised no significant new initiatives; his tone was defensive, his style defiant. He acted as a party leader speaking to the faithful, not a statesman struggling with the problems of a complex society. Although Botha later explained that it was a party event and that he was talking to a domestic audience, he was fully aware of the extraordinary international attention. His determination not to bend to pressure was well received by his party, as were his assurances that reform would not be speeded up to satisfy external opinion and that he would not 'lead white South Africans and other minority groups on a road to abdication and suicide'.[54] For his international audience, however, his insensitivity to world opinion at a time of severe crisis in the country was inexplicable.

Botha called the speech his 'manifesto for the future of our country'. 'I believe', he said, 'that we are today crossing the Rubicon. There can be no turning back.' In effect the speech set out the parameters of the reform policy developed in the Botha years. The starting point was 'a country of minorities'. 'We are not prepared to accept the antiquated, simplistic and racist approach that South Africa consists of a white minority and a black majority.' The nature of the population was 'multi-cultural and poly-ethnic', and the NP 'rejects any system of horizontal differentiation which amounts to one nation or group . . . dominating another or others'. Between these groups there should be economic interdependence and 'the properly planned utilisation of manpower'. Within this context of interdependence the government had accepted 'the principle of ownership rights for blacks in urban areas' and the need to consider 'improvements' to the 'outdated and too costly' system of influx control, and it had modernised labour laws.

On the constitutional front Botha simply reiterated that a 'constitutional dispensation providing for participation by all South African citizens should be negotiated'. Therefore, he concluded, 'it would be wrong to be prescriptive as to structures' and 'wrong to place a time limit on negotiations'. He made it clear that he was talking about participation of groups on matters of common concern, not participation by all individuals in one political system. While he believed that independence for 'various black peoples within the context of their own statehood' represented 'a material part of the solution', he accepted that those 'black national states not wishing to have independence would remain part of the South African nation and would have to be accommodated in political institutions within the Republic . . . But I know for a fact that most leaders . . . and reasonable South Africans will not accept the principle of one-man one-vote in a unitary system', which would lead to 'domination of one over the others . . . and to chaos. Consequently, I reject it as a solution.' He also rejected the idea of a fourth chamber of parliament to represent black groups.

Botha avoided the question of restoring citizenship to blacks deprived of it by homeland independence, but he did accept the permanence of black communities in urban areas outside the national

322

states, and he recognised the need for constitutional arrangements to accommodate their 'legitimate rights'. This acceptance of the realities of industrialisation and urbanisation was the most far-reaching deviation from Verwoerdian apartheid. Botha's emphasis on acceptance of the principle of negotiations was also important: even though confined to groups rather than parties (let alone the ANC), that principle had been accepted. He spoke of 'letting the people speak' through their leaders in negotiations 'in which there will be give-and-take'. He added: 'We will not prescribe and we will not demand.' From this stage the debate on South Africa's future came increasingly to focus on the question of how negotiations could be promoted and less on the process of unilaterally imposed reform.

Botha's justification of existing policies was met by criticism from many South Africans. Bishop Tutu was 'devastated', and he also criticised Western governments which, by failing to use their influence, had made sanctions the only alternative to violence. Botha was able to use his military strength 'to bludgeon the Blacks into submission' and knew he would be supported by Thatcher, Reagan and Kohl. 'They have made it clear that in their view Blacks are expendable.'[55] Homeland leaders joined the chorus of criticism. President Lennox Sebe of Ciskei even accused Botha of 'betrayal' and said he had been misled by Pik Botha who had led him to believe that there would be an announcement about common South African citizenship, embracing all blacks in and out of the homelands.[56] Businessmen were also very critical. P. W. Botha himself expressed amusement at the 'confusion of Babel' surrounding his speech and blamed the press for the false predictions. Speculation arose over the role of ministers, especially Pik Botha, who had fuelled the expectations. There were suggestions of divisions in the Cabinet, which might have led P. W. Botha to change the speech at the last moment, but no divisions emerged publicly, and Pik Botha, far from resigning, vigorously defended the speech. In the final analysis P. W. Botha was not prepared to take a dramatic leap in the reform process. There was an element of wishful thinking which allowed Western governments and businessmen to read too much into what Pik Botha told them, but there was little doubt that the President drew back at the last moment because of conservative reaction and because he resented the advice showered on him from home and abroad.

THE ECONOMIC IMPACT

The international economic impact of the Rubicon speech was immediate. The following day share prices dropped and the value of the rand fell from 44.5 US cents to 38.5. The downward pressure on the rand's external value had been marked since 1983 when exchange controls had been relaxed to reflate the depressed economy, but that was premature and resulted only in the mini-boom of 1984 while accelerating the rand's depreciation and thus fuelling inflation.[57] As the economy declined again in the second half of 1984, the rand fell further, depreciating by over 40 per cent against the US dollar during that year. Political factors then aggravated the economic pressures and, when the state of emergency was declared in July 1985, the rand dropped below the 50 US cents level, and after Rubicon it dropped to under 35 US cents by 28 August. The Johannesburg Stock Exchange was closed for three days (the first such closure since the Sharpeville crisis), while restrictions were placed on the outward flow of capital. This followed the decision of major foreign banks, following the lead of Chase Manhattan in New York, not to 'roll over' maturing short-term loans to South Africa. The Governor of the Reserve Bank claimed that this decision was not economically justified, but was based on 'distorted perceptions of the nature, extent and possible consequences of South Africa's domestic political problems'.[58] The US banks maintained that their decisions were based on regular 'country risk' procedures, but it was also clear that domestic political pressure from shareholders, clients and public interest groups in the US played an important role.

Pretoria imposed a four-month 'standstill' on repayments of foreign debt (not on interest payments), and reintroduced a two-tier exchange rate comprising a commercial and a financial rand. The moratorium applied to about $13.5 billion (about half carried by US banks) of South Africa's estimated total foreign liabilities of about $23.8 billion. The level of South Africa's foreign debt had risen sharply following the economic upswing of 1979–80, when the increase in imports was not matched by exports. A degree of vulnerability had arisen which was now exposed by the foreign banks, and Pretoria faced growing criticism of its handling of the economy. It was suggested that 'the conduct of economic policy reflected a degree of confidence both about South Africa's political future and about its position in the world economy which . . . appears to have been misplaced'.[59]

Pretoria now aimed to reschedule the debt with a Swiss banker, Dr Fritz Leutwiler, acting as intermediary. He made proposals whereby the banks agreed to extend their loans for a further year to the end of March 1987, with token repayments of principal being made to them (about 5 per cent of the total owed) in that year. The banks had little choice but to accept. For its part Pretoria wanted to repair its international financial reputation and gave Leutwiler political support in his negotiations. Botha was forced to recognise that without political concessions the US banks especially were subject to pressures which might prevent rescheduling. At two NP provincial congresses in September 1985 he announced further reforms. In Bloemfontein he said he was prepared to negotiate with the four 'independent' TVBC states for the restoration of South African citizenship to those who had lost it, but he made clear that the sovereignty of these 'states' was not in dispute. In Port Elizabeth on 30 September he referred to the interdependence and possible co-operation with the TVBC states in an overall constitutional framework, which would allow for one collective South African citizenship. This promised a shift in government policy as did Botha's statement that he was willing to include black leaders (not only from the homelands) in the President's Council. He also referred again to the need to change the influx control system. These two speeches went some way. to restoring Botha's reformist image but they were too late and too little to stem the tide of adverse international reaction to the continuing violence.

Two important developments followed the banks' action. First, Western governments took reluctant steps on the sanctions road. The US Congress in September adopted a compromise bill to impose limited sanctions. Reagan vetoed the bill but at the same time imposed executive bans on bank loans to the government; export of computers to government agencies; nuclear exports; import of South African produced arms; and export marketing support for US companies not adhering to the Sullivan code. In addition there was provision for prohibiting the import of krugerrands (later implemented) and for increasing educational assistance to blacks. Although these measures were widely regarded as mainly symbolic, they were enough to prevent Reagan's veto from being overridden by Congress. The Executive Order was intended to demonstrate, as Reagan said, the seriousness of American concern, and it meant that the Administration's opposition in principle to economic sanctions had been breached. A few days later the EC countries, with the exception of Britain, agreed on mild sanctions which included a ban on oil and arms exports, curtailments of cultural and sporting links and the withdrawal of military attachés. Following this joint action, Britain soon agreed to comply.

Japan followed suit a month later by placing a ban on computer sales to government agencies and discouraging the import of krugerrands, to add to existing restrictions on investment, and bank loans. On the diplomatic level the Japanese government had always refused to exchange ambassadors, maintaining only consular relations, but the trading relationship thrived and by 1987 Japan became South Africa's main trading partner. This trade constituted only about 1 per cent of Japan's total foreign trade, but it was of vital importance to South Africa, particularly for the export of coal and other primary products, and the balance was in South Africa's favour. Tokyo, sensitive to possible repercussions in the UN, had consistently maintained a low political profile on South Africa, and was concerned not to be singled out for being 'soft' on Pretoria, or criticised for taking advantage of Western problems with South Africa. In late December 1985 the Japanese Foreign Ministry criticised both Pretoria's 'terrorist activities' and the 'intensification of suppression'. It urged Pretoria 'to make a courageous decision toward the abolition of apartheid' and 'to release Nelson Mandela and all other political prisoners, in order to start talks with widely representative black leaders, including those of the ANC, as expeditiously as possible'.[60]

16 THE SEARCH CONTINUES

The introduction by the West and Japan of sanctions as a serious option in addition to the banks' 'private sanctions' and the growing disinvestment trend brought a new low in South Africa's search for status and security, and caused grave concern in Pretoria and in business circles. This international pressure also served to fuel militant black expectations and resistance, and to cause a further erosion of economic confidence. At this stage a new international initiative was launched which briefly promised to provide a means of resolving the conflict.

THE COMMONWEALTH MISSION AND ITS AFTERMATH

When Commonwealth leaders met at Nassau in October 1985, South Africa dominated the proceedings. Sanctions were the central issue, with only Mrs Thatcher standing firmly against them. While Thatcher argued that sanctions would mainly harm blacks and South Africa's neighbours and would not change government policies, her Commonwealth critics pointed to the support for sanctions from black leaders in South Africa and neighbouring states. In fact this support was not unanimous, either within South Africa or in the region, but in the international clamour the voices opposed were muted or simply ignored. All Commonwealth members knew – and so did Pretoria – that a decision at Nassau without British participation would have little significance, and Thatcher therefore came under great public pressure to agree on economic measures. In private discussions, however, intense diplomatic activity, promoted by Canadian Prime Minister Mulroney, was directed at finding a compromise acceptable to Thatcher and the Frontline States (FLS). The latter were clearly not in a position to apply sanctions themselves, and Thatcher made it clear that Britain would not underwrite the FLS. A similar message was conveyed from Washington.

The Accord eventually adopted on 20 October preserved Common-wealth unity at the expense of not committing members to any significant new sanctions.[1] Thatcher boasted that she had only given way 'a tiny little bit', but for Pretoria it was another half turn on the sanctions screw. In the 'programme of common action' all members reaffirmed strict observance of the UN arms embargo and the Glenea-gles sports agreement, and they took further steps, including a ban on the import of krugerrands – in Britain's case worth some £500,000 p.a. Britain also ended official funding of trade missions to South Africa, of which there had already been nine in 1985. In addition, it was agreed that, after six months more stringent measures would be considered if there had not been concrete progress, but there was no commitment to such further action. More significant was the agreement to call on Pretoria to take a number of steps, including initiating (with a suspension of violence on all sides) a 'process of dialogue across lines of colour, politics and religion, with a view to establishing a non-racial and representative government'. Towards this end the Common-wealth established a small group of eminent persons: Malcolm Fraser (Australia), Dame Nita Barrow (Bahamas), Archbishop Edward Stott (Canada), Swaran Singh (India), Lord Anthony Barber (Britain), John Malecela (Tanzania) and General Olusegun Abasanjo (Nigeria). Fraser and Abasanjo were co-chairmen. The formation of this Eminent Persons Group (EPG) was greeted initially in South Africa with scepticism because it was felt that Botha would not tolerate such interference and that the Group did not have sufficient 'clout' to persuade him to alter course. Scepticism was also apparent in the initial ANC comment that the EPG was a repetition of the ineffective Western contact group on Namibia. However, at the end of 1985 neither side could afford to be unbending. In Pretoria's case the dispute with the foreign banks was unresolved, the sanctions threat was a reality, the economy was in serious trouble and confidence was low. Moreover, Thatcher and Reagan favoured the EPG and brought their combined influence to bear on Botha not to reject the initiative. In particular, Thatcher's personal communications helped to overcome Botha's deep reluctance to accept this intervention.

Although the ANC was riding high internationally, it also faced problems. The external leadership was not in control of young activists – the 'comrades' – in the townships, who were now setting up their own structures to replace official local authorities. The ANC call to make the country ungovernable by Pretoria was more a reflection of the situation than the cause of it. Nor was the diffuse leadership of the UDF able to exercise overall control. A terrible illustration of the

ANC's dilemma was the increasing use of the 'necklace' (a burning tyre as a form of execution) against black 'collaborators'. This barbaric practice was condemned by Bishop Tutu and UDF leaders, but the ANC hesitated to denounce it, trying rather to explain it away as a reaction to oppression. Pik Botha repeatedly accused the ANC of using the necklace as part of its 'terrorism' campaign, and it was not until Western revulsion was undermining the ANC's image that in September 1987 it unequivocally dissociated itself from the practice.[2] A further important factor for the ANC was that it was dependent on the FLS for bases and support, and they favoured the EPG mission.

P. W. Botha suggested in a letter to the EPG that a visit could 'serve a useful purpose', if the EPG promoted 'peaceful political dialogue' and was 'unbiased'. He agreed with the Nassau Accord that 'a suspension of violence' was required for dialogue, and he hoped that the EPG would discourage violence by word and action. He expressed determination to proceed with his reform programme, and to 'get moving with the negotiations . . . Our political programme provides for power-sharing, subject only to the protection of the rights of all minorities, and we are reconciled to the eventual disappearance of white domination.' In this letter,[3] which went much further than his public statements, Botha also referred to the need for the co-operation of 'all our communities in constructing an alternative system of government for South Africa'. Although Botha's receptive attitude to the EPG was not publicly known, it was known to Thatcher and Reagan and must have encouraged them.

The EPG paid several visits to South Africa and the FLS during February to May 1986, meeting a wide range of leaders, including the President, Pik Botha and other ministers, Nelson Mandela in Pollsmoor prison, and Tambo with other ANC leaders in Lusaka. In mid March the Group presented the government with a 'possible negotiating concept' which required meaningful steps towards ending apartheid, removal of military forces from the townships, and the restoration of black political activity, by lifting bans on the ANC and PAC and releasing political prisoners, including Nelson Mandela. On their side the black parties were required to enter negotiations and suspend violence. The EPG believed that this concept offered 'a real chance of establishing productive negotiations'. Six weeks later Pik Botha conveyed an encouraging reply in which he asked for a further exchange of views on how to achieve a suspension of violence and facilitate discussions. The political climate had been improved by the lifting of the partial state of emergency in March and by the President's mid April announcement ending application of the pass laws and promising repeal of influx control legislation. Pik Botha referred to these steps and also claimed that forced removals in pursuit of a political ideology were ended. He made clear, however, that the key issue for Pretoria was the suspension of violence, and he pointed out that violence might recur during the negotiating period, requiring action to restore order.

Although still concerned about sanctions, P. W. Botha's confidence was by this time returning. His reform speech of late January 1986 had been well received by Western governments and businessmen, a reasonably favourable agreement on the debt issue had been reached with the foreign banks, Reagan and Thatcher stood firm against further sanctions and, although township violence continued, the security forces could contain it. Moreover, a long term strategy had been developed for dealing with the unrest, based on the network of Joint Management Centres established in the early eighties under the control of the SSC, as part of a nationwide 'security management system'. For these reasons the need for concessions was less compelling, and Pik Botha's reply to the EPG, while suggesting further discussions, reflected a hardening of attitude. The introduction of doubts about a 'suspension', rather than a renunciation, of violence was to avoid a commitment to negotiate with the ANC.

The hardening attitude became clearer when the EPG returned for final discussions in mid May. P. W. Botha, in a public statement, spelt out emphatically 'certain important principles which are not negotiable' and he warned against outside interference. He said a negotiated settlement would be possible only within the 'democratic ideal' which 'must accommodate the legitimate political aspirations of all South Africa's communities', providing for the 'effective protection of minority groups and the right against domination and for self-determination for such groups and communities'. He renewed the commitment 'to devise such democratic solutions' with those 'who reject violence as a means of achieving political goals'. He also referred to the protection of the integrity of borders, the defence of the people 'against internationally organised terrorism' and the maintenance of law and order.[4] The timing of this statement suggested that Botha had concluded that the EPG's discussions had gone too far, arousing unrealistic expectations abroad and exposing him to right-wing opponents at home. Nevertheless the EPG's role was further boosted by its meetings with Mandela in Pollsmoor prison and other ANC leaders in Lusaka. Mandela accepted the 'negotiating concept' as a starting-point and confirmed his desire to see violence end. He said Pretoria knew of his commitment to help restore peaceful conditions. The leaders in

Lusaka evinced intense mistrust of Pretoria, but they indicated tentative acceptance of the 'negotiating concept' and said that a firm answer would be given to the EPG within about ten days.[5]

Then on the morning of 19 May, when the EPG was due to meet the Cabinet's Constitutional Committee, news broke of SADF raids the previous night in Gaborone, Harare and Lusaka. Malan, justifying the raids, referred to the recent US air attacks on Libya which were defended in terms of article 51 of the UN Charter, whereas similar action by South Africa was called aggression or destabilisation. An army statement reasserted Pretoria's determination to combat terrorism: 'Neighbouring countries', it said, 'cannot plead ignorance regarding the presence of terrorists in their countries', and they had been repeatedly asked not to assist them.[6] In response Presidents Masire and Kaunda denied that the houses attacked were ANC facilities. In Botswana the houses were largely deserted and one person was killed with three, including a Botswanan soldier, wounded. Masire said the attack was completely undeserved, especially as his government was committed to discussions with Pretoria later that week. In Lusaka two people were killed and several wounded at what Kaunda said was a refugee camp. He condemned the raid as 'state terrorism' saying that Pretoria was apparently afraid of the progress being made by the EPG. In Harare the houses were deserted and there were reports that the ANC had been warned beforehand by Zimbabwean intelligence. Mugabe accused Pretoria of aggression and terrorism, called for comprehensive and mandatory sanctions and said everything possible would be done to reduce Zimbabwe's economic reliance on South Africa. There was widespread international condemnation, some of which was directed at the West, with Tutu blaming Reagan, Thatcher and Kohl for their 'protection' of Pretoria, and Kaunda denouncing constructive engagement for encouraging the attacks. In both Washington and London particular regret was expressed about the effect on the EPG mission.

In Cape Town the EPG members doubted that any agreement could be reached, but nevertheless they met with Heunis and other ministers in the constitutional committee. The meeting reinforced the doubts, as Heunis insisted on a 'renunciation' of violence and that the phrase 'suspension of violence', originally adopted by the President, 'had to be interpreted not in the temporary sense, but as a public commitment to reject violence as a means of attaining political goals'. The EPG regarded this demand for a one-sided 'renunciation' of violence as 'unrealistic and wholly unreasonable'. This in effect marked the end of the Group's mission and its 'negotiating concept'.

In its report the EPG argued in favour of imposing further measures mentioned in the Nassau Accord, believing that Pretoria was concerned about economic sanctions and that, if it concluded 'that it would always remain protected from such measures, the process of change in South Africa is unlikely to increase in momentum and the descent into violence would be accelerated'.[7]

Such concern was not apparent when Botha declared a full state of emergency over the whole country on 12 June 1986. He met the sanctions threat head-on, saying he would not 'crawl' to prevent them. 'Neither the international community at large, nor any particular state, will dictate to us what the contents of our political programme should be . . . we ourselves will find solutions to our problems and we will make them work.' He would continue with reform, but he would not beg the world to grant recognition to the reform already taken and planned. 'We deserve encouragement and understanding – not punishment of any sort', but, if punishment in the form of sanctions had to come, 'we will make sure that it is to our advantage in the long term'.[8] Condemnation of the emergency decision came from all major Western states and Japan. But Botha had reached a turning point; no longer would he allow external criticism and threats to influence him or dictate the pace of reform. His personal inclination had always been to resist international pressures, and his experience since Rubicon, with little international recognition of his reform announcements, had further hardened him. From now on his priorities were to restore and maintain order and to promote economic recovery in the face of sanctions. In the latter regard, he needed – and increasingly obtained – the co-operation of the business community. Above all, he had to show that the sanctions wave which was now building to a crest would not work as a means of changing his government.

The seven Commonwealth leaders selected at Nassau met in London in early August to consider the EPG's report. Thatcher still stood alone against sanctions. Again a compromise was reached in which Thatcher 'reluctantly' agreed to a voluntary ban on new investment and the promotion of tourism to South Africa. She also agreed to a ban on future imports of coal, iron and steel, if the EC adopted it, which meant weakening her 1985 EC stand. The other leaders approved the additional measures adopted at Nassau and called on the rest of the Commonwealth and the wider international community to implement them urgently. The next step on the sanctions road was taken by the EC Foreign Ministers in mid September, but it was a smaller step than anticipated because of opposition from

Germany and Portugal to a ban on coal imports. Geoffrey Howe, as President of the Council of Ministers, visited southern Africa in July to promote the dialogue which the EPG had proposed. This unsuccessful visit left Howe in no doubt about Botha's defiant mood, or about the negative attitude towards Thatcher's government of the UDF, the ANC, and President Kaunda who accused the British and American governments of 'kissing apartheid'.[9] The eventual EC agreement included a ban on new investment – which had already dried up – and on imports of iron, steel and gold coins, which was a small proportion of South Africa's exports to the EC. This weak compromise strengthened the belief in South Africa that the threat of sanctions was worse than the reality. US action was still to come, however, and Japan was an unknown factor. Pik Botha, after visiting Tokyo in early September, acknowledged that Japan was under great pressure and could not afford to stand alone against the US and EC on sanctions. After the EC decision, Tokyo announced its own package, including a ban on iron and steel imports and on tourist visas for South Africans, but, following the EC lead, it did not ban coal imports.

In the US a confrontation developed between Congress and the President, in which Congress eventually overrode a Presidential veto in passing the Comprehensive Anti-Apartheid Act of 1986 (CAAA). *Inter alia* this forbade the import of South African coal, iron, steel, uranium, arms and ammunition, textiles and agricultural products. New investment and the export of oil were banned, and the landing rights of South African Airways were revoked. The CAAA also directed the President to impose further sanctions after a year if Pretoria made no progress in ending apartheid, or to lift the sanctions if Pretoria took steps similar to those in the Nassau Accord. It allocated $40m. to aid victims of apartheid, and it required the Administration to make a study of the ANC's use of violence and the influence of communism on the ANC. The sanctions were welcomed in South Africa by the UDF, AZAPO and some trade union leaders, while businessmen expressed shock tempered by an estimate that they were unlikely to affect more than 5 per cent of total exports. There were also some expressions of determination that sanctions would not only be overcome but would even help to stimulate domestic economic activity.

The CAAA marked the crest of the sanctions wave. A year later Reagan reported, as required by the Act, no sign of significant progress towards ending apartheid, but claimed that the impact of the CAAA had been negative 'causing increased unemployment for Blacks and worsening the country's economic stagnation, without having a positive effect on the government itself'. Instead of additional sanctions, he proposed 'a period of active and creative diplomacy' to bring about negotiations.[10] Although his report was strongly criticised by advocates of sanctions, attempts to have stronger measures adopted by Congress were abandoned. In the Commonwealth, too, a stalemate was reached. At the meeting in Vancouver in October 1987 there was again a confrontation between Thatcher and the others, but no new sanctions were adopted. Instead, all members except Britain agreed to set up a committee of Foreign Ministers to monitor developments and to commission a study on South Africa's relationship with international finance houses.

REGIONAL FLUX

A new development at the Vancouver meeting was the presence of Mozambique's Foreign Minister as an observer, reflecting the importance of the Commonwealth in southern Africa. (Of the nine SADCC members, only Angola and Mozambique were not members.) Britain, keen to emphasise its regional and Commonwealth role rather than concentrating only on South Africa, had developed a close relationship with Mozambique since Zimbabwe's independence. Her aim (along with the EC, the US and the Scandinavian countries) was to reduce the FLS dependence on South Africa by offering technical and financial assistance, much of which was concentrated on restoring transport routes, particularly through Mozambique. At Vancouver Britain publicised her substantial aid to the SADCC states, which included military training for Zimbabwe, Mozambique, Lesotho and Swaziland, and stated that her aims were 'to work for peaceful dialogue in South Africa' to end apartheid, replace it with a 'non-racial, representative system of government', and to 'promote the peaceful, stable and prosperous development of all states in the region'.[11] Although this involvement did not satisfy those demanding further sanctions, the growing British and Western regional commitment imposed a significant constraint on Pretoria, particularly in its relations with Mozambique and Zimbabwe. Any economic or military actions against them ran the risk of adversely affecting Western interests and, in particular, of offending Thatcher. This constraint was reinforced by the visits of Chancellor Helmut Kohl to Mozambique in late 1987, of the French Foreign Minister in February 1988, and the announcement in early 1988, during a visit by Franz Joseph Strauss, of German financial aid to Maputo. In contrast, the Reagan Administration was unable to balance its continued opposition to sanctions by granting substantial aid to Zimbabwe and Mozambique because of Congressional resistance to helping 'marxist regimes'. But Crocker prevented aid being given to the MNR and arranged some help for the Mozambique government, in spite of concerted pro-MNR efforts by Senator Helms and others.[12]

Working relations between Pretoria and Maputo gradually improved as the after-effects of Machel's death receded and West European initiatives influenced both sides. In spite of lingering mutual suspicions, support for the Nkomati Accord was re-affirmed by Presidents Chissano and Botha, several meetings at ministerial and official level were held in the first half of 1988, and agreement was reached to resuscitate the joint security committee. In June an agreement was reached on Cahora Bassa, covering the financing of repairs to the powerlines, the tariff to be paid by South Africa and the future security of the lines, including non-lethal logistic support from South Africa for a 'protection force'. This tentative *rapprochement* culminated in a summit meeting of the two Presidents near Cahora Bassa in September, after which Botha paid a state visit to Malawi.

There was no similar improvement in relations with Zimbabwe. During 1987 tension increased with the active promotion of sanctions by Mugabe (who had become chairman of the Non-Aligned Movement in September 1986). Mugabe was eager to show his Commonwealth colleagues, not least Thatcher, Zimbabwe's willingness 'to put its money where its mouth is'. However, attempts in late July 1987 to cut off all but essential imports from South Africa were quickly abandoned after the consequences for the economy and the risks of retaliation by Pretoria were more carefully considered. Instead a policy of disengagement by persuasion was adopted, and businessmen were advised to find alternative trading partners and trade routes. The shortest route was to Beira in Mozambique, and international financial aid was readily available for restoration of the railroad, road and port. However, progress on increasing the volume of traffic was slower than expected, because of the low capacity of the port, inefficiency and the disruptive activities of the MNR. Better prospects were envisaged for the line to Maputo which was being restored with British assistance, provided disruption by the MNR could be prevented. Meanwhile, South African trade and other links with Zimbabwe were maintained and the SADF refrained from further overt strikes in Zimbabwe, but the tension was not relieved. Accusations that the ANC was using Zimbabwean territory continued from Pretoria, with counter-accusations from Harare that

South Africans were responsible for various attacks and bomb blasts in Zimbabwe.

EFFECTS OF AMERICAN PRESSURE

In the US the Administration scrupulously applied the CAAA. Any country selling arms to Pretoria was liable to be denied future American military assistance, and this threw the spotlight on Israel which, according to a Congressional report in April 1987, 'appears to have sold military systems and sub-systems and provided technical assistance on a regular basis', as well as upgraded major South African weapons systems, contrary to the UN arms embargo.[13] The Israeli Cabinet, aware of the US threat, agreed that no new defence contracts would be signed with Pretoria and that cultural and tourism links would be curbed. Existing contracts would not be broken but would not be renewed. Foreign Minister Shimon Peres said that Israel would 'gradually reduce our relationship with South Africa following policies that other democratic countries pursue'. He strongly denied allegations of co-operation in producing nuclear weapons but would not elaborate on possible trade sanctions. In this regard the most substantial item was coal, with South Africa supplying 50 per cent of coal needs for electricity generation, but Peres did say that coal from China could be substituted.[14] Although it was uncertain how rigorously Israeli sanctions would be applied, they were a considerable psychological blow to Pretoria, and Pik Botha blamed American pressure.

In the business field American links were reduced. Even though no further sanctions were adopted in 1987, the tide of disinvestment continued and trade decreased between the two countries. By the end of 1987, 143 American companies (about half the total) had left South Africa, 94 of them since the beginning of 1986.[15] Although the disinvestment campaign weakened during 1987, together with the marked decrease in media attention to South Africa, an unexpected development introduced new problems for companies still in South Africa. A last-minute amendment to a domestic finance bill (being rushed through Congress before the 1987 Christmas recess) was adopted without debate and reportedly without most Congressmen knowing about it. Although the Administration was strongly opposed, Reagan could not veto the whole bill for the sake of this one item, which meant that US firms in South Africa would have to pay both South African and American taxes on their profits. Pik Botha said it would further reduce US influence and he accused the sanctions advocates in

Congress of trying to destabilise South Africa economically, and of promoting conflict.

As the Americans moved out, others moved in. A Commonwealth report revealed that in 1987 both Japan and Taiwan in particular had substantially increased their trade with South Africa. The report also revealed that, while South Africa's coal exports should have fallen by 10m. tons because of the steps taken by the US, France and Denmark, they had only fallen by 3m. tons because Spain, the Netherlands, Portugal and Greece took advantage of low South African prices, while Turkey re-exported South African steel as 'Turkish steel'.[16] Yet the economy continued to falter. Unlike previous periods of crisis it did not recover quickly from the political/security pressures, which revealed their effects in balance of payments problems and the outflow of capital (in both cases sanctions playing a part), and inside the country the government's attempts to encourage black economic development as part of its reform programme met with suspicion from blacks and resistance from right-wing whites. Underlying the economic problems was the 'inability of economic forces to escape the shackles of the apartheid legacy'.[17]

WHITE REACTION

The hardening of white opinion towards the US and towards outside interference generally was evident in the second half of 1986, following the rash of sanctions. When P. W. Botha hinted that he was considering a white general election, it was assumed that he was taking advantage of this reaction, although he said the election was to test support for reform. However security, not reform, came to dominate the campaign. Botha placed reform third in the government's order of priorities, after the restoration of order in the country and the revival of the economy. In the long campaign before the election on 6 May 1987 the NP faced the CP and HNP (which also fought each other for some seats) to its right, and an alliance between the PFP and the small NRP to its left, plus a group of three independents who included a former Nationalist MP, Wynand Malan, and the former ambassador in London, Denis Worrall. An intensive government media campaign accused the PFP of being 'soft' and the CP of breaking ranks in the face of an external revolutionary threat.

At the election the PFP/NRP alliance suffered a severe setback, with the number of PFP seats dropping from twenty-five to nineteen, the NRP from five to one, and Malan was the only independent elected. On the far right the HNP lost its only seat, but the CP gained five and

337

with a total of twenty-two seats replaced the PFP as the official opposition in the white House. The NP marginally increased its number of seats, but the growth in CP support, particularly in the Transvaal, came as a shock. The number of seats did not tell the full story: although the NP received over 52 per cent of the vote, the far right increased its share to nearly 30 per cent, while those to the left had only 16 per cent, a drop of about 10 per cent from 1981.[18] After the election the white political battle shifted to the right as the NP and CP locked horns. The CP constantly attacked Botha's reforms and opposed any deviation from separate development. In these circumstances the government became less inclined to take political initiatives. Instead, emphasis was placed on economic needs, encouraging greater support and co-operation from the business community, together with continued emphasis on security. The state of emergency was re-imposed in June 1987, and the overt unrest continued to decline under the draconian security regulations which *inter alia* severely restricted the media, including foreign correspondents. As a result Pretoria's confidence in its ability to control the situation steadily returned, and internationally the South African issue became less prominent. The economy also showed signs of recovery, although this was not strongly sustained in 1988 when new measures were required to counter the threatening balance of payments problem.

For the government and the business community a continuing source of concern and of pressure for change was also the black trade unions. The Congress of South African Trade Unions (COSATU), formed in November 1985 and politically aligned with the UDF, was by far the biggest grouping. The biggest single union and a major component of COSATU, the National Union of Mineworkers (NUM), called a strike in August 1987 which lasted three weeks. Although the results were mixed and the mineworkers gained little, it was the biggest strike in South African history, involving at least 40 per cent of the workforce on the mines, i.e. 230,000 workers, according to the employers. (NUM claimed 340,000 were on strike.) 11 miners died and over 500 were injured in clashes, and the strike attracted wide international attention. It underlined the growing strength and militancy of unions, as well as their overt political motivation. The government threatened to introduce controversial amendments to legislation which the unions considered would restrict their recently gained rights. Then, in February 1988, COSATU was included among seventeen organisations prohibited from engaging in any politically related activities.

The organisations affected by this severe clampdown included also the UDF and AZAPO, which were accused by the Law and Order Minister, Adriaan Vlok, of promoting a 'revolutionary climate' and of fostering 'civil disobedience and revolt'. Although the government avoided an outright banning of the organisations, the effects of the restrictions were similar, and there was strong criticism from Western governments which feared increased pressure for sanctions. In a more limited arena there was concern about the violent conflict between the UDF and Inkatha supporters in the Pietermaritzburg area of Natal, a conflict which had cost more than 400 lives in less than a year from mid 1987. Talks to end the violence were promoted by church and business leaders, but the effective banning of UDF groups, while Inkatha was not affected, threatened to undermine these efforts.

One dimension of violence that the emergency had not brought under control was the increasing incidence of bomb explosions in urban centres with a rising number of civilian casualties, black and white. These terrorist attacks were ascribed to the ANC by the government, but the ANC did not always accept responsibility. Its policy of 'soft' targets was unclear, even ambiguous, reflecting internal differences. Tambo maintained, in early June 1988, that it was still official policy that police and army personnel and installations were the primary targets, with civilian deaths in such attacks being regretted but unavoidable in a 'war' situation. On the other hand, Chris Hani, chief of staff of Umkhonto we Sizwe, argued that more civilian deaths, black and white, were inevitable as attacks in white-zoned city centres increased. He argued that the emergency and the clampdown on black organisations left the ANC no option but to intensify armed action, because most whites would stop supporting the government only when it was no longer seen as able to guarantee their safety.[19] By the end of 1988, however, ANC policy of not attacking purely civilian targets was being more clearly stated, and the number of such incidents decreased.

The ANC strongly promoted a boycott of the municipal elections for all race groups in October. Pretoria wanted to demonstrate increased black support for local institutions and then use these to provide participants for consultation at a national level. To this end revamped proposals for a national council, intended as a negotiating forum, were published in June. The local elections were thus an essential part of the overall constitutional plan, and an official advertising campaign urged participation of all groups. One of the reasons for the February clampdown may have been to stop the UDF from pursuing a boycott campaign similar to that which had been so effective in the Indian and Coloured elections of 1984, and it was made an offence under emergency regulations to advocate a boycott. In the event the elections on 26 October confirmed the lack of support from the vast majority of blacks for government-established local authorities, with particularly low polls in Soweto (11 per cent) and townships in the Eastern Cape. But Pretoria took comfort from much higher participation in other areas which had been less affected by the unrest and violence. The overall national participation was estimated to be about 27 per cent of blacks who had registered to vote, but this was less than 6 per cent of those calculated to be eligible. More satisfying for the government were the results of the bitterly contested elections for white municipalities, where the NP managed to restrict the CP threat largely to the Transvaal. Even there, the CP lost some of the ground gained in the 1987 general election and was unable to demonstrate that it posed any serious threat to the NP's continued domination of white politics. Once again, the government had used the security issue to retain its white support, Afrikaans and English, in spite of general concern about the weak economy and disillusionment on its left about the lack of purpose and will in implementing reform.

The idea of a national council was opposed by white and black opposition to the left of the government, including Buthelezi who said he would not participate before Nelson Mandela was freed. It was also strongly opposed by the CP to the right, because of the aim to include blacks in central government. Nevertheless, the government proceeded with enabling legislation, arguing that it could wait no longer and that those who would not participate would simply be left out. In June it also introduced controversial amendments to the group areas legislation, which promised to open up some areas for mixed occupation but at the same time give more teeth to the law forbidding blacks to own or occupy property in white residential areas. Although Botha faced up to opposition from the right, which opposed mixed residential areas and other reforms, these new steps did not gain him any plaudits internationally, given the lack of black support for a policy which promised no fundamental change. They did not help to counter the highly negative impact abroad of security actions and threats, including the renewal again in June 1988 of the emergency regulations in an even stronger form. The international sanctions campaign was reinvigorated, particularly in the US during an election year. A bill which would effectively end economic links with South Africa was passed in the House of Representatives with strong support. Although it did not have sufficient support in the Senate to override an inevitable veto by Reagan (and was eventually not brought to a vote), there was growing concern in business circles that further negative incidents in South Africa could produce enough support for at least a watered-down version of the bill in 1989. This would in turn have an effect on the EC and on Japan where a policy of reducing the level of trade was already being implemented.

Although the election of George Bush ensured that the Administration would for the time being continue to oppose further measures, this opposition was likely to weaken if there were no positive steps by Pretoria. Some improvement in the international climate resulted from P. W. Botha's decision not to proceed with the restrictive group areas legislation, after the Coloured House had refused even to consider the bill, and his decision to commute the death sentences on the 'Sharpeville Six' who had been convicted for involvement in the group murder of a local council member during the disturbances in 1985. But more significant was the positive change in the region and the renewed hope of early independence for Namibia.

LIMITS TO REGIONAL POWER

In the first half of 1988 security measures within the country were matched by actions across the borders, where there were several incidents in Zimbabwe, Botswana and Mozambique. For instance, in March 1988 an SADF raid on an alleged ANC base in Gaborone left four dead and aroused bitter anger. In June Botswana claimed to have stopped a South African commando group, capturing two members and charging them in court. In addition, South African agents were allegedly active with clandestine attacks on ANC leaders in countries outside southern Africa. In France the assassination of a senior ANC official, Mrs Dulcie September, led to anti-South African demonstrations and strained French–South African relations. While Pretoria's involvement in many of these terrorist incidents could not be proved, questions were raised as to 'whether the cost of adventurism in foreign affairs can be justified by the results. Nearly a dozen South Africans, so far as can be determined, are in detention in neighbouring countries, accused of complicity in some or other skullduggery. These detentions, if they do nothing else, lend credence to the long list of assassinations, bombings, raids and kidnappings attributed to "South African agents". These incidents are not perceived outside this country as isolated events. They are perceived as a concerted policy of enmity and aggression . . .'[20]

The main attention, however, from late 1987, was focused on the conflict in Angola. In September/October the Angolans, with Cuban support and more strongly armed than in 1986, renewed their offensive against UNITA. They were repulsed by UNITA with South African support which on this occasion was explicitly admitted. An SADF statement said the 'limited action' was taken against 'surrogate forces' (named as Cubans and Russians) to prevent MPLA control of Cuando-Cubango province which would have given SWAPO and the ANC greater freedom of movement, thus increasing the 'terrorist' threat to South West Africa and South Africa.[21] Savimbi claimed UNITA's 'biggest victory'. He said he was 'very surprised' by the statement that the SADF had intervened, and he even suggested that Pretoria was trying to share the credit for UNITA's success. Malan nevertheless confirmed the intervention, claiming that it was necessary to halt a Cuban–Russian offensive which would otherwise have resulted in the defeat of UNITA. If that happened, South West Africa, Botswana, Zimbabwe and Zambia 'would then be overwhelmed by Russian–Cuban aggression . . . The whole of Southern Africa would be destabilised and subjected to Russian domination.' As a regional power, he said, South Africa was 'committed to countering the destabilisation of the region'.[22] Allowing that Malan's statement may have been intended to head off criticism within South Africa of growing involvement in another Angolan war, and as an appeal to conservatives in the West, it did reflect real concern about the increased strength of Angolan and Cuban forces armed with sophisticated Soviet equipment. The balance of forces was shifting away from UNITA and South Africa, especially in the vital dimension of air power.[23] This aggravated Savimbi's dilemma: militarily he was more reliant than ever on Pretoria (even with US aid), while politically the alliance was becoming more and more embarrassing.

Fighting in Cuando-Cubango province continued in the early months of 1988 around the key town of Cuito Cuanavale, but eventual military stalemate was followed by a new round of negotiations which began formally at a meeting in London in early May between South African, Angolan and Cuban officials, with Crocker as chairman and mediator. The South African team was headed by Foreign Affairs Director General Neil van Heerden, assisted by the SADF Chief, Gen. Jannie Geldenhuys, and the head of the National Intelligence Service (NIS), Dr Neil Barnard.

The London meeting was the first of a long series – held in Cairo, Brazzaville, Geneva and New York – which continued until December. These protracted negotiations, focusing on the Cuban presence in Angola and Namibian independence, were conducted mainly by senior officials with ministers drawn in only at crucial junctures. The US continued to play a prominent mediating role but was now encouraged by the USSR with its new spirit of 'glasnost' and its policy of disengagement from regional conflicts. The President of Congo and other African leaders also played an important supportive role. Pretoria's greater readiness to look for a settlement was influenced by new developments, including recent military experience in Angola where UNITA, assisted by the SADF, had been undefeated but also unable to dislodge large Cuban and Angolan forces using sophisticated weapons, and where a major move by the Cubans into the southern Cunene province threatened the Namibian border and the hydroelectric schemes on the Cunene River, as well as the military's ability to counter SWAPO. There was also white concern over the growing losses from the escalating conflict (still small in comparison to those of the Angolans, Cubans and UNITA) and over the costs of the war and the occupation of Namibia for a weak economy.

In the negotiations, the linkage between withdrawal of Cuban troops and Namibia's independence was accepted, and in July the three governments agreed on fourteen 'principles for a peaceful settlement in south-western Africa'. These included the full implementation of UN resolution 435 leading to Namibian independence and the withdrawal of foreign troops from Angola. The prospects for a settlement now seemed much better than at any time in the past becasue it would serve the differing interests of the major parties involved – US, USSR, Angola, South Africa and possibly even Cuba. Yet the uncertainty about Cuba's willingness to agree to a withdrawal timetable acceptable to Pretoria and Washington was only one of the many factors that could lead to another breakdown. The activities and interests of UNITA and SWAPO – not included in the negotiations – could spark off renewed conflict, as could instability in the Angolan government or in South Africa itself. With the CP opposed to withdrawal from Namibia, the government might back away because of fear of adverse white political reaction or of resistance from the security establishment. However, this threat was balanced by the positive international response to the prospects of peace in the region and by wide domestic support for the diplomatic initiatives, especially from the business community. The local elections showed that there was no strong white reaction to the idea of Namibian independence, despite the withdrawal of South African forces from Angola, in terms of an agreement reached during the negotiations.

In mid December the three governments signed a protocol in Brazzaville, which was formalised by a treaty signed at the UN in New York on 22 December. The date of 1 April 1989 was set for the start of the implementation of resolution 435 (1978) which would lead to elections for a constituent assembly seven months later, with the number of South African troops (estimated at over 50,000) reduced by then to 1,500. In a separate accord between Angola and Cuba provision was made for the withdrawal, in carefully monitored stages, of all 50,000 Cuban troops from Angola by July 1991. In all these arrangements the UN was designated to play a central role with the support of the US and the USSR, which reflected the improving international climate. The climate was improved for Pretoria, too, and the ice had now been broken even with the Soviet Union. Crocker referred to the end of a long and difficult chapter of African history.

At the end of 1988, therefore, possibilities existed for great changes on South Africa's borders, although the expectations by the achievement of the Treaty still had to be fulfilled in Namibia's actual independence. But within the Republic itself the search for the status and security of a white-controlled state had not been abandoned; nor had a solution been found to the issue which had plagued South Africa since 1945: that of black rights within the state. The agreement with Angola and Cuba, like the Nkomati Accord with Mozambique, included principles which Smuts had laid down in the 1940s and which each government that followed had repeated, namely respect for sovereign status and territorial integrity, and non-interference in internal affairs. They had been the bedrock of the government's policies over forty years. The search for status and security continued in a world that was still largely hostile to white-dominated South Africa.

APPENDIX OF POPULATION, ECONOMIC AND DEFENCE STATISTICS

Graph 1 South Africa – population increase: total and racial breakdown, 1945–1985

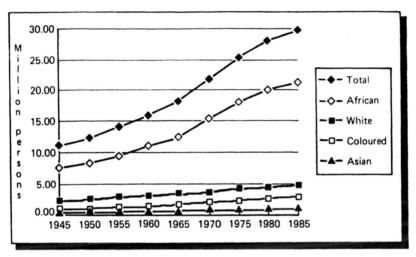

Year	Total	African	White	Coloured	Asian
1945	11.15	7.70	2.30	0.90	0.25
1950	12.35	8.45	2.60	1.00	0.30
1955	14.05	9.60	2.90	1.20	0.35
1960	15.85	11.00	3.10	1.35	0.40
1965	18.15	12.40	3.50	1.75	0.50
1970	21.80	15.35	3.75	2.10	0.60
1975	25.40	18.10	4.25	2.35	0.70
1980	28.05	20.10	4.50	2.65	0.80
1985	29.65	21.15	4.80	2.80	0.90

Note: Population statistics for Transkei, Bophuthatswana, Venda and Ciskei are excluded from recent South African population statistics but have been included in the above graph and table.
Sources: South African Labour Statistics, 1986, Central Statistical Services, Pretoria, 1986; South African Institute of Race Relations, Annual Surveys, 1974 to 1986, SAIRR, Johannesburg; Report of the Science Committee of the President's Council on Demographic Trends in South Africa, Government Printer, Cape Town, 1983; Central Statistical Service, Statistical News Releases, selected issues during 1987

Graph 2 South Africa – percentage annual change in real gross domestic product at constant 1988 prices, 1947–1988

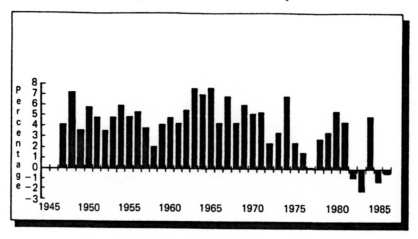

Graph 3 South Africa – emigration and immigration, 1945–1986

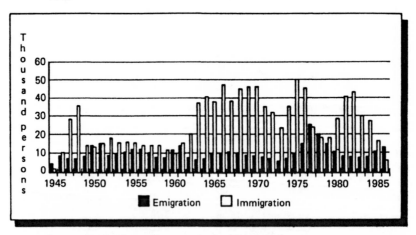

Sources: South African Statistics, 1982, Central Statistical Services, Pretoria, 1982; Bulletin of Statistics, vol. 16, no. 4 (Quarter Ended December 1982), Central Statistical Services, Pretoria; Race Relations Survey, SAIRR, 1985; Central Statistical Service, Statistical News Release, 15 June 1987, Pretoria

Graph 4 South Africa – expenditure on defence as a percentage of total government budget expenditure, 1946–1987

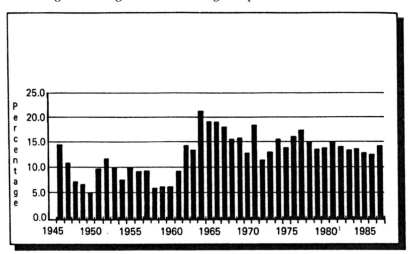

Source: estimate of the Expenditure to be Defrayed from State Revenue Account 1946–1987 to 1947–1988 inclusive

Graph 5 South Africa – total imports, free on board, 1945–1985.

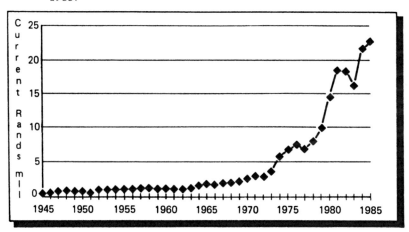

Year	Imports
1945	0.2
1950	0.6
1955	1.0
1960	1.1
1965	1.8
1970	2.5
1975	6.7
1980	14.4
1985	22.7

Sources: South African Statistics 1986, Central Statistical Service, Pretoria, 1986; Bulletin of Statistics, vol. 21, no. 3, September 1987, CSS, Pretoria

347

Graph 6 South Africa – total produce and gold exports, 1945–1985. (Produce includes re-exports.)

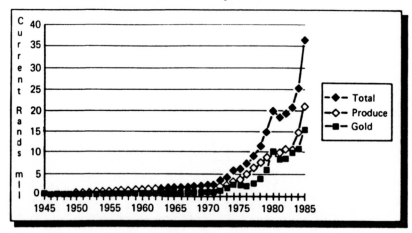

Year	Total	Produce	Gold
1945	0.6	0.2	0.5
1950	0.8	0.5	0.2
1955	1.1	0.7	0.4
1960	1.4	0.9	0.5
1965	1.8	1.1	0.8
1970	2.4	1.5	0.8
1975	6.2	3.7	2.5
1980	20.0	9.8	10.1
1985	36.3	20.8	15.5

Sources: South African Statistics 1986, Central Statistical Service, Pretoria, 1986; Bulletin of Statistics, vol. 21, no. 3, September 1987, CSS, Pretoria

Table 3. *South Africa – import sources by country (1946–85)** [leading five]

Year	Federal Rep. of Germany	France	Japan	United Kingdom	United States of America
1946	0.1	2.7	–	148.3	113.6
1950	13.8	9.4	16.9	252.7	98.1
1955	57.7	12.6	20.7	332.6	200.8
1960	111.2	23.8	40.6	314.4	217.7
1965	191.4	46.9	100.1	494.5	330.9
1970	374.0	88.1	220.8	561.2	423.4
1975	1,033.8	244.9	611.5	1,094.3	984.1
1980	1,853.4	541.6	1,287.0	1,738.4	1,949.2
1985	3,807.2	1,040.1	2,280.1	2,772.1	3,159.5

*In current Rands million.
Sources: Statistical Yearbook 1964, Bureau of Statistics, Pretoria. South African Statistics, Central Statistical Services, Pretoria (1970, 1974, 1978, 1982). Monthly Abstract of Trade Statistics, January–December 1985, Commissioner for Customs and Excise.

Table 4. *South Africa – export destinations by country (1946–85)** [leading five]

Year	Federal Rep. of Germany	France	Japan	United Kingdom	United States of America
1946	0.4	6.8	–	35.4	34.5
1950	19.2	54.4	1.4	120.0	39.7
1955	32.2	25.4	10.8	204.5	53.2
1960	35.3	28.3	30.3	226.6	54.5
1965	55.7	37.2	76.1	357.8	99.8
1970	106.3	37.8	181.0	446.6	127.9
1975	269.4	115.1	191.7	783.6	349.6
1980	658.9	421.4	1,199.7	1,226.3	1,032.0
1985	1,258.4	814.1	2,829.1	2,124.6	3,029.7

*In current Rands million.
Sources: Statistical Yearbook 1964, Bureau of Statistics, Pretoria. South African Statistics, Central Statistical Services, Pretoria (1970, 1974, 1978, 1982). Monthly Abstract of Trade Statistics, January–December 1985, Commissioner for Customs and Excise.

Table 5. *South Africa – import sources by region (1946–85)**

Year	Asia	Europe	North America	South America	Oceania	Africa
1946	25.3	187.0	146.9	32.8	4.4	32.4
1950	86.6	324.5	126.3	9.7	5.4	60.8
1955	115.6	509.0	239.9	–	–	72.3
1960	156.6	595.9	253.7	–	14.0	76.9
1965	240.9	969.7	380.6	–	28.1	108.9
1970	409.3	1,393.0	497.8	18.0	65.2	131.1
1975	787.9	3,271.1	1,070.0	38.2	95.0	253.6
1980	1,802.6	5,701.6	2,100.3	120.8	107.7	287.9
1985	3,413.5	10,885.1	[3,886.1]		281.0	456.8

*In current Rands million.
Sources: Statistical Yearbook 1964, Bureau of Statistics, Pretoria. South
African Statistics, Central Statistical Services, Pretoria (1970, 1974, 1978,
1982). Monthly Abstract of Trade Statistics, January–December 1985,
Commissioner for Customs and Excise.

Table 6. *South Africa – export destinations by region (1946–85)**

Year	Asia	Europe	North America	South America	Oceania	Africa
1946	7.8	83.7	35.9	4.7	1.7	40.1
1950	19.5	286.4	50.4	7.6	7.7	93.4
1955	26.7	372.0	56.1	–	6.9	144.6
1960	71.1	389.7	61.0	–	14.0	141.6
1965	99.1	621.0	115.8	–	13.7	147.1
1970	220.7	788.4	167.9	7.5	15.3	263.6
1975	699.1	1,680.3	487.2	51.9	35.2	423.8
1980	1,932.0	4,412.1	1,240.7	259.1	96.2	1,091.5
1985	5,246.0	9,293.3	[3,477.7]		277.9	1,577.9

*In current Rands million.
Sources: Statistical Yearbook 1964, Bureau of Statistics, Pretoria. South
African Statistics, Central Statistical Services, Pretoria (1970, 1974, 1978,
1982). Monthly Abstract of Trade Statistics, January–December 1985,
Commissioner for Customs and Excise.

Table 7. *South Africa – imports by standard international trade classification sections and divisions in SA Rands million (1946–85)*

	Total	Food & livestock	Beverages & tobacco	Inedible raw material except fuel	Mineral fuels & lubricants	Animal & vegetable oil & fats	Chemicals	Manufactured goods (by material)	Machinery transport equipment	Misc. manufactured goods	Not classified by kind
1946	430.2	52.8	4.8	29.3	15.7	3.7	20.0	151.0	84.9	66.5	1.5
1950	613.6	42.7	2.6	57.9	54.1	8.1	27.2	223.4	156.5	36.2	4.9
1955	961.9	42.7	8.9	70.4	73.4	8.4	65.5	298.7	305.8	75.4	12.7
1960	1,111.1	48.7	7.6	73.9	75.9	8.6	78.1	316.8	409.0	82.4	10.1
1965	1,752.5	63.8	13.0	131.8	92.3	10.8	123.7	425.8	738.1	122.1	31.1
1970	2,540.1	102.9	25.8	245.8	NA	11.5	199.1	495.4	1,186.9	225.1	47.6
1975	5,551.7	202.1	49.5	298.1	NA	22.5	516.0	1,036.1	2,950.1	425.3	52.0
1980	14,380.5	289.7	65.7	629.1	NA	55.1	1,226.6	1,508.7	5,484.1	819.2	4,302.3
1985	22,690.6	887.5	205.9	1,035.6	NA	345.4	2,756.0	2,631.9	9,180.6	1,584.7	4,063.0

Sources: Statistical Yearbook 1964, Bureau of Statistics, Pretoria. South African Statistics, 1970, Department of Statistics, Pretoria. Bulletin of Statistics, vol. 7, no. 3, September 1973, Department of Statistics, Pretoria. Bulletin of Statistics, vol. 10, no. 4, December 1976, Department of Statistics, Pretoria. Bulletin of Statistics, vol. 16, no. 3, September 1982, Central Statistical Services, Pretoria. Bulletin of Statistics, vol. 21, no. 3, September 1987, Central Statistical Services, Pretoria.

Table 8. *South Africa – exports by standard international trade classification sections and divisions in SA rands million (1946–85)*

	Total	Food & livestock	Beverages & tobacco	Inedible raw material except fuel*	Mineral fuels & lubricants	Animal & vegetable oil & fats	Chemicals	Manufactured goods (by material)	Machinery transport equipment	Misc. manufactured goods	Not classified by kind
1946	179.9	18.1	4.6	78.8	10.0	0.9	8.4	41.8	2.9	10.9	3.5
1950	457.6	53.1	5.0	172.8	11.6	5.8	21.4	90.4	13.3	12.8	71.4
1955	663.2	140.6	4.4	286.7	10.4	5.4	28.9	132.5	28.2	22.9	3.1
1960	799.5	170.6	6.0	328.9	12.9	8.9	31.3	180.5	36.2	19.9	4.2
1965	1,056.3	224.8	11.2	368.1	30.9	9.3	36.4	282.3	47.4	15.0	31.0
1970	1,533.6	302.4	13.7	434.8	NA	8.9	63.2	470.3	110.0	17.7	112.4
1975	3,325.5	1,016.0	19.4	737.1	NA	22.4	138.9	885.2	197.1	42.7	266.6
1980	9,774.8	1,641.4	41.2	2,230.8	NA	35.8	443.7	3,079.1	400.2	135.3	1,767.3
1985	20,844.9	1,692.6	46.4	6,573.2	NA	74.4	1,016.9	7,004.6	903.6	332.6	3,200.6

*Gold *not* included.

Sources: Statistical Yearbook 1964, Bureau of Statistics, Pretoria. South African Statistics, 1970, Department of Statistics, Pretoria. Bulletin of Statistics, vol. 7, no. 3, September 1973, Department of Statistics, Pretoria. Bulletin of Statistics, vol. 10, no. 4, December 1976, Department of Statistics, Pretoria. Bulletin of Statistics, vol. 16, no. 3, September 1982, Central Statistical Services, Pretoria. Bulletin of Statistics, vol. 21, no. 3, September 1987, Central Statistical Services, Pretoria.

Table 9. *South Africa – mineral production: total and global percentage and ranking (1984)*

Commodity	Unit	Total S. African production	Percentage of global production	Global ranking
Alumino-silicates	kt	145	31	3
Antimony[a]	t	7,440	14	3
Asbestos	kt	191	5	3
Chrome Ore	kt	3,407	36	1
Coal[b]	kt	163,000	5	5
Copper[c]	kt	207	2	11
Diamonds[d]	kcar	10,121	16	4
Ferrochromium	t	894,190	32	1
Ferromanganese	kt	381	6	5
Ferrosilicon	kt	89	3	10
Fluorspar	kt	319	7	5
Gold[i]	t	682	46	1
Iron Ore	Mt	15	3	8
Lead[c]	kt	95	3	12
Manganese Metal[e]	kt	37	54	1
Manganese Ore	kt	3,049	13	2
Phosphate Rock	kt	2,496	2	10
Platinum-group Metals	kt	*	45	2
Silicon Metal	kt	35	6	6
Silver[c]	t	220	2	10
Titanium Minerals[f]	kt	328	19	2
Uranium[c]	t	5,734	NA	NA
Vanadium[g]	t	22,345	40	1
Vermiculite	kt	158	31	2
Zinc[c]	kt	106	2	15
Zirconium Minerals[h]	t	153,123	20	2

* Classified
[a] metal in concentrate
[b] bituminous and anthracite
[c] contained metal
[d] gem and industrial, rough
[e] electrolytic
[f] metal content of minerals, excluding slag
[g] contained V_2O_5
[h] concentrate
[i] provisional
NA   not available
t   tonne
kt   kilotonne
kcar   kilocarat
Mt   megatonne
Source: Minerals Bureau of South Africa, August 1986.

Table 10. *South Africa – mineral reserve base:* total and global percentage and ranking (August 1987)*

Commodity	Unit	Total S. African reserve	Percentage of global reserve	Global ranking
Alumino-silicates[a]	kt	51,600	38	1
Antimony[b]	t	254,000	6	4
Asbestos[c]	kt	7,800	6	4
Chromium[a]	Mt	3,200	74	1
Coal[d]	Mt	58,404	11	4
Diamonds[e]	kcar	365	24	2
Fluorspar[f]	kt	31,000	6	6
Gold[b]	t	20,000	50	1
Iron[b]	Mt	5,987	7	5
Lead[b]	kt	5,000	4	5
Manganese[a]	Mt	12,700	79	1
Nickel[b]	kt	5,860	7	6
Phosphate Rock[g]	Mt	2,310	7	3
Platinum-group Metals[b]	t	30,200	79	1
Titanium Minerals[b]	kt	31,100	13	3
Uranium[b][h]	t	256,600	NA	NA
Vanadium[a]	kt	7,800	47	1
Vermiculite[a]	kt	73,000	NA	NA
Zinc[b]	kt	15,000	5	4
Zirconium[b]	kt	6,900	16	3

*Reserve base: that part of an identified resource that meets specified minimum physical and chemical criteria related to current mining and production practices, including those of grade, quality, thickness and depth. The reserve base is the in situ demonstrated source from which reserves are estimated. It may encompass those parts of the resources that have a reasonable potential for becoming economically available within planning horizons beyond those that assume proven technology and current economics. The reserve base includes those resources that are currently economic (demonstrated reserves) and marginally economic (demonstrated marginal reserves).

[a] ore, in situ
[b] contained metal
[c] contained fibre
[d] bituminous and anthracite – proven recoverable reserves
[e] gem and industrial
[f] contained CaF_2
[g] contained concentrate (38 per cent P_2O_5)
[h] recoverable at a cost of less than US $80/kg
NA   not available
t   tonne
kt   kilotonne
kcar   kilocarat
Mt   megatonne
Source: Minerals Bureau of South Africa, August 1986.

Table 11. *South Africa – African source countries of migrant labour to South Africa in thousands of persons (1972–86)*

Year	Total	Botswana	Lesotho	Malawi	Mozambique	Swaziland	Zimbabwe	Other[1]
1972	441,148	31,960	131,749	131,231	121,708	10,108	*	14,392[2]
1973	485,100	46,192	148,856	139,714	127,198	10,032	3,258	9,858
1974	482,313	33,357	134,667	137,676	139,993	9,984	5,961	20,675
1975	414,586	37,016	152,188	39,308	150,738	16,390	8,890	10,049
1976	390,010	43,159	160,634	12,761	111,257	20,750	32,716	8,733
1977	357,356	43,527	173,867	12,412	68,232	18,195	37,919	31,195
1978	327,051	34,464	155,623	38,525	49,168	14,054	27,494	7,574
1979	326,709	32,463	152,023	35,803	61,550	13,005	21,547	10,308
1980	287,230	32,200	140,746	32,319	56,424	19,853	10,377	4,311
1981	300,758	26,169	150,422	30,602	59,391	13,417	16,965	1,792
1982	282,272	26,262	140,719	27,558	52,323	13,659	11,332	3,419
1983	358,035	25,967	145,797	29,622	61,218	16,773	7,742	70,916
1984	351,620	26,433	138,443	29,268	60,407	16,823	7,492	72,334
1985	371,008	27,814	139,827	30,144	68,665	22,255	7,428	74,875
1986	385,405	28,244	138,193	31,411	73,186	29,194	7,304	77,873

*Negligible amount.
[1] Other includes Angola and Zambia and other African countries not listed separately on this table.
[2] Includes Zambia.
Source: South Africa Yearbook, 1973 to 1981. Geregistreerde Trekwerkers en Pendelaars in die Blankegebied, 30 Junie 1986, Department of Home Affairs.

NOTES

1 Introduction

1 House of Assembly Debates (H. of A.), 5 Feb. 1948, col. 1007–8.
2 Quoted by Kenneth Grundy, *Confrontation and Accommodation in Southern Africa* (University of California Press, 1973), p. 3.
3 H. of A., 5 Feb. 1965, col. 636.
4 Kenneth A. Heard, *General Elections in South Africa 1943–1970* (Oxford University Press, 1974), p. 196.
5 Quoted by Jan Botha, *Verwoerd is Dead* (Cape Town: Books of Africa, 1967), p. 55.
6 H. of A., 15 Sept. 1970, col. 4210.
7 *The Times*, 22 Nov. 1946.
8 H. of A., 16 May 1983, col. 7045.
9 Deon Geldenhuys, *The Diplomacy of Isolation: South Africa's Foreign Policy Making* (Johannesburg: Macmillan, 1984), pp. 247–9.
10 See Ronald T. Libby, *The Politics of Economic Power in Southern Africa* (Princeton University Press, 1987).
11 Botha, *Verwoerd is Dead*, pp. 55–6.

2 Smuts and the aftermath of war

1 Roughly 200,000 South Africans had joined the armed forces and of these 6,840 had been killed, 1,841 were missing, 14,363 had been wounded and 14,589 had been taken prisoner. Nicholas Mansergh, *The Commonwealth Experience* (London: Weidenfeld and Nicolson, 1969), p. 296.
2 D. Hobart Houghton, *The South African Economy*, 3rd edn. (Cape Town and London: Oxford University Press, 1973), pp. 16–17.
3 The 'race problem' at that time was seen as the relationship between the Afrikaners and the English-speaking whites, as distinct from the 'native problem' which was concerned with the black man's position.
4 Quoted in conversation by an ex-Nationalist minister.
5 Ralph Horwitz, *The Political Economy of South Africa* (London: Weidenfeld and Nicolson, 1967), p. 4.

6 For the major biography of Smuts, see Sir Keith Hancock, *Smuts*, vol. I, *The Sanguine Years 1870–1919*; vol. II, *The Fields of Force* (Cambridge: Cambridge University Press, 1962, 1968).
7 House of Assembly Debates (H. of A.), 27 Jan. 1950, col. 244.
8 Smuts's philosophical views are discussed by Hancock, *Smuts*, vol. I, ch. 15 and vol. II, ch. 9.
9 H. G. Nicholas, *The United Nations* (London: Oxford University Press, 2nd edn., 1962), Appendix, p. 196. The actual draft made by Smuts read: 'To re-establish faith in fundamental human rights, in the sanctity and ultimate value of human personality, in the equal rights of men and women.' (Quoted by J. C. Smuts, *Jan Christian Smuts* (London: Cassell, 1952.)
10 *The Times*, 23 June 1945.
11 *The Times*, 22 June 1945.
12 *The Times*, 1 June 1946.
13 Mansergh, *Documents and Speeches on British Commonwealth Affairs 1931–1952*, 2 vols. (London: Oxford University Press for the Royal Institute of International Affairs, 1952), vol. I, p. 568.
14 Jean Van Der Poel, *Selections from Smuts Papers*, vol. VII (Cambridge: Cambridge University Press, 1973), p. 203.
15 H. of A., 14 April 1947, col. 2661.
16 Mansergh, *Documents*, vol. I, p. 575.
17 H. of A., 19 March 1945, col. 3720.
18 Poel, *Selections from Smuts Papers*, vol. VII, p. 88.
19 Hancock, *Smuts*, vol. II, p. 450.
20 Poel, *Selections from Smuts Papers*, vol. VII, p. 47.
21 *Ibid.*, p. 101.
22 Quoted by A. Vandenbosch, *South Africa and the World: The Foreign Policy of Apartheid* (Lexington: The University Press of Kentucky, 1970), p. 129.
23 Tom Lodge, *Black Politics in South Africa* (London: Longman, 1983), ch. 1.
24 Thomas Karis and Gwendolen M. Carter, *From Protest to Challenge: A Documentary History of African Politics in South Africa*, vol. II (Stamford, Calif.: Hoover Institution Press, 1973), p. 210.
25 E. Walker, *A History of South Africa* (London: Longmans, 1968), p. 762.
26 Poel, *Selections from Smuts Papers*, vol. VII, p. 129.
27 Personal information from Mr Douglas Mitchell.
28 Mandated territories were those previously administered by Germany and Turkey which were transferred to allied countries; R. W. Imishue, *South West Africa: An International Problem* (London: Pall Mall Press for the Institute of Race Relations, 1966), p. 5.
29 Article 2 of Mandate. Quoted by J. E. Spence, in *Oxford History of South Africa* (Oxford: University Press, 1971), vol. II, pp. 505–6.
30 Article 22, League of Nations Covenant.
31 Sara Pienaar, *South Africa and International Relations between the Two World Wars: The League of Nations Dimension* (Johannesburg: Witwatersrand University Press, 1987).
32 H. of A., 15 March 1946, cols. 3676–80.
33 The actual figures given by Pretoria for the 'natives' referendum was 208,850 in favour and 33,520 against (*Round Table*, vol. 37 (146),

March 1947, p. 133). The question did not give an option of independence, for at that time it was assumed that such poor, backward territories would never become sovereign states.

34 Poel, *Selections from Smuts Papers*, vol. VII, p. 113.

35 Heaton Nicholls, *South Africa in My Time* (London: Allen and Unwin, 1961), p. 320.

36 *The Times*, 22 Nov. 1946.

37 *UN Year Book 1946–47*, p. 146.

38 In the 1927 agreement India agreed to arrange the voluntary repatriation of Indians, while South Africa agreed to improve educational and other facilities for Indians who stayed as part of the permanent population. (See *Oxford History of South Africa*, vol. II, p. 449.)

39 Mansergh, *Documents*, vol. I, p. 851.

40 *The Times*, 28 May 1947.

41 Hancock, *Smuts*, vol. II, p. 449.

42 Nicholls, *South Africa in My Time*, p. 387.

43 Smuts, *Jan Christian Smuts*, p. 507.

44 Hancock, *Smuts*, vol. II, p. 447.

45 *The Times*, 9 Dec. 1946.

46 H. of A., 5 Feb. 1948, cols. 1007 and 1008.

47 *The Times*, 9 Dec. 1946.

48 H. of A., 21 Jan. 1947, cols. 10911 and 10915.

49 H. of A., 21 Jan. 1947, col. 10932.

50 H. of A., 2 Feb. 1946, col. 1224.

51 H. of A., 21 Jan. 1947, col. 10899.

52 Poel, *Selections from Smuts Papers*, vol. VII, p. 117.

3 The NP establishes its rule and looks to Africa

1 Deon Geldenhuys, 'The Effect of South Africa's Racial Politics on Anglo–South African Relations 1945–1961', unpublished Ph.D. dissertation, University of Cambridge, p. 338.

2 Seats won at elections:

1943		1948	
National Party	43	National Party	70
United Party	89	Afrikaner Party	9
Labour Party	9	United Party	65
		Labour Party	6

1953		1958	
National Party	94	National Party	103
United Party	57	United Party	53
Labour Party	4		

3 See John Barratt, 'The Department of Foreign Affairs' in Dennis Worrall (ed.), *South Africa: Government and Politics* (Pretoria: J. L. van Schaik, 1971).

4 Geldenhuys, *The Diplomacy of Isolation: South Africa's Foreign Policy Making* (Johannesburg: Macmillan, 1984), pp. 31–2.

5 Geldenhuys, Ph.D. dissertation, p. 115.
6 G. R. Berridge, 'The Ethnic "Agents in Place": English-speaking Civil Servants and Nationalist South Africa, 1948–57' in *Intelligence and National Security*, 4 (2) April 1989.
7 Quoted by Gail Cockram, *Vorster's Foreign Policy* (Pretoria: Academica, 1970), p. 89.
8 House of Assembly Debates (H. of A.), 27 Jan. 1957, col. 28.
9 Thomas Karis and Gwendolen M. Carter (eds.), *From Protest to Challenge: A Documentary History of African Politics in South Africa: 1882–1964* (Stanford: Hoover Institution Press, 1973), vol. II, pp. 337–8.
10 Tom Lodge, *Black Politics in South Africa* (London: Longman, 1983), p. 43.
11 Mokgethi Motlhabi, *The Theory and Practice of Black Resistance to Apartheid* (Johannesburg: Skotaville, 1984), p. 59.
12 *Ibid.*, p. 45.
13 *Ibid.*, p. 47.
14 H. of A., 7 May 1957, cols. 5554–6.
15 H. of A., 1 Sept. 1948, cols. 1323–4.
16 H. of A., 25 Jan. 1951, col. 180.
17 Quoted by A. G. Barlow – H. of A., 12 May 1949, col. 5666.
18 H. of A., 11 Aug. 1953, col. 1327.
19 *Ibid.*, col. 1328.
20 H. of A., 16 May 1951, col. 6820.
21 G. C. Olivier, 'South Africa's Relations with Africa' in Robert Schrire (ed.), *South Africa: Public Policy Perspectives* (Johannesburg: Juta, 1982), p. 272.
22 Quoted by U. O. Umozozurika, 'International Law and Namibia', *Journal of Modern African Studies*, 8 (4) Dec. 1970.
23 H. of A., 7 July 1953, col. 1312.
24 A. Vandenbosch, *South Africa and the World: The Foreign Policy of Apartheid* (Lexington: The University Press of Kentucky, 1970), p. 162.
25 Colin De B. Webb, 'The Foreign Policy of the Union of South Africa' in J. E. Black and Kenneth Thompson (eds.), *Foreign Policies in a World of Change* (New York: Harper and Row, 1963), p. 440.
26 H. of A., 23 April 1956, col. 4104.
27 'Fact Paper' (South African Information Service), April 1957.
28 Geldenhuys, *Diplomacy of Isolation*, p. 13.
29 *The Times*, 8 March 1957.
30 H. of A., 20 Mar. 1959, cols. 2940–1.
31 Geldenhuys, *Diplomacy of Isolation*, p. 13.
32 *The Times*, 30 April 1957.
33 Ritchie Ovendale, 'The South African Policy of the British Labour Government 1947–51' in *International Affairs*, vol. 59 (1) 1982–3.
34 Nicholas Mansergh, *Documents and Speeches on British Commonwealth Affairs 1931–1952* (Oxford: Oxford University Press for the Royal Institute of International Affairs, 1952), vol. II, pp. 928–9.
35 H. of A., 11 Aug. 1953, col. 1328.
36 Quoted by Lord Hailey, *The Republic of South Africa and the High Commission Territories* (Oxford: Oxford University Press, 1963), p. 93.

37 John Redcliffe-Maud, *Experiences of an Optimist* (London: Hamish Hamilton, 1981), p. 81.
38 Ovendale, 'South African Policy', pp. 57–8.
39 Mary Benson, *Tshekedi Khama* (London: Faber and Faber, 1960), pp. 200–1.
40 Kenneth O. Morgan, *Labour in Power: 1945–51* (Oxford: Oxford University Press, 1984), p. 416.
41 *Optima*, Johannesburg, March 1959.

4 The Nationalists search for an international role

1 *The Times*, 25 Nov. 1952.
2 House of Assembly Debates (H. of A.), 25 Jan. 1951, col. 180.
3 Kurt Campbell, 'Soviet Policy towards South Africa' (Oxford University Ph.D. Thesis).
4 H. of A., 1 Feb. 1956, cols. 733–4.
5 H. of A., 16 April 1951, col. 7017.
6 Ritchie Ovendale, *The English Speaking Alliance* (London: George Allen and Unwin, 1985), p. 264.
7 H. of A., 3 April 1954, col. 4496.
8 *UN Year Book*, 1951, p. 350.
9 Deon Geldenhuys, 'The Effect of South Africa's Racial Politics on Anglo–South African Relations 1945–1961' (Cambridge University Ph.D. Thesis), p. 202.
10 H. of A., 27 Jan. 1950, col. 242.
11 Heaton Nicholls, *South Africa in my Time* (London: George Allen and Unwin, 1961), p. 405.
12 Ovendale, *The English Speaking Alliance*, pp. 260–2.
13 *The Times*, 7 Jan. 1957.
14 Thomas Karis, 'United States Policy Towards South Africa' in Gwendolen M. Carter and Patrick O'Meara, *Southern Africa the Continuing Crisis* (Bloomington: Indiana University Press, 1979).
15 H. of A., 10 June 1957, col. 7600.
16 H. of A., 11 May 1959, col. 5520.
17 Ralph Horowitz, *The Political Economy of South Africa* (London: Weidenfeld and Nicolson, 1967), p. 283.
18 Duncan Innes, *Anglo-American and the Rise of Modern South Africa* (New York: Heinemann, 1984), pp. 147–8.
19 See Susan Strange, *International Economic Relations of the Western World 1959–1971*, vol. II: *Monetary Relations* (Oxford: Oxford University Press, 1976), pp. 302–3.
20 H. T. Andrews et al. (eds.), *South Africa in the Sixties* (Johannesburg: South Africa Foundation, 1965), pp. 34 and 41–3.
21 Geoffrey Berridge in his *Economic Power in Anglo–South African Diplomacy* (London: Macmillan, 1981), argues that Pretoria used its economic muscle directly in relations with Britain. We have found no evidence for this.
22 South African Institute of Race Relations Annual Survey (IRR), 1951–2, p. 10.
23 *The Times*, 22 Oct. 1953, and Gary van Staden, 'Return of the Prodigal Son:

Prospect for a Revival of the Pan African Congress' in *International Affairs Bulletin*, 12 (3) 1988.

24 H. of A., 10 June 1957, col. 7604.

25 *The Times*, 25 Sept. 1948.

26 H. of A., 5 May 1955.

27 H. of A., 15 July 1958, col. 351.

28 IRR, 1956–7, p. 235.

29 R. W. Imishue, *South West Africa: An International Problem* (London: Pall Mall Press, 1966), p. 51.

30 H. of A., 31 Aug. 1948, col. 1228.

31 Quoted by Eric Walker, *A History of South Africa* (London: Longmans, 1964), p. 790.

32 Quoted by Carter, *Southern Africa*, p. 386.

33 H. of A., 16 May 1951, col. 7021.

34 Ovendale, *The English Speaking Alliance*.

35 *La Revue Française*, Nov. 1952.

36 G. R. Lawrie, 'The Simonstown Agreement: South Africa, Britain and the Commonwealth', *South Africa Law Journal*, vol. 85 (2) May 1968, pp. 157–77.

37 *The Times*, 21 Aug. 1951, and 23 Aug. 1951.

38 *The Times*, 9 April 1954.

39 *Southern Africa*, 3 Jan. 1959.

40 W. C. B. Tunstall, *The Commonwealth and Regional Defence* (London: Athlone Press, 1959), pp. 12 and 47.

41 Alexander Steward, *The World, the West and Pretoria* (New York: David McKay Company, 1977), pp. 25–6.

42 J. E. Spence and G. R. Berridge, 'South Africa: The Roads to Simonstown' in John W. Young (ed.), *The Foreign Policy of Churchill's Peacetime Administration* (Leicester University Press, 1988).

43 Cmd. 9520 (London: HMSO, 1955). Also see Lawrie, 'The Simonstown Agreement', and C. J. R. Dugard's article, 'The Simonstown Agreements: South Africa, Britain and the United Nations' in the same number of *South African Law Journal*, May 1968, pp. 142–56.

44 *The Times*, 25 June 1956.

45 H. of A., 20 March 1959, col. 2940 (Nigeria had not then attained independence but it was in prospect).

46 James Eayrs (ed.), *The Commonwealth and Suez: A Documentary Survey* (Oxford: Oxford University Press, 1964), pp. 62 and 190–1.

47 *Ibid.*, p. 394.

48 *The Times*, 24 Feb. 1951.

5 The state under threat

1 Deon Geldenhuys, *The Diplomacy of Isolation: South Africa's Foreign Policy Making* (London: Macmillan, 1984), p. 26.

2 Kenneth A. Heard, *General Elections in South Africa 1943–1970* (Oxford: Oxford University Press, 1974), ch. 6.

3 Fred Barnard, *Thirteen Years with Dr H. F. Verwoerd* (Johannesburg: Vortrekkerpers Ltd., 1967), p. 63.

NOTES TO PAGES 69–82

4 See Nicholas Mansergh, *Documents and Speeches on Commonwealth Affairs 1952–1962* (London: Oxford University Press, 1963), pp. 347–51.

5 Jan Botha, *Verwoerd is Dead* (Cape Town: Books of Africa, 1967), pp. 55–6, and Henry Kenney, *Architect of Apartheid: H. F. Verwoerd – An Appraisal* (Johannesburg: Jonathan Ball, 1980), p. 178.

6 South African Institute of Race Relations Annual Survey (IRR), 1959–60, p. 55.

7 See Leonard Thompson, *Politics in the Republic of South Africa* (Boston: Little Brown, 1966), p. 165.

8 Thomas Karis and Gwendolen M. Carter, *From Protest to Challenge*, vol. III, *1953–1964* (Stanford: Hoover Institution Press, 1977), p. 322.

9 House of Assembly Debates (H. of A.), 23 March 1961, col. 3500.

10 Nelson Mandela, *The Struggle in my Life* (International Defence and Aid Fund for Southern Africa, 1978), p. 160.

11 Karis and Carter, *From Protest to Challenge*, vol. III, p. 684.

12 Edward Feit, *Urban Revolt in South Africa 1960–1964* (Evanston: Northwestern University Press, 1971), Appendix 1, pp. 325–45.

13 Karis and Carter, *From Protest to Challenge*, vol. III, p. 762.

14 H. of A., 10 June 1964, cols. 7634–6.

15 Stephen M. Davis, *Apartheid's Rebels: Inside South Africa's Hidden War* (New Haven: Yale University Press, 1987), pp. 18–19.

16 See Karis and Carter, *From Protest to Challenge*, vol. III, pp. 657–9.

17 IRR, 1964, p. 75.

18 Karis and Carter, *From Protest to Challenge*, vol. III, p. 671.

19 Filt, *Urban Revolt*, pp. 236–7.

20 Mandela, *No Easy Walk to Freedom*, ed. Ruth First (New York: Heinemann, 1965), p. 174.

21 Tom Lodge, *Black Politics in South Africa* (London: Longman, 1983).

22 H. of A., 20 April 1960, col. 5626.

23 H. of A., 5 Feb. 1965, col. 628.

24 Sir Robert Menzies, *Afternoon Light* (London: Cassell 1967), pp. 200–1 and 206–7.

25 H. of A., 24 April 1964. col. 4831.

26 Kurt Campbell, 'Soviet Policy Towards South Africa', Oxford University, unpublished Ph.D. thesis, ch. 4.

27 *Ibid.*, ch. 5.

28 Geldenhuys, *The Diplomacy of Isolation*, p. 18.

29 For accounts of the various groups see James Barber, *The Uneasy Relationship: Britain and South Africa* (London: Heinemann, 1983), ch. 5; George Shepherd, *Anti-Apartheid* (London: Greenwood Press, 1977); and Abdul Minty, 'The Anti-Apartheid Movement' in Peter Willets (ed.), *Pressure Groups in the Global System* (Frances Pinter, 1982).

30 Ronald Segal (ed.), *Sanctions against South Africa* (Harmondsworth: Penguin, 1964), p. 7.

31 The phrase is taken from a letter sent to voters. See Alexander Hepple, *Verwoerd* (Harmondsworth: Penguin, 1967), pp. 177–8.

32 J. D. B. Miller, 'South Africa's Departure', *Journal of Commonwealth Political Studies*, vol. I, 1961–3.

33 Geldenhuys, 'South Africa's Racial Politics', p. 414.
34 H. of A., 23 March 1961, cols. 3501–2.
35 Hepple, *Verwoerd*, p. 9.
36 H. of A., 29 March 1962, col. 3466.
37 Colin De B. Webb, 'Foreign Policy of the Union of South Africa' in J. E. Black and K. W. Thompson (eds.), *Foreign Policies in a World of Change* (New York: Harper and Row, 1963), p. 499.
38 Z. Cervenka, *The Organization of African Unity* (London: C. Hurst and Co., 1968), p. 17.
39 H. of A., 26 Feb. 1960, col. 2334.
40 Quoted by J. E. Spence, *Republic Under Pressure* (Oxford: Oxford University Press, 1965), p. 106.
41 Geldenhuys, *The Diplomacy of Isolation*, p. 24.
42 IRR, 1964, pp. 108–10.
43 The South African case is outlined in Mr Justice J. T. Van Wyk, *The United Nations, South West Africa and the Law* (Cape Town: University of Cape Town Press, 1968).
44 IRR, 1962, pp. 233–7.
45 IRR, 1964, pp. 366–7.
46 H. of A., 5 May 1964, col. 5446.
47 Quoted by G. Cockram, *Verwoerd's Foreign Policy* (Pretoria: Academica, 1970), p. 22.
48 Pakistan delegate to General Assembly – quoted by Spence, *Republic Under Pressure*, p. 103.

6 The government's response

1 Alexander Hepple, *Verwoerd* (Harmondsworth: Penguin, 1967), p. 134.
2 Fred Barnard, *Thirteen Years with Dr H. F. Verwoerd* (Johannesburg: Vortrekkerpers, 1967), p. 61.
3 House of Assembly Debates (H. of A.), 5 Feb. 1965, col. 611.
4 Sam C. Nolutshungu, *South Africa in Africa: A Study in Ideology and Foreign Policy* (Manchester: Manchester University Press, 1975), p. 104.
5 Quoted by John Redcliffe-Maud, *Experiences of an Optimist* (London: Hamish Hamilton, 1981), p. 104.
6 South African Institute of Race Relations Annual Survey (IRR), 1959–60, pp. 103–5.
7 Quoted by Deon Geldenhuys, *The Diplomacy of Isolation: South Africa's Foreign Policy Making* (Johannesburg: Macmillan, 1984), p. 23.
8 Henry Kenney, *Architect of Apartheid: H. F. Verwoerd – an Appraisal* (Johannesburg: Jonathan Ball, 1980), p. 186.
9 A. Vandenbosch, *South Africa and the World: The Foreign Policy of Apartheid* (Lexington: The University Press of Kentucky, 1970), p. 243.
10 Personal communication.
11 Kenneth A. Heard, *General Elections in South Africa 1943–1970* (London: Oxford University Press, 1974), ch. 7.
12 IRR, 1961, p. 14.
13 H. of A., 5 Feb. 1965, col. 636.

14 'Bantu' replaced 'Native' in the government's vocabulary.
15 *Optima*, Johannesburg, March 1959.
16 Quoted by Kenney, *Architect of Apartheid*, p. 206.
17 H. of A., 10 April 1961, col. 4191.
18 Kenney, *Architect of Apartheid*, p. 206.
19 Robert Scott Jaster, *The Defence of White Power: South African Foreign Policy Under Pressure* (London: Macmillan/Institute of Strategic Studies, 1988), p. 32.
20 Geldenhuys, *The Diplomacy of Isolation*, p. 24.
21 Heard, *General Elections in South Africa*, p. 121.
22 Personal communication.
23 H. of A., 23 April 1964, col. 4817.
24 Quoted by J. E. Spence in *Oxford History of South Africa*, vol. II, (Oxford: Oxford University Press, 1969), p. 501.
25 H. of A., 23 April 1963, cols. 4599–600.
26 Quoted by H. W. van der Merwe, 'What Middle Road for the Coloureds?', *New Nation*, Pretoria, June 1971, p. 10.
27 IRR, 1961, pp. 135 and 141.
28 *Ibid.*
29 Alexander Steward, *The World, the West and Pretoria* (New York: David McKay, 1977), pp. 172–3.
30 Greg Lanning, *Africa Undermined* (Harmondsworth: Penguin, 1979), p. 148.
31 Quoted by Merle Lipton, *Capitalism and Apartheid: South Africa 1910–1986* (Aldershot, Hants: Gower, 1985), p. 286.
32 Lanning, *Africa Undermined*, p. 150.
33 *Ibid.*, p. 149.
34 L. D. Hobart Houghton, *The South African Economy* (Oxford: Oxford University Press, 1973), p. 198.
35 International Defence and Aid Fund – South Africa Information Service (IDAAF), Jan.–June 1968 (Economics section), p. 43, and *Bulletin of Statistics*, Dec. 1969.
36 Quoted by J. E. Spence, *Republic Under Pressure* (Oxford: Oxford University Press, 1965), p. 45.
37 IDAAF, Jan.–June 1970 (Economics section), p. 94, and Jan.–June 1971 (Economics section), p. 111E.
38 H. of A., 6 June 1961, cols. 7398–9.
39 H. of A., 6 Feb. 1964, col. 871.
40 H. of A., 18 May 1961, cols. 7005–7.
41 IRR, 1963, p. 33.
42 H. of A., 18 May 1961, cols. 7005–7.
43 Philip H. Frankel, *Pretoria's Praetorians: Civil–Military Relations in South Africa* (Cambridge: Cambridge University Press, 1984), chs. 2–3.
44 H. of A., 29 Sept. 1966, cols. 3261 and 3245.
45 Richard Leonard, *South Africa at War: White Power and the Crisis in Southern Africa* (Westport, Conn.: Lawrence Hill, 1983), p. 132.
46 *Ibid.*, p. 133.
47 Robert S. Jaster, *South Africa's Narrowing Security Options* (International Institute of Strategic Studies – Adelphi Paper No. 159, 1983), p. 16.

48 Frankel, *Pretoria's Praetorians*, pp. 81–2.
49 *Ibid.*, p. 80.
50 H. of A., 24 June 1963, cols. 8625–6.
51 H. of A., 27 April 1964, col. 5008.
52 *Report – South Africa and World Strategy* (London, June 1969).
53 Editorial comment in *Die Volksblad*, 6 May 1969.

7 The internal setting

1 Kenneth A. Heard, *General Elections in South Africa 1943–1970* (Oxford: Oxford University Press, 1974), p. 164.
2 Merle Lipton, *Capitalism and Apartheid: South Africa 1910–1986* (Aldershot, Hants: Gower, 1985), p. 305.
3 South African Institute of Race Relations Annual Survey (IRR), 1972, pp. 1–2.
4 *Southern Africa*, 10 June 1968, p. 371.
5 Personal communication.
6 *Report from South Africa* (Department of Information, Pretoria), June 1969, pp. 3–4.
7 *Rand Daily Mail*, 12 Sept. 1966.
8 Quoted by Gail Cockram, *Vorster's Foreign Policy* (Pretoria: Academica, 1970), p. 124.
9 See Christopher R. Hill, *Change in South Africa: Blind Alleys or New Dimensions?* (London: Rex Collings, 1983), ch. 15.
10 House of Assembly Debates (H. of A.), 14 April 1969, cols. 3879–83.
11 Lipton, *Capitalism and Apartheid*, p. 307.
12 See Leonard Thompson, *The Political Mythology of Apartheid* (New Haven: Yale University Press, 1985).
13 Heard, *General Elections in South Africa*.
14 O. Geyser (ed.), *B. J. Vorster: Select Speeches* (Bloemfontein: Institute for Contemporary History, 1977), p. 112.
15 H. of A., 23 July 1970, cols. 292–3.
16 H. of A., 25 April 1973, cols. 5098–9.
17 Deon Geldenhuys, *The Diplomacy of Isolation: South Africa's Foreign Policy Making* (Johannesburg: Macmillan, 1984), p. 123.
18 *Ibid.*, p. 110.
19 H. of A., 8 Aug. 1974, cols. 4283 and 4302.
20 *White Paper on Defence* (Pretoria, 1973), p. 1.
21 *The Observer*, 12 Dec. 1971. For a general account see James Barber's 'BOSS in Britain', *African Affairs*, vol. 82 (328) July 1983.
22 Gordon Winter, *Inside BOSS* (Harmondsworth: Penguin, 1981).
23 *The Sunday Times*, 4 Oct. 1981.
24 See Barrie Penrose and Roger Courtiour, *The Pencourt File* (London: Secker and Warburg, 1978).
25 Winter, *Inside BOSS*, p. 312.
26 Geldenhuys, *The Diplomacy of Isolation*, p. 148.
27 *Ibid.*, pp. 147–9.
28 Ken Flower, *Serving Secretly: Rhodesia into Zimbabwe 1964–1981* (London: John Murray, 1987), p. 154.

29 Kenneth W. Grundy, *The Militarization of South African Politics* (London: I. B. Tauris, 1986), p. 81.

30 Thomas Karis and Gwendolen Carter, *From Protest to Challenge*, vol. III, *1953–1964* (Stanford: Hoover Institution Press, 1977), p. 688.

31 Mokgethi Motlhabi, *The Theory and Practice of Black Resistance to Apartheid* (Johannesburg: Skotaville, 1984), ch. 4.

32 Steve Biko, *I Write What I Like* (London: The Bowerdean Press, 1978), pp. 23–4.

33 *Ibid.*, p. 146.

34 Gail M. Gerhart, *Black Power in South Africa: The Evolution of an Ideology* (Berkeley: University of California Press, 1978), p. 269.

35 Geyser, *B. J. Vorster*, p. 146.

36 H. of A., 10 Sept. 1974, col. 2591.

37 H. of A., 23 April 1968, cols. 3947–8.

38 H. of A., 27 May 1968, col. 6031.

39 International Defence and Aid Fund – Southern Africa Information Service (IDAAF), Jan.–June 1969, p. 258.

40 IDAAF, July–Dec. 1970, p. 401.

41 H. of A., 15 Sept. 1970, col. 4211, and *Today's News* (South African Embassy, London), 10 June 1971.

42 IRR, 1973, p. 165.

43 IRR, 1974, p. 183.

44 H. of A., 4 Feb. 1974, col. 58.

45 *Ibid.*, cols. 321–3.

46 IDAAF, July–Dec. 1972, p. 548.

47 *First Report of the Select Committee on Bantu Affairs* (Cape Town: Government Printer, 1975).

48 IDAAF, Jan.–June 1971, p. 444.

49 IDAAF, July–Dec. 1971, p. 478.

50 H. of A., 7 Feb. 1974, col. 305.

8 The African setting

1 International Defence and Aid Fund – Southern Africa Information Service (IDAAF), Jan.–June 1970, p. 348.

2 IDAAF, July–Dec. 1971, p. 464.

3 House of Assembly Debates (H. of A.), 27 April 1973, col. 5333.

4 *Southern Africa*, 11 Nov. 1968.

5 H. of A., 1 Sept. 1970, col. 3117.

6 Adrian Guelke, 'Africa as a Market for South African Goods' in *Journal of Modern African Studies*, 12 (1) 1974. For an alternative view, see Sean Gervasi, 'South Africa's Economic Expansionism' in *Sechaba*, 5 (6) June 1971.

7 Gail Cockram, *Vorster's Foreign Policy* (Pretoria: Academica, 1970), p. 126.

8 IDAAF, Jan.–June 1971, p. 427.

9 *Southern Africa*, 6 Dec. 1969.

10 Robert Jaster, *Southern Africa: Regional Security Problems and Prospects* (Aldershot, Hants: Gower, 1985), p. 54.

11 South African Institute of Race Relations Annual Survey (IRR), 1967, pp. 328–9.
12 Jaster, *South Africa in Namibia: The Botha Strategy* (Lanham, Md.: University Press of America, 1985), p. 7.
13 IRR, 1964, pp. 362–5.
14 IDAAF, July–Dec. 1973, col. 407.
15 Duncan Innes, *Anglo-American and the Rise of Modern South Africa* (London: Heinemann, 1984), p. 238.
16 IDAAF, July–Dec. 1973, col. 412.
17 IDAAF, Jan.–June 1973, col. 147.
18 Innes, *Anglo-American*, p. 239.
19 Barbara Brown, 'South Africa's Foreign Policy Towards its Black Neighbours', Boston University, unpublished Ph.D. dissertation, 1979, p. 94.
20 IDAAF, July–Dec. 1972, col. 149E.
21 O. Geyser, 'Détente in Southern Africa', *African Affairs*, 75 (299) April 1976.
22 *Journal of Modern African Studies*, 8 (1) April 1970, pp. 123–8.
23 IDAAF, Jan.–June 1970, p. 348.
24 H. of A., 11 April 1967, cols. 3957–8.
25 IRR, 1972, p. 121.
26 Geyser, 'Détente in Southern Africa', p. 189.
27 IRR, 1975, p. 289.
28 Carolyn MacMaster, *Malawi: Foreign Policy and Development*, (Julian Friedmann, 1974), p. 23.
29 *Africa Report*, Washington, 13 (8) Nov 1968, pp. 26–9.
30 H. of A., 9 Feb. 1971, col. 548.
31 G. R. Berridge, *The Politics of the South Africa Run: European Shipping and Pretoria* (Oxford: Clarendon Press, 1987), pp. 198–9.
32 Kenneth W. Grundy, *Confrontation and Accommodation in Southern Africa* (Berkeley: University of California Press, 1973), p. 48.
33 Quoted by J. A. Lombard, J. J. Stadler and P. J. Van der Merwe, *The Concept of Economic Cooperation in Southern Africa* (Pretoria: Econburo, 1968), p. 57.
34 IRR, 1975, p. 287.
35 H. of A., 21 April 1971, col. 4932.
36 Quoted by Cockram, *Vorster's Foreign Policy*, p. 156.
37 Quoted by MacMaster, *Malawi*, p. 90.
38 H. of A., 23 April 1963, col. 4599.
39 Martin Meredith, *The Past is Another Country: Rhodesia UDI to Zimbabwe* (London: Pan, 1980), p. 145.
40 Ken Flower, *Serving Secretly: Rhodesia into Zimbabwe 1964–1981* (London: John Murray, 1987), p. 32.
41 Private communication.
42 H. of A., 25 Jan. 1966, col. 53.
43 IDAAF, Jan.–June 1973, col. 169.
44 IDAAF, Jan.–June 1968, p. 51E.
45 *Cape Argus*, 2 Jan. 1966.
46 *Report on the Supply of Petroleum and Petroleum Products to Rhodesia – The Bingham Report* (London: HMSO, 1978).

47 Martin Bailey, *Oilgate: The Sanctions Scandal* (Philadelphia, Pa.: Coronet, 1979), p. 11.
48 H. of A., 23 April 1969, col. 4580.
49 Flower, *Serving Secretly*, p. 157.
50 Personal communication.
51 H. of A., 15 Sept. 1970, col. 4210.
52 H. of A., 29 Sept. 1966, col. 3236.
53 David Martin and Phyllis Johnson, *The Struggle for Zimbabwe* (London: Faber, 1981), p. 10.
54 IDAAF, July–Dec. 1973, col. 448.
55 *The Star*, Johannesburg, 7 Sept. 1968.
56 Flower, *Serving Secretly*, p. 108.
57 See J. K. Cilliers, *Counter Insurgency in Rhodesia* (Beckenham, Kent: Croom Helm, 1985).
58 Tom Lodge, *Black Politics in South Africa* (London: Longman, 1983), p. 312.
59 Flower, *Serving Secretly*, pp. 118–19 and 140–1.
60 IDAAF, Jan.–June 1973, col. 79.
61 Martin and Johnson, *The Struggle for Zimbabwe*, p. 161.
62 Quoted by G. C. Olivier, 'South Africa's Relations with Africa' in Robert Schrire (ed.), *South Africa: Public Policy Perspectives* (Johannesburg: Juta, 1982), p. 280.
63 IRR, 1974, p. 125.
64 H. of A., 1 Sept. 1970, col. 3123.
65 Edwin Munger, 'New White Politics in South Africa' in William A. Hance (ed.), *Southern Africa and the United States* (New York: Columbia, 1968), p. 59.
66 Quoted by MacMaster, *Malawi*, p. 96.
67 *Ibid.*, p. 99.
68 H. of A., 22 April 1971, col. 4994.
69 H. of A., 30 May 1968, col. 6524.
70 H. of A., 15 Sept. 1970, col. 4208; and Cockram, *Vorster's Foreign Policy*, p. 152.
71 H. of A., 4 April 1971, cols. 4930–8.
72 Grundy, *Confrontation and Accommodation*, pp. 318–9.
73 Olivier, 'South Africa's Relations with Africa', p. 282.
74 H. of A., 14 May 1971, col. 6857.
75 H. of A., 7 May 1969, col. 5450.
76 *Southern Africa*, 28 Nov. 1970, p. 291.
77 *Africa*, London, 2 July 1972, p. 14.
78 IDAAF, July–Dec. 1970, p. 530.
79 H. of A., 22 April 1971, col. 4976.
80 IDAAF, July–Dec. 1971, p. 464.
81 Olivier, 'South Africa's Relations with Africa', p. 285.
82 John Barratt, 'Dialogue in Africa: A New Approach', *South Africa International*, 2 (2) 1971, p. 102.
83 IDAAF, July–Dec. 1970, p. 383.
84 IDAAF, July–Dec. 1972, p. 530.
85 IRR, 1974, p. 124.
86 *Ibid.*
87 H. of A., 30 April 1973, col. 5418.

88 Colin Legum, *The Battlefronts of Southern Africa* (New York: Africana Publishing Company, 1988), p. 15.
89 Olivier, 'South Africa's Relations with Africa', p. 280.
90 IRR, 1975, p. 286.
91 Legum, *Battlefronts* p. 15.
92 S. Nolutshungu, *South Africa in Africa* (Manchester University Press, 1975), ch. 1.

9 The international setting

1 Personal communication.
2 Sheridan Johns, 'Obstacles to Guerrilla Warfare: A South African Case Study' in *Journal of Modern African Studies*, 11 (2) 1973.
3 International Defence and Aid Fund – Southern Africa Information Service (IDAAF), Jan.–June 1967, p. 14.
4 IDAAF Jan.–June 1971, p. 449.
5 Tom Lodge, *Black Politics in South Africa* (London: Longman, 1983), p. 311.
6 Johns, 'Obstacles to Guerrilla Warfare'.
7 *ANC Speaks*, p. 180.
8 *Ibid.*, pp. 2 and 172.
9 *Ibid.*, p. 52.
10 *Ibid.*, p. 146.
11 IDAAF, 1967 (Economic Section), p. 20.
12 Anthony Sampson, *Black and Gold: Tycoons, Revolutionaries and Apartheid* (London: Hodder and Stoughton, 1987), p. 96.
13 *Ibid.*, p. 96.
14 *The Star*, 29 June 1967.
15 *Sunday Times*, London, 1 Feb.1987.
16 Sampson, *Black and Gold*, p. 102.
17 *Ibid.*, p. 87.
18 *Southern Africa*, 12 July 1969, p. 15.
19 House of Assembly Debates (H. of A.), 7 May 1969, col. 5451.
20 James Adams, *The Unnatural Alliance: Israel and South Africa* (London: Quartet Books, 1984), p. 23.
21 IDAAF, Jan.–June 1974, p. 579.
22 IDAAF, July–Dec. 1973, p. 86.
23 H. of A., 2 Feb. 1967.
24 IDAAF Report (1968), 'The British Embargo on Arms for South Africa'.
25 *Ibid.*
26 Robert Jaster, *The Defence of White Power: Foreign Policy Under Pressure* (London: Macmillan, 1988).
27 IDAAF Report (1968), p. 2.
28 *Southern Africa*, 20 Sept. 1969, p. 150.
29 IDAAF, Jan.–July 1967 (Economic Section), p. 2.
30 *The Times*, 27 Sept. 1967.
31 Personal communication.
32 *The Guardian*, 12 March 1973; and subsequent reports.
33 H. of A., 30 April 1973, col. 5432.

34 James Barber, 'The EEC Ccde of Conduct for South Africa: Capitalism as a Foreign Policy Instrument' in *The World Today*, March 1980.

35 Richard Bissel, *South Africa and the US* (New York: Praeger, 1982), p. 25.

36 *Ibid.*, p. 17.

37 Barry Cohen and Mohammed A. El-Khawas, *The Kissinger Study of Southern Africa* (Nottingham: Spokesman Books, 1975).

38 *Ibid.*, p. 66 *et seq.*

39 IDAAF, Jan.–June 1971, p. 436, and IRR, 1972, p. 116.

40 Christopher Coker, *The United States and South Africa 1968–1985* (Durham N.C.: Duke University Press, 1986), pp. 72–5.

41 Southern Africa Institute of Race Relations Annual Survey (IRR), 1972, p. 119.

42 IRR, 1974, p. 148.

43 Geldenhuys, *The Diplomacy of Isolation: South Africa's Foreign Policy Making* (Johannesburg: Macmillan, 1984), p. 115.

44 H. of A., 4 May 1972, col. 6532.

45 H. of A., 9 Aug. 1974, col. 420.

46 IRR, 1962, p. 213.

47 IRR, 1971, p. 320.

48 Guy Beresford, 'Playing Apartheid to Win or Lose?' in *International Affairs Bulletin*, SAIIA, 10 (3) 1986.

49 Peter Hain, *Don't Play With Apartheid* (London: George Allen and Unwin, 1971).

50 *The Times*, 26 Aug. 1981.

51 Geldenhuys, *The Diplomacy of Isolation*, p. 217.

52 Richard E. Lapchick, *The Politics of Race and International Sport: The Case of South Africa* (London: Greenwood Press, 1975), pp. 87–8.

53 *Ibid.*, p. 298.

54 IRR, 1974, p. 395 and IRR, 1975, p. 275.

55 Quoted by Gail Cockram, *Vorster's Foreign Policy* (Pretoria: Academica, 1970), p. 24.

56 Newell M. Stultz, 'The Apartheid Issue at the General Assembly' in *African Affairs*, 86 (342) Jan. 1987.

57 Cockram, *Vorster's Foreign Policy*, p. 47.

58 H. of A., 16 Feb. 1968, col. 714.

59 H. of A., 7 May 1969, col. 5443.

60 *Southern Africa*, 1 Nov. 1969.

61 John Barratt, 'South African Diplomacy at the UN' in G. R. Berridge, *The UN and Diplomacy* (London: Macmillan, 1985), p. 196.

62 H. of A., 10 Sept. 1974, col. 2584.

63 IRR, 1975, p. 285.

64 *Southern Africa*, 26 Sept. 1970.

65 Stultz, 'The Apartheid Issue'.

66 IRR, 1968, p. 59.

67 *Today's News*, Department of Information, 24 June 1971.

68 Jaster, *South Africa and Namibia: The Botha Strategy* (Lanham, Md.: University Press of America, 1985), p. 7.

10 The watershed years in southern Africa

1 Al J. Venter, *Portugal's Guerrilla War* (Cape Town: John Malherbe Pty Ltd., 1973), p. 194.
2 Antonio de Spinola, *Portugal and the Future* (Johannesburg: Perskor Publishers, 1974).
3 *South Africa: Time Running Out*, Report of the Study Commission on US Policy Toward Southern Africa (Berkeley: University of California Press, 1981), p. 136.
4 *Ibid.*, p. 140.
5 Anthony Lake, *The 'Tar Baby' Option: American Policy toward Southern Rhodesia* (New York: Columbia University Press, 1976), p. 277.
6 *Race Relations News*, South African Institute of Race Relations, October 1974.
7 Quoted in Martin Meredith, *The Past is Another Country: Rhodesia UDI to Zimbabwe* (London: Pan Books Ltd, 1980), p. 151.
8 *Ibid.*, p. 151.
9 House of Assembly Debates (H. of A.), 10 Sept. 1974, cols. 2588–94 (Muller's statement).
10 Kenneth W. Grundy, *The Militarization of South African Politics* (Indiana University Press, 1986), p. 91; and Eschel Rhoodie, *The Real Information Scandal* (London: Orbis South African Pty Ltd, 1983), p. 72.
11 John Barratt, 'Détente in South Africa', in *The World Today*, March 1975, p. 122.
12 *Southern Africa Record*, South African Institute of International Affairs, 1975, vol. 4, p. 3.
13 Meredith, *The Past is Another Country*, p. 154.
14 For full speech see *Senate Debates* (Official Report), First Session – Fourth Senate, cols. 3335–46.
15 *Southern Africa Record*, SAIIA, vol. 2, 1975, p. 17.
16 David Smith and Colin Simpson, with Ian Davies, *Mugabe* (Sphere Books Ltd., 1981), pp. 74 and 78.
17 Meredith, *The Past is Another Country*, p. 152.
18 *Rand Daily Mail*, 6 Nov. 1974.
19 Personal communication.
20 *Ibid.*
21 Meredith, *The Past is Another Country*, p. 188.
22 *Ibid.*, p. 189.
23 Personal communication.
24 John A. Marcum, *The Angolan Revolution* (The MIT Press, 1978), vol. II, pp. 229 and 252.
25 *Ibid.*, p. 248.
26 *Ibid.*, p. 237.
27 *Ibid.*, p. 230.
28 *Ibid.*, pp. 252–3.
29 *Ibid.*, p. 257.
30 Fred Bridgland, *Jonas Savimbi: A Key to Africa* (Edinburgh: Mainstream Publishing Co., 1986), p. 181.

31 Robin Hallett, 'The South African Intervention in Angola, 1975–76' in *African Affairs*, 77 (308) July 1978, pp. 355–6.

32 Crawford Young, 'The Portuguese Coup and Zaire's Southern African Policy' in John Seiler (ed.), *Southern Africa since the Portuguese Coup* (Colo.: Westview Press Inc., 1980), p. 209.

33 See, for instance, John Stockwell, *In Search of Enemies* (New Jersey: André Deutsch Ltd., 1978), ch. 9 and Postscript.

34 From interview reproduced in *Africa Report*, 21 (1), Jan.–Feb. 1976, pp. 13–15.

35 William Colby, *Honourable Men: My Life in the CIA* (London: Hutchinson and Co., 1978), p. 422.

36 Stockwell, *In Search of Enemies*, p. 161.

37 Maurice Halperin, 'The Cuban Role in Southern Africa' in John Seiler (ed.), *Southern Africa*, pp. 77–8.

38 *Ibid.*, p. 35.

39 Marcum, *The Angolan Revolution*, p. 443, note 256.

40 *Ibid.*, p. 443, note 255, and Halperin, 'The Cuban Role in Southern Africa', p. 35. It is possible that the training camps were first set up a few months earlier by a smaller group of 230 Cuban advisers – see Marcum, *The Angolan Revolution*, p. 273, and Hallett, *The South African Intervention in Angola*, p. 355.

41 Hallett, 'The South African Intervention in Angola', p. 359.

42 *Ibid.*, pp. 351–3.

43 *Die Burger*, Cape Town, 8 Feb. 1977. Article by Robert Moss on the Angolan war.

44 *Windhoek Advertiser*, 30 May 1975, *The Times*, London, 8 Dec. 1975, and Gordon Winter, *Inside BOSS: South Africa's Secret Police* (Harmondsworth: Penguin Books, 1981), pp. 537–8.

45 Hallett, 'The South African Intervention in Angola', p. 358.

46 Marcum, *The Angolan Revolution*, p. 269, and SADF Press Release, 3 Feb. 1977.

47 Winter, *Inside BOSS*, pp. 544–5.

48 Stockwell, *In Search of Enemies*, pp. 86–90.

49 Regarding positions taken within government, see Deon Geldenhuys, *The Diplomacy of Isolation: South African Foreign Policy Making* (Johannesburg: Macmillan, 1984), pp. 78–84, and Rhoodie, *The Real Information Scandal*, p. 144.

50 Geldenhuys, *The Diplomacy of Isolation*, p. 79.

51 Rhoodie, *The Real Information Scandal*, p. 142 et seq.

52 Stockwell, *In Search of Enemies*, p. 181.

53 *Ibid.*, pp. 179–80.

54 Winter, *Inside BOSS*, pp. 534–41.

55 See, for instance, Hallett, 'The South African Intervention in Angola', p. 370.

56 Geldenhuys, *The Diplomacy of Isolation*, pp. 81 and 262, note 46.

57 Grundy, *The Militarization of South African Politics*, p. 127, note 7.

58 Even a Pro-Cuban writer admitted subsequently that the South African advance in October/November had been like a 'Sunday drive'. Hallett, 'The South African Intervention in Angola', p. 369.

59 Hallett, 'The South African Intervention in Angola', p. 370.
60 Stockwell, *In Search of Enemies*, pp. 186–7.
61 Hallett, 'The South African Intervention in Angola', p. 371, and Marcum, *The Angolan Revolution*, p. 274.
62 Hallett, 'The South African Intervention in Angola', p. 371.
63 *Ibid.*, p. 272.
64 *Ibid.*, p. 377.
65 Bridgland, *Jonas Savimbi*, p. 163.
66 *Ibid.*, p. 168.
67 André du Pisani, *SWA/Namibia: The Politics of Continuity and Change* (Johannesburg: Jonathan Ball, 1985), pp. 273–4.
68 *Ibid.*, p. 234. In another reference, p. 231, du Pisani gives a figure of 'some 4,500' for the exodus of SWAPO supporters from Ovambo in 1974.
69 *Ibid.*, p. 227.
70 Department of Foreign Affairs, *South West Africa Survey 1974*, (Pretoria: 1975), p. 29.
71 du Pisani, *SWA/Namibia*, pp. 289–90.
72 *Ibid.*, p. 297.
73 *Ibid.*, p. 284.
74 *Ibid.*, pp. 311–12.
75 *Die Transvaaler*, Johannesburg, 19 Aug. 1976.
76 du Pisani, *SWA/Namibia*, p. 321.
77 Geldenhuys, *The Diplomacy of Isolation*, p. 81.
78 For full text of Lusaka speech see *Southern Africa Record*, SAIIA, vol. 5, 1976, pp. 1–10.
79 Cyrus Vance, *Hard Choices: Critical Years in America's Foreign Policy* (New York: Simon and Schuster, 1983), p. 273.
80 du Pisani, *SWA/Namibia*, p. 318.
81 Vance, *Hard Choices*, p. 273.
82 du Pisani, *SWA/Namibia*, p. 319.

11 Soweto – the domestic and regional impact

1 House of Assembly Debates (H. of A.), 21 June 1976, col. 10013.
2 Full text of speech in *Southern African Record*, SAIIA, vol. 5, 1976. See also Richard E. Bissell, *South Africa and the United States* (New York: Praeger, 1982), pp. 29–30.
3 John D. Brewer, *After Soweto: An Unfinished Journey* (Oxford: Oxford University Press, 1986), p. 7.
4 H. of A., 21 Jan. 1977, cols. 3–4.
5 H. of A., 20 April 1977, col. 5644.
6 H. of A., 2 Feb. 1978, cols. 325 and 338.
7 South African Institute of Race Relations Annual Survey (IRR), 1976, p. 59.
8 H. of A., 18 June 1976, col. 9696.
9 H. of A., 20 April 1977, col. 5644.
10 IRR, 1976, p. 57.
11 Mokgethi Motlhabi, *The Theory and Practice of Black Resistance to Apartheid* (Johannesburg: Skotaville, 1984), p. 146.

12 IRR, 1978, pp. 32–3.
13 IRR, 1977, pp. 129–30.
14 IRR, 1977, p. 31.
15 IRR, 1978, p. 36.
16 Brewer, *After Soweto*, p. 256.
17 Thomas Karis, 'The Resurgent African National Congress' in Thomas M. Callaghy (ed.), *South Africa in Southern Africa* (New York: Praeger, 1983), p. 214.
18 Brewer, *After Soweto*, p. 133.
19 Tom Lodge, *Black Politics in South Africa* (London: Longman, 1983).
20 Stephen M. Davis, *Apartheid's Rebels: Inside South Africa's Hidden War* (New Haven: Yale University Press, 1987), p. 128.
21 Précis of US Congressional Report on ANC, Jan. 1987.
22 Karis, 'The Resurgent African National Congress', p. 199.
23 Lodge, *Black Politics*, pp. 343–4.
24 *ANC Speaks: Documents and Statements of the African National Congress* (no publisher or date), pp. 198–211.
25 Callaghy, 'South Africa's Relations with Angola and Mozambique' in *South Africa in Southern Africa*, p. 274.
26 H. of A., 18 June 1976, col. 9696.
27 Kenneth W. Grundy, *The Militarization of South African Politics* (London: I. B. Taurus, 1986), p. 11.
28 Philip H. Frankel, *Pretoria's Praetorians: Civil–Military Relations in South Africa* (Cambridge: Cambridge University Press, 1984).
29 IRR, 1977, p. 90.
30 IRR, 1976, p. 49.
31 Frankel, *Pretoria's Praetorians*, p. 58.
32 *Ibid.*, p. 136.
33 *Ibid.*, p. 112.
34 IRR, 1978, p. 55.
35 James Adams, *The Unnatural Alliance: Israel and South Africa* (London: Quartet Books, 1984), p. 82.
36 H. of A., 28 Jan. 1977, cols. 387–8.
37 IRR, 1977, p. 322.
38 Deon Geldenhuys, *The Diplomacy of Isolation: South African Foreign Policy Making* (Johannesburg: Macmillan, 1984), pp. 96–9.
39 Matthew Midlane, 'The South African General Election of 1977' in *African Affairs*, 78 (312) July 1979. The seats held by each party after the election were: NP 135 (117); PFP 17 (18); NRP 10 (24); SAP 3 (6) (1974 seats in brackets).
40 H. of A., 11 Feb. 1977, col. 1280.
41 H. of A., 20 Feb. 1977, cols. 5648 and 5651.
42 Callaghy, *South Africa in Southern Africa*, pp. 300–3.
43 Robert Scott Jaster, *The Defence of White Power: South African Foreign Policy Under Pressure* (Macmillan/Institute of Strategic Studies, 1988), p. 55.
44 Martin Meredith, *The Past is Another Country: Rhodesia 1890–1979* (N.J.: André Deutsch, 1979), pp. 242–3.
45 Dickson A. Mangazi, *The Cross Between Rhodesia and Zimbabwe* (N.Y.: Vantage Press, 1981), p. 135.

46 Personal communication.
47 Ken Flower, *Serving Secretly: Rhodesia into Zimbabwe 1964–1981* (London: John Murray, 1987), p. 132.
48 *Ibid.*, p. 153.
49 Colin Legum, *The Battlefronts of Southern Africa* (New York: Africana Publishing Company, 1988), p. 51.
50 Meredith, *The Past is Another Country*, p. 243.
51 IRR, 1977, p. 81.
52 H. of A., 30 Jan. 1978, cols. 69–70.
53 H. of A., 12 April 1978, col. 4627.
54 Cyrus Vance, *Hard Choices: Critical Years in America's Foreign Policy* (N.Y.: Simon and Schuster, 1983), p. 276.
55 *Southern Africa Record*, SAIIA, vol. 9, 1977, p. 14.
56 South West Africa Constitution Amendment Act, No. 95 of 1977, passed in June.
57 André du Pisani, *SWA/Namibia: The Politics of Continuity and Change* (Johannesburg: Jonathan Ball, 1986), p. 355.
58 *The Star*, Johannesburg, 11 July 1977.
59 UN Document S/12827 of 29 Aug. 1978.
60 du Pisani, *SWA/Namibia*, p. 404.

12 Soweto – the international impact

1 James Mayall, 'The Soviet Union, Zimbabwe and Southern Africa' in Olajide Aluko and Timothy M. Shaw (eds.), *Southern Africa in the 1980s* (London: George Allen and Unwin, 1985), p. 114.
2 Keith Somerville, 'The USSR and Southern Africa since 1976' (unpublished paper), p. 9.
3 House of Assembly Debates (H. of A.), 31 Jan. 1978, cols. 103–4.
4 See W. Scott Thompson and Brett Silvers, 'South Africa in Soviet Strategy' in Richard E. Bissell and Chester A. Crocker (eds.), *South Africa into the 1980s* (Colo.: Westview Press, 1979).
5 *Ibid.*, p. 148.
6 South African Institute of Race Relations Annual Survey (IRR), 1977, p. 575.
7 Robert Jaster, *Southern Africa: Regional Security Problems and Prospects* (Aldershot, Hants: Gower, 1985), p. 67.
8 IRR, 1977, p. 558.
9 *Keesing's Contemporary Archives*, 12 Aug. 1977, col. 28507.
10 James Barber, 'The EEC Code of Conduct for South Africa: Capitalism as a Foreign Policy Instrument' in *World Today*, March 1980, and Richard E. Bissell, *South Africa and the United States* (New York: Praeger, 1982), pp. 85–91.
11 IRR, 1977, p. 576.
12 Personal communication.
13 J. E. Spence, 'South Africa, the World Powers, and Southern Africa' in Thomas M. Callaghy, *South Africa in Southern Africa* (New York: Praeger, 1983), p. 111.

14 IRR, 1978, p. 145.
15 Owen Ellison Kahn, 'South Africa and the Political Economy of Minerals in Southern Africa' in Callaghy, *South Africa*, ch. 4.
16 Richard J. Payne, 'Japan's South Africa Policy' in *African Affairs*, 86 (343) April 1987.
17 H. of A., 17 April 1978, cols. 4852 and 4948.
18 H. of A., 13 June 1977, col. 10007.
19 H. of A., 27 May 1977, col. 8738.
20 Bissell, *South Africa and the United States*, p. 31.
21 H. of A., 2 Feb. 1978, col. 337.
22 H. E. Newsum and Olayiwola Abegunrin, *United States Foreign Policy Towards Southern Africa* (New York: St Martin's Press, 1987), p. 64.
23 IRR, 1977, p. 1.
24 Bissell, *South Africa and the United States*, p. 12.
25 *Ibid.*, pp. 34–5.
26 IRR, 1977, pp. 572–4.
27 IRR, 1977, p. 574.
28 H. of A., 27 May 1977, cols. 8738 and 8744.
29 H. of A., 27 May 1977, col. 8718.
30 H. of A., 5 June 1978, cols. 8461 and 8571.
31 Newsum, *United States Foreign Policy*, p. 63, and Bissell, *South Africa and the United States*, p. 85.
32 H. of A., 21 April 1977, col. 5827.
33 H. of A., 21 April 1977, col. 5814.
34 James Adams, *The Unnatural Alliance: Israel and South Africa* (London: Quartet Books, 1984), p. 110.
35 *Ibid.*, ch. 4.
36 Philip H. Frankel, *Pretoria's Praetorians: Civil–Military Relations in South Africa* (Cambridge: Cambridge University Press, 1984).
37 *Ibid.*, p. 90.
38 Deon Geldenhuys, *The Diplomacy of Isolation: South African Foreign Policy Making* (Johannesburg: Macmillan, 1984), p. 116.
39 IRR, 1976, p. 405.
40 Adams, *The Unnatural Alliance*, p. 25.
41 *Ibid.*, p. 122.
42 Jaster, *The Defence of White Power*, p. 155.
43 Bissell, *South Africa and the United States*, p. 116.
44 Ronald W. Walters, *South Africa and the Bomb: Responsibility and Deterrence* (Mass.: Lexington Books, 1987), p. 9.
45 Bissell, *South Africa and the United States*, p. 106.
46 *Ibid.*, p. 108.
47 *Ibid.*, p. 115.
48 Zdenek Cervenka and Barbara Rogers, *The Nuclear Axis: Secret Collaboration Between West Germany and South Africa* (New York: Julian Friedman, 1978).
49 Walters, *South Africa and the Bomb*, p. 92.
50 J. D. L. Moore, *South Africa and Nuclear Proliferation* (New York: St Martin's Press, 1987), ch. 5.
51 Bissell, *South Africa and the United States*, p. 109.

52 IRR, 1977, p. 87.

53 J. E. Spence, 'South Africa's Nuclear Option' in *African Affairs*, 80 (321) October 1981.

54 Bissell, *South Africa and the United States*, p. 119.

55 *The Sunday Times*, London, 14 Aug. 1988.

56 Walters, *South Africa and the Bomb*, p. 103.

57 Jaster, *The Defence of White Power*, p. 82.

13 P. W. Botha's advent and the return of confidence

1 Mervyn Rees and Chris Day, *Muldergate* (Johannesburg: Macmillan, 1980), p. 75.

2 Regarding this 'personalisation' of the policy role, see Deon Geldenhuys, *The Diplomacy of Isolation: South African Foreign Policy Making* (Johannesburg: Macmillan, 1984), pp. 72–3.

3 Rees and Day, *Muldergate*, p. 96.

4 *Ibid.*, p. 122.

5 Eschel Rhoodie, *The Real Information Scandal* (London: Orbis South African Pty Ltd., 1983), pp. 2 and 14.

6 Rees and Day, *Muldergate*, p. 134.

7 Rhoodie, *The Real Information Scandal*, pp. 719ff.

8 Rees and Day, *Muldergate*, p. 133.

9 Eschel Rhoodie was in fact arrested in France in July 1979, extradited to South Africa, tried and convicted by the Supreme Court in October and sentenced to 12 years imprisonment. The conviction was, however, overturned by the Appeal Court in September 1980, and Rhoodie was acquitted on all charges.

10 After his forced resignation from the Cabinet and from the National Party, Dr Mulder founded the National Conservative Party, but it failed to win a seat in the 1981 elections. He then joined forces with Dr A. P. Treurnicht in 1982, when the latter left the National Party to establish the Conservative Party, Mulder was returned to parliament as an Opposition Member in May 1987. He died in January 1988.

11 Rees and Day, *Muldergate*, p. 135.

12 During the few years until his death in September 1983, Vorster made occasional statements critical of the Botha government and indicating some support for Dr Treurnicht and the Conservative Party. As with many other aspects of this affair, questions remain to be answered about the nature and extent of Vorster's role.

13 Geldenhuys, *The Diplomacy of Isolation*, pp. 90 and 91.

14 *Ibid.*, p. 93.

15 Kenneth W. Grundy, *The Militarization of South African Politics* (Bloomington: Indiana University Press, 1986), p. 35.

16 Grundy, *The Rise of the South African Security Establishment: An Essay on the Changing Locus of State Power* (Bradlow Series No. 1, SAIIA, 1983), p. 17.

17 Geldenhuys, *The Diplomacy of Isolation*, p. 92.

18 Grundy, *The Militarization of South African Politics*, p. 51.

19 Geldenhuys, *Some Foreign Policy Implications of South Africa's 'Total National*

Strategy' (Special Study, South African Institute of International Affairs, 1981), p. 3. The following summary of the implementation of the TNS relies on this study, from which the quotations by Malan and Botha are also taken.

20 *Die Transvaaler*, Johannesburg, 24 Sept. 1976.

21 House of Assembly Debates (H. of A.), 21 March 1980, col. 3321.

22 Republic of South Africa, Department of Defence, *White Paper on Defence*, (1977), p. 5.

23 See Philip H. Frankel, *Pretoria's Praetorians: Civil–Military Relations in South Africa* (Cambridge: Cambridge University Press, 1984), pp. 46–70; and Grundy, *The Militarization of South African Politics*, p. 118, note 27.

24 *Ibid.*, p. 18.

25 See Geldenhuys, *Some Foreign Policy Implications*, pp. 9–10, and Grundy, *The Militarization of South African Politics*, pp. 53–4. Further development of the joint management system at the local level took place in the mid 1980s, in response to internal unrest.

26 For the full text of the 'twelve-point plan', with amendments subsequently announced, see Geldenhuys, *Some Foreign Policy Implications of South Africa's 'Total National Strategy'*, pp. 60–3.

27 H. of A., 29 April 1980, col. 5087.

28 Hermann Giliomee, *The Parting of the Ways: South African Politics 1976–82* (Cape Town: David Philip, 1982), p. 17.

29 Grundy, *The Militarization of South African Politics*, p. 45, quoting Philip H. Frankel.

30 Deon Geldenhuys and Denis Venter, 'Regional Co-operation in Southern Africa: A Constellation of States?', in *International Affairs Bulletin*, 3 (3) Dec 1979, p. 46.

31 Geldenhuys, *The Constellation of Southern African States and the Southern African Development Co-ordination Council: Towards a New Regional Stalemate?*, (Special Study, South African Institute of International Affairs, 1981), p. 2.

32 The concept of a central 'triangle' was not explicitly expressed but was implicit in government statements and policies on Namibia and Rhodesia.

33 From text issued by the South African Department of Foreign Affairs and Information.

34 See Geldenhuys, *The Neutral Option and Sub-Continental Solidarity* (Occasional Paper, South African Institute of International Affairs, March 1979), pp. 1–5.

35 See T. D. Venter, *Suid-Afrika: 'n Onverbonde Buitelandse Beleidsrigting?* (Occasional Paper, SAIIA, 1979), pp. i and ii.

36 See, for instance, Peter C. J. Vale, 'South Africa as a Pariah International State', in *International Affairs Bulletin*, 1 (3) 1977, pp. 121–41.

37 Geldenhuys, *The Neutral Option*, pp. 4–5.

38 *Ibid.*, p. 9.

39 Cyrus Vance, *Hard Choices: Critical Years in America's Foreign Policy* (New York: Simon and Schuster, 1983), p. 276.

40 André du Pisani, *SWA/Namibia: The Politics of Continuity and Change* (Johannesburg: Jonathan Ball, 1985), p. 410.

41 Vance, *Hard Choices*, p. 311.
42 Brian Urquhart, *A Life in Peace and War* (New York: Harper and Row, 1987), pp. 320–1.

14 Regional power and constructive engagement

1 On SADCC's further development see, for instance, Gavin Maasdorp, *SADCC: A Post-Nkomati Evaluation* (Special Study, South African Institute of International Affairs, 1984).
2 Simon Jenkins, 'Destabilisation in Southern Africa', in *The Economist*, 16 July 1983, p. 15.
3 'Coercive diplomacy seeks to undermine the opponent's will.' It involves an escalation of pressure 'from verbal threats to use of force' in order to 'induce the opponent to behave in a specific way'. Tim Zimmerman, 'The American Bombing of Libya: A Success for Coercive Diplomacy', in *Survival*, 29 (3) May–June 1987, IISS (London), p. 195.
4 Phyllis Johnson and David Martin (eds.), *Destructive Engagement: Southern Africa at War* (Harare: Zimbabwe Publishing House, 1986), p. 94.
5 Fred Bridgland, *Jonas Savimbi: A Key to Africa* (Edinburgh: Mainstream Publishing Co. Ltd., 1986), pp. 297–8.
6 Johnson and Martin (eds.), *Destructive Engagement*, p. 13. See also Ken Flower, *Serving Secretly: An Intelligence Chief on Record, Rhodesia into Zimbabwe 1964 to 1981* (London: John Murray, 1987), pp. 140–1. The background to the origins of the MNR is given in a 'Top Secret' memorandum – Appendix, pp. 300–2.
7 Johnson and Martin (eds.), *Destructive Engagement*, p. 6.
8 *Ibid.*, pp. 13 and 345, note 25.
9 See Kenneth W. Grundy, *The Rise of the South African Security Establishment* (Bradlow Series No. 1, South African Institute of International Affairs, 1983), pp. 12 and 13, and Deon Geldenhuys, *The Diplomacy of Isolation* (Johannesburg: Macmillan, 1984), p. 141.
10 Johnson and Martin (eds.), *Destructive Engagement*, pp. 5 and 342, note 10.
11 Flower, *Serving Secretly*, p. 257.
12 *Ibid.*, p. 262.
13 Johnson and Martin (eds.), *Destructive Engagement*, pp. 13–16. Most of the information about the SA Defence Force's involvement with the CIO and MNR prior to Zimbabwe's independence was obtained from Ken Flower himself and other CIO officers. Flower gave considerably less detail in his own book.
14 Johnson and Martin (eds.), *Destructive Engagement*, p. 19.
15 *Ibid.*, p. 12.
16 *Ibid.*, p. 20.
17 A variation of this argument is given in Christopher Coker, *The United States and South Africa, 1968–1985: Constructive Engagement and Its Critics* (Durham, N.C.: Duke University Press, 1986), p. 227: 'Since it was in Pretoria's interest that there should be no successful black government in Southern Africa, it was enough to impede their success.' This is an unlikely explanation.

18 Geldenhuys, *Destabilization Controversy in Southern Africa*, Position Paper 18, vol. 5 (1982), Johannesburg: South African Forum.
19 *Sunday Tribune*, Durban, 24 Feb. 1980.
20 Gavin G. Maasdorp, 'Squaring up to Economic Dominance: Regional Patterns', in Robert I. Rotberg et al., *South Africa and its Neighbors* (Lexington, Mass.: Lexington Books (D. C. Heath and Co.), 1985), p. 106, and Johnson and Martin (eds.), *Destructive Engagement*, p. 18.
21 Flower, *Serving Secretly*, p. 262.
22 Zbigniew Brzezinski, *Power and Principle: Memoirs of the National Security Adviser 1977–1981* (N.Y.: Farrar Straus Giroux, 1983), p. 143.
23 Coker, *The United States and South Africa*, p. 138.
24 Jimmy Carter, *Keeping Faith: Memoirs of a President* (N.Y.: Bantam Books, 1982).
25 Alfred O. Hero Jr, 'The American Public and South Africa', in Alfred O. Hero Jr and John Barratt (eds.), *The American People and South Africa* (Lexington, Mass.: Lexington Books (D. C. Heath and Co.), 1981), p. 8.
26 Desaix Myers III, 'US Domestic Controversy over American Business in South Africa', in *ibid.*, p. 67.
27 *Ibid.*, p. 74.
28 *Ibid.*, p. 69.
29 South Africa (Republic of), *Report of the Commission of Inquiry into Labour Legislation, Part 1* (Pretoria: Government Printer, 1979), p. 2.
30 Robert M. Price, 'US Policy toward Southern Africa', in Gwendolen M. Carter and Patrick O'Meara (eds.), *International Politics in Southern Africa* (Bloomington: Indiana University Press, 1982), p. 53.
31 Robert Legvold, 'The Soviet Threat to Southern Africa', in Robert I. Rotberg et al., *South Africa and Its Neighbors*, pp. 45–6.
32 Chester A. Crocker, 'South Africa: Strategy for Change', in *Foreign Affairs*, 59 (2) Winter 1980–1), pp. 323–51. The quotations by Crocker are from this article, except where otherwise indicated.
33 Coker, *The United States and South Africa*, p. 160.
34 Crocker, 'The US Policy Process and South Africa', in Hero and Barratt (eds.), *The American People and South Africa*, p. 143. (This article was based on a paper prepared in May 1980.)
35 Sanford J. Ungar and Peter Vale, 'South Africa: Why Constructive Engagement Failed', in *Foreign Affairs*, Winter 1985–6, p. 235.
36 Quoted by Price in Carter and O'Meara (eds.), *International Politics in Southern Africa*, pp. 71–2.
37 From statement before Senate Foreign Relations Committee on 27 April 1981. See *Southern Africa Record*, vol. 23, June 1981, p. 49.
38 *Ibid.*, p. 49.
39 Coker, *The United States and South Africa*, p. 257.
40 André du Pisani, *SWA/Namibia: The Politics of Continuity and Change* (Johannesburg: Jonathan Ball, 1986), p. 470.
41 IRR, 1981, pp. 451–2.
42 du Pisani, *SWA/Namibia*, p. 474.
43 Bridgland, *Jonas Savimbi*, pp. 329–30.

44 *Ibid.*, p. 341.
45 *Ibid.*, p. 342.
46 du Pisani, *SWA/Namibia*, pp. 477–8.
47 Coker, *The United States and South Africa*, pp. 260–1.
48 Colin Legum, 'The Southern Africa Crisis', in Colin Legum (ed.), *Africa Contemporary Record*, vol. 14 *1981–82*, (New York: Africana Publishing Co. (Holmes and Meier Publishers Ltd.), 1981), p. A31.
49 du Pisani, *SWA/Namibia*, p. 481.
50 *Ibid.*, p. 483.
51 Samuel P. Huntington, 'Reform and Stability in a Modernizing, Multi-Ethnic Society', in *Politikon*, 8 (2) December 1981, Political Science Association of South Africa, pp. 11 and 24.
52 *South Africa: An Appraisal*, 2nd edition (Nedbank Group Economic Unit, 1983), p. 49.
53 See, for instance, business comments in *The Good Hope Plan for Southern Africa*, issued by the Department of Foreign Affairs and Information, December 1981, pp. 33 and 35.
54 Steven Friedman, *Building Tomorrow Today: African Workers in Trade Unions, 1970–1984* (Johannesburg: Ravan Press, 1987), pp. 166–7. Because of the white miners' resistance, the reservation of certain jobs on the mines for whites was not removed until 1987.
55 The leader of the white Mine Workers' Union, Arrie Paulus, was elected as a CP MP in 1987.
56 South African Institute of Race Relations Annual Survey (IRR), 1981, p. 1.
57 *The Good Hope Plan for Southern Africa*, p. 32.
58 It was estimated that during the 1979–80 year the per capita expenditure on school pupils of the racial groups (including capital expenditure) was: R1,169 for whites; R389 for Indians; R234 for Coloureds; and R91 for blacks in 'white' areas. Five years later (1984–5) these figures had changed to: R1,926, R1,182, R708 and R294, respectively. IRR, 1981, p. 334, and IRR, 1985, pp. 367–8.
59 IRR, 1981, p. 344.
60 J. P. de Lange, 'Recent Changes in Education', in D. J. van Vuuren, N. E. Wiehahn, J. A. Lombard and N. J. Rhoodie (eds.), *South Africa: Plural Society in Transition* (Durban: Butterworths, 1985), pp. 210 and 220.
61 *The Good Hope Plan for Southern Africa*, p. 13.
62 South Africa (Republic of), *First Report of the Constitutional Committee of the President's Council* (Government Printer, 1982).
63 See, for instance, Arend Lijphart, *Democracy in Plural Societies: A Comparative Exploration* (New Haven, Conn.: Yale University Press, 1977).
64 Lijphart, *Power-Sharing in South Africa* (Berkeley: Institute of International Studies, University of California, 1985), pp. 56–64.
65 South Africa (Republic of), *First Report*, p. 19.
66 T. R. H. Davenport, *South Africa: A Modern History*, 3rd edition (South Africa: Macmillan, 1987), p. 452.
67 *Ibid.*, p. 470.
68 *Ibid.*, p. 464.
69 *Rand Daily Mail*, 17 Nov. 1982.

70 IRR, 1983, p. 567.

71 *Sowetan*, Johannesburg, 17 Aug. 1981.

72 Comment by Dr Tom Lodge, after the explosions at Koeberg. IRR, 1982, p. 230.

73 L. J. Boulle, 'The RSA Constitution: Continuity and Change', in van Vuuren, Wiehahn, Lombard and Rhoodie (eds.), *South Africa*, p. 7. If all potential voters were included, not only those registered, the percentages would be 19.3 and 17.9, respectively.

74 Geldenhuys, 'South Africa: A Stabilising or Destabilising Influence in Southern Africa?', in Calvin Woodward (ed.), *The Razor's Edge* (Africa Institute of South Africa, 1986), p. 62.

75 See Marge Holness, 'Angola: The Struggle Continues', in Johnson and Martin (eds.), *Destructive Engagement*, pp. 102 and 361–2, note 60.

76 See John Barratt, 'Foreign Policy 1983–85: The Regional Context', in van Vuuren, Wiehahn, Lombard and Rhoodie (eds.), *South Africa*, pp. 425–6.

77 For full text of Nkomati Accord, see *Southern Africa Record* (SAIIA), vol. 35, April 1984, pp. 6–10.

78 *Southern Africa Record* (SAIIA), vol. 33, Oct. 1983, pp. 61–72.

79 *The Good Hope Plan for Southern Africa*, p. 28.

80 See *Southern Africa Record* (SAIIA), vol. 36, Aug. 1984, pp. 3 and 4, for text of relevant Exchange of Letters.

81 Johnson and Martin (eds.), *Destructive Engagement*, pp. 27 and 28.

82 *The Economist*, London, 24 March 1984, p. 13.

15 Crisis and Pretoria's response

1 *Address by the Hon. P. W. Botha*, Occasional Paper, SAIIA, Sept. 1984.

2 *Sunday Times*, Johannesburg, 6 May 1984.

3 *The Star*, Johannesburg, 26 April 1984.

4 Harald Pakendorf, Editor of *Die Vaderland*, Johannesburg, from article reproduced in *Sunday Tribune*, Durban, 27 May 1984.

5 *The Citizen*, Johannesburg, 28 May 1984 claimed that Botha had pushed back the USSR and opened the door for the West.

6 Editorials in *Sunday Times*, Johannesburg, 6 May and 10 June 1984.

7 *The Times*, London, 4 June 1984.

8 *The Citizen*, Johannesburg, 12 June 1984.

9 *Sunday Tribune*, Durban, 17 June 1984.

10 South African Institute of Race Relations Annual Survey (IRR) 1984, pp. 190, 240–1 and 244.

11 *Ibid.*, pp. 71–2.

12 *The Citizen*, 19 Nov. 1984.

13 Tom Lodge, '"Mayihlome! – Let Us Go to War!"': From Nkomati to Kabwe, The African National Congress, January 1984–June 1985', in *South African Review* vol. III (Johannesburg: Ravan Press Ltd., 1986), pp. 238–43.

14 Statement by Mr Thami Mali, chairman of the Transvaal Regional Stay-away Committee, IRR, 1984, p. 77.

15 Randall Robinson, 'Investments in Tokenism', in *Foreign Policy*, vol. 38, Spring 1980, p. 267.

16 Senator Lowell Weicker, August 1986, quoted in Anthony Sampson, *Black and Gold: Tycoons, Revolutionaries and Apartheid* (London: Hodder and Stoughton, 1987), p. 165.

17 Michael Clough, 'Beyond Constructive Engagement', in *Foreign Policy*, vol. 61, Winter 1985–6, p. 14.

18 Anthony Sampson, *Black and Gold: Tycoons, Revolutionaries and Apartheid*, p. 166.

19 *The Sunday Star*, Johannesburg, 2 Dec. 1984.

20 *International Herald Tribune*, 9 Nov. 1984.

21 Interview with Bishop Desmond Tutu, in *Leadership SA*, First Quarter, 1985, p. 62.

22 From summarised version of speech issued by US Information Service office, Johannesburg, 17 Dec. 1984.

23 From interview with SABC-TV (Johannesburg), 13 Dec. 1974. Transcript issued by US Information Service office, Johannesburg.

24 Quoted in *The Star*, Johannesburg, 27 Jan. 1985.

25 Patrick 'Terror' Lekota (UDF) and Imran Moosa (AZAPO), quoted in *The Star*, Johannesburg, 26 Jan. 1985.

26 *The Citizen*, Johannesburg, 26 Jan. 1985.

27 Tertius Myburgh, *Sunday Times*, Johannesburg, 27 Jan. 1985.

28 From article by Allister Sparks in the *Observer*, London, 27 Jan. 1985.

29 IRR, 1985, pp. 328 and 330.

30 *Ibid.*, pp. 4–5.

31 *Ibid.*, p. 491.

32 Proclamation R120 of 21 July 1985.

33 *Sunday Times*, Johannesburg, 21 July 1985.

34 IRR, 1985, pp. 440–1. These figures do not include the estimated 19,153 people detained during 1985 in the TVBC states, according to figures of the Detainees' Parents Support Committee.

35 André du Pisani, *SWA/Namibia: The Politics of Continuity and Change* (Johannesburg: Jonathan Ball, 1986), p. 534.

36 IRR, 1985, p. 429; and Fred Bridgland, *Jonas Savimbi: A Key to Africa* (Edinburgh: Mainstream Publishing Co., 1986), pp. 441–2. After his release in September 1987, the officer said he had had 'no other choice but to go along with' the Angolan 'accusations'. His press conference in Luanda 'had all been scripted beforehand'. Allan Soule, Gary Dixon, René Richards, *The Wynand du Toit Story* (Johannesburg: Hans Strydom Publishers, 1987), pp. 35 and 49.

37 *The Star*, Johannesburg, 27 Sept. 1985.

38 *Financial Times*, London, 2 Oct. 1985.

39 *The Observer*, London, 13 Oct. 1985.

40 Fred Bridgland, *Jonas Savimbi*, p. 445.

41 In opinion surveys of white opinion in 1982, 1984 and 1986 a consistent positive response of about 81 per cent was received to the question whether terrorist/guerrilla bases in neighbouring states should be attacked. See *What Do We Think? A Survey of White Opinion on Foreign Policy Issues*, No. 3 (SA Institute of International Affairs, May 1986), p. 14.

42 *Sowetan*, Johannesburg, 17 June 1985.

43 *City Press*, Johannesburg, 16 June 1985.
44 House of Assembly Debates, 28 May 1985, col. 6378.
45 IRR, 1985, pp. 432–3.
46 *The Citizen*, Johannesburg, 29 June 1987.
47 *The Times*, London, 18 Jan. 1986.
48 *The Citizen*, Johannesburg, 25 Jan. 1986.
49 See, for instance, 'Back-door Relations Key to South African Trade' in the *Observer*, London, 6 July 1986.
50 Malcolm Rifkind, 'Britain is Concerned', in *Leadership South Africa*, 4 (2) 1985, p. 19.
51 *Ibid.*, pp. 24 and 26.
52 *The Citizen*, Johannesburg, 25 July 1985, and *Beeld*, Johannesburg, 30 July 1985.
53 *Argus*, Cape Town, 12 Aug. 1985.
54 Quotations from text of Durban speech as reproduced in *Business Day*, Johannesburg, 16 Aug. 1985.
55 *The Star*, Johannesburg, 16 Aug. 1985, and the *International Herald Tribune*, 17 Aug. 1985.
56 *The Star*, Johannesburg, 17 Aug. 1985.
57 See Jesmond Blumenfeld (ed.), *South Africa in Crisis* (Croom Helm, 1987), pp. 18–19.
58 *Financial Times*, London, 30 Aug. 1985.
59 Blumenfeld (ed.), *South Africa in Crisis*, p. 19.
60 *The Citizen*, Johannesburg, 27 Dec. 1985.

16 The search continues

1 Text of Commonwealth Accord on Southern Africa in *Mission to South Africa: The Commonwealth Report* (Penguin Books for the Commonwealth Secretariat, 1986), Annex 1, pp. 142–5.
2 Tambo told a group of black South Africans at a meeting in Harare that he was opposed to necklacing and he asked them to spread this message in South Africa. *Sowetan*, 8 Sept. 1987, and *Beeld*, Johannesburg, 1 Oct. 1987.
3 *Mission to South Africa*, pp. 148–9. Subsequent letters between the EPG and the government, referred to below, appear on pp. 103–9 and 121–4.
4 *Ibid.*, p. 111, and pp. 195–6 (Annex 7).
5 *Ibid.*, pp. 112 and 115.
6 *The Star*, Johannesburg, 19 May 1986.
7 *Mission to South Africa*, pp. 119, 120 and 140.
8 *Argus*, Cape Town, 13 June 1986.
9 *The Times*, London, 25 July 1986.
10 *International Herald Tribune*, 5 Oct. 1987.
11 *British Aid to Southern Africa: A Force for Peaceful Change and Development* (London: Central Office of Information for the Foreign and Commonwealth Office, 1987).
12 Report by Heritage Foundation in early 1988 said US had covertly provided military equipment to the Maputo government from 1982 until 1986, despite

ban by Congress on initiative of Helms. *Business Day*, Johannesburg, 18 Feb. 1988.

13 *The Star*, Johannesburg, 16 April 1987.

14 *The Wall Street Journal*, 20 March 1987, and *Financial Times*, London, 27 March 1987.

15 Study by David Hauck of the Investor Responsibility Research Center (IRRC), Washington, reported in *The Star*, Johannesburg, 22 Dec. 1987.

16 *The Independent*, 4 Aug. 1988.

17 Jesmond Blumenfeld, 'South Africa's Economy: Apartheid's Latest Political Prisoner?' in *The World Today*, 44 (8–9) 1988.

18 For an analysis of the various interpretations of the results, see Eugene Lourens and Hennie Kotzé, 'The South African White General Election of 1987: Shifting Deckchairs or Burning Boats?' in *International Affairs Bulletin*, 11 (2) 1987, pp. 19–43.

19 *The Times*, London, and *International Herald Tribune*, 7 June 1988.

20 Editorial in *Business Day*, Johannesburg, 7 July 1988.

21 *Business Day*, Johannesburg, 12 Nov. 1987.

22 *The Citizen*, Johannesburg, 13 Nov. 1987. (Savimbi's and Malan's statements in separate reports.)

23 *Strategic Survey 1987–1988* (International Institute for Strategic Studies, 1988), pp. 194–5.

INDEX

communist states, 78; AAM formed and growth, 79; and OAU, 84; and Verwoerd, 90, 110; and Bantu, 92; government confirms attitude to, 107; and Vorster, 109–10, 149; homelands and movement of people, 122; foreign attitudes to, 123; blacks in urban areas, 123; and Namibia, 127, 197, 200, 313; Oppenheimer and economic growth, 154; and US, 160, 231–2, 239, 275, 277, 307–8; and sport, 164–8; and reform, 212; and AAM, 229; and Japanese, 230; and Zionism, 236; petty, 256; and National Party, 256; and P.W. Botha's twelve-point plan, 256–63; and Crocker, 277; and internal opposition, 284; and Trade Unions, 285; and education, 287; and tricameral parliament, 291, 309; white support for change, 291; impracticability of, 300; and West Germany, Italy and Vatican, 302; and township unrest, 303; and forced removals, 310; and EPG, 329; influence on economy, 337; and Conservative Party, 338; Group Areas Act and property rights, 340

Arab states, 156–7, 237–7

Arikpo, Dr, 147

Arms ban, 79, 81, 85, 88, 102, 157–8, 160, 210, 214, 228, 232, 233–6, 237, 238, 258, 302, 303, 325, 328, 336

Arms Industry, 10, 12, 100–3, 125, 140, 235–7, 241, 258, 281, 314, 325, 336

ARMSCOR (see Arms Industry)

Ashe, Arthur, 166

Asians in South Africa (see Indians)

Asiatic Land Tenure and Indian representative Act, 23

Atlantic Charter, 21

Australia, 5, 156, 228, 320

AZAPO (Anzanian Peoples'

Organization), 209, 300, 304, 309, 333, 339

Ball, George, 161

Bamford, F.H.Y., 159

Banda, President Hastings, 144, 149

Bantu Authorities Act, 32

Bantu Education Act, 32

Bantu Homelands Act, 120

Bantu Self-Governing Act, 93

Bantustans, implementation of and black rejection, 3; emphasis on, 9; and independence, 10, 120; instability of, 11; greater autonomy, 43; and 'Bantu', 92; population table, 93; land allocation, 93; legislation, 93, 120; and Verwoerd, 94, 118; Transkei, 94–5; and potential danger, 107; Black States Constitutional Act, 109; and foreign policy, 118; and P.W. Botha, 120; forced resettlement, 121–2, 310; defence of, 121; division among leaders, 122; Bantu Investment Bank, 122; policy, 122; and blacks in urban areas, 123; and Namibia, 197, 200; Bophuthatswana, 213; economic links with, 230; leaders of, 288; and citizenship, 309, 322; and Swazis and Zulus, 319; and Rubicon speech, 323

Barber, Lord Anthony, 328

Barnard, Fred, 68

Barnard, Neil, 342

Barrow, Dame Nita, 328

Basutoland (see Lesotho and BLS states)

Bechuanaland (see Botswana and BLS states)

Becker, J.J., 114

Berlin Air Lift, 46

Biko, Steve, 9, 117–18, 206, 211, 214, 229

Black Consciousness, 9, 117, 154, 206–9, 304

Black Peoples' Convention, 118, 212, 291

Powell, Colonel C.B., 30
Pratt, David, 90
President's Council, 288–9
Progressive Federal Party (PFP), 214, 216, 286, 290, 300, 337
Progressive Party (PP), 91, 113
Prohibition of Mixed Marriages Act (1949), 32
Prohibition of Political Interference Act, 109

Qoboza, Percy, 316

Rajbansi, Amichand, 310
Reagan, Ronald, 274, 276–9, 330–1
Redcliffe-Maud, Sir John, 42
Referenda (see also Constitutional Reform), 1960 on Republic, 66–7; 1983 on constitution, 289–90
RENAMO (see Mozambique National Resistance)
'Revolutionary Onslaught', 306
Rhodesia (Southern), 5–6, 8–9, 19, 40–1, 47, 74, 91, 107, 115, 120, 125, 130, 135–42, 149, 157, 159, 175–6, 178, 180–6, 190, 197, 202, 204, 216–21, 229–30, 271
Rhoodie, Eschel, 114, 143, 149, 237, 249–51
Riebeck, Jan Van, 16
Rifkind, Malcolm, 320
Riotous Assembly Act, 211
Robben Island, 72
Roberto, Holden, 186, 196
Robinson, Randall, 307
Rubicon Speech (P.W. Botha), 320–4
Russia (see USSR)

SADCC (see Southern African Development Co-ordination Conference)
Sanctions, 7, 9, 11, 24, 27, 68, 79–81, 85, 88, 136–9, 147, 151, 155–6, 159, 169–71, 227, 229–320, 325, 327–8, 330–3, 336–7, 340
SANROC (South African Non-Racial Olympic Committee), 164–8 (see also Boycotts)

SASOL (see South African Coal, Oil and Gas Corporation)
Satherthwaite, Joseph, 81
Sauer, Paul, 20, 56–7, 90
Savimbi, Jonas, 187, 190–6, 281, 312, 315, 341
Scandinavian states, 334
Schoeman, B.J., 159
Schwarz, Harry, 112
Scott, Revd Michael, 34
Segal, Ronald, 80
Senghor, President Leopold, 147, 149, 192
September, Dulce, 341
Sharpeville, 8, 69–70, 84, 90, 98
Sharpeville Six, 341
Sibeko, David, 209
Simonstown Agreement, 55, 58, 158
Singh, Swathan, 328
Sisulu, Walter, 32
Sithole, Revd Ndabiningi, 183, 185
Slovo, Joe, 154
Smith, Ian, 135–6, 138–9, 142, 178, 183, 216
Smuts, General Jan, and racial separation, 2; and human rights, 2, 26; and UN, 8, 17, 22; and World War Two, 15; and United Party, 15–16; and Commonwealth, 15, 17–18; and National Party, 16; as Foreign Minister, 17; and expansion, 18–19; and UN Charter, 19; and Dr Xuma, 21; and South West Africa, 22; and British Labour Party, 26; and India, 26; and sovereign status, 27; and criticism of racial policies, 27; and Malan and Strijdom criticism, 27; as international figure, 28; principles and policies, 344
Sobukwe, Robert, 70, 207, 209
Société d'Etudes et de Recherches d'Uranium, 238
Solodonikov, Vasily, 226
South Africa–Britain Trade Association, 159
South Africa Broadcasting Corporation, 127, 290

.

Lightning Source UK Ltd.
Milton Keynes UK
24 March 2011

169785UK00001B/90/P

9 780521 388764